ANTONIO GRAMSCI

ANTONIO GRAMSCI:
Towards an Intellectual Biography

by ALASTAIR DAVIDSON

MERLIN PRESS: LONDON
HUMANITIES PRESS: NEW JERSEY

First published in 1977
by The Merlin Press Limited
2/4 West Ferry Rd., London E.14

Printed in Great Britain
by Whitstable Litho Limited
Millstrood Rd., Whitstable, Kent

First published in U.S.A. in 1977
by Humanities Press Inc, Atlantic Highlands N.J. 07716

Library of Congress Cataloging in Publication Data
Davidson, Alastair, 1939—
Antonio Gramsci: towards an intellectual biography.
Bibliography: p. 356
Includes index.
1. Gramsci, Antonio, 1891-1937.
2. Communists—Italy—Biography. I. Title.

HX288.G7D32   335.4'092'4[B]   76-42190
ISBN 0-391-0067-1

Table of Contents

Note: The Standard abbreviations of the titles of Gramsci's works
will be used in this book.

Acknowledgements

Among the many people who have read and commented on various drafts of this book, I owe particular thanks to Professor Norberto Bobbio of Turin who has devoted many hours of his time to commenting on this work both when I was teaching the Gramsci seminar in Turin and for some five years thereafter. I was also able to discuss the work with Massimo Salvadori, Sergio Caprioglio, Elsa Fubini, Giuseppe Tamburrano and others — not least the Gramsci Seminar I taught at the Gioele Solari Institute in 1970. I must also thank Professor Stuart Woolf and Dr P. Allum who commented on early parts of the book. In 1972 at the TELOS Gramsci Conference in St Louis, Missouri I was able to meet American scholars writing on Gramsci. In particular I appreciated comments from, and discussion with, Carl Boggs and David Sallach. Again in 1973-4 I was able to benefit from the criticisms of colleagues in France, including Hugues Portelli, Dominique Grisoni, Robert Paris and M.A. Macciocchi. I would like to express special thanks to Professor Lucian Marquis, the "pink cyclist" of Claremont, California, who bought his deep knowledge of Italy to bear on some parts of the thesis. Finally my thanks go to Bronwyn Fooks and Joy Smith who typed the draft and to Joan Kirsop who translated some of the French and checked the manuscript.

This book is for Mary, Francesca and Rjurik

Preface by Norberto Bobbio

Eric J. Hobsbawm recently wrote that Gramsci was "an extraordinary philosopher, perhaps a genius, probably the most original communist thinker of the twentieth century in Western Europe". It is a judgment which can be accepted or rejected. What cannot be denied — because it is simply a matter of fact — is that, if we except the great protagonists of the Soviet revolution, there is no personality in the history of the workers' movement of these last fifty years whose person and work have aroused greater interest than Gramsci's. Indeed, we must recognize that this interest, instead of slowing up, has grown rapidly in recent years, and is spreading ever more widely from Italy overseas. If the ideal life of a militant marxist is a unity of theory and practice, then Gramsci presents us with an example of this unity which is difficult to beat. A leader and organizer of the workers' struggle in Turin during the fiery years between the end of the First World War and the advent of fascism, as well as one of the founders of the Italian Communist Party, during his years in prison Gramsci wrote — midst enormous difficulties and cruel physical suffering, which in time killed him — a series of notes on literary, philosophical, historical and political subjects, which in the recent "critical" edition published a few months ago amounted to about two thousand five hundred pages. It is now common opinion that these notes constitute one of the most original contributions of the last half century to a marxist analysis of Italian and European society, as well as philosophical reflection on some crucial themes of our time, like that of the intellectuals and their relation with society, and that of the revolutionary party and the transitional State. However, it is also necessary to recognize that a great part of the literature on the work and thought of Gramsci has been strongly influenced and continues to be strongly influenced by the debate (which has never slackened) on the historical significance of the October revolution and on the strategy of communist parties, particularly in Western countries. In particular, the fact that after the liberation of Italy from fascism Gramsci was considered the man who inspired the policies of the Italian communist party, and his work, especially the *Prison Notebooks*, as a sort of canonical text for the strategy of the Italian workers' movement in the period of transition, contributed to feed a literature which was orientated more towards political polemic than towards dispassionate study.

Those people who did not share the party line involved Gramsci in the polemic in two ways: either through accepting the official interpretation and thus denying that Gramsci was an authentically revolutionary writer, a true and real leninist, or through denying the official interpretation and thus claiming that Gramsci was a genuine leninist against the revisionism of the party. Both the official interpretation and that which opposed it were too often marred by the fact that Gramsci's work was transformed into a pretext for political battle, with the consequence that an irksome research for orthodoxy on the one hand and heresy on the other prevailed over an analysis of the man and his life in all its aspects, and a sterile debate over whether and how much Gramsci was a leninist or marxist — or, as some members of the new left who see revisionists everywhere were inclined to believe, he might perchance have been neither a marxist nor a leninist, but a masked idealist — prevailed over historical understanding. It goes without saying that being dragged hither and thither is the price great writers pay, because everyone wants to gain some advantage from being allied with them. But it is also true that to take up only the threads which serve ones own cause is a way of repressing greatness, and diminishing the intrinsic value of a work.

The publication of the *Lettere dal carcere* (*Letters from Prison*) and the six volumes of the *Quaderni del Carcere* (*Prison Notebooks*) between 1947 and 1951 constituted a true and real discovery for both marxists and non-marxists. For some years Gramscian studies were directed in great part to analysing the themes which Gramsci had dealt with in his solitary musings, especially the confrontation with the philosophy of Benedetto Croce, the judgments on the Italian Risorgimento, the problem of the intellectuals, and the theory of the party and of the State. Only when the articles written by him for socialist newspapers and *L'Ordine Nuovo* between 1914 and 1926 began to be published in chronological order, did the organizer and political agitator who had played such a part in the formation of a new class of leaders of the workers' movement again begin to be known and studied. But a certain rupture remained between the Gramsci who spent ten years in the political struggle and the Gramsci who spent ten years in the rigours of prison. One of the favoured themes of Gramscian literature for some time was the confrontation between the party man and political leader who was struggling in a difficult situation without ever losing hope in victory, and the ideas of the thinker compelled to silence who meditated on defeat, and who passed from the occasional bit of writing to historical essays, from journalistic exchanges to philosophical reflection. People asked themselves: is there a continuity or a contradiction between the two periods?

Alastair Davidson's book has the merit of not falling into either of the two defects which have weighed down Gramscian studies for some time: neither into that of a search at all costs for orthodoxy or heresy, nor into that of counterposing the Gramsci of *L'Ordine Nuovo* and the writings of his youth to that of the *Notebooks*. What interests our author is the personality in his complexity and his interests. With a deep human sympathy he follows him from his earliest years to his death through five fundamental stages: his birth and adolescence in Sardinia (1891-1911); his university studies in Turin and first political battles during the war (1911-1918); in the formation of the Turin group and the foundation of *L'Ordine Nuovo* (1918-1920); from the foundation of the new party to his arrest (1921-1926); in prison and death (1926-1937). The author keeps away both from an apologia and from an interested polemic for partial ends. He is not concerned so much with establishing exactly the extent of Gramsci's adhesion to this or that thesis of Lenin or Trotsky with the view of inserting him into a certain line of thought; but with getting inside a strong personality guided by a lucid intelligence and sustained by an untameable will, whose life was inspired by an ethic of intransigency, sacrifice, and domination of his own passions. He admires his profound intellectual honesty and his moral strength. He does not call into question his revolutionary passion but seeks to show how this passion was never separate from a critical mind and an independence of judgment. He insists on the theme of the humanist conception of history according to which men are the makers of their own destinies, but at the same time he underlines the importance attributed by Gramsci to the dominating will which leaves nothing to chance or to spontaneity, and relies on the efficiency of organization (hence the central place which the theme of the party — the "Modern Prince" — has in his thought).

However, we should not think, despite the sub-title, that Davidson's book is an intellectual biography only: the author never forgets that Gramsci was a historical person, who played an important part in some events of his time. The story of his life continually alternates with the story of the historical events with which it was historically intertwined. The book is also a picture of the history of Italy from the First World War to the advent of fascism, with particular attention paid to post-war workers' struggles, even if they are seen through the actions and reactions of one of their protagonists. To me it seems that one of the characteristics of the book is that it does not fall into the temptation of a point by point record of a life, even though the events which mark it were extraordinary, and, in many respects, fascinating. Nor does it fall into the opposite excess so frequent among writers of strict marxist persuasion, of going so far into the heaven of concepts that it loses sight of the world of facts. The battle of ideas cannot be separated from the events in which the ideas germinated and clashed with each other, from the battle of men. This book has tried to show both things are interdependent, and overcome this problem.

Finally, I am pleased to add that the book is written in an engaging manner. For this reason I foresee that it is destined to have readers who will read about the events recounted with the same human sympathy with which the author describes them.

New Year 1976   Norberto Bobbio

Introduction

Why another biography of Gramsci? The first reason is that much more information about him has been unearthed among the stony hills of Sardinia, in the musty archives of the Partito comunista italiano, and in an ageing revolutionary's study near Neuchâtel, since Cammett[1] published his excellent introductory work in 1967, and even since Tom Nairn's equally excellent translation[2] of Giuseppe Fiori's *Vita* (1966) appeared in 1970. Four particularly important new sources are the collection of Gramsci's writings in 1921-22 which appeared under the title *Socialismo e fascismo* in 1967 and those from 1923-26 which were published in 1972[3]; the first volume of Paolo Spriano's history of the Italian Communist Party, also published in 1967[4]; and finally the *Archives*[5] and the second volume of *Mémoires*[6] of Jules Humbert-Droz, which were published in 1970 and 1971 respectively.[7] Together they fill a gap in information about Gramsci's life which is immediately apparent when we pick up Cammett's and Fiori's books and flip over to the sections on 1921-22. Moreover, they do so in a fashion which immediately suggests that both biographies would have to be revised if they were rewritten today, because they make quite clear that Gramsci was a "leftist" in those early years, a thesis advanced by socialist historians of the "right" for some time,[8] but dismissed too rapidly by Cammett and Fiori, who tended to reinforce the communist thesis that Gramsci was not a "deviationist".

We can, of course, attribute the brevity of both authors' treatments of this stage in Gramsci's development to the paucity of evidence available to them, but for Gramscian scholarship more hinges on their treatment of those years than is first apparent. Like good historians they made the best use of what evidence was available to them to fill the gap. It was nearly all from later periods and influenced in particular by accounts of 1921-22 given in the letters between Gramsci and Togliatti and others in 1923-24 published in 1962 under Togliatti's editorship, under the influence of necessity.[9] We need not accuse either the letter writers or the publishers of dishonesty or distortion to see the problems which such evidence in the future past tense posed for these historians: the situation of the letter writers in relation to the problems of 1921 and 1922 was different in 1923 from what it was in 1921-2. They discussed these problems from a different angle: as if the events of those years were a preparation for their attitudes at the time of writing. In 1923-24 Gramsci was intent on creating an opposition to Bordiga, the "leftist" leader of the PCI, so the whole frame of reference of the letters of these years was "against Bordiga", and the fact that he was "for Bordiga" in 1921-22 was seen only in terms of the later frame of reference. Their shared positions were therefore easily reduced by both Cammett and Fiori to matters of "tactical" support and not agreement on matters of principle. This had further implicit results for the overall interpretation of Gramsci, who now seemed always a loyal exponent of his party's (the Communist International's) policy, to at least 1923 and therefore necessarily an exponent of the Leninist orthodoxy, against "deviations". In sum, a picture of the early Gramsci was created which was very close to that desired by the PCI. Gramsci became the exponent of party policies, and, by inversion the party became the exponent of Gramsci's theory. A more detailed examination of why he supported Bordiga, instead of accepting the glib argument where "tactical" means many things because its content is not established, may reveal that Gramsci was far from orthodox from the beginning of his career and thus call into question the whole thesis that he was a "Leninist" which *prima facie* rests on his loyalty to the party.

So, when the new evidence about Gramsci in 1921-22 is put into his biography the whole constellation or structural unity of the other evidence changes to some degree, and this in itself is reason for a new biography. No pretence is made that a final picture will emerge as a result of incorporating the new evidence. Gramsci's biography will always have to be updated when further crucial new evidence is discovered, (which today really means when the PCI is ready to make its next "drop" to confirm or discredit some thesis).

The second reason for another book on Gramsci is that the two earlier works were pioneer works written by historians[10] with consequent particular aims, methods and techniques. Each gave particular emphases as a result of his style and the different evidence available to him, but perhaps it is not misstating the position to say that Cammett and Fiori were content to put the facts together and let the reader make his meaning of them. Together they accumulated sufficient complementary evidence (and corroborated much of each other's evidence) to allow a more considered examination of its implications to be made. Fundamentally, we all start from the same facts, and, as Marxists, see what is in history rather than see through history, as is the wont of philosophers,[11] but I will ask the significance of this or that fact starting from the view that knowledge is a unity, and that to separate disciplines results in subtle and erudite mystifications.

These reasons are perhaps trite. The third is substantial. Readers of my article in *Political Studies*[12] will recall that in 1967: 1) many Italians decided that all interpretations of Gramsci's *Prison Notes* (*Quaderni*) available were premature as too little was known about his intellectual biography to allow anyone to put together the fragmented notes in an order which corresponded with Gramsci's overall view and intentions; and 2) Italian writers have acted on this premise, putting together the material which allowed Paggi[13] to publish the first volume of an intellectual biography, covering the years 1918-1922. My biography attempts to be the first intellectual biography in English, which not only clothes with substance the abstract categories of Gramsci's "Croceanism", Gramsci's "Leninism" and Gramsci's "National-popularism", so that the reader can see how each developed from earlier positions into a particular view when he wrote his notes, allowing a useful reading of the notes, but is also an implicit criticism of many of the interpretations and anthologies at present available, which are, to say the least, ideologically biased because the very way the notes have been ordered by some editors constitutes an interpretation which in marxist terms can only be justified by reference to the real man with real views who wrote them.

What then is it to write an intellectual biography? As I have already intimated, the growth of an outlook, a *Weltanschauung*, cannot be understood isolated from the total experience of the individual. Marx pointed out many times that a "consciousness" is always located in a sensuous being, and, if we are to establish a hierarchy between concepts and feelings, that is, the content of the vessels consciousness and sensuous being, it is the sensuous which precedes the conceptual. The development of Marx' theory away from its Hegelian origins into an autonomous system, would not be comprehensible unless we accepted that he took as his ruptural starting point the Feuerbachian notion that "Suffering precedes thought", often glibly referred to as Feuerbachian anthropological materialism, the definitional beginning of the slippery path back to philosophy. It follows that it is because a man suffers and wants to free himself from this suffering that he searches from a knowledge to help him understand his situation and to change it in an act of will. This is so, whether the individual is conscious of doing this or not. But this is not what is substantial in Marx' theory, as it only reformulates a commonplace which men have lived for millenia. What is substantial is that the suffering man is no empty abstraction isolated from the social reality around him. He is the ensemble of the social relations at a particular stage of their historical development. *Autant dire* that the content of those vessels of sensuousness and consciousness does not come from some well-spring within him, some Human Nature, but comes from without him and is social in origin. Each man is given a particular structured set of conditions with which to cope and a certain finite, structured mode of coping with them which includes an intellectual apparatus, with which he will talk, and within whose structure he will think, like it or not. Provided we remember that these structures are dynamic, historical and therefore changing, we can specify them with precision. Grasping them historically means realising that they do not present themselves to each individual uniformly, and that they are simultaneously both historical and spatial, so that each individual is located differently within them. In sum, we begin to grasp how much each individual can only be explained by his position in a particular historical and social structure, which is *his*.

So to make Gramsci's intellectual choices comprehensible, our account of the changing shape of intellectual attitudes in their development is rooted not only in an account of his life qua sensuous being, but also then rooted in his inheritance from the past: the social and economic structure which "produced" him, which in turn can only be grasped structurally if it is grasped historically.

The major problem in this technique of biography is deciding in what way the past is internalised in the individual. Readers will only see the tip of an iceberg of research into the theoretical work on this issue. In particular I have been stimulated by the work of J.-P. Sartre who is the only major Marxist theoretician to attempt to establish a theory of the individual by case-study, but I cannot agree with the pessimism of Sartre's conclusions about the interaction of the conditioning environment and the personality, precisely because it is too deterministic and does not allow men to make their own destinies.

Per contra I hope that this account of Gramsci's life not only does justice to a great man, but by throwing attention on the inherent nobility of his desire to "struggle and overcome" in various ways, some more successful than others, will redirect attention to the centrality in Marxism of the III Thesis on Feuerbach which reads: "The materialist doctrine that men are the products of circumstances and upbringing, and that, therefore changed men are products of other circumstances and changed upbringing, forgets that it is men who change circumstances and that it is essential to educate the educator himself. Hence, this doctrine necessarily arrives at dividing society into two parts, one of which is superior to society (in Robert Owen, for example).

"The coincidence of the changing of circumstances and of human activity can be conceived and rationally understood only as revolutionising practice."

ALASTAIR DAVIDSON

Postscript: The critical edition of Gramsci's *Prison Notebooks*, edited by V. Gerratana, appeared too late to be used for the final chapter of this book. This is regrettable, since the new edition may necessitate some modifications to existing understanding of Gramsci's theory, including that of this author.

AD

CHAPTER 1

A Country Boy

I

Antonio Gramsci's life began at Ales in Sardinia on 22 January 1891. On the sixth day of his life he was carried to the Cathedral and baptised into the Roman Catholic faith of his fathers by the Vicar-General, Sebastiano Frau, in the presence of his father and his godfather's deputy. His godfather was *cavaliere* Francesco Puxeddu of Masullus. His spiritual nourishment had begun.[14] Not so his more urgent infant demands. His Sardinian mother, née Giuseppina Marcias, could not nurse him because she was afflicted with mastitis. So, some two weeks after he was born he was given to a neighbour, a close friend of the family, Signora Melis, to nurse together with her own new-born son.[15] The adult pomp of the baptism was cancelled out by the more mundane aspects of child-bearing and the pomposity of the Southern inteilectual bourgeois was already pricked by the reality common to all men.

Gramsci's initiation into the world was a wry commentary on the state of life in the bulk of Sardinians of his time: too much spiritual, and not enough fleshly, succour. It was, moreover, a reminder that whether he later accepted or rejected Sardinia and all that it entailed, he could not escape its influence: born there of a Sardinian mother, he was already at two weeks of age immersed in its social culture on the level 'of religion and relations with neighbours: the *rito della Santa Romana Chiesa* and *u bixinau*. So it is with Sardinia that the story of Gramsci's intellectual formation begins.

II

Every Sardinian was the dialectical product of the interaction between his personality and imperialism and its products: the

1

economic and political force of feudalism and its legacy, and the social and ideological mores of the society. How these forces affected him depended on his precise social situation in this structure. It was, of course, a situation he inherited from the past.

Foreign rule had been Sardinia's lot for eleven hundred years before Antonio Gramsci was born. First there came the Carthaginians. The Romans ousted them in the second Punic War. In turn the Roman Empire lost the island to Byzantium several centuries later. Then the Eastern Empire's nominal rule was contested by all comers until 1297 when the Aragonese were appointed rulers by Papal fiat. Eventually when Spain was united, the Spaniards ended up ruling the island. In their turn they went: The new imperialists were the Piedmontese, whose king succeeded to the throne of Sardinia in 1720, and they were joined by other Italians when the Italian peninsular was united in 1861.[16]

This succession of conquerors came for different reasons, but, once in possession of the island their common object was to exploit the land and the men who lived in it. The pattern of this exploitation was set by the Carthaginians and Romans who established huge grain farms on the plains of the west and south and worked them on an exploitation basis with indigenous and imported slave-labour. Both the land and the slaves were drained of life in a savage and senseless exploitation. In the short run high yields were made, but the combination of exploitation farming of grain in a very dry climate, on unprotected land lashed by the hot winds of Africa, eventually exhausted the soil in this part of Horace's *tria frumentaria subsidia rei publicae*. Feudalism emerged gradually on the ruins of these *latifundia* and an indigenous baronage grew up. It was already fully-fledged when thirty-eight Aragonese grandees inherited nearly all of the island, and, dividing it up among themselves, continued to farm grain on the traditional exploitation basis.

For these barons, the island and the Sard serfs existed to provide them with quick returns from grain and sheep. To obtain the maximum return from the minimum investment their middle-men started to let the land in small plots at rack-rents in kind or in coin to the serfs, who then farmed it in the manner they thought fit. Since the serf had a very limited acquaintance with progress in agricultural science, he continued for six hundred years after the Aragonese arrived to work the land in the time immemorial way, using Roman technology. On the plains, the Campidano, he grew grain on his plots of land, supplementing the staple with an occasional vine, olive tree, and a few food-producing animals; in the jagged mountains he continued the tradition of nomadic pastoralism, grazing his sheep on ridges so close to heaven that it is difficult to realise today — when farming is much the same — that his terrestrial life is hell. Both grain growers and shepherds lived "in Franciscan communion" with their animals in sparse huddles of foul, fetid dens. The cities were small and contained almost no industry. Commerce was deliberately made the preserve of foreigners like the Genovese and Pisans.[17]

Very little of the soil which the Sard serf put under grain was suited to anything but pasturing animals, so his crops were small and frequently failed completely. In the hills drought often killed the flocks. Since his livelihood depended on this subsistence farming, his life was no more than a cycle of misery. The lack of an adequate diet mean he was very susceptible to disease. Malaria, from the swamps of the Oristanese and elsewhere, was endemic and on several occasions the plague struck. Mortality rates were so high that the Sard population dwindled with each century of Spanish rule. Doctors and hospitals were virtually unknown even at the end of the nineteenth century.[18]

Frequently the Sards rebelled against their foreign exploiters. In the sixth century B.C. they fought a long and bloody battle against the Carthaginians before they were defeated. Some were enslaved and others fled to the mountains. For centuries afterwards the mountaineers descended onto the plains in marauding raids. In 177-176 B.C. the Romans united in a savage punitive expedition against the marauders. The guerilla war between the Sards and their rulers grew in intensity as Rome's power dwindled before the Vandals. When the Aragonese arrived the Sards again fought a bitter war of resistance against the hated foreigner. Under Spanish rule there was relative peace until 1708, when Spain was challenged, and they again rose in rebellion. The Piedmontese fared no better. Popular risings in 1725-35, 1747-51, the 1760s, 1795, 1802 and 1835 were crushed by the punitive expeditions of the Piedmontese Viceroys.[19] These risings were almost always crushed with the greatest of brutality. The rebels were torn to pieces by savage dogs, burnt alive, hanged from the gallows which dotted the landscape of the Nuorese in the eighteenth century, and tortured for their "treason". Jean François Coffin, a contemporary observer of the repression of the rebels of 1795, spoke of the most frightful reaction.[20]

The forces of repression did not always win outright, and their

3

failure encouraged Sards to react to injustice. One Viceroy was forced to come to terms with the "bandit" leader, Leonardo Marceddu of Pozzamaggiore. Each era had its bandit hero who passed into legend among the Sards. In between the more substantial risings and repressions were minor reactions against Piedmontese soldiers collecting dues for the Spanish lords, something which had to be done practically every year. In Solanas in August 1789, "About eighty persons of both sexes reacted violently when five soldiers of the Sardinian regiment tried to force payment [of feudal dues]; the soldiers, before the menacing pressure of popular action, were obliged to withdraw, refraining from any action against the populace ..."[21] In the nineteenth century mass arrests, imprisonment on suspicion, execution of whole groups of peasants, and shooting of "escaping" prisoners continued to be part of the style of rule. Accounts like this of an episode in 1899 are too illustrative not to be told:

"That devilish captain had already thought up a siege plan. The city was divided into seven sectors, the personnel, *carabinieri*, police, into seven groups, holding bases for prisoners made ready, heaps of handcuffs, chains, rope: everything worked out and prepared for months without a living soul knowing, all planned with meticulous care down to the candles for the stairs, to the pencils and forms for the unloading. Midnight struck and *carabinieri*, guards, soldiers launched out in all directions....
From the central holding base, every few minutes a long file of handcuffed people, flanked by the glinting of bayonets and followed by a queue of wailing women, made their way to the railway station where a train awaited them.... So arrived the batches from all the stations of the Nuorese; at Bitti 33, Lula 27, Dorgali, 40...."[22]

Antonio Gramsci was eight when this occurred.

In the crucible of this millenial oppression and struggle against foreign invaders Sardinia's social relations were moulded. Invasion and domination marked the beginning of Sardinia's history. Foreign rule was not grafted onto a long-existing economic, social and political culture like many other conquered peoples of history. Sardinia's culture was formed in the dialectic of the struggle. Foreign domination determined what Sardinia and the Sard would be.

Imperialists had compelled him by their mode of production to eke out his life on a plot of barren soil insufficient for his needs. They had provided him with no technological innovations to offset the exhaustion of the soil and the vagaries of nature. They had kept him in the barbarous and ignorant state in which they had originally found him. Feeling at the mercy of a capricious natural and social world in which there were no rules or justice, he had become a fatalist. He knew what *Chie cumandat fachet lezze* and that *sa lege mai obblighat chie la faghet*.[23] He also knew that there was no point trying to control destiny, or as he put it: "You don't get olive chips from a cork tree". The inexplicable and the magical, the supernatural and the absurd lay all around him. The ethic of *sa balentia* enabled him to remain a subject in a world which was "implacable and hopeless, in which to exist is to resist, to resist a destiny which is always against him...." This added up to his living by a set of social norms, inculcated from childhood, which taught him to suffer and endure his lot on the one hand, and on the other, to react to each capricious, inexplicable, mishap owed to men or nature, with an equally irrational response.

His social world was naturally wild, cruel and brutal, for the dialectic of the master and slave permeated into even the slaves. The men ruled with an iron fist in the homes and the women taught their children that in the vulpine world outside they must seek to maximise their self-interest at the expense of others. The doctrines of Christianity had little effect on him although there was one priest for every fifty people in 1826. Naturally there was always a tension in Sard society as the corollary of psychological health at one social level was a continual offence and defence on another social level. It was dangerous for an offended party to tolerate the offence as this showed that he was weak in a society where weakness meant destruction. "Vengeance became the basic ethos of the country".[24] Rustling, and murderous blood feuds were a part of life to which the entire population was bound in one way or another. What laws were introduced by the foreigners could not compete with the deeply rooted law of the vendetta.

Having made the Sards these "barbarous", "slothful", "unlawful" people each successive ruler both treated them as such, reinforcing the ethic through their own brutality and capriciousness. At some time they forbade the Sards to live the way they did. Tyndale, who visited the island in 1843, relates:

"The father of a nobleman now holding one of the highest

appointments under the Piedmontese government ... was walking with his friend in one of his feudal estates on the island, and feeling tired, called to one of his vassals then digging in the field, to come to him. The poor peasant obeyed, and was immediately ordered to ... place himself 'on all fours' ... upon the ground, which having done, the feudal Baron leisurely sat upon his back till he was rested. His friend, unable to suppress his feelings at such an act, subsequently spoke to him about it, to which he merely replied in Spanish, 'No es nada; dexelo hacer; es bueno que asi se mantengan en el respecto che deven a los Senores-estos picaros' (That is nothing — let him do it, it is quite right that they should thus behave themselves with the respect they owe to their lords — wretches that they are!)"

"A similar demand was made by another feudal baron; but the peasant — drawing his long knife — a species of bayonet — from his girdle and sticking its handle in the ground, indignantly replied, 'Sezat si subra di essa bayonetta' — 'There, sit down upon that knife' and afterwards told him that he would sooner put his knife through his own, or the baron's body, than submit to being a footstool."[25]

By 1897 Niceforo had rationalised this treatment by 'proving' with bogus science that the Sardinians skills had "atavistic stigmata" and "dolichocephalic survivals".[26] In sum, what united the *nazione fallita* of the Sards was not only that there was on the forehead of every Sard "the mark of the most hideous slavery", but a common and abiding antagonism towards their foreign rulers and any Sards associated with them in the popular mind. This antagonism ranged from incomprehension at the best of times to savage hatred at the worst. The most hated section of the society were those Sards who had made common cause with the *straniero*, either through marriage, education, position, or through being "different".

Since the coming of the Spanish there had always been such people, the agents of the imperialist power. The Spaniards had started a deliberate policy of "divide and rule" and gradually turned the indigenous nobility into "loyal subjects" who spoke Catalan and met in their own estates, the *Stamenti*, whose political function was more dignified than real. In 1795 the middle-class leader of the celebrated rising of that year wrote: "The Archives of the towns in Sardinia are filled with monuments to the fidelity of the Sards to the kings of Spain and the immense privileges given by these monarchs to the Sard nation for the great help and eminent service which she rendered them at all times, and particularly during the frequent wars which they had to fight."[27] The Spaniards also succeeded in creating abiding antipathy between the *barbaricini* of the mountains and the plainsmen. Even under the Piedmontese the townfolk of Sassari, the mountain capital, still spoke Catalan.[28]

The indigenous group associated with the rulers grew wider under the Piedmontese, when the small emerging middle class of notables and middle-farmers — the *cavaglieris* — and *massajos* were incorporated into the administration, law, and politics. This was done by the gradual abolition of feudalism and creation of private property in the land. It was a long process in which only the serfs suffered but it must be discussed at some length since it shows where the Gramscis fitted into Sardinian society.

III

According to the Treaty of Utrecht and agreement with the Spanish Government, the Piedmontese had agreed to leave all the Spanish barons in their feuds. In 1744 they considered buying them out but this was shelved for fear of offending the Spanish court. At the end of the century absentee Spaniards still held 198 feuds; resident Spaniards held 107, 68 belonged to the crown and 11 to residents of Turin. When feudalism was abolished in 1836-40 Spaniards still held most of the feuds.[29]

Throughout 1720-1836 their abuses of powers became more excessive and conditions continued to get worse for the Sards.[30] The Secretary of State for Sardinian affairs, Lorenzo Bogino, made only episodic and fragmentary reforms to the feudal system.[31] There was no alteration in the perennially backward methods of cultivation and grazing in Sardinia and no real diversification of commerce took place. Some private owners bought into the land and some of the lords lost their jurisdictions, but this meant little to the Sard for whom life was much the same.

Only at the very end of the century, after a serious revolt had almost ousted the Piedmontese, did they begin to reconsider the legal order of Sardinia on which feudalism was based. Some abuses were corrected in the criminal reforms of 1799. Then in 1819, hoping to stimulate the development of private property, the

7

Piedmontese passed an enclosure law allowing the barons to enclose. Finally in a series of edicts of 1835-38 the Piedmontese formally abolished feudalism and set up Royal Commissions to decide who had rights to what land.

By 1840 Piedmontese laws had formally abolished feudalism on the island. Momentarily the Sard peasants were overjoyed, as they had long desired to own the land that was their livelihood and to be free from the oppression of foreign barons.[32] The Piedmontese laws of 1819-20 allowed them to enclose the plots they worked and claim them as their own property. They were to be the class of petty proprietors whom the Piedmontese bourgeoisie hoped would develop the land and accumulate capital because of their interest in it. Momentarily the expropriated barons were hostile. They had not been consulted in their *Stamenti* or Estates as to the measure and all their unlimited rights had suddenly been removed. Both groups soon changed their minds.

The barons discovered first that they were getting far more from the indemnity the government was paying them, and whose cost the new Sard peasant proprietors would ultimately have to bear, than they had ever got from their dues.[33] Moreover, they too were able to enclose land (some of them had been doing this illegally since the beginning of the century anyway) and quickly enclosed not only the best, but also much of the common land.

In the area where Gramsci was born, Mura of Santu Lussurgiu enclosed a vast area around Paulilatino, a few miles from Ghilarza, cut off the well and refused to let the peasants drink from it. This abuse was abetted for some time by a provincial official.[34] Elsewhere other barons discovered that because of their power and the complacency of Piedmontese officials in the neighbourhood they could obtain the lion's share of the spoils. One Piedmontese viceroy wrote to Turin in 1832 that similar abuses were "almost general in the Nuorese". He claimed that on both the plains and mountains the large landowners had enclosed woods and the best pastures to oblige shepherds to pay very high rents; that they had cut off watering places and public fountains in order to ensure that they would make the law for the shepherds.

"In its execution the law suited only the rich and powerful, who were not ashamed to enclose huge areas of land of every sort, without any intention of improving the agrarian system, but with the sole object of making the peasants and shepherds pay dearly for their right to sow or graze their flocks."[35]

In fact, this meant the *de facto* retention of feudal political power — the right to make laws for his serfs — in the hands of the baron but the loss of serfs' rights to communal grazing and wood gathering rights. The worst of feudalism was being retained, the best lost.

Naturally, the peasants showed bitter resistance, especially in the mountains where baronial abuses when enclosing were worst. They concluded pacts with those barons who still opposed the abolition of feudalism and with bandits and started to hurl down the hated enclosures in a series of guerilla attacks and risings, shouting *pro torrare a su connottu* — "let us return to the known system of land tenure" — which in the mountains usually meant the continuance of communal pasturage.[36] These risings continued until well into the 1840s. Verses record peasant antipathy towards the enclosing.

> *Tanche chiuse a moro*
> *fatte all'arraffa arraffa*
> *se il cielo fosse stato in terra*
> *avreste chiuso pure quello* [37]

There was even one case where the disillusioned peasants entreated the baron to take them back into vassallage.[38]

The peasant faced much more than his baron. The whole force of modernising capitalism represented by Piedmontese imperialism was opposed to the communal ownership of the highlands. By the 1860s the violent opposition had been crushed down and the bulk of the island was private property. Between 1833-53, two thirds of the land around Gramsci's home, Ghilarza, was enclosed for example.[39] Only royal desmesne remained land held in common.

In the second half of the nineteenth century, most of the land was held by peasants in small holdings.

On the other hand there were still a few huge properties which correspond with the baronial lands of former times and the Sard peasant only had an agglomeration of tiny plots. There were thus still leading landowners in each district who retained the rights of the baron informally if not formally. They were often his blood heirs. The peasant still tilled his plots in the time immemorial fashion. This did not mean the end of feudalism as a system of political values, social organisation or cultivation methods. Its legacies remained and so did the legacies of the way it was abolished.

In the struggle between the conflicting interests of tiny peasant owner and baron, the Piedmontese unwittingly but effectively weighed the odds heavily in the favour of baron and the perpetuation of feudalism.

The indemnity paid to the barons for the loss of their rights lay heavy on the shoulders of the new peasant proprietors. 480,000 lire had to be found each year to pay off the public debt incurred, and, given the tax structure of the Italian state, the small holder or peasant paid it.[40] Tyndale wrote with great pertinence:

"The reality of the measure [abolition of feudalism] was soon tested, and the vassals, awaking from their credulity found the change to be merely a substitution of one inconvenience and evil for another; the burden of increased taxation sat with less ease than the old on their galled shoulders; payment was enforced by the violent hand of the government instead of the private measures of the baron, and as a climax of the evil, was extracted in specie instead of in kind."[41]

Indeed, the peasant had been suddenly launched into a money economy, something he hardly comprehended at all. Money was the new master of his destinies as much as the soil. The Piedmontese intention in abolishing feudalism had been to allow a new property owning middle class to grow up and to accumulate capital. It was, of course, their sincere belief that economic progress would come as well as agrarian innovation when men had a stake in the land. But there was no native middle class to buy into the land. Earlier imperialist policies had ensured that no local mercantile capitalist class would emerge. Capital was needed if the peasant was to improve his holding and there was no liquid capital available or made available to him by the government. The Piedmontese even destroyed the agrarian credit organisations which existed throughout Southern Italy in a series of reforms in the 1860s. On the other hand the communes collected the dues to pay the indemnity to the barons with great rigor from the peasant proprietors, who not only still faced the same agricultural problems that they always had, but had frequently enclosed the most unproductive land anyway.

They could not improve their holdings, in the absence of readily available money to borrow, and so they remained in the same precarious position, threatened by the elements and nature as they always had been. Now they were even worse off than under feudalism as they had to pay the tax to the commune as well.

Salaris[42] pointed out that in one commune in the Campidano they were paying a third of their income in tax. Most of them only survived in their tiny holdings at the price of indebting themselves more and more to usurers or to the commune itself. By 1870 Sardinia had a mortgage debt of 3000 lit to the hectare, four times the value of the land, as the peasants struggled not to go backrupt. In 1901, 41,661 still worked their own plots, another 24,031 were ploughmen, 15,408 were leaseholders.[43]

By 1900 the struggle had been too much and many went bankrupt. Already in 1870 forced sales reached 139 for every 100 thousand of the population, a significantly greater proportion than elsewhere in the *Mezzogiorno*. 17.1% of these sales were for debts of more than 50 lit; 64.7% for debts from 5-50 lit and 18.2% for tiny sums less than 5 lit. The property almost invariably found its way back into the hands of the large landowners, the former barons. By the middle of this century, when the process of reconcentration had reached a zenith, 1.8% of the proprietors owned 44% of the land and large holdings over 200 hectares were not rare.[44]

A large number of landless, and usually unemployed, labourers had grown up by the end of the nineteenth century. In 1901, there were 77,753 agricultural day labourers on the island.[45] Many others had found their way into the dreadful mines of the island, or denuded the island of timber. Particularly responsible for the great unemployment was the introduction of a protectionist tariff against France in 1887 which prevented Sards selling their stock on the Marseilles market, as had been the custom. Many farmers went bankrupt. Death by starvation was frequent.

Under feudalism these people would still have had rights to common pasture. But what royal desmesne had been reserved as common pasture fifty years earlier had nearly all been alienated to the larger proprietors. There was nothing left but to suffer and endure or to emigrate.

A visitor of 1840 who returned in 1900 would not have thought that anything had changed. Men still worked thousands of tiny plots in feudal style. There were still a few large landowners whose economic strength made them the social and political powers in particular areas. While he might have been surprised at the number of unemployed and a growing number of middle peasants, the *massajos*, he would have seen that most men survived as they had when they were feudal serfs, eking a living from the grain of their tiny plots, or grazing their sheep on the *tanche*, much as had been

11

the custom in Roman times.

A new group of people had been created to carry out the process of breaking up the feuds, or reorganizing agriculture on the basis of private property. They were particularly hated by the Sard peasant. There had always been the "perfidious feudal baron" of Mannu's national song. There had long been the collectors of feudal dues and taxes. To these there were now added the officials of any office associated with the agrarian reform, from the collectors of redemption payments, to those who decided which land had been held in common and which not, and what the old rights were. The land registries, and offices dealing with deeds and successions were particularly detested because throughout the nineteenth century title to land was continually being contested due to the complications about rights after the abolition of feudalism. On two separate occasions there were major revisions of the *Catasto*, or register of land property. On each occasion, the bureaucrats presented a threat to Sard peasants who feared that they would lose their right to a particular plot in a revision. The revisers of the roll were also particularly open to bribery and pressure from the more powerful interested families.[46]

It was into this society that a mainlander, a member of the foreign bureaucracy, came in 1881 to take the position of director of the registry. He was Antonio Gramsci's father, Francesco.

IV

Francesco Gramsci [47]

We can only speculate as to the state of mind of Colonel Gennaro Gramsci when his fifth son, Francesco, was born at Gaeta in the Kingdom of the Two Sicilies in March 1860. Unless he was unusually confiding we shall probably never know whether he still had that joy which Italian fathers show on the arrival of a *bel maschietto*, even though it was his fifth. We can infer that he was rather troubled at the time, if he was not unusually philosophical or lacking in perception, for his ordered world was crashing down all around him. Great events gripped Italy. Within a year, the state he lived in was to go out of existence, swallowed up in the new Italy ruled from Turin. It would be conquered by force from the South, where the flower of Italy's youth made common cause with the Sicilian peasantry and put the Neapolitan army to fight, and from the North, by the armies of Piedmont, ordered by older, more cautious, less idealistic men, fearful that Garibaldi and his Redshirts would give offence to the Pope. Indeed, within months of Francesco's birth, the city in which Colonel Gramsci lived would be besieged by General Cialdini's troops. If the invaders from the South and the invaders from the North had anything in common it was dislike and scorn of the state system of the Kingdom of the Two Sicilies in which Gennaro lived. In particular, the conquerors hated men like Gennaro Gramsci and what they stood for, the most reactionary, inefficient, inegalitarian state system in Europe. Among them the Bourbon kings of the Two Sicilies and their oppressive state machinery were anathema. Most of liberal, nationalist, capitalist bourgeois Europe was, metaphorically, applauding both sets of invaders as they dismantled Bomba's kingdom and stamped out the monstrous prison system and police regime which had so horrified Gladstone less than ten years before, when he had called it "the negation of God". To Gennaro Gramsci it must have sounded like the roar of Nemesis, for he was a colonel of the gendarmes, the worst of the offenders in the eyes of the invaders because they were the personnel of the police state. Whatever fanciful tales were circulating in the censor-ridden kingdom, one essential message must have been coming through: that he, his profession, and his type of people were *personae non gratae* in the Italy which was being made. Perhaps they were even doomed. He fought tenaciously in the siege against Cialdini and is reputed to have had his wife flee on foot through Cialdini's lines, carrying Francesco with her.[48]

Fate is capricious. The old ordered feudal world of the Italian South in which Gramsci, himself the son of a Greek Albanian who had fled Epirus in 1821, had found his niche (perhaps through marrying Teresa Gonzales, the daughter of a family of Spanish descent, in a country ruled by Spain until 1734) did not disappear in a blood bath of retribution. Instead, Garibaldi and his thousand quickly showed that they did not stand for social revolution by shooting peasants who occupied feudal desmesnes and so started that alliance between the middle-class of the North and the landowners of the South which continued the old order in the South which in turn perpetuated a backward agrarian system akin to that in Sardinia already described. Late in the century some idealistic souls were to call it the Southern problem. Although the Piedmontese were horrified by the state of Southern Italy and attempted to remove all Bourbon state structures, including the

13

administration (in 1865), they too, thought that the real enemies were the peasants and the Bourbons, and consequently fostered the continuance of the old order. While they proceeded formally to continue Bourbon efforts to abolish feudalism they encouraged the emergence of a new social group to take the place of the feudal barons, but to wield power as the barons had, as the real power of the *Mezzogiorno*. In no time people like Gennaro Gramsci, who could rightly have feared for his life in 1860, again filled most of the administration of the South. He himself became part of the *carabinieri*, retaining his old rank of colonel, and thus became part of the new ruling class of the South of united Italy. His children survived the turmoil to make successes of themselves. The only daughter married a native of Gaeta, a rich gentleman called Riccio. One son became a civil servant in the Treasury, another an Inspector of Railroads, the third, Nicolino, whom we will meet again, an artillery officer. Only Francesco fared less well. He had finished high school (*liceo*) and was studying to be a lawyer, when his father died. Compelled to give up his legal studies, he too joined the administration, and at 21 years of age found himself in what was regarded as an absolute hole, Sardinia.

Gennaro's grandson himself said in an interview: "Our father was thus of a typical well-off Southern family of the sort that supplies the middle ranks of the State bureaucracy."[49] He could have said little that was more damning about Francesco's social formation, and his social attitudes. This middle rank of the State bureaucracy became the mainstay in the new variety of the old system of rule in Southern Italy. The complex articulation of this system of rule need not be described at length here.[50]

Briefly it consisted of a situation in which the local middle-class, especially in the communes, being in possession of all the administrative, judicial and political offices of the South, became the intermediaries for a central government, which, washing its hands of the South except as an area of exploitation, deposited all real socio-economic power in the hands of the middle-class provided that the middle-class secured elections and taxes for it. In turn the only way in which the Southern peasant, who constituted the bulk of the Southern population in the second half of the nineteenth century, could obtain anything administratively, judicially or politically was by approaching these middle-class dispensers of power. And they did favours for favours. An elaborate *clientele* system developed around these groups of notables. They wielded almost absolute power and they wielded it in their own interests.

The resultant inequity caused enormous class hatred. In much of the twenty years when Francesco Gramsci lived on the mainland, law and order was kept in many places by martial law. Especially hated were the petty-bourgeois who controlled the villages and communes, for these were the people with whom the peasant had direct contact, while the more august lived far away in the cities.

Gaetano Salvemini characterised the petty-bourgeois of the villages this way in 1911.

"Go any afternoon to one of these clubs (*circolo di civili*) where the finest flower of these country idlers meet, listen for some time to the conversation of these corpulent people, with their blank eyes, their stupid half-broken voices, gross and vulgar in both words and acts, take note of the stupidity, the nonsense and the irreality of their *propos*. I don't know where this difference of intellectual capacity between the petty bourgeois and peasant populations of the South comes from.... Perhaps, manual work and life in the open air preserves the peasants from the degeneration which very quickly takes hold of these do-nothing families in that mild climate, largely infested with malaria. This much is certain: between the 'gentleman' and the 'bumpkin' there exist not only profound and easily visible differences in dress, dialect, everyday life, but also real somatic differences. The peasant is thin, ascetic and tenacious in his work: the Roman *miles quadratus* cannot have been very different. The gentleman is flaccid, inert, and good-for-nothing. The gentleman when he shouts at the peasant, tries to imitate his voice making it deep and masculine when it is normally feminine and false: he thinks he is satirising the peasant when, in fact, he is illustrating his personal degeneration. What allows the Southern gentleman to appear intelligent beside northerners, who are realist but slow, is his promptness of reply, an inferior quality which all neurotics possess ... "[51]

Salvemini could have been describing Francesco Gramsci at the time Antonio was born or a little after. He was corpulent, given to grandiose schemes of little practicality, to vanity and boasting, and was a typical authoritarian type.[52] He had also become one of the petty-bourgeois of the countryside, which was, in the hierarchy-conscious South, a cut below what he might have been, had he finished his law studies, always regarded by the Southern bourgeois as the way to *otium cum dignitate*.

At first, he hated the backwoods of the administration to which he's been condemned and wished to use his stay only as a stepping stone to something better than the position of Registrar in Ghilarza, possibly to return to the mainland.[53] After the delights of law school, Ghilarza, with its 2000 inhabitants, must have seemed the epitome of boredom to the young bourgeois. It had one street, a tiny square and a church. Other villages lay close around in the densely settled part of the Campidano, but they were even more dismal. The nearest town, Santu Lussurgiu, was still a horse, donkey, or the ox-cart ride away as there were no roads, and there was little to attract a young man there anyway. So Francesco was confined to the village and had to find his amusements there, and to the villagers he was a hated *straniero*, dignified by the appellation *Signore*.[54] Not that they would have been interested in him or had much time. To farm their tiny plots they left the village early and returned late. Most owned some land (*massajos*) but they also had to find labouring jobs at sowing and reaping time. For these people life was work. The year began formally in September, and that month had a Sard name derived from the Hebrew Rosh Hoshana but Ghilarza's life could be measured better in terms of the cycles of grain production. A successful sowing meant food for the next year and so it was accompanied with great pomp. Since the outcome depended so much on natural phenomena invocation of the incomprehensible deity who decided such events was common. To relieve Francesco's boredom there was the feast of the Archangel Michael on May 8, when the village's patron saint was invoked, in a solemn procession of villagers carrying ears of corn in their hands, to protect the newly sown crop against the flails of drought, hail and locusts.[55]

Then there came for him the boring, and for them the emotionally tiring wait until the grain could be harvested. It was very hot and the land became parched. If there was a drought the village would arise out of its torpor, the young men would enter the street and make a shelter of grass and branches and sing:

> *Maimone, Maimone,*
> *abba chere in laore,*
> *abba chere in siccau,*
> *Maimone, llau llau.*

Their godfathers would come from the doorways and sprinkle water upon the shelter. The invocation of the pre-Christian deity was supposed to break the drought. If the drought broke, and there was a harvest, in June the men would eat *su pane de sa rughe e de sos bracchedos*, bread baked and consecrated at Xmas. The purpose was to protect themselves from injury during reaping.

The reaping would involve the whole village and the crop would be carried in in festive fashion to the sound of songs. The night would be lit with fires and full of the smell of burning off. The reaping was done by hand, and even in 1900, there were few threshing machines: usually the grain was trampled by horses or oxen. Its conclusion marked another triumph of man over nature that year and consequently the poor were often given alms for fear of provoking bad luck. A harvest feast was held. The master and the servants sat at the same table, mutual toasts were given, and ribald jokes told.[56]

The active year, when men seemed to impose themselves on their environment, would end and there would begin the months-long period of comparative inactivity. There was, of course, some work to be done on the farms, but usually it was a period when all *massajos* and landless labourers looked for work and usually did not find it.

It was a dull period. The big religious festivals of Ghilarza, except of S. Serafino (24 October) all fell during the active period. So did the dancing and the putting on of best clothes; though in the eighties and nineties Sardinian peasants still wore traditional costume.[57] It was a hungry period, especially for the smaller farmers and the day labourers, who relied on work to eke out their meagre subsistence.

Without education or intellectual reserves to fall back upon, they lived a dreadful life of enforced idleness when they seemed completely victims of the outside world and their social environment.

This feeling of being victims of fate coloured their whole outlook on life. Their folklore was pervaded with the idea of their own objectivity and the ineluctability of whatever happened to them. They conformed very closely to the general picture of Sards already given. The laughter of their harvest feasts showed the hectic joy of the psychologically hopeless. Even in dance they wore no smiles — it savoured of a religious rite rather than a form of social relaxation.

For the Ghilarzese, if the anarchy of nature and the outside world had any unifying principle, it was Fate. There therefore seemed no escape from it and little could be done except to placate

17

the natural world. The whole society of the Campidano was riddled with witchcraft, spell-casting and belief in the supernatural; with fear of entities beyond the power of men to control except by further cabalistic appeals.

In Ghilarza were-wolves were greatly feared, and so were maleficent ghosts and witches. The first were known as *sa surtora*. The people believed that certain women had the capacity to transform themselves in various ways, and then to travel at night to *succianta su sangue is pippius*, "to suck the blood from babies." The most common form that these women took was that of a cat. Ghosts returned as Will-o'-the-wisps to squat on the breasts of sleeping people. The witches were believed to have powers to cast spells on adults, by sticking pins into effigies.[58]

In a world populated by such demons the poor peasant could only protect himself by further magic. For example, when a ghost squatted on his chest at night to oppress him, he could seize it by one of its seven berets if he woke suddenly, and the ghost would give him a treasure to secure its freedom. Again, if a spell was cast on him, he could obtain philtres and charms from the wise women of the village to counteract it. He could gather flowers and herbs on All Saints' Day and hang them in his house to prevent an evil befalling him.

Nighttime was especially dangerous and the fear of darkness was increased by the frequency with which stories of such supernatural creatures were told by the fire in folktales handed down from generation to generation.[59] Not only was a natural phenomenon like darkness feared, so too were harmless beasts like the frog and the toad, which according to legend had evil powers. Pity help the peculiar looking or cast-eyed member of the community for he would be a pariah suspected of having the evil eye. Hunchbacks were also treated unusually as it was believed that touching their hump would bring good luck.[60] When a dog bayed, as dogs are wont to do at night, it was a warning that someone in the house would soon die (*so canes ululant, malu signale*).[61]

In sum, it was a society in which abnormality of any sort brought suspicion, whether it were physical abnormality or not.

Ghilarza was, moreover, as ignorant societies are apt to be, cruel. At the source of this cruelty lay the poverty of men who had insufficient for their needs and those of their families.[62] The only attachments of men were to the land, the sole guarantee of life, the ox with which he worked it, and to his family. The family was an extended organisation rather like a clan and had ramifications beyond the limits of blood relations to "vicinati" or neighbours who had lived in long or close communion with him. Outside the clan everyone was a *straniero*.

Within the family the father ruled with a clenched fist. He was a jealous God who was addressed in the third person and before whom all dispute stopped. Even today wife-beating is common in the Ghilarza area.[63] It was affirmed with the surety of the authoritarian *Chi ha peccato non ha redenzione* — "there is no redemption for sinners."

Lacking in compassion, the affection within the family was undemonstrative, dry and formal. The relation of the villagers to the world was unwittingly expressed by their houses — for everyman *hat su casa*. Life took place in the courtyard at the rear, where the women baked the bread and weaved the cloth and where the youngest children played. In this courtyard there was often a donkey-worked mill. Facing the street was a wall with a doorway. It testified to the withdrawn nature of the Sards and the desire for privacy for their women.

Backward, ignorant, withdrawn and cruel, this society and its people presented little attraction for anyone, let alone a young man straight from the joys of university. Francesco turned to the 200 literates of the village and became part of the joking, card playing petty-bourgeois *circolo* of the village.[64] This society is an empty, emotionally unsatisfying life, and within a year he started to think of marrying. Few girls in the village were suitable matches, but one who particularly took his eye was Giuseppina Marcias, the daughter of a tax collector, who belonged to one of the best families of the neighbourhood.[65] His relatives were horrified and strongly opposed him in his desire to marry; for a mainlander, marrying a Sard bordered on miscegenation. Boredom breeds passion, and Francesco was not to be turned away from his intention. In 1883 he married Giuseppina Marcias.

V

Antonio Gramsci's mother was the most important formative influence in his life. She had been born at Ghilarza in 1861. Her father had been born at Terralba a few miles to the South. Hosts of relatives lived all around Ghilarza and in neighbouring villages. She belonged on her mother's side to the Corrias, one of the leading land-owning families of the area. In a word she was a Sard.[66]

While she inherited all the characteristics imposed on Sards, she was also one of the Sards who had associated with the imperial regime. Her mother's family were large landholders in an area where tiny plots were the norm. Her father was that most hated of all officials, the tax-collector.[67] He too had a small landholding. She belonged to the Sardinian petty-bourgeoisie, which, in common with the rest of the bourgeoisie of the Italian South, had an idea of its own importance which appeared greatly over-inflated when viewed from Olympian heights by those amused by the vanities of petty people, but which was accurate enough from the point of view of the parish pump politics in the Sardinia of the time. Though in most ways very similar, the Marcias and the average villager thought of themselves as different from one another. She was always addressed as Signorina Peppina not as Tzia Peppina because she was a "refined lady, to whom consideration was paid."[68] The villagers normally addressed each other familiarly as Uncle or Aunt.

The difference between the Marcias and the ordinary villager should not be stressed too much. Her father, as a landowner, shared the problems of all the villagers. He lived in a house without lighting or sanitation as everyone else did. All members of the family spoke the Campidanese dialect as well as Italian. Giuseppina learnt what all young Sard women did, how to cook and sew and, presumably, to remain silent in the presence of the men. She was as deeply religious as the other women of the village.[69] Her children were later named after the important saints of the district, and she was a regular church goer.

Giuseppina was as insular as the rest of the village. In her whole life she never travelled more than twenty five miles from the village.[70]

But it was what distinguished her which was important, as it was the criterion by which she established her difference from the villagers. Apart from the fact that her family was richer, and associated with the administration, she was also unusual. She could read, having been sent to school for three years at a time when only 200 or less people in the area could read. She could write, and she could speak Italian. She never lost her love of reading and devoured books avidly, including Boccaccio, a very worldly work for a young Sardinian girl.[71] She dressed in "European" clothes, eschewing the traditional dress favoured by others. She was one of the very few possible brides for the young mainlander who arrived in 1881. Her marriage to him was a step up the social hierarchy.

A Country Boy

Antonio Gramsci's infancy

When they were married, Antonio's parents moved to Ales, a larger cathedral town some miles to the South. In 1883, a son, Gennaro, had been born to them. At Ales two girls arrived, Grazia Antonia Serafina (1887) and Emma Potenziana Antonia (1889). Giuseppina Gramsci had well and truly embarked on her role of childbearing by the time Antonio was born in 1891. Francesco was intent on making his career and was mixing with the right people. Their friends and acquaintances numbered the court bailiff, notaries and other administrative notables. By 1892 there was a female domestic. Antonio was to be born to a privileged group by Sardinian standards.

But it was still to some degree part of the overall Sardinian culture. The differentiating quality of petty-bourgeois status was marginal in the small rural villages in which the Gramscis lived. The situation of Giuseppina especially cannot be grasped until it is realised that the peasants had a healthy and sometimes openly expressed scorn for the "white-faced" and "parasitic" bourgeois who did not work with his hands and who gave himself unacceptable airs. This attitude was owed possibly to the fact that there was so little real difference between peasants and women like Giuseppina. It was illustrated by a baptismal feast for Antonio which had all the qualities of the traditional Sardinian baptism. The proud parents, their three children, and friends and relatives from Ales and Ghilarza ate the traditional cakes and drank the wine either with the genuine gaiety of the extrovert or the forced gaiety of those for whom joy is more private.

Antonio Gramsci was "at home" with his people, who would dandle him on their knees and hold him in their arms, from whom he would learn his first lessons; lessons he himself had forgotten by the time he was an adult.[72]

The cacophony of voices, laughter, tinkling glasses; the smell of Sardinian baking, wine, and the people who consumed it; the white shapes surrounded him which were, in time, to become separate, identifiable personalities or to be lost to memory as his parents shifted away from Ales.[73]

The first person he knew in a continuous relationship was his mother, who, having recovered from her mastitis, started to breast feed him, as all Sardinian women did. She was then thirty, and photographs reveal a plump, Italianate, and slightly worn woman with an anxious smile. From childhood she had been prepared for

21

motherhood and she had already mothered three. This made her an excellent mother. Antonio was an attractive child, with his blond waves and light coloured eyes and much was made of him by visitors.[74]

She had little time to devote to him alone as soon after the family shifted to Sorgono, where Francesco had been transferred, she gave birth to Mario (1893), Teresina (1895) and then in 1897 to Carlo. But Antonio was not neglected by her and was the darling of his sisters. He also had a nurse-maid. Up to the age of three he was a very happy little boy.[75] All his life Gramsci was deeply attached to his mother and greatly admired her.[76] He hardly ever mentioned his father, rejected his values completely, and broke entirely with the conservatism of his background.[77] Where he could, as we shall see, he blamed him for his own afflictions and condemned him for lack of care.

Most biographers have noted a change in his life at this stage of his development. They have stressed that it coincided with his being injured in an accident, leaving spinal damage which developed in later life into a hunchback.[78]

VI

Sorgono was in the Barbagia, where the most backward of the Sards lived. The nurse maid came from the village. When Gramsci was three she was engaged in a torrid love affair with the local government doctor and had become pregnant. The intensity of the relationship was probably increased by the realisation on the part of both lovers of what retribution could befall them in this country of the vendetta. For Sards, though notably tolerant of love affairs which ended in weddings, were also prone to kill seducers of village maidens. The doctor decided that the danger was too great and fled the village. The languishing maid saw her chance to see her lover again when Antonio, then four, slipped and fell down some high stairs. At first she hid the fall from the parents but when a swelling developed and the fall was discovered she suggested that he be taken to see the doctor.[79] His parents, being agreeable, allowed him to be taken on the long, bumpy ride in an ox-cart, aggravating the hurt done by the fall. On his return the little boy started to pass blood through his mouth and anus. The haemorrhaging lasted three days, and marked the beginning of an illness lasting three months during which he hovered between life and death.[80]

Dr Cominacini advised his father to take him to the mainland for treatment but his father was apathetic and neglected to do so.[81] The boy's condition worsened and his distracted mother was told by the doctors to give up hope for his survival. A little coffin and shroud were even purchased for him and remained in the house until 1914 for the boy to see.[82] The backwardness of the country was revealed in his mother's treatment: she massaged the swelling on his back with iodine, only making it worse.[83] His aunt Grazia Delogu, prayed for him and annointed his feet with oil from a lamp dedicated to the Madonna.[84] His recovery was later attributed by her to the miraculous powers of the Virgin. We cannot help feeling that miracles happen in backward areas because science is so inefficient!

When the crisis was over the swelling remained. Now his father visited specialists in Oristano and Caserta and obtained a little harness from which the boy was suspended from the ceiling by his father or elder brother in an endeavour to straighten out what was becoming a hunchback.[85] By the age of six it was noticeable that hs rate of growth had declined considerably. He was going to be a dwarf hunchback in a society which was very cruel and unsympathetic about such defects. Only the superior status of his parents could protect him from the harsh realities of life.

They succeeded in doing so until he was seven. In the intervening years he attended the kindergarten of the nuns at Sorgono with his sisters. Teresina became particularly dear to him. To some degree the extent of his privilege can be gauged from this as there were then only eleven kindergartens in Sardinia.[86] He also regularly received presents on his birthday, something unheard of except in the most privileged families in Sardinia.[87] As the child of the *signore*, whose hunchback was not yet very noticeable, he was shielded from the misery which was to befall him as a result of his father's involvement in parish pump politics.

Like so many Southern Italian rural petty-bourgeois, Francesco Gramsci became deeply involved in local politics after he arrived to take up his new position at Sorgono. In 1896 Sorgono began to prepare for the Italian general elections of the following year. Two rival cliques of bourgeois contested the electorate. Neither really stood for any political position; both were interested in the rewards which would ensue for them when their candidate was elected.[88] Then plum jobs would be distributed, opponents punished for losing, and the grant of the central government would be passed on to the commune, which they now constituted, for administration as

23

they thought fit. The report of Francesco Pais Serra made to the Prime Minister Crispi in 1896, described local politics in Sardinia as a type of gradual vassallage worse than that which existed under feudalism:

" ... conservative, liberal democratic and radical are words without content; socialism and anarchy and political clericalism are not even known by name, yet parties are lively, tenacious, intransigent and aggressive: but they are not political parties, nor parties moved by a general or local interest, they are personal parties, cliques (in the strict meaning of the word).... Under the great wings of these larger personal parties... pullulate microscopic personal parties in the different Communes, all the more spiteful and violent because the reaons for disagreement are closer, and contact necessary every day.... They make themselves dependent on the major parties, from whom they receive in exchange protection and effective aid in little local contests and, above all, personal protection through obtaining favours and through avoiding the consequences of breaking the law, and, sometimes even of committing crimes."[89]

The two patronage systems which contested the electorate of Isili, which included Sorgono, were headed by Cocco Ortu and Enrico Carbone Boy. The sitting member Ortu had been a Member of Parliament for twenty-one years and Undersecretary of first the Agricultural Department and then the Department of Justice. Boy could rely on the local loyalties of his village, Nuragus and considerable sections of Sorgono and Tonara and threatened to unseat the existing *camarilla* whose clientele system culminated in Ortu. Naturally great bitterness existed.

Ortu was a powerful, unscrupulous man who cared not a whit for his electorate except as the prize which he could apportion to his local followers.[90] We need not, on the other hand, attribute any high-mindedness to Francesco Gramsci in supporting Boy in the elections. As Serra indicated, the *camarillas* which existed in these tiny villages were no better than one another and Francesco would have shared the prize if his candidate had won, to the detriment of the peasants of the area. Indeed, the registry was particularly open to manipulation in the interests of his group in any disputes involving property rights which were then rife in Sardinia.

In the elections Boy, and thus Gramsci's *camarilla*, was beaten. It knew what to expect from the victors. There is no reason to believe that it would not have done exactly the same had it won. The general rules of the game of Southern politics as described by Salvemini — which men knew involved framing, suborning, blackmailing and intimidating — were all borne out.[91]

Francesco Gramsci was a classical example of Salvemini's generalisation about electoral politics in Southern Italy. He left Sorgono briefly in December 1897 to attend the funeral of his brother, Nicolino, who had commanded the artillery at Ozieri. While he was absent the victors in Sorgono sent a telegram to Cagliari suggesting an inspection of the registry. An inquiry into his conduct of the registry was set in motion by the members of his opponents' faction.

As with nearly all meridional office holders there were matters for which he could be reproved: the office had not been run properly. But, as Salvemini suggests, even had it been impeccably run, evidence of "misconduct" might still have been found. Francesco Gramsci was suspended from his office.

The disaster which had befallen the family was crucial for Antonio's intellectual development. His father could not cope with his misfortune, and with much wringing of hands and shaking of heads withdrew into himself and awaited his fate. The family rallied round. It was decided that they would return to Ghilarza and live with Grazia Delogu in her house in the main street of the village. The eldest son, Gennaro, fifteen in 1898, returned from Ozieri, where he had been living with his late uncle, as soon as the school year ended. He alone was told of his father's predicament and that he would have to work when the school holidays finished.[92] On 9 August 1898 the *carabinieri* arrested Francesco on charges of embezzlement, extortion and falsification of documents while employed at Sorgono. He was transferred to Oristano gaol to await trial.

His wife showed the fortitude and resourcefulness which Antonio recalled to his sister many years later in these words:

"If she had been another woman, who knows what disastrous end we might all have come to as children? Perhaps none of us would be alive today."[93]

Scorning to turn for help to his mainland parents who had opposed the marriage, she sold instead the land which she had inherited from her father, took in a veterinary surgeon, Dr Vittorio Nessi, as a boarder, and started to eke out the fund with money earned as a seamstress, as she had always excelled at sewing. There is nobody so terribly human as the fallen petty-bourgeois, and none so easy to hurt. For the children there was a stiff upper lip and falsehoods to explain their father's absence. She did without sleep, sewing at night to help pay for the lawyers. At all costs the disgrace had to be hidden from as many as possible.[94] For solace there was the church — she became deeply religious — and for catharsis there were lonely weepings in the street on dark nights.

No doubt she prayed hard in the two years the authorities held Francesco before bringing him to trial in Cagliari in 1900. It was to no avail. He was sentenced on 27 October 1900 to five years eight months and twenty-two days in prison, a mandatory minimum sentence for a crime like his, where little public money was actually missing. He served his sentence near his birthplace, Gaeta. As the paper *Il Momento* indicated some years later, he was not alone in the terrible revenge which the *coccisti* inflicted on their opponents and the hate engendered led to terrible crimes even ten years later.[95]

What significance had his father's fall from grace for Antonio? The Gramscis had lived lives of comparative ease as members of the ruling group of Sardinia. He had been kept carefully shielded from the discrimination which could result from the fact that he was a hunchback. His mother had kept him at the kindergarten although he was more than seven. The sudden alteration of the family's circumstances meant that although Giuseppina attempted to maintain its status in the petty-bourgeoisie, in ways which we will see, it no longer had the social power which lies behind all status ranking. Lacking both a privileged foreign father in the administration or the material well-being of former times, it was at the mercy of a peasantry whose hatred had formerly been kept in bounds by this status. It was doubly disliked because it attempted to "Put on airs" as ridiculous as those of the quixotic hidalgo. While peasant animosity, whose origins were buried in the history and social culture of Sardinia, could now be loosed against the hapless Gramscis, Antonio also had reached the stage where he had to emerge from the womb-like family environment of friends, neighbours and relatives into the social world of the village. He first went to school at seven and a half years and thus met his peer groups, who were the children of peasants, and shared their social, ethical and cultural values. In meeting them, and their parents, in a social relationship, he met extreme cruelty and persecution born both of the social culture itself and realities such as class and the

26

concomitant class hatreds, and of the natural cruelty of children towards the abnormal. As a result he had become by 1900 a desperately lonely child, whose withdrawal from the normal life of his peers resulted in a sensitivity and capacity for fantasy which made him very socially aware of cruelty and injustice. Like most boys he did not make much of his loneliness and tried to hide it from his parents. We must be moved by this letter, written from the vantage point of adulthood, when the terrible griefs of childhood had faded into the subconscious.

"If she [his mother] knew that I know all that I know and how scarred these experiences have left me, it would poison her life...."[96]

If we stressed too much the lack of sanitation, running water and light in the house in which he now lived as the first mark of his new poverty, we would err through neglecting to view conditions in the cultural context.[97] Almost no Sardinian houses had light or sanitation or running water in villages like Ghilarza in the 1880s. The house was a typical Sardinian rural bourgeois house, large, with a good back yard in which the outside kitchen was located. Antonio's bedroom, upstairs, facing the courtyard, was light, airy and adequately furnished.[98] No doubt, from the outside the house needed a whitewash and appeared dark and cavernous, but Ghilarza was a damp place, and all houses need paint frequently. The poverty was not a matter of starvation either. There are no recollections in Gramsci's letters of great hunger but there are several of the varieties of bread his mother used to bake and of the home cooking. No doubt helpings were not palatable and the diet unbalanced, but, again seen relative to the situation of many Sardinians whose livelihood had been destroyed by the tariff war with France and who were eating grass and starving to death in the late nineties, the Gramscis did not suffer from hunger.[99] Their poverty seems to have been more that penny-pinching poverty of the bourgeoisie, which does not wish to appear to have come down in the world. His sisters used to gather the stumps of old candles and melt them down to make up new ones so that he could read.[100] He used to stand for hours waiting to get the best coffee.[101] At other times he used to collect firewood or acorns to feed the pig.[102] It appears that his mother attempted to shield the children as much as possible from hardship by pulling in her own belt and working late at night making clothes which were then sold.

The change in the Gramscis' circumstances could not be hidden in a small village where a large proportion of the inhabitants were closely related. This constituted their real poverty. Antonio had not been told what had happened to his father and the miserable boy appears to have discovered that his father was in gaol through the jeers of the village children. He was mortified and years after instructed his own wife[103] to tell his seven-year-old son that he was in gaol so that he would not discover fro a others the situation of his father:

"I don't know why it has been hidden from Delio that I am in prison, without any thought that he might learn of it indirectly, that is, in the most unpleasant way for a child, who begins to doubt the truthfulness of his teachers and is beginning to think for himself and make a life of his own. At least that is what happened to me when I was a child: I remember it perfectly.... Therefore, we must convince [Giulia] that it is not right or useful to hide the fact that I am in prison from the children: it is possible that on first being informed they might have unpleasant reactions, but the way in which they are told must be chosen with care. I think that it is best to treat children as reasonable beings, with whom one speaks seriously about the most serious matters; this leaves a very great impression with them, reinforces their character, but especially avoids leaving the development [*formazione*] of the child to the luck of the environment and the mechanics of chance encounters. It is really strange that grown-ups forget having been children and do not keep their own experience in mind: I, for my part, remember how every discovery of subterfuge used to hide even matters which could hurt me offended me and induced me to close myself in myself and live by myself; I had become, at about the age of ten, a real torment for my mother, I had become so fanatical about frankness and truth in reciprocal relationships that I even made scenes and caused scandals."[104]

The truth was out, but the mother continued to protest that the father was visiting his grandmother at Gaeta and used to address letters to forwarding addresses.

This duplicity was particularly irritating, not only to sons, but to people in general. Everybody in the village knew that Francesco Gramsci was in jail, and yet the mother maintained the farce. Faced with the dull-looking collection of peasant children with whom he

28

went to school, Antonio would have had to make a choice about loyalties. As it was his peers gave him no choice. He was persecuted mercilessly by them, hardly ever joined in their games, and turned instead to books, games of fantasy, pets, and his mother and sisters, especially Teresina.

Today surviving villagers, especially boys, try to forget the miserable time Antonio had either by maintaining that he could not join in because he was injured, or he was too small (big) or that in fact he did join in the games of village children. Alternatively they maintain that he did not wish to join in because he was "the quiet type", withdrawn.[105]

Antonio Gramsci recalls that he was never allowed to join and was persecuted. What interests us in a story of his intellectual formation, or learning process, is what he felt was happening. It may be true that on occasion he joined in the boys' games and in time he made a few friends, often girls or adults, who showed more compassion, but the general truth for us is:

"When I was a child the boys of the town never came near me except to make fun of me. I was almost always alone. Sometimes, finding me by chance among them, they hurled themselves against me, and not only with words. One day — and while he told me this his great eyes shone with an inner light — ... they started to throw stones at me with more violence than usual, with the evilness which is found among children and the weak. I lost patience, and grabbing stones I too started to defend myself with such energy that my attackers were put to flight. Mario, I succeeded in beating them: I terrified them to such an extent that from that day they respected me and no longer annoyed me. I ran to my mother ... and told her of my first victorious battle: she kissed me tenderly and it was the best prize that I could have wanted."[106]

The result was a withdrawn little boy whom photographs reveal as solemn faced, with introspective eyes. He is recalled by his family and others who knew him as a child as "quiet", "reserved", and "melancholy".[107] He, himself, told us more, when he likened himself to a "bear".[108] Although his childhood friend Nenetta Cuba recalls that she "never saw him laugh with joy" and that his smile was that of an adult not a boy, on occasions the desperate desire to belong, to join in, to be loved, provoked laughter from him.[109]

Long lonely walks through the country with his noisy and vivacious little brother, Mario; a number of pets, including a parrot, hedgehogs, and a little dog which he loved and tormented by turns; drawing and model-making; and, above all, reading, filled in the hours for Antonio.

It appears that he ascribed the persecution more to the fact that he was deformed than to class hatred. He had already become aware of his deformity before he came to live in Ghilarza permanently[110] but now he set out to combat his affliction. He made himself some barbells and used to exercise frequently with them in the courtyard.[111] He showed considerable ingenuity in making them from pieces of stone. His brothers helped him cut them out from masses of rock and shape them. Iron was, of course, too expensive for the penny-pinching family. He also turned this constructive and patient facility towards model-making: his speciality was model boats, made of paper, cane rushes, cork and wood, which he played with in the courtyard together with a little boy called Luciano. The boats were destroyed in great battles fought with homemade airguns.[112] Then there were cages to be made for the injured animals he brought home.[113] There was the Abbyssinian parrot who was nasty because he didn't know how to do anything but eat beans and chickpeas,[114] and the little dog "he had gone half mad over getting, it made him so happy". This little dog, who compensated for so much, was clipped, climbed all over his master, even made *pipi* on him in his excitement. The favourite game was to go for a walk in the country, place him on a high rock from which he could not get down, run away and hide. The tiny dog would then find the way down and look under every unlikely bush and stone until he found his master.[115] The hedgehogs were found one night raiding an apple orchard, captured and carried home to play some months in the courtyard before somebody stole them for the pot.[116]

Much of his time he spent drawing, laboriously copying pictures from the newspapers and taking care to get the colours right. He recalled to his own son that one drawing took him almost three months. It was a picture of a peasant who had fallen into a grape vat and was being looked at alarmedly and amusedly by another.

"The picture belonged to a series of adventures whose protagonist was a terrible billy goat (Barbabucco) who, butting treacherously and suddenly, made his enemies and boys who made fun of him fly through the air."[117]

What filled most of his spare time was reading. This he did with his sister Teresina, his favourite, and future ally against the adult world. The Gramscis, being literate and privileged, had always had a few books on the bookshelves in addition to the various Criminal Codes and manuals used by Francesco. Antonio recalled that one of the first books he read, *Quintino Sella in Sardegna*, was from the family shelves. However, this was a weighty tome, and after his school books to which he devoted what time was needed, his preferred reading was romantic. At seven he had read *Robinson Crusoe*, which so impressed him that he never went out without matches thereafter in case he was marooned, and *Treasure Island*. He read Emilio Salgari's novels about pirates so much that he knew them by heart (hence the naval battles in the courtyard). *Uncle Tom's Cabin* he found mushy, but Kipling, and Rikki Tikki Tavi impressed him greatly. *Pinocchio* was a favourite. Many of the brothers Grimm's fairytales were devoured: *Rumpelstiltskin, Three Men in the Forest* and others.[118] Many of these books had been given to him by the wife of the tax-collector, Signora Mazzacurati, before her husband was transferred elsewhere.[119]

This passion for reading benefited him when he started school, although he started a year late. With his mother helping him with his spelling and learning his lines, he was able to stand out in a class of peasant children, many of whom could not even speak Italian.[120] He did not even have to spend much time at his lessons, although his mother took special care to foster his interest.[121] He wrote later to his son:

"At your age I was very undisciplined, I spent many hours roaming around the country, however I got along well at study because I had a good and ready memory, and nothing escaped me which was necessary for school: to tell you the whole truth I must add that I was smart and knew how to get myself out of difficulties even when I had studied very little. But the school system which I attended was very backward; moreover almost all my fellow pupils only spoke Italian very badly and with difficulty and that placed me in an advantageous position because the teacher had to take into account the average student and knowing how to speak Italian was already a matter which made many things easier (the school was in a country village and the great majority of the pupils were of peasant origin)." [122]

He and his sister were always reading whatever they could lay their hands on, and this made them somewhat marvellous in a village of illiterates.[123] He was always first in his class in the first two years he was there, although there were forty-nine pupils in the charge of Igniazio Corrias, the teacher in his first year of primary. His marks were always nine or ten out of ten. In second year, under a new teacher, Celestino Baldussi, he got three "tens", one "nine", two "eights" and a "seven". This encouraged him to attempt to skip a class. At this stage, his estimates of his own ability outstripped his capacity. On presenting himself before the headmaster, *cavaliere* Pietro Sotgiu, who was to teach him in 1901-02, to ask for permission to sit the appropriate examination, he was sent off with an intellectual clip on the ear. Sotgiu asked him "Do you know all the eighty-four articles of the Constitution?". He did not, and mortified to the brink of weeping, he went home.[124] Up to the age of eleven, when he had completed fifth class (1902-03) he did extremely well in his exams, coming down only in gym and craft.[125]

"Remember how mad we were about reading", he later reminded his sister, and bosom companion, Teresina, who rivalled him for scholarly fame in the village.[126] This love of books earned him a reputation as a "swot".[127] On the other hand it was a compensation for his rejection by his peers and it enabled him to feel superior to the peasants who attended the school with him.

His outward social life followed much the same pattern as that of his peers and as the years slipped by he became more and more accepted, and part of the community, to whom a role was accorded. He took part in the various religious and national celebrations of the village, either in the processions or as a spectator.[128] At least once he went to the seaside.[129] He used to go, on occasion, on the religious pilgrimages too common in Sardinia, to this or that rural church.

Living in the village, he gradually got to know its people and its culture. With some adults and a limited number of younger people, he made friends. This was almost unavoidable. His aunt, Grazia Delogu, brought the local Sard culture into her house with her corruptions of religion: her appeals to the holy Donna Bisodia (a corruption of *ora pro nobis hodie*), her belief in miraculous cures, and magical properties of certain substances.[130] Antonio became aware of the values and beliefs of the villagers through learning their folklore, and hearing their folktales. Although some of his relatives lived in Abbasanta, he knew that the *abbasantesi* were

stranieri for the residents of Ghilarza.[131] (Now both villages were
joined together.) He saw how they worked in their distant plots and
what effect this had on the village. He heard folktales and local
stories and in prison proposed to write a poem about his
acquaintances along the lines of the excommunication of *predi
Antiogu a su populu de Masuddas*, which castigated the prejudices
of rich and poor of the village. In this the principal actors were to
be childhood acquaintances *"tiu Remundu con Ganosu e Ganolla,
maistru Andriolu e tiu Millanu, tiu Micheli Bobboi, tiu Escorza
alluttu, Pippetto, Corroncu, Santu Jacu zilighertari ecc ecc...."*
[132] He too heard the tales of monstrous flies, of toads which sat
on the chests of sleeping peasants, and of other demons which filled
the air after dark.[133] He too made heroes of the bandits of
Sardinia, Derosas and Tolu, who were symbols of resistance
against the foreign imperialist.[134] Like the rest of the village, he
spoke dialect. He got to know the travelling salesmen who in those
"uncivilised" times were one of the few contacts with the outside
world. Later he remembered that one had a horse, whose ears had
been eaten off by a wolf; how he put false ears and a false tail on his
horse on Sunday so that the children would not make fun of
him.[135]

It would be wrong to ignore the incessant pull of the local culture
on Antonio through his mother and her less educated or esteemed
relatives. It would be equally wrong to ignore the fact that while
belonging to the culture through his mother — "we are only half
Sard", he wrote later — he never regarded himself as a peasant.
Most of the villagers were so far below him and his family, on a
social level, even while his father was in prison, that they were only
good for passing *salaam aleikums*.[136] Where, very early he
thought he might become a carter, by the time he was asked the
ill-fated question about the Constitution he had already decided on
a career as usher at the Pretura (court usher), something which
would never have occurred to the peasant who knew he was born to
die a peasant. Though no longer one of the leading families of the
neighbourhood, his mother and he were still acquainted with such
people as the Sannas, whose father was at one time mayor of
Ghilarza, the Porcellis, the local surveyors, as well as with the
Corrias family.[137]

Many years later, Antonio Gramsci was to refer to himself as a
Sard without psychological complications.[138] At about the same
time a doctor examining him on behalf of the Italian State made a
report in which he said that Gramsci had:

"... always dominated his own unhappiness with an iron will for study, making efforts way beyond the strength of his organism". [139]

There is no man without psychological complications, but Antonio certainly learned to dominate or master himself very early, though he was probably not conscious of this until much later.[140] With each step he took adjusting himself to his environment, he learned. This development was not completely chronological. He was still engaged in self-flagellation (hitting himself with a rock until he drew blood) and believed that nobody loved him when he was ten.[141] By this time the family was not in such straits as in the previous two years as Gennaro had found a job at the *catasto* in 1900 and the initial shock of cruelty from peer groups must have died down — Antonio was more accepted but he still recalled:

"I was forced to make too many sacrifices because my health was so poor, I persuaded myself that I was merely something to be tolerated, an intruder in my own family. Such things are not easily forgotten, and leave much deeper traces than we might think."[142]

He learned to cope with his loneliness and feeling of inferiority which flowed from rejection by his peers by excellence at study, and by living a private existence. His own experience of the cruelty of the world led him to a heightened awareness of the cruelty of the society around him, and a compassion for the sufferers who were his fellows. At eight he saw something which impressed him and aroused his compassion despite his own hurts.

"It is all a matter of comparing one's own life with something worse and consoling oneself with the relativity of human fortunes. When I was eight or nine I had an experience which came clearly to mind when I read your advice. I used to know a family in a little village near mine: father, mother and sons: they were small landowners and had an inn. Very energetic people, especially the woman. I knew (I had heard) that besides the sons we knew, this woman had another son nobody had seen, who was spoken of in whispers as if he were a great disgrace (*disgrazia*) for the mother, an idiot, a monster or worse. I remember that my mother referred to this woman often as a martyr, who made great sacrifices for this son, and put up with great sorrows. One Sunday morning about ten, I was sent to this woman's: I had to deliver some crocheting and get the money. I found her shutting the door, dressed up to go out to mass, she had a hamper under her arm. On seeing me she hesitated and then decided. She told me to accompany her to a certain place, and that she would take delivery and give me the money on our return. She took me out of the village, into an orchard filled with rubbish and plaster; in one corner there was a sort of pig sty, about four feet high, and windowless, with only a strong door. She opened the door and I could hear an animal-like howling. Inside was her son, a robust boy of 18, who couldn't stand up and hence scraped along on his seat to the door, as far as he was permitted to move by a chain linked to his waist and attached to the ring in the wall. He was covered with filth, and his eyes shone red, like those of a nocturnal animal. His mother dumped the contents of her basket — a mixed mess of household leftovers — into a stone trough. She filled another trough with water, and we left. I said nothing to my mother about what I had seen, so great an impression it had made on me, and so convinced was I that nobody would believe me. Nor when I later heard of the misery which had befallen that poor mother, did I interrupt to talk of the misery of the poor human wreck who had such a mother."[143]

This experience was but an early isolated instance of Gramsci's awareness of the social cruelty which existed everywhere in Sardinia, and which mattered to him as he himself suffered from it, even though he was not of the same class. Later on when at school at Santu Lussurgiu, he observed similar social cruelty. He lodged with a woman and her mother, who was a trifle senile. The daughter, intent on having her commit some gross extravagance so that she could have her committed to the lunatic asylum, treated her with great harshness, while, of course, observing the Sard convention of addressing her in the third person. The old lady used to cry with asperity "Call me thou and treat me well".[144]

Living in a Sard society of brigands, vendettas and social cruelty Gramsci could not but have "almost always known only the most brutal aspect of life."[145]

His father, released three months before the due date, returned to find a son who had become so accustomed to living an isolated life that he was on many accounts a stranger; a son who had learned to hide his feelings behind an impassive face or an ironic smile; a son who himself said that "his relationships with others were enormously complicated."[146] Almost immediately he generated extreme hostility between himself and Antonio by insisting that the boy, who had done so well at school, be taken away and start work. He insisted with heavy-handedness, as the salary of nine lire a month meant an extra two pounds of bread a day for his family. Nino worked ten hours a day, six and a half days a week for this, shifting heavy registers around the land office. This exhausted him and at nights he used to cry with pain. He himself claims that what prevented his becoming a "wrung out rag" (*cencio inamidato*) was his rebellious instinct, first against the rich, who were able to go to school, when he who had been so bright could not: the son of the butcher, the pharmacist, the haberdasher.[147] This later widened, he claimed twenty years later, to include all the rich who oppressed the peasants of Sardinia. He then thought that a war of national liberation with the slogan "Into the sea with Italians" should be fought. He reported nothing of his resentment against his father, though perhaps his father was included in the rich. Certainly his father quickly found his feet again. The bourgeoisie of the village did not discriminate over much against him for his fall. They knew the style of politics and that it was luck who ended in prison. So though he could no longer hold a position in the government, they found him work. First he was secretary of the cooperative for cattle raising, then he became, as a result of his early legal studies, a councillor to the Magistracy; finally, he became an amanuensis at the *catasto*. He was readmitted immediately to the petty-bourgeois clubs of the village. But he could no longer play the *signore* as far as the villagers were concerned, and in time became known as *tiu*. Since Gennaro was doing his military service and Mario was now in a seminary in Oristano, Francesco and Antonio were the only bread winners, although Giuseppina continued to sell her sewing and the eldest sisters helped out. The family was still in comparatively straitened circumstances in 1904-05. The father, now somewhat more timid, though still strong willed and old fashioned, and his reserved, crippled son began to come into conflict more and more and Gramsci, growing into puberty, withdrew more and more from the rest of the family. Later he claimed that he detested family life and he certainly had little time for the vacuousness of the petty-bourgeois clique of the village.[148] Perhaps both his father and he were relieved when it was decided that the family now had enough money to send the boy to *ginnasio* in Santu Lussurgiu, about eleven miles away.

The lack of transport or adequate roads obliged Antonio to lodge in the Sa Murighessa area with a middle-aged peasant, Giulia Obinu, the mother of the senile old woman who used to call out "Call me thou and treat me well". For five lire each month he was given lodging, frugal board, and linen.[149] The ambience was probably worse, and certainly no better, than that at Ghilarza, though he no longer had to see his father except at weekends. The old lady, who really took care of him, used to forget who he was, and regularly, on meeting him on the stairs would ask who he was.

The school, the Carta-Meloni *ginnasio*, was run by the municipality, who had inherited it from the religious order of the Scolopi when the order was stripped of its holdings by the Piedmontese in 1866. The original endowment was the cause of a lawsuit between the State and the Commune which lasted until 1901 when the school was finally opened. Naturally, it was no school to emulate, but by Southern Italian standards early in this century it was typical. The five classes were taught by three "self-styled" professors. In 1905 two totally unqualified teachers were dismissed, because they had done nothing about obtaining qualifications, and positions were advertised. The expected teachers did not arrive, and Antonio only began school when the academic year was well advanced, after supply teachers had arrived. An engineer taught him science and French. Two supply teachers taught him the literary subjects so important in Italian schools. They were so inept and gave the school such a bad record that between them these teachers destroyed in him any of his early love and ability for the natural sciences.[150]

Their intellectual dishonesty and stupidity entirely destroyed in him any respect for teachers and the Italian middle-school system. He remembered cases where he was told that certain reptiles did not exist except in myth (by the engineer) when all the boys of the neighbourhood knew that they did as they had seen them,

"You know how angry a boy gets when he is told he is wrong when he knows he is right or is mocked as superstitious when it is a matter of reality."[151]

and suggested that it was "authority in the service of ignorance". He was good at school and was always at the top of his class, displaying particular talents in literary matters. Despite his early rejection by the villagers of Ghilarza, here among the children of bourgeoisie, he was accepted and frequently visited the homes of school companions.[152]

At first, most of his time between his arrival by horse wagon on Monday morning, and his departure for Ghilarza, sometimes on foot, on Saturday mornings, was spent in school, or studying. He had the previous two years to make up when, with the exception of the acquisition of some Latin through private study, he had not had time to keep up with his studies. His sisters always despatched him with some provisions, to eke out his meagre board, and the money for his rent which they had earned making stockings.[153] The love and devotion of his sisters was something he could always count on. However, both they and their mother in time realised that the naughty Nino often sold part of his provisions to raise money to buy books and papers. He was especially interested in history. They did not forgive him for this.

On the weekends his homecomings were mixed affairs of joy and disapproval. Relations with his father were particularly strained. He despaired of his sons. Gennaro, the eldest, was doing his national service in Turin, and having learned some more advanced views before he left from the young technicians in the *catasto* where he had worked in 1901, was rapidly becoming a socialist. His object was to convert people to his new faith and he regularly sent home socialist material in the hope of converting his family. Nino was the only one who responded. He read everything avidly, demanding the mail as soon as he arrived home. The reactionary father wrung his hands over these two, and Nino teased him about his Bourbon antecedents. Perhaps the distraught father, aware that socialism had spelt jail in the Crispi period, feared another family disgrace. Antonio was compelled to catch the postman before the dread subversive material was seen by his father and to read it secretly.[154] Mario, the seminarian, was no cause for joy either. He had returned home too, because he felt that his lusts were stronger than his faith, and suggested that Nino be made the priest instead, "as he has no thought of women". His religious mother was particularly disappointed.[155]

In 1905 Nino's life changed slightly. He was still receiving the inadequate education of the Carta-Meloni school, which was now in such straits that there were proposals that the school be closed, but now he was reading *Avanti* regularly, thus becoming one of the first bridgeheads of socialism in Sardinia.[156] He also took a part-time job in the holidays as an accountant at about this time to eke out his existence and started coaching students.[157]

Poor teaching, and neglect of his studies, combined with a general debility, added up to poor marks when he took his *licenza ginnasiale* in Oristano at seventeen. Only in history did he receive eight out of ten. In French, learnt from the engineer, he received three; in Italian six for written work and seven for the oral; in Latin six and seven respectively and in geography, seven. He put off sitting mathematics and sciences until later in the year 1908. Then he passed both and the French which he had failed.[158]

For the first time he was about to be incorporated into the Italian state school system and to leave the area where he was born. Both meant going to Cagliari, the small, backward capital of Sardinia, where he would attend the Giovanni Maria Dettori *liceo* for three years. He went to live with his brother Gennaro, known affectionately as Nannaro, who was working in the ice factory of the Fratelli Marzullo as a cashier, and with whom Nino now had most in common.[159] Gennaro and he lived at 24 via di Principe Amadeo. After the first month, Nino received no money and they had to live on Gennaro's 100 lire a month. Again and again his father's allowance was to prove insufficient. Naturally poverty was once more his lot. He tightened his belt, always wore the same suit and could not afford books. In 1908 and 1909 he sent several letters to his father asking for money and books. He reported to his father that he was in dire straits, and his plea in these years was: "Remember that I must study if I am to get my matric. (*licenza*) and that I shouldn't have cause for worry."[160]

After the poor teaching at Santu Lussurgiu he made a bad start at *liceo* Ashamedly, he tried to explain away his failure as due to poor teaching there and as a result of a three day absence from school. In history, his predilection, he could only manage five out of ten. In the other subjects, with the exception of chemistry, he could manage little better. However, vain about his intellectual ability, he promised something better by the end of the year.[161] This he did, for despite an average of six at the end of the year, he was promoted.[162]

He returned to Ghilarza for the summer vacation of 1909, if not in triumph, at least uncrushed. After the holidays, the brothers changed their boardinghouse for a cheaper place at 149 Corso Vittorio. His room had lost all its plaster because of the damp and overlooked a courtyard which to him seemed more like a latrine.[163] His brother Gennaro still had to support Nino on his low salary as his father's allowance was insufficient and this caused strained relations between them. Again feeling that he was a burden

39

on his relatives, he tried to impose as little as possible by missing out on the morning coffee and reducing the number of meals he ate to one each day.[164]

His poverty meant that he could not join in the extra-curricular activities of his fellow students as much as he liked. He could not buy them a coffee in return for theirs and regularly turned down their hospitality. He never went to the billiard room with them although this was part of Italian bourgeois adolescence.[165] Again, as in his youth, the young man started to live by himself, never speaking to his fellow guests.[166]

And again he compensated for his loneliness by reading and working hard. In 1910 his marks started to improve. At the end of the first term he received 7 and 8 for Latin, 8 for Greek culture, 8 for Greek, 8 for history, and 6 in physics, natural history and philosophy.[167] He received no mark in Italian because there was no teacher in Italian. Eventually the new professor of Italian arrived. Raffa Garzia immediately made Gramsci his favourite because the young man was now excelling in his compositions, which were read to the class as models. It is interesting to read a summary of them.

"... curious essays in which something new can be noted: a singular sense of history as it was going on, something not common in a young man of his age, getting close to men and facts which are distant temporally and spatially. You feel that the most burning problems of culture and Italian life of that time are not unknown to the young man who is writing those pages. Here and there you can feel the eagle move his wings. This eagle, however, does not know how to fly yet."[168]

Togliatti overstates Gramsci's awareness and understanding of the world outside, but it is clear that Gramsci's life experience, what he had learnt, was about to be expressed.

In 1911, through his friendship with Garzia, normally a harsh man, but who was gentle with Gramsci, Antonio emerged from the school world into the limited intellectual world of Cagliari. Garzia was thirty-three. He had published an essay, *Il canto di una rivoluzione*, which compared the Sard national anthem of '95 and Parini's *Giorno*. He was the manager of the most widely read paper on the island, *'Unione sarda'*, which he owned, and in which he advanced his radical and anti-clerical views, though he was not a socialist. His paper supported Cocco Ortu who was indirectly responsible for Gramsci's father's disgrace. In 1910 the paper's main target was the Luzzatti government because Ortu had been excluded from the Ministry. The paper attacked the government both from the right and the left. It also took up strongly Sardist positions, especially after the royal visit of 23-25 May 1910, asking what the government had done to improve conditions in Sardinia.

In July 1910, Gramsci requested a post for the summer vacation as journalist for this paper. Garzia, now a friend, made him correspondent at Aidomaggiore, a village near Ghilarza. He had passed his second year well.[169] Gramsci's first published work appeared five days after the journalist's pass was issued to him, in the *Unione sarda* of 26 July 1910. It ran:

"In the surrounding villages the word had spread that terrible things would happen at Aidomaggiore on election day. The populace wanted to introduce manhood suffrage at one fell blow, that is, elect the mayor and the Council by plebiscite, and seemed ready to commit all sorts of outrage. The Lieutenant of the *carabinieri* at Ghilarza, cav. Gay, seriously worried by these symptoms, sent a whole army platoon, 40 *carabinieri* and 40 infantrymen, thank heavens without cannon, and one policeman (who would have been enough on his own). When the polling began the village was deserted; electors and non-electors, fearing arrest, had made themselves scarce, and the authorities had to go from house to house to flush out those who remained. Poor mandarin growers of Aidomaggiore. The infantry is different from the phylloxera."[170]

Late in 1910 Antonio Gramsci returned to Cagliari again to start his last year of *liceo*.[171] He was almost 21. He was still very short of money and since he felt that Nannaro had done enough to support him, this year too was full of pleas and letters to his parents asking for money.[172] When, as on one occasion, an acquaintance stole his money, he was in dire straits.[173] In the last eight months of the year he was so poor that he started to eat only one meal a day again and was in a state of severe malnutrition at the end of the academic year when he had to sit his exams. At *liceo*, his mentor Garzia had taken sick leave and had been replaced by Vittorio Amadeo Arullani. Gramsci continued to show the same excellence at studies. On one occasion, he even surprised the mathematics master by his ingenuity in solving a final examination problem on the board. Amid the friendly jeers of this man, who was an acquaintance of Gennaro's and a militant socialist, he covered himself with chalk as he laboriously and successfully worked out some mathematics which he needed for physics. Thereafter Maccarone called him the *"fisico grecizzante."*[174]

His forte was, without doubt, languages and literature and he had decided to be a teacher (*professore*) of literature.[175] In his final examinations he received nine from Arullani in Italian and eight in all the other subjects.

Only then did he discover that there existed a scholarship from the Collegio Carlo Alberto, which if won, would take him to the University of Turin. He would be examined in all his *liceo* subjects.[177] His uncle Serafino Delogu was the only one who realised the poor state of health and invited him to act as a tutor of his son Delio. Gramsci spent six weeks in Oristano before leaving for the mainland to sit the scholarship examinations. He had had no time for personal study having devoted all his time to his charge and he described his state of mind on departure as "somnambulism".[178]

During his last year in Cagliari he continued to become more extroverted although the basic pattern of life was one of the withdrawn scholar. Garzia had left, but he still read *Unione Sarda* which was Sardist. He read widely; both Sardinian literature and the papers and journals of the mainland. He did not like Deledda and preferred the poems of Sebastiano Satta which dealt with the contemporary problems of the Sardinian, especially those about bloody incidents at Bugerru a few years before.[179] He started to read *Domenica del Corriere* regularly and the socialist *Viandante* of the "revolutionary Tomaso Monicelli".[180] His favourite authors, Benedetto Croce, Gaetano Salvemini, Emilio Cecchi and Giovanni Papini, he read in what were naturally his favourite journals, both non-political, *La Voce* and *Il Marzocco*.

The socialist literature he obtained through his brother Gennaro who had been elected to the Council of the Camera del Lavoro in January 1911. Gennaro acted as cashier and a secretary of the local section of the Socialist party. He stated in an interview:

"I used to meet the young leaders of socialism in Sardinia: Cavallera, Battelli, Pesci, often, and sometimes Nino happened to be with us. A large quantity of propaganda material, papers, pamphlets ended up in the house. Nino who most evenings remained at home without going out for even a few moments, took little time to read those books and papers ..."[181]

On the few evenings when he did go out, and he was now better integrated in city life, he sometimes used to go to the opera, where, with a complete change of character he came alive, shouted, and gave cheek to the police. He was now covered in a mane of flowing locks, so that the police thought on one occasion that the noisy theatre-goer was a girl.[182]

His brother's incorporation into the organised leadership of the socialist movement was a cause for some concern at home. The police, vexed by a strike and by the growing separatist feeling of the Sards, were checking with even more care than normal into the activities of the "subversives" and made inquiries from the distraught parents at Ghilarza. Francesco and Giuseppina feared another family disgrace and Francesco was only dissuaded from visiting Cagliari to see what offence his son had committed by a letter from Nino which said:

"Nannaro has accepted some jobs at the Camera del lavoro; thus his name, not known until now, has come to the notice of the police, who want to know about this revolutionary, this new butcher of police spies who is coming up: and they asked for information. Are you happy now? As you see nothing bad has happened, and it is all over. There having been a strike and Nannaro being treasurer of the Camera del lavoro, the police wanted to know his address so that they could confiscate the funds and stop the strike; but the strike stopped of its own accord, and the funds are still there...."[183]

He went on that the police were something to make fun of and to be pitied: they spent so much time chasing socialists and anarchists that they had no time for the thieves.

Obviously among his new acquaintances he numbered his brother's friends and companions, the local socialists. He did not always feel great affection for them and recalled later that the teacher Maccarone used to torment him to school.[184]

The "bear" Antonio was starting to peep out of his "lair" in the last year of his schooling. In time he would come right out, but he would still remain the "bear" his early life had made him.

VII

His basic attitudes, values and beliefs had been formed in the previous twenty one years. The first significant attitudes, on which he had built later, had been formed in the very early years of his life. Cammett has written about the series of "accidents" which made him what he was. [185] The most notable of these were his fall and consequent hunchback and his father's imprisonment. The first was obvious by the time he was five and the second took place when he was seven. Gramsci himself laid stress on the importance of such "accidents" in a man's mental formation, though he considered what led up to the "accident" more important.[186] What caused the development of significant personal qualities in Gramsci by the time he was eight was not so much the "accidents" themselves, but the reaction of the human social environment to them and the way in which he reacted to this reaction. In this sense, as events in a historical context, neither his injury, nor his father's imprisonment, were strictly speaking "accidents" as their effect was socially and culturally determined. Had Sardinia and Sardinians not been the cruel society with its intolerance of abnormality and lack of charity, and had it not been characterised by the particular class structure and feeling which I described earlier, neither the injury, nor the father's disgrace and consequent loss of status of the family would have had the dimensions of importance which they had. The fall itself may have been "chance" but the father's imprisonment was certainly not, as he was playing according to political rules which possibly included jail for the losers and certainly included sanctions. In turn, as I have pointed out, the nature of the Sardinian social culture was owed to the backward mode of production fostered by imperialist exploitation. We cannot understand Gramsci independent of history.

As we have seen, as a little boy he met great social cruelty as a result of who he was both physically and socio-economically. Only the women of his family seemed to have treated him with the compensatory affection he needed. Very early on he became socially alienated: he withdrew into himself to avoid hurt, he avoided his peers and lived an emotionally and physically solitary existence. The accounts of contemporaries and Gramsci himself are riddled with references to the solitariness of his existence. Only one, Garuglieri's *Ricordo di Gramsci* provides a satisfactory and non-face-saving reason for what can only have been extreme loneliness. It was not that he wanted to be alone, but that he was forced to be alone. Consequently the little boy was extremely unhappy. He was convinced that nobody loved him, and that he was incapable of being loved.[187] He even felt in time that his family resented him and that he was a burden on them. His manifest reactions varied. At times he punished himself through self-inflicted injury, at others he had dreadful fights with the members of his family, and especially his father, but most of the time he compensated by reading and escape into fantasy. Later this early reading became an advantage at school and since it was compensatory and earned approval, he became devoted to study.

The solitariness, or apartness of his early life was reinforced both in his adolescence and his young manhood. Both in Santu Lussurgiu and Cagliari he lived a lonely life, hardly ever going out, and without close friends. This life was imposed on him not only by his earlier acquired psychological attitudes of shyness and diffidence but by his poverty and his growing studiousness.[188] Here too he spent almost all his time reading and excelled at study.

The two emotional crutches which enabled him to survive "the sewer of his past"[189] were withdrawing into himself and study. At twenty-one he had already been a solitary scholar for fourteen years.

From his experience of the reality of life, he must have already developed his unstructured world-view. He himself was wise enough to recognise that all men have a world view. Quite simply, in the Sardinia whose ubiquitous cruelty he knew personally and through observation of the condition of others, he could only evolve a view of man and society which was pessimistic. As Togliatti pointed out later, where he had only known Sardinians "from above" Gramsci knew them and their culture "from below" in a very profound way.[190] Much of the detailed knowledge of their customs was acquired from reading both at *liceo* and afterwards, but already as a child he knew the immediate life of Ghilarza and its peasants through direct personal knowledge. He had even been shot at by bandits, who were in the habit of bringing their rustled animals down into the Oristano from the mountains.[191] His letters from prison are full of references which show his deep personal knowledge of the average Sard peasant and his customs. He was no believer in the nobility of the poor or the mass, for him they were cruel and backward.

At first he must have feared and hated them. Then he became contemptuous of them[192] an almost universal attitude for a person of his class — though in his case he had reason. It was a family game to make fun of various village personalities and their rural foibles.[193] More privately, he detested their cruelty and insensitivity.

While he was in no way tied to the masses by loyalty, although he did have a similar experience, he certainly had no affection for his father and for the typical Southern intellectual he epitomised. Thus he had little time for the *gente da bene* who ruled the island.[194] From his father he had met just about as much insensitivity and neglect as he had met cruelty from the peasants. He rejected his father.

Neither the peasants, nor his father was respected or loved by him. If he felt any sense of kinship with anybody in the society he lived in, it was with the sufferers: those like the deranged boy in the pigsty, who suffered from the cruelty of the others. Perhaps one of the most perceptive statements about Gramsci was that made by Garuglieri:

"... to be mocked at because of his deformity developed in him a great love for all those who suffer unjustly and the need to succour them drove him to sacrifice himself generously for their cause."[195]

The sacrifice had not begun at twenty-one, but the feeling of community almost certainly had, if his own letters written later are reliable.

If there was anything he wished to emulate or attain to, it was the teacher and proficiency in study. He was almost invariably top of whatever class he was in and used to study to the point of exhaustion. He was not a genius as his hagiographers have portrayed him. He was merely a good country school student who was doing as well as was possible in the circumstances. He was, as we have seen, proud of his ability and ashamed when he failed to excel. He also had an exaggerated notion of his own abilities. Intellectual excellence was what made him superior to the "peasants" at an early age, when he was inferior and rejected because of his physical deformity.

When he left Ghilarza and *ginnasio* at Santu Lussurgiu to go to Cagliari none of these attitudes and values would have been conceptualised or conscious, though all existed on a spontaneous level. He knew about class and class feeling by the time he left and he knew the reality of life in Sardinia[196] but they were still not completely thought out concepts united in a general view of the world either of his own or derived from reading. (The effect of early reading is discussed at length in the next chapter).

Both Romano and Fiori have stressed the enormous importance of his departure from the only world, "the brutal" "uncivilised", "backward" world to use his own words, he had known until he was seventeen.[197] It is without doubt true that his own earlier attitudes were gradually given more order, assembled, conceptualised and added to while he was at Cagliari where he found his first intellectual heroes, those writers who most appealed to him because their world view which was coherent, articulated and conceptualised, approached closest to his own derived primarily from real experience, and this is discussed at length in the next chapter of this book.

What has interested us, and been discussed, is the fact that his own life style did not change much. As Gennaro described, he still lived a lonely, reserved existence, the only signs that he would like to join in being moments like those where he made fun of the policeman at the theatre, moments of mad hilarity which paralleled those described by childhood playmates who accompanied him on a trip to the seaside in 1900.[198] For him the world was still a hostile environment, in which there were those who inflicted suffering and those who suffered. He dreamed of a life in which his mind and his will were the only guides.[199] His programme for action, based on his view of the world, probably included these notions, both expressed many years later:

"expect nothing from anyone, and you will avoid delusions. We must do only what we know we can do and go our own way. We must always be superior to the environment we live in without despising it or thinking we are superior. To understand and reason, not whimper like women."[200]

CHAPTER II

Making the Country Boy
an Italian

I

We need not be child psychiatrists to realise that the misery of Gramsci's life, as described to this point, must have led him to wish that life would change, that somehow, someday, he would wake to find his hunchback gone, his family rich and respected, and his father never having been in jail.

His fear and hatred of life as it was led to his first political beliefs, at first incoherent, but settling into a definite structured understanding and critique of society by the time he was in his teens. Naturally it was antithetical to the *status quo*. We must avoid the unsophsticated notion that he developed his earliest views of the world directly from his life experience.

A large number of institutions and personalities operated on the child Gramsci with the object of having him accept their definition of who he was. The Church tried to have him accept from birth the supranational Christian view of the world, and, as the story of the articles of the constitution and the national holidays where he cried "Viva il leone di Caprera" showed, the State, through the medium of schooling, was intent on making him an Italian nationalist. No doubt there were other ideologies presented to him. But in the Sard society described earlier, such supranationalism and nationalism were doomed to have little effect, when they competed with the nationalism which everybody in the society believed in, Sard nationalism, to which the Church was subordinated and for which Italians were the enemy.

Contradictory though it may seem, Gramsci's self-identification with the Sards and the society which caused him so much misery was quite natural for a small boy. For him, life was wrong; at this juvenile stage of his development only concrete persons could be blameworthy (the notion that the system was responsible was beyond his intellectual capacities) and so someone or some group was obviously to blame for the inequities of life; practically everybody in the society believed that it was the foreigners who were to blame. What more natural than that a tiny boy, who desperately wanted to belong anyway, should agree.

At first his "nationalism" was a nebulous generalisation: the feeling of being a Sardinian could not have been explained. He identified with others because he lived there; because he spoke a Sard dialect; because of the common life he had with the villagers of Ghilarza.

When Antonio first went to school he was taught songs by his school master about the resistance of Sards to the "haughty Aragon". Nothing of course, was said about the immediate oppressor, the Italian State, but such general emphasis on national history, and, especially, past national glory, began to give coherence to the inexplicit Sardism of the boy. He, like the other boys in the school made the feeling more immediately relevant himself by inserting into the generalisation about Sard resistance and defeat of exploiters, particular, then popular, local heroes,[201] the bandits Derosas and Tolu, who opposed the Italian government.[202]

His identification with Sardinia increased greatly when he was taken away from school by his father. He could still see the other sons of the bourgeoisie going to school, and this inequity provoked in him that feeling of resentment for the rich, which in Sardinia was quickly converted into dislike of all "continentals", on whom with some justice all Sardinia's inequities could be blamed.[203]

In the dialectic of personal experience and all-pervasive ideology there emerged, by the time he was at school in Santu Lussurgiu, an abstracted political attitude which we may describe as Sardism and define as a view of politics in which the foreign imperialism was responsible for the inequities in life, and the remedy was to liberate Sardinia from foreign oppression.[204] By 1908, when Gramsci first went to Cagliari, this strong identification with Sardinia had developed into an obsession with Sard folklore and literature. He read whatever he could lay his hands on and knew the works of the two leading literary figures of the Sard world, Grazia Deledda and Sebastiano Satta, profoundly. So far did his Sardism extend that he even sought a position on *Unione sarda*, the paper of his teacher and protector Grazia, which was adopting strongly Sardist positions in 1910-11.[205]

Gramsci himself stated that his world view was strongly Sardist

49

when he first left the island[206] and many of those acquainted with him at that time also remarked on his Sardism.[207] Moreover, we may at least infer from his activities and preferred reading shortly before he left the island, what was his personal variety of Sardism. We know that he preferred the poems of Satta to the novels of the more prestigious Deledda, and we have indications why. Deledda was the novelist of the Sard peasant, the Sard national writer *par excellence*, Satta wrote poems about the nascent Sard proletariat working in the mines. Gramsci said that Sardinia was not merely *tanche*, sheep, and the dead man's mother[208] but miners working for foreign capitalists in dreadful conditions.[209]

At this time the proletariat was a tiny minority of the Sard working classes and we have no evidence that Gramsci knew of their conditions of life personally. It is curious that he chose to regard them as more important than the peasants he knew so well. One possible explanation was that he was deliberately choosing an unrepresentative group in preference to the peasants because he found it difficult to love or identify with those who had caused him so much suffering. The notion that his Sardism was not really a defence of the mass of working people, in Sardinia the peasants, is reinforced by his association with Grazia's paper which was one of the more conservative (it supported the "ministerialist" Cocco Ortu) and by the one article he wrote in it, which was decidedly patronising about the peasantry and their "democratic" pretensions.[210]

It is difficult to discover any evidence that there was a populist or democratic ingredient in his Sardism before 1911. On the other hand, his own life experience and his choice of allies and reading suggest at least marginally that the contrary was the case. This reading allowed him to relate the problems of the Sard to the wider Italian scene.

His favourite writers were Emilio Cecchi, Ugo della Seta, Giovanni Papini, Gaetano Salvemini and Benedetto Croce, whose writings he used to collect and put in files.[211] The last two were particular heroes. He read them all mainly through *Il Marzocco* and *La Voce*, the first a literary journal and the second cultural, and increasingly political, in its interests.

La Voce, which started publication in 1908, was undoubtedly the more important source for political opinions. The editors had first collaborated because they wished to tear the veil of their parents' hypocrisy from the face of Italy: "One thing united us, the cult of truth. Italian life, Italian poetry and Italian philosphy seemed to us to lack truth", wrote Guiseppe Prezzolini, one editor.[212] But the views of the other editor, Papini, and many of its contributors were the acme of Italian middle-class juvenile outrage. Rolland wrote on meeting some of them: "... they went from one fad to another, with the same intolerance."[213] Papini, one of Gramsci's heroes, set the flavour for the *lavociani* of 1908-11. He has been described as "genial and disordered, vain to almost shameless exhibitionism, inventor of the most useless and complicated cerebrations, endless fabricator of cultural scandals, given to exercising a real and frightening intellectual terrorism at moments of tension."[214] Under his influence the journal hid a host of implicit prejudices beneath a cloak of shouting the truth about Italy. The open hatred of anything to do with Italy's nascent industrial society from capitalism to its products "democracy" and the proletariat and its parties, and the hatred of "positivism, erudition, *arte verista*, historical methods, materialism and the bourgeois collectivist idea of democracy ... the stink of carbolic acid, of grease and smoke, of popular sweat, of the screech of machinery, the commercial game ..." united around the journal "socialists tired of Marxism", "republicans bored by Mazzinianism" and monarchists who wanted something different from the monarchy that then ruled.

In 1908-11 *La Voce* was more *against* than *for* anything, but in 1911 it became nationalist, national-socialist and, finally, ended up supporting fascism. The logic of that development was already there when Gramsci read it. In those years its targets were: the Giolittian government "which had been parliamentary and not national, that is surrounded by the solid obedience of clienteles in parliament and widespread dislike in the country": the extreme left which supported him and was against universal suffrage: "Sad to say this above all about the socialist party, morally undone earlier than normal for a young party, dominated and weakened by the masonry, reduced to a huddle of hungry and noisy petty bourgeois, now incapable of attracting any but *arrivistes* without conscience or ideals": Giolitti, the ally of the Southern *camorre*, against whom it favoured the arch-conservative Sonnino who knew the South well: and it announced that since the Southern question was the key question in Italy it would work for its solution as this would change the face of the country.[215]

Gaetano Salvemini, one of the "socialists tired of Marxism" and the PSI, wrote regular articles for the journal. In these he tied all the hatreds together in a synthesis which explained how the

Southern question and its solution was linked to the system of rule in Italy.

In particular he singled out the petty-bourgeois cliques of the villages of the South — men like Gramsci's father — for his attacks, revealing with pitiless scorn their hypocrisy and shallowness and the misery that they caused to others.[216] These *camorre* owed their position to the unholy alliance which they had made with the ruling Giolitti-Zanardelli governments of the North, whose position in turn was shored up by the support of an overwhelming majority of socialists.

Since Salvemini felt that the Southern peasant was too backward and lacking in socialist consciousness to overcome his own misery — universal suffrage could only be the "plough" which would make this virgin soil of value — he ended up arguing that the only honest and credible alternative to Giolitti was Sonnino, the arch-conservative.[217]

The journal projected this sort of argument into a general disbelief in the possibility of solving Italy's problems through parliament — at least in the short run. It argued in 1910 that: "The present democracy is no longer pleasing to honest minds.... Everything is collapsing. All ideals are vanishing. Parties exist no longer, only groups and patronage systems. The sad state of Parliament has repercussions in the country.... Young men who are not *arrivistes* do not join political parties."[218]

The alternatives it proposed were general, dogmatic and uncompromising: idealists would have to go into this quagmire and combat their destructive enemies. This added up to arguing for action before everything else — action for which no guidelines could be drawn up: "Action must be taken in historical situations, whence arises its infinite variety."[219] Such proposals brought the journal close to the nationalists who later became national-socialists but their positions were not identical until more than ten years later. In 1911 the journal still pointed out that while it shared the aspirations of nationalism, it felt that Italian nationalism would not be beneficial until "the sense of discipline, of punctuality, of cleanliness, and of personal dignity had become a national patrimony."[220] It therefore could not support generic calls for war.

The restraining influence on the journal — before it threw its support behind the Libyan war — seems to have been Benedetto Croce, who, by 1908, was already Italy's leading literary critic and philosopher. Croce agreed with the journal's view that positivism was not philosophy and that socialism was corrupt, and after an initial period when Papini and Prezzolini resisted his teachings, began to write articles for *La Voce*.[221] He particularly influenced Prezzolini through his *Filosofia della pratica*, which appeared in December 1908. Many articles based on its theme appeared in *La Voce*.

The *Filosofia della pratica* argued that practical action was never more than a continuous operation of the will to change what existed (an idea which appealed to *La Voce*) since there were no foreordained plans of historical and moral development or final truths for men to discover and follow. But it also argued that men had to accept even so that:

1) they always did what they intended, and there were no errors in good faith. "Exquisite and delicate souls" found even their mistakes "a biting bitterness and they blame themselves with them.";
2) they would always be judged and have to judge "to continue to act, that is, to live";
3) and they would therefore have to create an adequate philosophy in order to judge.
4) In order to act effectively, with judgement, "to will the good", they had to dominate themselves through self-knowledge of their weaknesses and this was a "hard labour ... as all life, 'sweet life' is hard".
5) This did not mean that they had to accept life as it was. Indeed, life was progress — "It is not a fact that men hope and live, although in the midst of their sorrows?" — and knowledge existed to serve life.
6) And, Croce concluded, men driven by a desire to improve what was could only make their better future collectively.[222]

Many of these themes permeated Prezzolini's writings, which also emphasised the need for practical action to be responsible, that is, based on knowledge, and on loyalty to the motto "know thyself".

We have no evidence that Croce's views directly influenced Gramsci during his Sardist stage, but, given his commitment to the journal and its writers, we are not surprised that while in Sardinia "things by Marx" were no more than an intellectual curiosity to him.[223] The "things by Marx" reached him distorted through the socialist press, dominated after 1908 by the discredited "reformists" of the doubly-discredited PSI. No doubt, as an omnivorous reader who read everything from the mushy novels of Invernizio to *the* bourgeois newspaper, *Domenica del Corriere*, he was aware of the view of the various factions of socialists in 1905-1911.[224] It would, however, have been impossible to reconcile his Sardism, let alone his commitment to *La Voce*, with the "Marxists" of his youth and the economic determinist views they held.

Under the leadership of Filippo Turati, the PSI, in part because of its view of "Marxism", threw in its lot with the Northern capitalists completely deserting the oppressed masses of the South and Sardinia, which Turati contemptuously called the "Vendée of Italy."[225] Gaetano Salvemini, Gramsci's hero, expressed the Southern reaction to socialism: "socialist parliamentarians have become the spokesmen of the petty-interests of their constituents, hanging around the table like dogs for whatever morsel the capitalist government would throw them in return for their support": and declaring in 1910 that there had been "a universal degeneration of our movement" withdrew from the party. Despite such outrage, the "reformists" continued to support Giolitti both in his Southern policies, and his aggressive foreign policy, and endorsed the notion that it was marxist to "await [the] events" which would automatically bring about the revolution.[226]

If anything Gramsci felt more affinity for the revolutionary syndicalist wing of socialism than for the exponents of what passed for "Marxism" in 1905-11. The former, led by men like Enrico Ferri, Oddino Morgari and Enrico Leone, had dominated the PSI in 1905-08. In the short three years they had built up support in the South by overtly backing the nascent working-class movement there. In particular they had supported a celebrated but disastrous strike of miners at Bugerru in Sardinia in 1904. Not only did Satta, Gramsci's favourite poet, write about the strike in a fashion subtly confusing the views of Sardism and syndicalism, but many of the men Gramsci got to know in Cagliari were associated with syndicalism. Cavallera had led the strike in 1904. The editor-in-chief of *Unione sarda*, when Gramsci worked for it, was Jago Siotto, who had run *La Lega*, the periodical around which the first workers' organisations had formed at Bugerru six years earlier and whose formation underlay the Bugerru strike. The others his brother brought home were often romantically inclined towards syndicalism. So, by 1911, Gramsci was a subscriber to the revolutionary syndicalist newspaper, *Il Viandante*.[227]

The views of syndicalism in 1905-11 were mainly the views of Georges Sorel as interpreted by Enrico Leone and Arturo Labriola who modified them to respond to Italian conditions and to oppose the views of their "reformist" opponents. They corresponded closely with those found in *La Voce*, stressing wilful action by 'superior beings' — as this speech of 1910 reveals:

"In the revolutionary act the Union acts as a *creator* ..., as an artist who depicts the new order of reality. An inventor is a superior being. The miseries of the trifles of everyday life should be strange to him. He must scorn the vulgar interests of everyday things ... men concerned with their comfort will never be revolutionaries. Classes who think (*calcolano*) are incapable of creation. Because creation is the unknown and escapes calculation. The psychology of the rationalist, of the dealer, of the calculator, is anti-revolutionary.

Revolution is the thunderbolt which comes from a conflagration of forces. It is the outburst of the exuberant and plethoric soul."[228]

The empirical evidence of how this Sardism, syndicalism, Lavoceanism, Croceanism and Salveminianism blended together on the eve of Gramsci's departure from Sardinia can only be deduced from one school essay of 1910, "Oppressed and Oppressors".[229] Even the little evidence it presents compels us to accept that in his last year of school he was still much more Sardist and pragmatically oriented than committed to the philosophy of Croce or to *La Voce*. The theme contains no obvious Crocean notions, though we can at times see something of Salvemini in its overall Sardism.

Gramsci does not indicate clearly in the essay whether he considers oppression to be that of an individual, a class, or an entire people, showing an inclination however, to the belief that oppression is innate in man, who hypocritically asserts that he conquers and oppresses to bring civilisation and not to destroy.

He suggests that there is usually a conspiracy that the oppressed nation is barbarous, (though it never shares this fiction), when the reality is that wars of conquest are for commercial reasons, to exploit colonies. No-one has the moral courage to cry shame.

He concludes that men are still only varnished with civilisation, and that stripped, they are wolves. The vaunted French revolution only replaced one class oppression by another. It did not introduce civilisation to the world, revealing only that inequities were social and not natural. "Humanity needs another bloodbath to erase the existing injustice: let the oppressors beware having left the masses as ignorant and ferocious as they still are".

These are the words of a Sard, down to the concluding southern theoretical flourish. A *barbaricino* might have nodded, Croce would surely have shook his head.

From it we may make the following conclusions about Gramsci's world view before he left his rocky island home for the mainland. He was above all a Sardist, and he found his main solution to his personal and national misery in throwing the Italians off the island. The important and interesting fact is how he proposed that this should be done. Whether we look at his Sardism, his revolutionary syndicalism, his Lavoceanism or his passing knowledge of Croce, the solutions he espoused depended on men themselves. Conditions were matters to be overcome, and not determining. More particularly, they were to be overcome by an élite of men who dared to challenge what existed, not by the mass of men. Gramsci's own sneering in *L'Unione sarda* at the pretension of the villagers of Sardinia was paralleled by Salvemini's belief that the peasant could only become useful once the intellectuals had educated him, by *La Voce's* sneering at the "Nazarene herd of sheep", by the syndicalist stress on the men who created, and their anti-democracy, and by Croce's belief that philosophers made history. None of these theoreticians believed in democracy *tout court*, and all except Salvemini attacked it.

This élite of men would change the world by understanding both themselves and their context, by daring and by creation, the stress being more on the element of imposing their wills on what was by whatever methods than on comprehension and reason. While Gramsci promised another "blood bath", the syndicalists promised a "revolutionary thunderbolt" in their aspiration to dominate, and the common hatreds of *La Voce* spelt an "intellectual terrorism" in practice. Only Croce provided a moderating influence with his near-Puritan (but stripped of religion) demand for responsibility and reasonableness.

Lest we think that the young Gramsci, on the eve of his departure from Sardinia, was nothing but a romantic revolutionary firebrand who would soon be purged of all this voluntarist posturing, we must remember his dour personality with its seething resentments against the world, and his stress on domination of himself. It is certain that Gramsci really believed these violent "dark thoughts" and that he shared in the desire to bludgeon reality with truth. In this intransigency lay one element of his future greatness.

II

Gramsci had shared in the intellectual life of the mainland through reading these journals which were in vogue among the young Italian intelligentsia, but this did not mean that Sardinia stopped influencing him when he started at university. After he arrived on the peninsular a combination of his traditional Sard fears of the "continent"; his natural surprise at the strangeness of life there; and his personal reticence, only drove him into an evermore solitary existence divorced from the intellectual life of his peers.

On his way to Turin, he stopped for an evening with relatives in Pisa.[230] When he arrived at his destination he was lucky to have one of the beadles at the College find him a cheap *pensione*, because the traffic and noise of the little provincial capital terrified him.[231] Eschewing the delights, rather too expensive for him, of a city holding the fiftieth anniversary celebrations of Italian unity, he buried himself in his books, swotting madly for the scholarship examinations, which started in exactly a week's time.[232]

Turin represented misery and hardship. It was appallingly expensive by Sardinian standards. He moved from restaurant to restaurant trying to find somewhere cheap enough to eat on the paltry allowance of three lire a day which the College gave him while he was taking his examinations. He wrote to his father asking for money, pointing out that he could not make ends meet because prices had gone up since the Exposition had started — his three lire barely bought him a meal.[233] To compensate he again pulled in his belt, and this did not make the bitter, damp cold of the onset of winter at the foggy "foot of the mountains" any easier to bear.

He made himself ill, suffering from fainting spells and the first manifestations of what would in time become a recurrent nervous illness due to his excessive disregard of his physical and emotional needs.[234]

His performance at the examinations was not good. Fortunately for him, neither was that of the other seventy candidates for scholarships, almost all of whom made it to the orals which followed the written examinations. The examination board reported:

"The results of the competition were not very flattering. Nor were the marks an indication of particular merit.... On this occasion too, the youths will reach university ill-prepared".[235]

Thirty-nine scholarships were being contested. Gramsci came ninth with an average of 7.51 in a list headed by Lionello Vincenti, later a professor of German. Palmiro Togliatti, another candidate from Sardinia, was second.[236]

By this time, Sardinia, which had been the source of so much misery to him, had become his "beloved Sardinia",[237] and Zucàro speculates that he may have fled back there after the examinations. Certainly in November he was back in Turin. He enrolled at the University on 16th of the month, already some days late because the necessary documents and money had not arrived.[238] He found a room overlooking the Dora river, whose bitter cold permeated everywhere: Shortly before Christmas he wrote home: "Think how nice it is to go out and across the city shivering with cold, then come back to a cold room and sit shivering for hours, unable to warm oneself up. If only I'd known, I would not have come here to suffer this glacial existence, not at any price".[239]

The misery of cold, hunger and lack of money encouraged him to retreat into himself. "When first at university, the young Sard, a withdrawn and prickly character, had neither friends nor acquaintances".[240] Needing to belong, he sought out the haunts of Sardinian expatriates, eating regularly once a day in the Latteria Milanese, which was owned by a Sard and frequented by his compatriots. Here too, he always ate alone: a frugal repast which he seldom varied: pasta, two eggs and a bread roll for eighty *centesimi*.[241]

He studied very hard at the glottology, geography and Latin and Greek grammar which he was taking in his first year.[242] To fill in his loneliness he also attended other courses which interested him, in law, Italian literature and the history of art.[243] Most days he was at the University or the National Library: a solitary figure, shivering with cold in his threadbare coat, but determined to overcome his disabilities. Very soon some of the other men using the reading room at the National Library noted the studious, hunch-backed figure and before he really knew any of the students at the University, he had become acquainted with Professor Matteo Bartoli, professor of glottology, Professor Umberto Cosmo, professor of literature, and Professor Gustavo Balsamo-Crivelli, a socialist activist.[244]

Bartoli, who believed that the study of Sard dialects could throw considerable light on the development of the Latin vernacular into its early derivatives, was especially interested in the student and after they had walked home together spent long hours talking before the front door of Bartoli's house in Corso Vinzaglio about the Sard language. At first he appears to have picked Gramsci's brains somewhat as only months after Gramsci arrived in Turin his letters became filled with this sort of request:

"I am sending a list of words: would someone undertake to translate them into the Fonni dialect ... marking in clearly when the *s* is soft as in the Italian *rosa* and when hard as in *sordo*. Please don't make any mistakes, because it is for a professor whose exams I have to do this year, and I don't want to spoil matters by some idiocy ... it is for a work on linguistics by this professor."[245]

He was soon sincerely interested in the student, for whom he developed great expectations as a linguist, and, possibly, as the future promulgator of some of his own unspoken beliefs.[246] Naturally Gramsci benefited from this contact with Bartoli and decided to specialise in glottology.

Cosmo was also greatly impressed by Gramsci, whom he later recalled as one of his two best students of Italian literature.[247]

Where Bartoli encouraged Gramsci's study of linguistics, Cosmo, a specialist in Franciscan and Dantean studies,[248] further developed in him his love of literature. Later Gramsci recalled long arguments about Dante in Cosmo's seminars. Cosmo became deeply attached to him, lending him books and money, but only in 1922 did Gramsci understand the depth of this attachment.[249]

Balsamo-Crivelli was, it appears, a lesser influence. These three men were the only people who befriended him until April 1912.

Between them these professors strengthened in him the intellectual views he had obtained from reading *La Voce*, and Croce and Salvemini. Later he wrote:

"It seemed to me that I and Cosmo, and many other intellectuals of this time (say the first fifteen years of the century) occupied a certain common ground: we were all to some degree part of the movement of moral and intellectual reform which in Italy stemmed from Benedetto Croce, and whose first premise was that man can and should live without the help of religion — I mean, of course, without revealed religion, positivist religion, mythological religion, or whatever other brand one cares to name".[250]

Not only did Cosmo emphasise to him the merit of Croce and Salvemini, but he also had him study in depth the thinkers who provided Croce with his inspiration. Gramsci started to master not only Machiavelli, but de Sanctis and Hegel.[251] Bartoli further increased the Crocean influence on Gramsci since he too had been greatly influenced by the linguistic theories of Croce and brought to his teaching of glottology an idealist theoretical framework.[252]

Overall the teachers Gramsci heard or met with at Turin strengthened the orientation his more direct mentors were cultivating in him, for while they represented other points of view, nearly all were ardent moralists, preaching the doctrine that men were responsible for their actions and made their own destinies.

Thus Farinelli, whom Gramsci described as "a true master of humanism and life"[253] was recalled by Togliatti in these words:

"I recall a lecture room ... where we used to gather from our various faculties, and with our various outlooks, united by a common eagerness to find meaning in our lives. This was where that remarkable man Arturo Farinelli used to read and comment on the classics of German romanticism. There was something volcanic in his lectures.... Every now and then he would turn his head toward the window to the left, and the light that fell on him, together with his laugh and the curly locks on his forehead, gave him a strange look, the look of an angel or a devil who was showing us the way. It was a new morality which he taught us, whose laws were complete sincerity to ourselves, the spurning of convention, and sacrifice for the cause to which we had dedicated our lives."[254]

Arturo Graf, his protégé Ćosmo, Einaudi, Solari and other teachers were remembered by other students in much the same terms.[255] In time many of these scholars were to become renowned.[256]

Under their direction, but still very lonely, often ill and underfed, Gramsci worked himself into a condition of nervous prostration by May 1912 and decided to return to Sardinia, postponing his examinations until autumn.[257] July and August he spent in Sardinia, away from these new influences. Part of that time he coached a local youth for his examinations and then he took a seaside holiday at Bosa Marina.

He returned to sit his examinations in early November. He passed brilliantly in glottology (*trenta e lodi*) (first class honours) and also obtained marks of thirty/thirty in geography and twenty-seven in Latin and Greek grammar.[258] Bartoli, convinced that he had the linguist of the next generation, asked him to help draw up the courses for 1912-13.[259] Gramsci naturally decided that his *forte* was in the field and started to prepare himself for a teaching career, writing his first learned articles. The letters which came home spasmodically were nearly always about Sard dialects.[260]

For years Gramsci had seen the way out of his national and personal predicament in the attainment of a teaching career. It was to be the reward and compensation for years of lonely study and deprivation. The dignity and eminence of his teachers only enhanced the teaching profession in his eyes. But when the prize was finally within his grasp, he slowly, and with vacillating indecision, started to change his mind about whether it was what he should do.

His teachers were unwittingly responsible for this change of mind. They not only preached idealism and a cult of personal ethical responsibilty, but many were able to reconcile their beliefs, which reflected either directly or indirectly the Crocean atmosphere of the second decade of the century, with an adhesion to socialism and a rejection of the semi-racism which had characterised the Italian socialist party since 1900. Farinelli was a "near revolutionary", Cosmo, Balsamo-Crivelli and Bartoli were active in socialist circles.[261] They made it clear that in practice the two viewpoints of idealism and socialism were not mutually incompatible and they taught their students that it was their duty to take the new philosphy and its morality into the socialist movement and the working class. Their example influenced the young Sard.

More importantly, one of his first acquaintances, and they were very few and far between in his first lonely year at university, was Angelo Tasca, also an arts student, but also the son of a Turinese working man and a socialist activist of some years standing. Tasca had taken the implicit message of his teachers particularly to heart and was already neglecting his studies in favour of socialist activism.

Tasca started to cultivate Gramsci early in 1912. In April of that year he gave Gramsci a copy of the French edition of Tolstoy's *War and Peace* in which he inscribed a few lines expressing the hope that his fellow student of today would be his "fellow combatant of tomorrow".[262] When Gramsci shifted into digs in the same street as he lived he was able to work for the Sardinian's conversion to socialism with regularity.

He must have been somewhat daunted by Gramsci's resistance. To explain Gramsci's resistance we must start with his Sardism. In 1912 he still had the same outlook that he had developed in his years on the island. Embittered by the belief that was current, even among many socialists, that Sards were racially inferior, he used to spend hours under the porticos of the University talking to his new found friend Togliatti about the injustice of this.[263] He tended to romanticise Sardinia, posing, not without justice, as the campus expert on Sardinia. He collected whole libraries of books on Sardinia and its history.[264] A host of ingrained presuppositions about the attitude of socialists towards Sardinia had to be overcome by Tasca. This took time.

Gramsci was also loth to give up the time he devoted to his studies, through which he could attain to the teaching position he had always hoped for. Palmiro Togliatti, whom he had met at a law seminar in April 1912 after a fleeting acquaintance when both were sitting the scholarship examinations in 1911, was very much the studious intellectual,[265] and his bookish influence countervailed that of the less diligent Tasca.

Finally, and this was perhaps the crucial reason for Gramsci's refusal to be inveigled too quickly into the socialist movement, Gramsci became very suspicious about Tasca's personal probity when he got to know him better, both in a short period when he shared digs with him late in 1912, and when they lived close to each other near Piazza Carlina. He disliked his avarice, the way he treated his father (which no doubt evoked memories of earlier cruelty observed in Sardinia), and his lack of scholarly integrity — "he wasted his money buying books which he never opened".[266] It was difficult to believe in the moral idealism of a man who acted like this, and it was over a bridge of moral idealism that Tasca had to lead Gramsci to socialism.

In 1913 these stumbling blocks were overcome and what Togliatti correctly characterised as a period when Gramsci "seemed rather narrow in his concerns, and still full of doubts about what course to pursue"[267] appeared over.

First, in the middle of 1913, he was again too ill to sit his examinations, and returned to Sardinia where the first elections under universal suffrage were to be held. Gramsci observed them with interest:

"There was a widespread mystical conviction that after the vote everything would be changed utterly, as in a sort of social palingenesis: or so it was in Sardinia at least."[268]

But, Gramsci noted with fascination, the property-owners of Sardinia rapidly made common cause with the ruling class on the mainland and subordinated their erstwhile Sard nationalism to their class interests because they feared a threat to property by the socialists (who gave vent to a violent anticlericalism more than anything else). The object lesson about the narrowness of a Sardism with the slogan "Into the sea with the continentals" greatly impressed him: his story in which he likened Sardinia to fertile land which had become parched and unfruitful because someone had cut off the water from the spring, and in which the "continentals" were the evil-doers, had to be mentally re-examined. Were all continentals responsible for Sardinia's ills, or merely the property-owning class and their class-allies on the island?[269]

Then, his continual ill-health and consequent failure to appear for examinations was putting his scholarship in jeopardy and making his academic progress less rosy.

Finally, despite his continuing doubts about Tasca, he had met other young socialists in their bars and haunts in the neighbourhood, and he had been greatly impressed by their "force of character and moral rectitude".[270]

In June or July 1913 he made his intellectual commitment to the ideal of socialism by applying for membership on Tasca's recommendation in the Italian Socialist Party. At the end of the year he was accepted.[271] It was not nearly so decisive a commitment as Tasca suggests. Rather it was a commitment to the ideal of a socialism which would solve the problem of Sardinia and the Italian South — an extension of Gramsci's Sardism, via a moral idealism, to a Salveminian position, like that propounded by Tasca himself: "Gramsci was a warm champion of the importance of the southern question in socialist politics. We shared his view, and like him made this one of the key points in the political changes we were looking for".[272]

Indeed the only time Gramsci was at all active in the Socialist movement in the next year was when it concerned Southern politics. He started to attend meetings of the Youth Federation in a desultory fashion, sometimes in the company of his young friend Togliatti, but usually he sat alone, as withdrawn a figure as he had always been, prickly and with a scornful self-deriding laugh. The world of the industrial proletariat was as far away as it had been the year before, when he and Togliatti, had noted striking workers as if they were from a "different" race.[273]

Moreover, he did not see his decision to join the Socialist Party as sacrificing his university career. Indeed, in the first months after he joined the party, he neglected it to prepare for his examinations, especially after the scholarship board told him in February 1914 that his scholarship would be suspended if he did not pass all his subjects by April.[274] Only the intercessions of Bartoli had saved him from an immediate suspension anyway. In March and April he sat the biennial examinations in Greek literature and modern history, receiving 24 and 27 marks respectively, and in moral philosophy, receiving 25.[275] While this meant that his scholarship was renewed for another year, it was a decided disimprovement in his achievement. His near constant ill-health throughout 1913 and his dabbling with socialism are among the obvious explanations for this disappointment.

Once the hurdle of the examinations was over he began to spend more time with the socialist youth group to which he belonged. He recalled later how:

"We often left Party meetings in a group around our leader. We continued our discussions through the streets of the now silent city, while the few later passers-by stopped to watch us, amazed at our ferocious assertions, our explosive laughter, our sallies into the realms of dreams and the impossible."[276]

and many of his "assertions", his friends recalled, were about Sardinia and the South of Italy.[277] When, however, it became more than a matter of assertions, but a matter of action, he was deluded in his desire to link the traditional moral concern of socialist intellectuals for the South with the destinies of the Northern working class.

Tasca, with Gramsci's support, suggested to the local socialists that the candidacy in the by-election for the Turin constituency held by the late Pilade Gay, a socialist, be offered to the Grand Old

Man of Southern Italian socialism, Gaetano Salvemini. Salvemini was approached by Ottavio Pastore but obliged to decline because he had not renewed his socialist party card after the elections of 1913.[278]

An attempt to make an active contribution to the debate on national policy was even more disastrous, sending Gramsci scuttling back to university for a year, and leaving an overall impression that he was not very active in the socialist·movement even in 1914.[279] This disaster can only be understood against the background of Socialist Party politics of the time.

III

In 1911 Giolitti's government had embarked on the conquest of Libya. The "reformist" leaders of the PSI, who had supported his government, maintaining that they were thereby advancing democracy and the development of the conditions precedent for socialism, were in a quandary about what to do. They split into two groups. One, led by Turati, proposed withdrawing support from the ministry. The other, led by Leonirda Bissolati, thought that a condemnation of the government's action would be sufficient. Both had miscalculated the feeling of the mass of the party and the working class, and, divided among themselves, they lost control of the party at the Reggio Emilia Congress of 1912. The new secretary was Benito Mussolini, who wished to build the party into a large, homogeneous monolith intent on making revolution. Consequently, he proposed that Bissolati and his followers be expelled from the party; that the party stop working for democracy or in alliance with the so-called democratic parties and revert instead to an attack on the system based on the fundamental notion of the class struggle. Ciccotti expressed the position of the group supporting him this way:

"We believe that the Socialist Party is eminently anti-democratic. Democracy is a bourgeois expedient. Democracy is the negation of the triumph of the social antithesis, and the negation of the triumph of the proletariat. And, as to the expedient of those comrades who claim that they wish only to enter the democratic fortress to conquer it, we reply: when they are inside the fortress its doors will close behind them. We do not wish the proletariat to become prisoners with them.[280]

A concomitant of this new intransigent revolutionary position in which the Socialist Party would unite the masses for an uncompromising struggle along class lines, was a recognition that the proletariat would have to be prepared to act on its own behalf. Angelica Balabanoff said: "The socialist party must remember that it has the function of a teacher vis-à-vis the masses".[281]

In the favourable situation presented by the crisis of the Giolittian system of government Mussolini's policies met considerable success. The party doubled its numbers in two years, greatly strengthened and centralised its organisation despite the cadre's crisis, and again started to attract large sections of youth.[282] *Avanti* was read by Turinese "automobile workers" and Sicilian "sulphur miners".

Moreover, the party won this unprecedented support while pursuing policies of aggressive strike action for political purposes. When the workers were forced to strike for economic or social reasons during these years, State repression was particularly harsh. Mussolini called for general strikes in response and this activity was supported by the anarcho-syndicalist trade union federation, which for years had been hostile to the Socialist Party.

At the Ancona congress of the PSI in 1914, Mussolini boasted

"Five general strikes in two months at Milan. A real record. I did not wish to desert the masses: I couldn't: it would have been suicide for the paper [*Avanti*]. They'll say the strikes were led by syndicalists. Of course they were led by syndicalists, and why? Because [Turati's group] haven't done what they should have done. The Milanese proletariat, especially because it is in the process of formation, and is experiencing urbanisation after six or seven years peace, felt an almost physical as well as a moral need to come into the streets: and we were unable to benefit because we could not feel what was in the proletarian mind."[283]

The pursuit of these policies provoked accusations from his opponents that he was a Stirnerian, a Bergsonian and a Nietzschean whose methods had nothing to do with Marxism (as they understood it). He had, indeed, brought a new theoretical flavour to the party. He was not going to be ruled by the "dogmas, formulae and rites" which the old leaders had used to guide their actions; he believed in the making of revolution through the class struggle, that class consciousness was something that emerged from

.the proletariat itself and was expressed through their party of "soldiers and warriors".

Attracted by the superficialities of his position, and especially by the uncompromising position the party was taking towards the capitalist State, young people started to look to the PSI as the party of idealists once again. Mussolini became their hero. As Montagnana wrote of Turin's young socialists:

"... we were all enthusiastic supporters of Mussolini; a little because he too was young, a little because he had done in the reformists, and finally because his articles in *Avanti* seemed strong and revolutionary to us."[284]

There seems little doubt that Gramsci shared this enthusiasm for Mussolini.[285]

After the Ancona conference Mussolini continued to gain prestige among the young by posing as the arch-opponent of Italian participation in the war which started to rage over Europe. He was, however, caught up in the toils of his own belief that what the masses believed or "felt" was far more important than any theorising by "intellectuals". He had said at Ancona that it was good riddance if all the "brains" of the PSI left as a result of his attacks on masonry, because the PSI was not "a showcase for famous men".

Mussolini realised that if the Italians entered the war on the side of the French and British, which was possible, he would have to face the possibility of an invasion by Austria and the consequent mass, popular, patriotic feeling. So, in October 1914 in a famous article calling for "active, operative neutrality" he suggested that in that situation the PSI should support a national war of defence against invaders, and inferred that · the party should support military efforts which would bring the war to a speedy end.[286] It was a call for a temporary truce with capitalism to pursue a national goal and in practice spelt a complete desertion of all his earlier positions.

This was not immediately clear to the rank and file, and in the following month, while the implications of Mussolini's new proposal were being thought out, Gramsci engaged in the debate on the side of Mussolini. With Togliatti's support he sent a letter to the *Grido del Popolo*, Turin's socialist newspaper, replying to an earlier letter by Tasca which condemned Mussolini's desertion of the socialist principle of never supporting capitalist wars.

Gramsci started out from the presupposition that the PSI was first and foremost a national party because "its immediate task gives it special national characteristics". On this level it was autonomous of the International's decisions which laid down only broad guidelines. The PSI had to decide what type of neutrality it would adopt in accord with national conditions.

National conditions dictated a departure from the original useful slogan of "absolute neutrality" in favour of an active operative neutrality somewhere between that of the "concrete realism" of the "Italian socialist" Mussolini and the position of the rest of the party leaders.

"Mussolini doesn't want a fusion of all parties into a national unanimity — this would make him an anti-socialist. He wants the proletariat, when it has a clear idea of its own strength and sees that it is at present too weak to take the helm of state, ... to allow those forces which it recognises as the strongest, and which it cannot supplant, to operate".

And in their operation, the bourgeoisie would discredit itself because it would indicate that the nation could only survive if the existing social system were discarded. In other words, Mussolini's position was still antithetical to the bourgeois State, and not collaborationist.

The key words in this article suggest that Gramsci had reached this position in favour of Mussolini, because, like the leader from Romagna, he did not wish to be ruled by little formulae: "... revolutionaries understand history as the creation of their spirit, made through a series of active efforts worked upon the passive elements in society."[287] It did not mean that like Mussolini he believed that "loosing the horde"[288] would bring the revolution.

Soon after Gramsci's article was published it had become clear that Mussolini's position was regarded as intolerable treachery by the mass of the proletariat in the party. Despite some attempts to keep him in the party, he was "spat upon by thousands of workers", reduced to tears, declared that the die was cast, and was expelled from the party. Almost immediately he started extremely interventionist propaganda through his new paper, *Popolo d'Italia*, with which, according to Tasca, Gramsci briefly proposed to collaborate.[289] The moral discredit which fell on him, also fell on Gramsci, who fled back to the University and those who might understand what he had said.

He sat only one examination in November 1914, and despite Bartoli's pleas on his behalf, his scholarship was suspended for failure to sit two others.[290] Again he fell nervously ill.

There is only Tasca's record of how he survived the next year. He almost certainly coached people and was helped out by a few student friends, who did not ostracize him like the bulk of the Turinese working-class leaders, to whom he referred bitterly and contemptuously as "peasants".[291] He also continued to go to the University, where Bartoli had introduced him to the professor of philosophy, Annibale Pastore, hoping that philosophy would help him get over his crisis in the socialist movement. We are tempted to see in this a repetition of Croce's emotional rehabilitation at Rome under Spaventa's guidance.

It was under Pastore's direction and guidance that he returned for the first time in years to the study of Marx, who had been no more than an intellectual curiosity for him when he was in Sardinia.[292] Pastore's course involved a reconsideration of the Marxist dialectic, which Pastore reformulated with a notion of his own that between the Thesis and the Antithesis there was a period of incubation while "material conditions developed within the womb of existing society".

It appears from Pastore's somewhat superficial description of his ideas that he was maintaining that in reality there was no automatic transition (or reversal) of the Thesis when it had created the conditions for its own transcendence, but that there was a period (the preparation for revolutionary reversal) when both the ruling and antithetical forces would coexist. This, of course, conflicted with the notions of the dialectic advanced by Croce, Gentile and Labriola, and immediately attracted the attention of Gramsci, who Pastore said was still Crocean, and who also was influenced by Gentile's thought.[293] It appears that Gramsci interpreted this incubatory period as a period when the idea of revolution became a practical force. At one stage he asked Pastore to write down G.M. Guyau's words "La pensée est en nous comme l'amour", and became concerned about how one made these ideas practical forces.

This course, and one other in Latin literature, occupied him until April 1915 when he sat the last examination he was to sit at Turin University. For some years afterwards he toyed with the idea of returning to the University and completing his degree but he had reached a turning point in his life.

It was probably in following months that he retrieved his lost credit among socialists by his anti-nationalist activities on campus, which had become a hotbed of nationalist activity.[294] Late in 1915 he began to write anti-nationalist articles for *Grido del Popolo*[295] and to give lectures to the Youth Federation and later to other socialist organisations about Romain Rolland, the Swiss anti-war activist, the socialist anti-war conferences at Zimmerwald (1915) and on Marxist theory.[296]

Listeners remembered his "quiet, unemphatic, inexorable" voice and his reliance on the content of his lectures rather than on histrionic ability to win his audience.[297]

By 1916 he was writing a regular column for the newspaper *Avanti*. It was called *Sotto la Mole* (*Beneath the Mole Antonelliana* — Turin's landmark, a few hundred yards from his digs and the newspaper office). His life as a student had ended, and his life as a socialist activist had begun.

IV

Up to 1916 Gramsci had remained much the same person, with the same emotional problems and the same aspirations as he had had while a youth in Sardinia.

He had remained alienated from his fellows and from society. In 1916 he wrote these words to his sister:

"For two years I have lived outside the world: in a dream world. One by one, I let each strand tying me to the world and to my fellow men be cut.

"I live entirely for the mind, for the heart not at all .... I turned myself into a bear, inside and outside ... other people did not exist for me. For perhaps two years, I didn't laugh once and I didn't cry ... but I never hurt anyone but myself".[298]

Indeed, everywhere we find records of a quiet, withdrawn, sometimes testy, Sard, who was too appallingly miserable for people even to want to approach him.[299] Alone in the library, alone at the university, alone at socialist meetings — the tale of loneliness and withdrawal was just the same as it had been in Sardinia.

And again, for compensation there was the excessive study: "I have worked too much, more than my strength allowed me"; the deprivation and the resulting illness: "For at least three years a day has not passed when I have not had a headache, some giddiness or dizziness".[300]

If the drive behind all this work was lost to Gramsci's memory, its aim was to make him a teacher in some school or other. His teachers expected great things of him.

He was not merely an unhappy man, he was miserable. He hated the world and he expressed his hatred in a barely watered-down Sardism. Even years later, Gobetti, who met him in 1918, wrote: "His socialism was first of all a reply to the offences of society against a lonely Sard emigrant" and "he joined the socialist party, probably for humanitarian reasons which matured in the pessimism of his loneliness as an emigrant Sard".[301] He posed as an exponent of Southern Italian interests in the socialist movement, and his attachment to Mussolini, though nebulous, may be explained by the support Mussolini enjoyed from Salvemini and other southerners. For years after joining the PSI he kept up close contact with other Sards, got jobs for them on the various socialist newspapers, and spent much of his time educating the mainlanders he knew about the facts of Sardinian life.[302]

In 1916 we see the beginnings of a change. On New Year he writes:

"I would like every morning to be New Year. I would like to come to terms with myself every day, to renew myself every day. No day of rest decided on in advance. I will choose myself when to stop, when I am drunk with the intensity of living, and want to dive into the animal life in order to reemerge with new vigour. [303]

Some days later he writes:

"I hate so-called serious people.... I prefer shameless cheek, a ragamuffin happiness".[304]

Of course these lines could be interpreted as wishful thinking by Gramsci, and in 1916 we can still find much to show the scars of youth, especially when he is in contemplative mood. But even the accounts of his personality change. The men who knew him at this time remember him as a man who joked a lot, who was always full of talk and surrounded by people.[305]

Moreover, now he left the university, turned down a position as a schoolmaster at Oulx in favour of much worse-paid job on *Avanti*, giving up his old aspiration to be an academic,[306] and his

Sardism became tempered with something else, as if he realised that he had to go beyond that explanation for his own predicament and that of his fellows. For several years he had no further emotional illness.

There had been a quite obvious change in his personality. Why had it taken place? It appears from Gramsci's intentional and unintentional revelations that he was in the process of remaking himself in what Marxists call *praxis*. By engaging in a practical and active rather than a contemplative life, he was purging himself of the emotional and ideological incrustations of this past.[397] He wrote that his "suffering" was a form of "egoism", that it harmed him to be alone, and that active life alone overcame that retreat into religion which came from the feeling that something was missing, which, if there, would make matters right.[308] "Returning to the active life, one feels the reality of history in a plastic sense", where mere attempts to understand it without overcoming it were insufficient.[309]

There are writers who suggest that the important change in Gramsci's life came earlier than 1916. For example, Romano points out that the words "active and operating neutrality" are taken from Marx's theses on Feuerbach, the 11th of which reads: "Philosophers have only interpreted the world, in various ways, the object is, however, to change it", and there are early writings of Gramsci which suggest that he believed in actively changing it. Even if his intellectual commitment to socialist activism came earlier than 1916, as they suggest, he most certainly did not act on his belief until late in 1915, when having started to impose his will on the world and not on himself he rapidly emerged from the intellectual *cul-de-sac* in which he had found himself when he vacillated between the university and socialism. In future years it was not what he read which was important — he read practically everything he could lay his hands on — but how he synthesised and modified the ideas he obtained from his reading in the practice of socialism, as he became an active part of the working class intent on changing the world for itself.

V

He worked hard as a journalist, chain smoking and drinking endless cups of coffee. Each day his regimen was the same. He would arrive at the office of the newspaper in the Corso Siccardi late in the morning; order a lunch basket from the restaurant opposite, eat half and put the other half aside for his evening meal. Since his column concerned Turinese life and theatrical criticism, he spent a lot of his afternoons and evenings at plays, at the cinema, at art exhibitions and at public lectures. The night was for conferences and writing. He wrote his articles in the same way. He would get up, walk around, smoking and thinking, take a piece of yellow paper, sit down suddenly and write out his article usually without a single mistake or deletion. He returned home early in the morning, perhaps at five o'clock, nearly always accompanied by someone who wished to talk to him, and perhaps to protect him from the nationalists who frequented the coffee bar he often went to.[310]

Gramsci's office was more than a place of work: it was the place he lived in, piled so high with books and papers that there was virtually no room to fit guests in. In this mess Gramsci always knew where everything was and could find a book with ease. His reading was omnivorous, from the worst paperback romances to the most abstruse books of philosophy.[311]

He rapidly earned the reputation for being an intellectual to whom the workers could speak without fear of revealing their own ignorance, and visitors from the nearby Casa del Popolo were always dropping in to find out what they should read, and what this or that meant. Gramsci used to listen with care and interest to what they said and then "he used to speak and he had the great gift of knowing how to speak to everyone".[312] This was a gift he would always retain. Giovanni Parodi recalled:

"When a worker said things that were wrong ... Gramsci knew how to reprove him both dryly and severely if it was needed; but always in a fashion which convinced him that he had made a mistake, without offending him, much less humiliating him." [313]

Perhaps it was his natural talent as a teacher which encouraged Gramsci to support the policies which Angelo Tasca, now away at the war, had introduced in the Youth Federation; and which up to this time, had been the only "socialist" policies which Gramsci had been involved in directly.

Tasca had, together with Gino Castagno and Giuseppe Romita, formed the first group (*fascio*) of the Socialist Youth Federation of Turin in 1909.[314] The Youth Federation as a whole was then in a state of crisis caused by the defection of the bulk of its members with the syndicalists who split off from the parent body. Since 1907 it had been led by Arturo Vella, and expressed its views through the newspaper *Avanguardia*. No clear policy existed for the organisation which had been left in a state of disarray by the defection.

In Turin, Tasca rapidly became dominant in what was initially a tiny organisation, and imposed on it a stamp which bore the marks of his own personality and inclinations. He was a man of somewhat romantic and undisciplined turn of mind, who believed that the Gospel combined more human solidarity, ethical import and the moral ideal of love than the works of Marx and Engels.[315] Strongly influenced first by Darwin, Spencer, and other positivists and then by Salvemini, Croce, *La Voce*, and the moralising of his teachers at Turin University, he encouraged young socialists to go forth into the countryside and "preach the word". Every Sunday groups of "red cyclists" led by young Turinese workers who had come from the particular area would go into the outlying towns to propagandise among the "recalcitrant" peasantry. They concentrated on cultural propaganda which would bear long-term fruits and not on the more short-term electoral propaganda, which was what socialist political activity amounted to in those years. By the time Gramsci got to know Tasca, he had given up sowing positivist theory among the peasants, and neglecting Marx, but his commitment to the new Crocean theory and to anticlericalism still appeared "empty moralising" to observers.[316]

Tasca suggested in 1912 that this policy of cultural propganda was designed to give to the workers that "know-how" which would allow them to become aware of their own separate and antagonistic interests to those of capitalism because, like all Croceans, he did not believe that they would arrive at this knowledge automatically. He proclaimed:

"Theories advance, but culture, that is men, are standing still. Our party is composed in great part of men who make judgements according to criteria which prevailed ten or twenty years ago: the party which wants to remake the world cannot even rejuvenate itself. We can no longer proclaim the truth of socialism in the name of science, not because there is a contradiction between them, but because socialists no longer know where to find science."[317]

One matter Tasca was certain of by 1914, was that science was not to be found in the texts of positivists.[318] He and his followers, both in the university and outside, spent much time attacking Professor Achille Loria, who had been the proponent of positivism in the socialist movement.[319]

This policy was limited to the young socialists of Piedmont[320] and because of its intellectual and elitist overtones was rejected outright at the Bologna national conference of the Young Socialist Federation in 1912. The bulk of young socialists, who were finding their leader in Amadeo Bordiga of Naples, preferred Mussolini's anti-intellectualism and belief that class experience gave birth to class consciousness to any "culturalist" policy.

Gramsci had been attracted to socialism by the same moralising and the same reading as Tasca, and shared at least that part of his road to socialism with him. Both also shared in the dislike of positivism and in the belief that socialism could be refurbished by contemporary knowledge. So, despite Tasca's defeat in 1912, he returned soon after his appointment as a journalist to Tasca's proposals to bring theory to the workers. In an article of January 1916, "Socialism and Culture", he suggested that a correct understanding of the relationship between culture and socialism could be grasped by starting from Novalis' proposition that attaining self-knowledge was the supreme problem of culture, and Vico's proposition that the "self-knowledge" which resulted from contemplation of oneself would lead to demands for equal political rights.

Culture, for these men, and for Gramsci, had nothing to do with encyclopaedic knowledge. Men were not to be seen as receptacles for "heaps of facts". "This form of culture is really dangerous, especially for the proletariat" Gramsci wrote, precisely because it created unjustifiable notions of superiority on the part of men with more "facts".

"Culture is something quite different. It is organisation, disciplining our own interior ego, it is taking possession of our own personality and winning a higher awareness through which we can succeed in understanding our own historical value, our own function in life, our own rights and our own duties."

But culture was not something obtained in a spontaneous evolution, according to a "fatal law". On the contrary, because Man was "above all, mind, historical creation and not nature", he

75

obtained awareness of his nature gradually through history as the result of "intelligent reflection", first by a few men, and then by a whole class, on the reasons for certain conditions existing and the best way of changing them from the conditions of slavery into the indicators of revolution and the coming remaking of society.

"This means that every revolution is preceded by an intense labour of criticism, of cultural penetration, of permeation of ideas among men who first resist them and who think only about how to resolve, from day to day and hour to hour, their personal political and economic problems, without uniting with others who find themselves in a similar situation."

To illustrate his point Gramsci pointed to the French Revolution which was made by the spread of "a bourgeois international of the mind", so that in Italy Napoleon found the way paved for him "by an invisible army of books, which had prepared men".

He concluded: "Today the same phenomenon is being repeated for socialism. It is through the criticism of capitalist civilisation that the united awareness of the proletariat has and is being formed, and criticism means culture, and not a spontaneous evolution".

"If it is true that all history is a chain of the efforts which man has made to free himself from privilege, prejudice and idolatry, we do not understand why the proletariat, which wishes to add another link to the chain, should not know who and why and by whom it was preceded and what it can get of use from this knowledge."[321]

In one hastily-written article Gramsci had given a theoretical dimension to Tasca's demand that socialist theory be up-dated.

Gramsci acted out his belief, encouraging the workers who visted him to start reading the greatest exponents of bourgeois culture: Bergson, Croce, Salvemini, *La Voce* and *Critica* as well as Marxists like Antonio Labriola.[322]

In the "First Stone", written at the end of 1916, he returned to the theme, making practical suggestions about the education of the masses, which gave point to a whole string of articles which he had published during the year. He wrote that because the existing school system was directed at making the views of the bourgeoisie universal, in particular the feeling of nationalism, socialism would have to create in opposition "a new education, which is simple, human and suitable for the popular classes" and which had a real content derived from an immediate, direct knowledge of their needs, desires, rights and duties.

"The history of education shows that every class which has sought to take power has prepared itself for power by an autonomous education. The first step in emancipating oneself from political and social slavery is that of freeing the mind. I put forward this new idea: popular schooling should be placed under the control of the great workers' unions. The problem of education is the most important *class problem.*"[323]

Given these beliefs, no sooner did Gramsci start to edit *Grido del Popolo* than he started to turn it, as Gobetti put it, into a "journal of culture"[324] instead of a paper of local news and evangelical propaganda. Gramsci's articles poured forth on a variety of cultural subjects: particularly important were those on what the workers should read and on the meaning of the Russian revolution. The workers frequently found the style difficult to understand, but despite their complaints, Gramsci refused to make concessions. [325] As one worker said later: "He didn't like amateurs",[326] and he was prepared to voice these unpleasant truths no matter what they were.

In February 1917 Gramsci also published the only issue of *La Città Futura* on behalf of the Youth Federation, at 2 *centesimi* a copy. The three main articles were by Croce, Salvemini and Carlini. Gramsci wrote all the rest. It was designed to show that the Youth Federation had lost none of its ardour because the war had torn so many young men away and declared that "History is made by the young". The Youth Federation's new paper affirmed that its first task was one of education. It showed clearly Gramsci's concern with education and his almost completely Crocean Salveminian orientation at this time.[327]

His main contribution was "Three orders and three principles" in which Gramsci considered what Pastore had denominated the "incubation of praxis". It was, he noted, extraordinarily difficult to overcome the feeling that a bird in the hand was worth two in the bush, a feeling which worked in favour of the maintenance of the *status quo*; even more difficult when the appeal was to kill the bird in the hand first. It was mankind's refusal to face up to the way new societies would have to be created which explained the ubiquity of utopias, which described the golden land in detail, but said little about how to get there.

In fact, socialists could only ever advance the most general idea of what would come after the revolution, and had to work for ideals rather than the concrete. The French revolutionaries "did not foresee the capitalist order. They worked to realise the rights of man", and it was from these ideals that the reality came in a fashion unforeseen by the utopian theorists.

In Italy socialists should work for "the possibility of all citizens realising a full human personality".[328]

He went on in another article that the main task therefore became to combat indifference to such ideals. Widespread popular apathy was due to the non-involvement of people in history, so that they saw themselves as its objects and victims.

"Some whimper pitifully, others curse obscenely, but none, or few, ask themselves: if I had done my duty, if I had attempted to impose my will, my opinion, would what has happened have happened."

"I hate the apathetic", he went on. Men should make efforts to arrive at the truth and realise that their failures started within themselves and were not the fault of others. There were no forces outside men and their wills which made life what it was. Like Tasca before him, Gramsci concluded that positivism and "scientificism" were discredited and that there were no social laws making matters inevitable. Laws were merely the *ex post facto* reduction of the complexity of events to simple standards. "For natural laws, the fatal progress of things of pseudo-scientists, has been substituted the tenacious will of men".

His practical directions were therefore that socialists should work among the non-aligned sections of the community and in winning these seek to raise their culture to that of professors "or their action will be sterile".[329]

It was not a policy calculated to appeal to the working class, with its excessively moralising overtones, and stress on self-help. Few were prepared to wait for Gramsci's revolution, which appeared to need more than a lifetime of preparation. So when in December 1917 a socialist proposed the creation of a cultural association for workers, Gramsci jumped at it and the *Club di Vita morale* was formed by Gramsci and three friends: Attilio Carena, a philosophy student, Carlo Boccardo, a municipal employee, and Andrea

Viglongo, a correspondent for the Youth Federation's newspaper, *Avanguardia*.

Some months after it was formed Gramsci gave this account of its activities to Giuseppe Lombardo Radice:

"At Turin we believe that preaching about the principles and moral maxims which should necessarily become established with the coming of a socialist civilisation is not enough. We have tried to give this preaching an organised form; to give new examples (for Italy) of how to work together. So the *Club di Vita morale* has recently emerged. Through it we propose to accustom young people in the socialist movement to dispassionate discussion about social and ethical problems. We want them to become used to research, to read methodically and disciplinedly, to expound their convictions simply and with equanimity. It works out like this: I, who have had to accept the role of excubitor, because I began the association, assign a paper to some young person: a chapter of Croce's 'Cultura e vita morale'; Salvemini's 'Problemi educativi e sociali', or his *French Revolution* or 'Cultura e laicità', the *Communist Manifesto* or the Commentary of Croce in *Critica*, or something else, which, however, reflects the existing idealist movement: then I or someone else replies."[330]

To encourage mutual trust the Club was run on the basis of participatory democracy.

It had few members, held only three meetings, and when the members were called to arms it died.[331]

We can discover what Gramsci considered important among his omnivorous reading by an examination of what he wrote in his newspaper columns and what he taught about in his lectures and in the *Club di Vita morale*.

It is quite clear that he was still heavily influenced by Crocean idealism.[332] Not only did he recommend Croce's writings to his readers and those who called on him at his home or at work, but he also stated that Croce's work was most important.[333] He also still took a great deal from Salvemini, as the letter to Lombardo Radice indicates. Furthermore, he suggested to the men associated with him that they read *La Voce*. In practically all cases the suggestions would not have been popular ones, because of the association in the minds of socialists of all these authors, either with Mussolini, or other sections of the nationalist movement.[334]

In *La Città Futura* we can see how far he had been influenced by Crocean principles. He rejected all positivist modes of thought in favour of Hegelian categories; he emphasised personal moral responsibility; he suggested that men could transcend themselves through thought. All these ideas can be traced back to books or articles written by Croce at about this time or a little earlier. We know that Gramsci had read some because he published them.[335] Other values may merely have been received indirectly from the men he admired, like Farinelli, who was also a moralist.

Gramsci also fostered the study and publication of the great works of European culture. In the *Club di Vita morale*, Wagner and Foscolo were discussed at length and on long walks he explained Marcus Aurelius' character to the workers.[336]

What was most interesting him at this time was the work of Romain Rolland, about whom he was always talking, and whose articles Pia Carena, his unofficial secretary, used to translate often for the newspaper. Gramsci knew the famous newspaper articles of 1914, "Au-dessus de la mêlée", and *Jean Christophe*, with whose childhood Gramsci could easily identify. He also read Charles Péguy in the *Cahiers de la quinzaine* and both read and personally met Henri Barbusse.[337]

And what of Karl Marx, whose theory provided socialism with its base? Dispute exists as to when Gramsci engaged in a systematic study of Marx. Certainly Pastore introduced him to some interesting ideas in 1914-15. By 1917 he had read Labriola's essays, *The Materialist Conception of History*, and *Discorrendo di Socialismo e filosofia*;[338] and he probably read some of Mondolfo's writings.[339] The first he recommended warmly to his friends in 1916-17.[340] From his articles about economic determinism, we know that he kept up with the writings of Turati, Treves and Modigliani.[341]

He and his circle probably went back to the study of Marx late in 1916 or early in 1917. Gramsci, who had studied German and English at the university, but who knew French better, used to read the French edition of Marx' works with their lemon-coloured jackets. Leonetti remembers that he read *The Holy Family, The Poverty of Philosophy, The Communist Manifesto, Revolution and Counter-Revolution in Germany, Introduction to the Critique of Political Economy*.[342] While he almost certainly read *Capital* as well, he did not read those as yet unpublished key works in Marx's intellectual development, *The Economic and Philosophical Manuscripts* of 1844 and *The German Ideology*.(343] Among the workers he appeared a master of Marxism, and he was already giving lectures on Marx in 1916.[344] This apparent mastery of Marx should not deceive us: the average worker who went back to Marx with him had to rely on a bad translation of the *Manifesto* and Cafiero and Fabietti's appalling edition of *Capital*, and was not a good judge.[345] Gramsci most certainly also knew many of the sources of Marx's thought since he republished matter from Hegel and the French socialists in 1917, and he was *au fait* with many of the interpreters of Marx, [346] but before 1917 Gramsci made very few direct references to Marx or Marxists in his newspaper columns, devoting much more space to the idealists and their work. He knew nothing of Lenin until 1917, and Lenin had not heard of him until after the Russian revolution of February 1917.

VI

Between 1915-17 Gramsci's *praxis* had been an intellectual *praxis* only: one in which he preached at the workers but was not active among them. He found it satisfying personally and was no longer the lonely, unsmiling, completely unfulfilled, alienated being he was before he became a journalist. It had enabled him to overcome some of the emotional encrustations of his past though not all, as he still lived in a society which thwarted full expression of his personality: one can never transcend one's fellows. But it was not a creative activity which was sufficiently *real* in the marxist sense to allow him to escape from all the ideological encrustations of his past. He still subscribed to the ideas of Croce, *La Voce* and Salvemini — which in practice meant an elitist notion of socialist activity where the intellectuals taught the workers what they thought the workers ought to know — because he had insufficient direct contact with the workers to learn how irrelevant many of idealism's theories were: in particular those about the relation between thought and action, or the intellectuals and the masses. While preaching had little or no effect on the workers because the *de haut en bas* cultural propagandising was irrational, inadequate to its object, it also did not allow Gramsci to discover what the workers thought they ought to know, or what he could discover a worker ought to know through being involved in their lives. Nor could be come involved in their lives while he was only a journalist.

To escape from the ideological encrustations of his past, to learn from the workers what they needed to know, and thus to go beyond his unproductive elitism, he had to add to the ideological praxis of his journalism the practical praxis of working among the workers, becoming involved, or living their lives. Then the workers could teach him if what he preached would have real meaning for them, and be satisfying on a collective as well as a personal level. His ideas would start to become real in the Marxist sense when masses of men took them up and they became social forces.

Gramsci started to unite his ideological practice with a practical practice early in 1917. This unification was what enabled him to start creating useful theory for the working class. It is important to note, in view of the traditional interpretation that Gramsci's thought escaped from fruitless idealism and he started to produce the new ideas which have made him famous, *after he discovered Lenin*, that in fact the process of unifying the two forms of praxis ante-dated his knowledge of Lenin by many months, and Leninism only became one ingredient in his journey towards making a successful theory. We note as an aside, which cannot be pursued here, that it is a lapse into idealism to assume that any system of ideas, Lenin's included, makes history, even Gramsci's history, by itself. We may also note that this assertion does not deny that ideas, including Lenin's, may have played a part which is empirically verifiable, together with other factors in a complexity, in Gramsci's history.

Among the threads we can trace back as one of the factors marking the beginning of his unification of the two praxes was Gramsci's reaction to the news of the Russian Revolution of February 1917.

VII

News of the Russian revolution of February 1917 only seeped past the censorship very slowly, and information about what was happening in that country was very vague. On the 18 March it was known that the Tsar had been overthrown. Gramsci expressed his first opinion about this over a month later,

> "The bourgeois press ... has told us how the power of the autocracy has fallen and been replaced by another power; they hope by a bourgeois power. They have jumped immediately at the obvious parallel, Russian revolution, French revolution, and

find that the two events are very like one another.... Nevertheless, we are persuaded that the Russian revolution is proletarian in character, as it has been so far in its deeds, and that it will naturally result in a socialist regime.''[347]

And the reason for this assertion, despite the lack of concrete information, was that the Russian revolution was inspired by an ideal which could not be the ideal of a minority, because a tremendously free and anti-authoritarian regime was being installed in Russia. Even criminals had been freed: something only possible when a new set of social standards were introduced.[348]

After April the information in the socialist press about events in Russia became even worse, because *Avanti* started to rely on the reports of an *émigré* Russian, Vassily Suchomlin, for its explanations of what was happening in Russia. Suchomlin's loyalties were to the Social Revolutionaries and he frequently misrepresented the role of other groups in the revolution. His articles were also strongly biased against Lenin. Like other socialists, Gramsci relied on Suchomlin's reports and in 1917 presented completely erroneous reports about what was happening in Russia.[349] On the eve of the Bolshevik revolution he wrote perceptively that the Russian revolution was about to enter its final stage but quite incorrectly reported that the leader of the revolution was Chernov.

"Russian maximalism [Bolshevism was nearly always referred to as maximalism in Italy, indicating a misunderstanding of its nature] has found its leader. Lenin was the master of life, the stirrer of consciences, the awakener of sleeping souls. Chernov is the realiser, the man with a concrete programme to put into practice, an entirely socialist programme, which permits no collaboration, which cannot be accepted by the bourgeoisie because it overthrows the principle of private property, because it finally begins the socialist revolution, the entry into world history of collectivist socialism.''[359]

But these errors of fact did not mean a corresponding error of the spirit. Gramsci shared in the popular enthusiasm for Lenin, which had become widespread by the middle of 1917.

"The Russian Maximalists are the Russian revolution. Kerensky, Tseretelli, Chernov are the present state. They have achieved an initial social equilibrium based on a balance of forces in which the moderates have retained much power. The maximalists represent the community, the tomorrow of the revolution; it is in this sense that they *are* the revolution. They incarnate the parameters of the idea of socialism; they want socialism in its entirety. And they have the task of preventing a compromise between the millenarian past and the Idea.''

Gramsci maintained that because the moderate socialists were no Jacobins, Lenin would not suffer the fate of Babeuf. Lenin had aroused energies which would not die away, and his comrades, nourished on a true revolutionary Marxist thought, believed that socialism could be introduced in Russia at any moment.[351]

Gramsci's enthusiasm for Lenin was shared by the Turinese working class. When the Goldenberg mission visited Italy on behalf of the Kerensky government in August 1917, they were greeted by a Turinese crowd of forty thousand, crying "Long live Lenin". Since the Russian delegation had made quite clear to the press a few days previously that they were the enemies of Lenin, this left no doubt where Turin working-class loyalties lay.[352] This coincidence of enthusiasm between Gramsci and the workers was symbolic in Gramsci's development. He had not been too unhappy in 1916-17; he was busy with his journalism and had made himself a limited reputation. *But*, he had only had contact with the working class as a teacher of theory, and his efforts to raise their culture, via the inculcation of Crocean concepts had had no success. For the first time, in the conjuncture of enthusiasm for the Russian Bolsheviks, Gramsci started to engage in political activity of an organisational sort, which was finally to enable him to resolve the vexing problem of the role of the intellectuals and cultural propaganda in the movement. This was something which Italian socialists had not been able to do, falling back on either Tasca's position (which, when all was said and done, had been Gramsci's position too for some years) of a *de haut en bas* system of education,[353] or on Mussolini and Bordiga's position of blaming the intellectuals for all the vicissitudes of the movement and saying that the proletariat could do without them.[354]

VIII

On September 30, 1917, Gramsci, who was already well-known in

Turin socialist circles as editor of *Il Grido*, was elected to the leadership of the Turin Socialist branch. Shortly afterwards he consolidated his position in the local leadership by winning control of the local co-operative (ACT) for the PSI. He had started to live the class struggle of the Turin working-class, and no longer contemplated it from outside.[355] The Turin working-class had a peculiar history which conditioned their outlook.

Up till 1900 most had worked seasonally in the country and in the city's main industries: textile and military production. Though their conditions of work were terrible, their wages were comparatively high. They had by 1900 formed their own self-help associations, co-operatives and unions, but contact with the countryside kept alive in them an individualist ethic and the Socialist Party won few to the cause of socialism.[356]

The burgeoning of the motor-car industry and the consequent growth of a proletariat which was completely urbanised did not alter the fortunes of the Socialist Party. The development of car manufacturing certainly created a class of skilled workers and sucked large numbers of unskilled workers into the city to supply the ancillary services, but the first received high wages and saw themselves as an aristocracy of labour and the second were still peasants with all the attitudes that entailed. The result was a city divided into three social strata: the capitalists, the skilled workers and the unskilled workers.

Although extremely reactionary, the industrialists of the automobile industry — who set the style for the city — made many concessions to the skilled workers to keep production high. The latter worked for wages which were directly related to profitability in the industry and in 1906 even won the right to organise shop stewards' committees (*commissioni interne*) at the place of work.[357] The skilled workers were able to insert their representatives — often Socialist Party members — into the organs of municipal and national government.

Even by 1906 the process of integrating the Turin proletariat into the ongoing system was well advanced. The metal workers' federation (FIOM) agreed with the ITALA company that there would be a moratorium on all strikes if the company recognised the union, and established a system of contractual negotiation. Such agreements subordinated working-class autonomy among the skilled workers to the needs of production, and separated the skilled workers more and more from the unskilled.

This integration and division did not matter when times were good — as they were generally until 1914, but they proved disastrous for established working class organisations when they were not. In 1907 and 1911 there were local recessions which affected workers' conditions. The workers pressed for strike action from their leaders, who, however, had become accustomed to working in a collaborationist fashion and attempted to restrain the workers from striking. As a result the syndicalists were able to lead more than 6,500 men out on a strike which lasted 65 days before it was defeated.

This strike, which showed that the system of collaboration with capitalism was breaking down, coincided with Gramsci's first year in Turin. By the time he had joined the PSI in 1913 the rapid inflation and the threat of war was making the rift between the rank and file and capitalism even deeper. The union leaders were obliged to some extent to take into consideration the workers' desires and break off the more blatant forms of collaboration with the capitalists. In particular, they rebuilt unity with the rank and file by encouraging the popular opposition to Italian participation in the war.

Italy's entry into the war only made class hatred more intense. The working class refused to abide by regulations banning demonstrations and continued to demonstrate their opposition. They were able to link this political action with social and economic issues because of the ubiquitous profiteering and rapid rise in the price of consumer articles.

The fact that the government made most work in the Turin factories a reserved occupation resulted in a continuity of personnel and the anti-war tradition after 1915. Even so, the number of workers organised grew rapidly: the FIOM had 20 sections with 7000 members in 1910; 50 with 11, 471 in 1914; 52 with 13,800 in 1915 and 62 with 22,445 members in 1916.[358] This showed that a large number of new workers were being incorporated into the unions, but it did not mean that the unskilled workforce was disappearing or that the bulk of it was organised.

Through its anti-war activity the Turin working class thus started to build up close links with the Socialist Party for the first time during the First World War, although formal alliances had existed since 1907.[359]

Under the leadership of Giacinto Serrati, a gifted unifier, the "maximalists" of the PSI had slowly rebuilt the party after Mussolini's defection. They had done this on a platform of anti-war agitation which won them the support of the Youth

Federation, led by Bordiga. In accord with their policy of rebuilding the party around opposition to the war, they supported international initiatives against the war and sent delegates to an anti-war conference at Zimmerwald in September 1915. At this conference Oddino Morgari and Angelica Balabanoff were exposed directly to Lenin's thesis that the anti-war feeling could be turned into a violent socialist revolution. They vacillated at the tone of some of the Russian's speeches, but they voted with the Bolsheviks and were elected to the executive of the anti-war movement. In April 1916 Serrati himself attended another anti-war conference at Kienthal, heard the Bolshevik theory that imperialist policies caused the war and how working-class opposition should and could be turned into a force for revolution and not peace, and his group again voted with the Bolsheviks on many issues.[360]

The theories of the Bolsheviks were then brought back to Italy, apparently with the stamp of approval of the maximalist leadership of the party and loudly applauded in Turin and elsewhere. There were huge pro-Bolshevik demonstrations throughout Italy when the Goldenberg mission visited to whip up support for the Russian Provisional government. This pro-Bolshevik feeling among the working-class of Turin took on a concrete form when the "revolutionary intransigent" faction in Turin led by Francesco Barberis, a carter with a syndicalist past, started to demand that the party do what had been done in Russia in February, and, at a conference in Florence created a national revolutionary wing to the left of Serrati himself. It also took on increasingly concrete form when the Youth Federation, having elected Bordiga its secretary, pronounced itself in favour of revolutionary solution to the country's problems.

Serrati and the maximalists had never given more than half-hearted support and verbal support to the positions of the Russian Bolsheviks and had, indeed, allowed the "reformists" not only to support the war effort but to attack the Bolshevik doctrines as "Blanquist", "anarchist" and the Bolshevik party itself as "doctrinal fanatics".[361] Popular pro-Bolshevik feeling finally obliged him to come out openly in support of Lenin in July 1917 and then to seek to establish a common ground with the pro-Bolshevik factions within his party. He therefore called a conference for November 1917 to work out a common policy for the future.

The Turin "rigids" — as the pro-Bolshevik Socialist workers were known — were doubly militant by the time the conference was held. First, there had been riots in Turin in August when bread supplies ran out and many clashes with the troops took place before the riots stopped. This prompted renewed demands that the workers "should do what had been done in Russia".[362] Then, in October, there came the first confused news of the Bolshevik revolution — the news was wildly applauded.

Two "rigid" delegates were chosen to go to Florence to put the views of the Turinese Socialists, but, when one suddenly could not go, Gramsci found himself on his way to the "secret" conference. Neither he, nor his newspaper, had ever been strongly revolutionary in any immediate sense but he was nevertheless chosen to represent the extreme left view at a conference of the left wing of the PSI.

At Florence he met Amadeo Bordiga for the first time. Bordiga, the son of a renowned professor, had belonged to the Neapolitan branch of the PSI and to the Youth Federation. His experience of politics had been in Naples where there was no real industrial proletariat, and where election struggles between socialists had been more corrupt even than those known to Gramsci in his youth in Sardinia. He had been responsible for the formation of the Karl Marx club in Naples, but, unlike Gramsci's *Club di Vita morale* in Turin, the Karl Marx club had denied the necessity for any cultural preparation of the masses at all: as far as its members were concerned the revolution was "actual" and the pressing task was to build a strong united party to carry it out.

Bordiga had brought these views into the Youth Federation. At the Bologna congress of 1912 he had clashed bitterly with Tasca, who was representing the Turin section. When Tasca suggested that what was needed among socialists was an updating of the theoretical tools necessary for revolution, and thus argued for an educatory programme among the workers, Bordiga had replied scornfully that:

"The need for study should be proclaimed in a congress of school teachers, not socialists. You don't become a socialist through instruction but through experiencing the real needs of the class to which you belong. And bourgeois socialists, I will call them exceptions, through sheer benevolence ..."[363]

Indeed, not only did he affirm that study was not needed, but he was prepared to ascribe much of the weakness of the socialist movement to the intellectuals who encouraged local and particularist interests to the detriment of general class interests based on "enthusiasm" and "faith".

Most young socialists, including those of Turin, shared his views. Until 1914 these corresponded closely with those of Mussolini. Like Mussolini, Bordiga believed that understanding came from class experience and, "that if you don't believe this any more, and want to substitute for it with schooling in theory, study, knowledge of practice", then you belonged outside the party. He like Mussolini wanted a compact centralised revolutionary party. He had broken with Mussolini when the latter proposed support of the war, arguing in terms reminiscent of those used by Lenin. Naturally, he was already a national figure by the time the Florence conference was held.[364] He was also one of the first Socialists to start reading Lenin.

For a multitude of reasons then, his views had differed from those of Gramsci. To these disagreements about policy, we can add the knowledge that he was tall, imposing, and one of those Southern orators of whom Gramsci had always been suspicious. Despite this background, Gramsci supported him at Florence when he called for the utilisation of the popular anti-war feeling to create revolutionary street actions. Gramsci too urged the "maximalist" leaders to "act now". The leaders curtly dismissed the almost unknown Gramsci's support for immediate revolutionary action as "Bergsonian voluntarism."[365]

Gramsci was not put off by such "maximalist" strictures and announced to his companion in the railway carriage carrying him back home, that: "What is happening in Russia shows us the road."[366] He referred to the recent triumphant seizure of power by the Bolsheviks as a lesson to be applied in the specific situation of the Turin working-class and the Italian socialist movement.

IX

Much depended on what he thought was taking place in Russia. It must be made quite clear that practically nothing at all was known about the Russian revolution, who its leaders were, what form it took, and what its specific aims were, either by Gramsci or anyone else in the socialist movement. The censorship still made anything happening in Russia obscure, and the misrepresentations of the press continued to give bias to what was known. So Gramsci, like everyone else, found what he wanted in the Russian revolution and Bolshevism.

He found in it the practical expression of the Marx he already believed in, who had found expression in *Città futura*, and whom he described in mid-1918 as "not a Messiah who left a string of parables laden with categorical imperatives and absolutely incontrovertible norms outside the categories of time and space. The only categorical imperative, the single norm, is 'Workers of the World unite'."[367]

And, as if to rebuke those who had castigated him for his views at Florence on the grounds that the objective conditions for revolution were not right, he stressed that "voluntarism" meant nothing. The Russian revolution, he wrote in an article now famous, was a revolt "against *Capital*", against the determinist interpretations which the bourgeoisie had given to Marx's *chef d'oeuvre*. The Bolsheviks were Marxist precisely because they had not made the work of the "Master" a collection of inscrutable, dogmatic affirmations,

"They live Marxist thought, the part of it which cannot die, that part which is the continuation of German and Italian idealism, and which in Marx himself became contaminated by positivistic and naturalistic incrustations. And this thought considers not economic facts the main force in history, but man, the society of men who are close to each other, who understand each other and develop through these contacts (civilisation) a social and collective will and understand, judge and order to their wishes those economic facts, so that their wishes become the motor of the economy ..."

and, able to see their future in England, were making the very conditions for their ideal.[368]

Again and again in 1918 Gramsci emphasised that the Russian revolution was practical evidence that men made their own destinies, a proposition he and others influenced by Croce had been preaching for years and which was a central theme in *Città Futura*.[369]

Illustrative is this, written in July:

"If you find Lenin a utopian, if you say that the attempt to set up the dictatorship of the proletariat in Russia is a utopian effort, you cannot be a socialist, who is aware, and who builds up his culture by studying the doctrine of historical materialism: you are a Catholic, bogged in the Syllabus; only you are the utopian really. Utopia consists precisely in not being able to see history as free development ..."[370]

In the Soviet Union liberty was being guaranteed by a new hierarchical order: "from the unorganised and suffering masses, through the organised workers and peasants, to the Soviets and the Bolshevik party and to one man, Lenin. A hierarchy based on prestige and trust, which formed spontaneously and is maintained by free choice,"[371] and in which the first groups could all belong to the Soviets which, in turn, were continuously integrated with the party. Apart from this generalisation, he did not feel at first that anything more specific could be learnt from the Bolshevik revolution until some years had gone by and it could be the object of mature reflection,[372] though he noted that there were great similarities between the Russian and the Italian proletariats, and that Lunacharsky's efforts to educate the Russian proletariat were almost the same as his own, somewhat earlier.[373] Gramsci wrote on 14 September 1918:

"Lenin, applying the methods shaped by Marx, finds that reality is the deep, unbridgeable abyss that capitalism has dug between the bourgeoisie and the proletariat, and the ever increasing antagonism between the two classes. In explaining social and political phenomena, and in deciding which path the party should follow, never in his life has he lost sight of the strongest spring of all political and economic activity: the class struggle."[374]

Gramsci not only spread this interpretation of the Russian revolution through his newspaper columns when press sales were rocketing upwards, but he also spread it in an organised way: "... the writings of Lenin, the documents of the Bolshevik party, were looked for, awaited with anxiety, translated, read and discussed collectively, explained, circulated in the factories. Gramsci was the soul of this work".[375]

But "matters were neither simple nor clear in those days"[376] and the material Gramsci had to distribute was mainly truncated versions of Lenin's *ad hoc* strategic speeches which came to him through French journals, and the translation which Togliatti and Leonetti undertook of Lenin's available work was not available for some time.[377] In Turin, Gramsci became known as the expert on Lenin. Even young bourgeois intellectuals, like Piero Gobetti, who used to visit him regularly in 1918, were greatly impressed and advanced almost the same interpretation of the Russian revolution as Gramsci did.

So influenced was Gobetti, that some years later he wrote:

"... Bolshevism is attacked because it is insufficiently socialist (of the infallible sort, which is symbolised in Italy by Treves, Turati, and others ...). In the polemics which our bourgeoisie has undertaken against bolshevism all methods have become valid. We willingly return to the old methodological prejudices from which our renovated historiographical culture freed us: again we scorn doctrines and ideas, and *facts* are exalted."[378]

Outside Turin, the "maximalists" did not share Gramsci's positive commitment to the Revolution or his assessment of its meaning. At first they maintained that it was not a marxist revolution but inspired by the anarchist teachings of Bakunin, Kropotkin and Tolstoy.[379] Then they moved, in somewhat confused fashion, into support of the ideas they believed it represented. On the whole, with most of the leaders in jail in 1918, they tended to wait and see, as they had in earlier years.

This inaction allowed the "reformists" to take the initiative and express determined opposition to the revolution, its leaders and their methods. Supported by many trade union leaders they even considered forcing the issue and splitting the party.[380] Where the official policy was to support the spread of revolution to the West, they supported the Wilsonian multi-national solution, and participation in a constituent assembly designed to re-establish capitalism in Italy after the war.

Threats by the leadership to expel the "reformist" leaders for indiscipline had little effect and nothing was done at the Rome congress of September 1918 to control them.[381]

Given the assertive, aggressive policies of the "reformists", the decision in December 1918 of the PSI leadership to adopt new policies inspired by what it thought was Leninism,

"the Socialist Party ... proposes as first objective the institution of a socialist republic and the dictatorship of the proletariat with the following aims: 1) socialisation of the means of production and exchange ... 2) distribution of products, made exclusively by collectives, by means of co-operatives and communal organisations; 3) abolition of military conscription and universal disarmament following the union of all proletarian republics in the Socialist International; 4) municipalisation of private habitation and hospital services, transformation of bureaucracy, entrusted to the direct management of the employees."[382]

was vacuous.

Faced by this situation, Gramsci attacked the reformists for supporting Wilson and the Constituent Assembly, claiming that they were deserting the party.[383] But he kept a decent silence about the maximalists and started to carry out party policy that "a socialist republic be instituted under the dictatorship of the proletariat".

CHAPTER III

A Philosophy of Praxis

I

Gramsci's Sardist world view of 1911 had been deeply rooted in his limited provincial experience of the miseries of Sardinia and developed before he had the advantage of a wider perspective from which to deduce possible solutions. In 1917 the problems he was concerned with were still the same, primarily personal and national problems, but the solutions he was finding had become modified by the perspective he gained from being in Turin with men who saw the resolution of life's problems differently from the Sardinians, and by his experience of the elections of 1913. He generalised these solutions, in his own words, as "a tendency towards Croceanism". [384]

He himself indicated that by this he meant that he had no faith in any religion which promised men salvation regardless of what they did, because he believed that men made their own destinies.[385] We can extend and give more specific content to these definitions by examining the content of the works of "Croceanism" to whose ideas he subscribed.

Gramsci knew Croce's work through reading the journals *La Critica*, which was written almost entirely by Croce himself, and *La Voce* and *L'Unità*. In 1910-11 Croce published several essays on socialism and democracy in *La Critica* (*Massoneria e socialismo* and *La Morte del socialismo* are the most important) in which he attacked socialism and democracy and declared that the theory of Marx was dead. But these were the last stages of an old argument belonging to the nineties, and in 1912-13 Croce was writing new important works which marked a development in his thought. They were historiographical essays which he published in *Critica* in 1916 and which, as Gobetti pointed out, influenced a whole generation of Italians. Gramsci read these essays too, declaring in 1916 that his

94

"dilemma came directly from the rigid historical realism" which the idealist philosophers Croce and Gentile had coined. Again in 1918 he declared that the central points which Croce reached in these essays were "undoubtedly right".[386]

Croce argued that "the wisdom of life warns us not to lose ourselves in an absurd desire" to know all that happened in the past, to create a universal history which "tries to form a picture of all the things that have happened to the human race, from its origins upon earth until the present moment". When men tried to do this they tended to fill "the abysses of prehistory" with "theological and naturalistic fictions" and to trace the future "either with revelations and prophesies, as in Christian universal history ... or with previsions, as in the universal histories of positivism, democratism and socialism."[387]

These commonsense warnings were designed to lead to the main object of his work, an attack on positivist and determinist history, which continued Croce's earlier attacks on positivist philosophy. Positivist history claimed to start with the facts and to have no theoretical presuppositions and thus to know what has happened in fact. It therefore imposed its history as a framework of the given upon man and merged into determinism. Croce typified the problems of the approach of starting with the "facts": "First collect the facts, then connect them causally; this is the way that the work of the historian is represented in the determinist tradition. But it is well known what happens when one fact is linked to another as its cause, forming a chain of causes and effects:[388] we thus inaugurate an infinite regression and we never succeed in finding the cause or causes to which we can finally attach the chain that we have so industriously put together".[389]

Despite their claim to start from the facts, by the implicit logic of their practice, they thus ended up sharing a common philosophy of history with transcendentalists. They, like every other historian, had a philosophical starting point, but theirs', like the transcendentalists', lay outside history in an unprovable proposition, that "brute facts" must be the starting point of any investigation.

"Methodological doubt will suggest above all things that those facts are a *presupposition* that has not been proved, and it will lead to the enquiry as to *whether the proof can be obtained*. Having attempted the proof, we shall finally arrive at the conclusion that *those facts really do not exist*."[390]

Croce's conclusion was arrived at by Hegelian logic as understood in his own *Essay on Hegel*. Briefly, he argued that since everything presumes its opposite in reality, both materialism and idealism are negations of reality.[391] If one started from reality, what created History[392] was "the mind who thinks and constructs the fact". Historians did no more than "select the facts" according to "choice itself, conditioned like every economic act, by knowledge of the actual situation, and in this case by the practical and scientific needs of a definite moment or epoch".[393]

If historians created rather than discovered History, then it followed that the status of three concepts which followed from a universal history (and which, we remark parenthetically, have relevance to Gramsci's and every other man's lives): *development, end* and *value* had to be re-examined. Croce recognised that within his theory of historiography these concepts could only exist as relative propositions and that therefore there could be no positive judgements. Nothing could be either finally good or bad. History had no adversaries, because, as a humanism, placing man as the creator at the centre of its conception, all its adversaries were also its subject. The inference he drew was that History never "metes out justice", it merely "justifies".

This whole theory has been characterised as "typically actual", by which phrase we should understand that it is what men are doing in the present which is of primary importance, not their reconstructed past which is ideological and existed to limit them only insofar as they had created it themselves.[394] Gramsci expressed this notion nicely and approvngly in 1918:

"To be History, and not simply graphic marks, or source material, or aids to memory, past events must be thought up again, and this rethinking brings them up to date, since the evaluation or ordering of those facts necessarily depends on 'contemporary' knowledge of the person rethinking the past event, about who makes history and made it in the past."[395]

Croce understood what men were *doing* in the present when making History primarily as what they created (thought), and this led him to dispute the different beliefs of Giovanni Gentile. Gramsci followed this debate, possibly in *La Voce* where Croce published in 1913 a long explanation of his disagreement with Gentile.

Gentile, who had co-edited *Critica* some years earlier, had advanced the theory that Thought was a "pure act". The substance of this theory was correctly typified by Croce as the reduction of what men were *doing* (always understood within the framework of the historiographical theory espoused by Gramsci) to the action or process of creation rather than its end result as conceptualisation. Thought thus became a *praxis* rather than a product.

Croce objected on two grounds. First he argued that Gentile's position was illogical (went against Hegel) because it started from the abstract notions of Thought and Being, as they were expressed in Hegel's *Logic* alone, and not from his whole system. This philosophical starting point in man's actual actions considered abstracted from history and society led it into these logical problems: If what was important was what men were doing in the practical sense when they thought, rather than the concepts they thought up, then in logic the material praxis was the same as the product itself, and when the idea of the object was the same as the object itself then everything was everything else. How then did people distinguish one thing from another?

Then he argued that it was immoral (went against Kant) because concern for what was "actual" to the exclusion of a historical pespective, which in Hegel was overridingly important, led to the position that the only way of distinguishing right from wrong, even in a relative sense, was to assume that what was past was wrong and what was present was right, for the same reason that the theory of knowledge implicit in the philosophy allowed no criteria for distinction of other sorts.

Given these logical and moral faults, Croce preferred to start from the Hegelian notion of the unity of the universe and believe in the primacy of the Mind and Reason rather than the Act.[396]

In fact, both men were caught up in the limitations of their philosophical idealism. The logic of Croce's position drove him to stress the "actual", and this immediately provoked an attack on Gentile's notion of what was the "actual". The only possible resolutions in philosophy were those which led both men back to positions they denied: Croce to the dominance of history over men (which was determinist and denied Hegel); Gentile to the dominance of men over history (which was transcendental and denied Hegel). Gramsci's own interpretation of Croce implied that he too thought that the actual was more important and he sided with Gentile in this debate. In 1918 he specifically singled out Gentile's theory of the "act" as what made the Palermitan "the Italian philosopher who has made the greatest contribution in the field of thought in recent years".[397]

From a reconstruction of Gramsci's writings and the references in them, we can infer tentatively that this support of Gentile showed that Gramsci was going beyond Croce in 1917. In the *Città Futura* of February 1917, Croce's *Religione e serenità*[398] was one of the three lead articles and Croce was referred to as the "greatest thinker in Europe at this time".[399] The first mention of Gentile which we meet comes a month later in *Sotto la Mole*, when Gramsci mentioned reading Gentile "a few days ago".[400] Then in May he started to use Gentilian terms in his writings:

"His system of philosophy is the latest development of the German idealism which culminated in G. Hegel, Marx's teacher, and is the negation of every transcendentalism, the identification of philosophy with history, with the act of thinking which unifies the true and the real in a dialectical progression which is never complete or perfect".[401]

By 1918 it was Gentile and not Croce whom Gramsci considered to have contributed most. This did not mark a negation of Gramsci's "croceanism" but an extension of it in a fruitful direction which will be indicated later. In the *Club di Vita Morale*, formed in December 1917, Croce's essays of 1910-11 published as *Cultura e Vita Morale* were still made recommended reading for members and the whole plan of reading still reflected the "existing idealist movement".

It should be understood on the other hand, that while Gramsci had read and continued to read other works of Croce[402] after 1917, there is no direct evidence that he espoused the theories in them in the way he did Croce's historiography and Gentile's development of the notion implicit in it.

Overall, his Crocean/Gentilean framework of 1917-18 informed his approach to all the other heroes of Sardinian days. This was particularly important in the case of Salvemini and his paper *L'Unità*, which Gramsci continued to read religiously both for the articles which Croce published in it,[403] and for the criticisms of the systems of exploitation of the South by the North through the unholy alliance of Giolitti, socialist "reformism," and the Southern intellectual *camarilla*. Salvemini's views could only be reconciled unilaterally with Gramsci's idealist beliefs: insofar as they were a critique of religious transcendentalism, they were acceptable. On the whole, however, Gramsci now saw Salvemini as falling into the grouping of false immanentists whom Croce attacked. Salvemini was attached too much to the values of the French Revolution, to liberal democracy, to be to Gramsci's taste any more:

"Jacobinism is a messianic vision of history: it always speaks in abstractions; evil, good, oppression, liberty, light, shade, which exist absolutely, generically and not in historical forms.
Jacobin messianism is completed by cultural messianism, which is represented in Italy by Gaetano Salvemini and has given birth to idealist movements like ... that of *La Voce* in the past and *L'Unita* at the present time.
Even cultural messianism abstracts from the concrete forms of economic and political life, and proposes an absolute outside time and space ... and ends up being utopian."[404]

Gramsci's recommendation to the *Club di Vita morale* of Salvemini's well-known *French Revolution*[405] can thus be understood as an endorsement of Salvemini's views insofar as the book is primarily an explanation of the Revolution as the spread of ideas, but not as an acceptance of the content of the ideas themselves or as philosophy. Similarly, his recommendation of *Problemi educativi e sociali d'oggi*[406] must be understood as an endorsement of the practical critique Salvemini made of aspects of the *Problema del Mezzogiorno* and the opposition he made to the Church (transcendentalists) being allowed to monopolise education [407] and not as an endorsement of his overall framework of reference.

Again, by 1917, Gramsci no longer subscribed to the views of *La Voce*, which was an "idealism of the past". The decision of Papini to support the Italian war effort and Mussolini meant that Gramsci could no longer see eye to eye with the journal after 1915. We may only speculate that *La Voce's* opposition in 1913 to anti-clericalism on the grounds that it was a conservative political weapon, permeated to Gramsci through the Youth Federation's activities. [408]

Gramsci's Croceanism did not prevent his finding new heroes to replace those who no longer satisfied him.[409] He now started to read the Frenchman Charles Péguy and the Swiss Romain Rolland, who advanced similar views to those of Croce, with a literary and emotional rather than a philosophical bias.

Gramsci knew Péguy's writings through reading the Frenchman's

Cahiers de la Quinzaine.[410] We do not know whether he read them first as part of his university studies of French or merely to escape from his provincialism via the only medium he had with facility — French (his German and English were still not very good), but he certainly read numbers which predated his arrival in Turin. Particularly influential was *Notre Jeunesse*, first published in the *Cahiers* in 1910, which Gramsci states he re-read in 1916.

"I have been re-reading a book which I really love, Charles Péguy's *Notre Jeunesse*, and I became drunk on its mystical religious sense of socialism and justice, which pervades it right through ... in the prose of Charles Péguy I feel many of the feelings which go through me expressed with a supernatural fullness, causing inexplicable shivers. In it I feel new life, a more vibrant faith than is usual, and the petty polemics of crassly materialist small-time politicos who decide how things will happen, only make me feel more haughty."[411]

The Péguy who appealed to Gramsci was "the man who wore himself out in a daily endeavour to educate himself, and sacrificed his own artistic personality, to give the youth of France a new consciousness, to send it on its way by the living example of his own toil to attain a world-view which was both more profound and would achieve more".[412]

In *Notre Jeunesse* there were two main themes, tightly linked. First Péguy maintained that it was never the great intellectuals nor what they thought which mattered but the common man and what he thought, as only he and his fellows constituted a real social force: "... it is peoples ... that make the strength and weakness of governments ..."[413] "The debate [about current political and social affairs] is not between heroes and saints, the struggle is against intellectuals, against those who despise heroes and saints equally."[414] "We must moreover grant these unfortunates [politicians] that they are generally very nice to us, except most of those who, since they come from the teaching profession, make up the intellectual party."[415] "What I *dispute*, what I deny, is that those that are conspicuous in the eyes of history (and that history, in return, takes hold of with so much alacrity) have a great importance in the depths of reality".[416]

Then Péguy maintained the need for an absolute honesty, loyalty and commitment, in which there was no room for the facile. "... he had this mystical attachment to the faithfulness that lies at the heart of friendship".[417] "... the question did not arise at all at that time for us, of knowing whether Dreyfus was innocent or guilty. But of knowing whether we would or would not have the courage to declare him innocent, to know he was innocent".[418]

So great was Péguy's influence on Gramsci by 1917 that he even wrote articles inspired by themes Péguy had discussed.[419] But it was Romain Rolland, whom Gramsci also read in the *Cahiers*, who became the most influential of Gramsci's mentors after Croce. Gramsci knew his work backward and the first lecture he ever gave was about him.[420] Rolland's enormous novel, *Jean-Christophe*, had started to appear in *Cahiers de la Quinzaine* in 1903 and was still appearing until 1912. It is the biography of a musician (who, Rolland warns us, should not be mistaken for Beethoven[421]) from his childhood to his death. It is a brilliantly perceptive account of the childhood of an ugly, friendless, sensitive boy, the progeny of a drunken father and a working-class mother, which leads to an account of his life as a composer, through University, war, revulsion against society, and finally to expectations of a newer and brighter future. Like all Gramsci's other favourite writers, Rolland too preached how men could find an immanent nobility in themselves which would enable them to overcome their difficulties and to create with honour.[422]

> "He saw that life is a truceless and merciless battle, where who-ever wants to be a man worthy of the name of man must struggle constantly against the armies of invisible enemies: the murderous forces of nature, confused desires, dark thoughts, which push him treacherously to debase and destroy himself."[423]

Gramsci almost certainly felt an identity with the hero, with his "dark thoughts", against which he had to struggle, though Rolland has himself suggested on the contrary that he had affinities with Emmanuel, another character (this comment compared a fictitious Gramsci with the working-class activist and poet of the novel).[424] There is a striking similarity between Christophe and Péguy's friend Bernard Lazare, both belonging to the sufferers of the world with whom Gramsci identified:

> "Because a man wears spectacles well planted on his fat nose, obstructing, glassing over two good big short-sighted eyes, modern man cannot see the look, the fire lit fifty centuries ago." [425]

Even more important for Gramsci were Romain Rolland's articles against the war, which appeared in the *Journal de Genève* in 1914-15 and which were published as *Au-dessus de la mêlée*. We know that Gramsci delivered a lecture on them when the Italian translation appeared in 1916, but he may have read the French version earlier.[426]

In these articles the familiar themes again emerge: Rolland, like Péguy, regarded men as responsible for their fates and affirmed almost identically: "Fatality is the excuse of souls without will. War is the fruit of people's weakness and their stupidity."[427] Like Péguy, he appealed to the youth and to the élite, to whom he counterposed the false intellectuals, to work together to stop the war and to create a new and better society for the future. Like Péguy he attacked pseudo-intellectualism, drawing a clear distinction between the intellectual classes and true intellectuals.

"As a European élite we have two cities; our native country and the other, the City of God. We are the guests of the one; the builders of the other. Let us give the first our bodies and our faithful hearts. But nothing of what we love, family, friends, fatherland, nothing has any right to our spirit. The spirit is light."[428]

"Certain slightly paradoxical passages of my books, have had me accused occasionally of being an anti-intellectual: which would be absurd .... But it is true that intellectualism has too often seemed to me a caricature of thought ... The intellectual lives too much in the realm of shadows, in the realm of ideas. Ideas have no existence by themselves, but by the experiences that may fill them: they are résumés or else hypotheses, outlines for what were or would be convenient formulas, necessary formulas; you cannot do without them in order to live and to act."[429]

What did all these Italian and French thinkers who appealed to Gramsci have in common? It would be a truism to state that all were directed to changing the world. Even the politically conservative Croce's philosophy was directed at supplanting the existing positivism, and remoulding men's opinions and consequent practice. What is important for Gramsci's intellectual biography is how they suggested this should be done. All were strong moralists, and advanced the proposition that men made their own destinies within a real historical context, which they made themselves. And the way that all suggested that changes could be effected for the better was by strength of Mind, or ideas, thus according paramountcy in history to thought, whether it was Salvemini with his bourgeois ideals, Croce with his neo-Hegelianism or Rolland with his idealism. This meant that all were concerned with the role the intellectual élite did and could play. On a practical level this concern reduced itself to a recognition that the existing intellectual groupings were somehow falling short of their obligation to tear the veils from the eyes of men, that they were corrupt through their alliances with the philistine materialist power groups of the society: as illustrations we have, on one hand, Salvemini's condemnation of the intellectual cliques of the South — on the other, Péguy's condemnation of the intellectuals of the Third Republic.

With one reservation, the corollary of this emphasis was that they were all élitist: historical progress was made in the minds of the philosophers. None really hid this orientation, and all, except one, tended to deprecate the common man's beliefs and capacity for acting without a leader. Yet most were or would become socialists.

Since for all, the true intellectuals were duty-bound to lead mankind, they demanded that intellectuals observe an absolute obligation to be honest in all their intellectual activities and struggle past the temptation of the Burning Bush.

They merely expressed what was characteristic of the idealist revival of the beginning of this century to which Gramsci said he belonged. The reservations we need to note to the generalisations made above are, however, very important in understanding Gramsci's further development beyond the positions described. First, Gentile's doctrine of the "pure act" could lead away from this idealist world view. It was, of course, prone to distortion in the direction of Faust's assertion that "In the beginning was the Act" rather than the Word, and in that form did become one of the rationalisations for mindless fascist activism, but it also could be translated from such emotionalism onto a rational level, from a unilateral material practice to a dialectical practice, and thus from the realms of resolution as the irrational activism of the mind, to that of resolution in the real world, [430] in the real minds of real men in society.

Then Péguy also departed from the élitist position, if not in what was implicit in his writings, at least in his expressed beliefs. By stressing the distinction between essence and appearance, which is fundamental to the Hegelian and the Marxist method, when he examined practical politics, he drew attention to the possibility that the motive force of ideas of history should be studied at the level not of great minds, but of little men.

Together Gentile and Péguy led the reader back to the society of men, to the real world, and already suggested a transcendence of the whole approach to the Marxist position.

While Gramsci devoted little space to Marxism in his writings before 1918 when compared with the emphasis he gave in theory and practice to the ideas of the idealists, we can trace the process of transcendence back to 1915, when Pastore's lectures drew his critical attention to the position of Gentile on praxis.[431] Pastore's utility was simply that he had had a positivist starting point and was concerned with what happened in history from a pragmatic rather than a Hegelian philosophical sense. His process was thus to counterpose what happened in the real world to what happened according to the neo-Hegelian philosophers. He observed that the reversal of praxis was not automatic in reality, as Gentile assumed, but involved a period of incubation. He was thus conducting a critique of the doctrine of the "pure act" by a similar method to that of Marx in his critique of Feuerbach when Marx referred not to philosophy to criticise the materialist theory of the production of ideas but to the real world. Pastore thus not only drew attention to the practical problems of Gentile's theory, but to the mistranslation which Gentile had made of the Theses on Feuerbach (Gentile translated the first Italian edition) to reach his notion that Marx had returned to idealist positions in his critique.[432]

So Pastore's lectures must have brought Gramsci face to face with the Theses on Feuerbach, which are so important in the development of Marxism beyond the idealist and materialist problematic. The implications of Pastore's thesis are very important. Where Gentile saw praxis as a philosopher and therefore maintained (because it could not be resolved otherwise within traditional philosophy) that Marx merely explained the relationship between man and his environment in the Theses on Feuerbach as the idealists did, according primacy to the subject,[433] Marx quite clearly understood praxis as a revolutionary praxis.[434]

It is not probable that Gramsci passed immediately from Gentile via Pastore to a Marxist humanism. In 1916 though, he did recommend Engels' *Anti Dühring* to the workers in a way which shows that he had considered even this in a "humanistic" fashion and Marxism as an anti-fatalism.[435]

Much more probable is that he returned to Pastore's ideas and thus to those of Gentile when he started in 1916 or 1917 to read the work of the neo-Hegelian Antonio Labriola, who was the leading Italian theoretical Marxist of the time after having passed through Hegelianism, Herbartianism and Völkerpsychologie. Despite Croce's denial, Labriola's position was easily reached from that of Croce with Gentile providing the bridge.[436] Labriola brought a similar Hegelian methodology to the interpretation of Marxism that Croce did to the interpretation of history, denying that Marxism was positivist, or determinist, or that it laid down immutable laws governing history. The *Communist Manifesto*, which he regarded as the key work of Marxism, though it had meaning in terms of the whole corpus:

> "Did not imply, and does not imply a chronological dating, or depict in advance the nature of society in a prophetic or apocalyptic manner."[437]

It made no attempt at a universal history as it was concerned only with what Labriola called "artificial history", or what men had created.[438] It was concerned with ongoing societies in their complexity and not with first causes, in which everything was a phenomenon of an essence and could be explained in terms of the essence. It followed that the "economic factor", the means of production in any society, was only significant when understood in terms of the complexity of all other phenomena, which were not reducible to it.

> "It is not a question of extending the so-called economic factor, abstractly isolated, to the rest, as opponents maintain (*favoleggiano*); but rather a question above all of conceiving the economy historically, and of explaining other historical changes by its changes."[439]

The knotty problem of the specific relationship between the economic and all other moments of history is fundamentally important, and Labriola had to come up with an explanation of the relationship. He stated:

> "All that has happened in history is the work of man; but it was

not, or is it, except very rarely, by critical choice, or the free will of the thinking mind; but it was and is *necessary*, that is, determined by needs and occasioned externally. What was necessary generated the experience and development of the internal and external organs. Among these organs are the intellect and reason, both results and consequences of repeated and accumulated experience".[440]

If we interpret this explanation as giving primacy to the material praxis of men, then it is philosophically inadequate for its purpose as it implies a theory of knowledge which has a materialist determinant. Labriola understood and intended it as a denial of fatalism or automatism and therefore regarded history as the process of development of understanding (via his notion of praxis) among men to the level marked by the *Manifesto*, in which they first produced an adequate understanding of its workings:

"The historical awareness of socialism lies today ... in the understanding of its historical necessity, or the awareness of the mode of its genesis...."[441]

This awareness was not reached automatically by all men. In Labriola's interpretation Marxism took into account the main difficulties it faced, in particular that everywhere conditions were not favourable for its success. Conditions he understood to include not only economic but all historical factors, especially what he regarded as the mediating "social psychology", or ideological factors.

To make a revolution, what was necessary was, and here he used Hegel's words, "to understand and overcome".[442]

Gramsci shared Labriola's theory that Marxism was a philosophy of praxis.[443] He recommended it to his friends again and again and studied Labriola carefully. What Marx he had available to him was the same Marx which Labriola had read and could only reinforce the interpretation, which we may dub, shorthand fashion, as a "humanist" Marxism, in which men made their own destinies and were responsible for their actions, and in which ideas, men's consciousness of themselvs, were the *political* motive force in history.

So even Gramsci's Marxism did not greatly depart from his "Croceanism". It was, of course, a lopsided Marxism, from which knowledge of the *Economic and Philosophical Manuscripts* and the

Grundrisse was absent. In Labriola this led to an undervaluation of *Capital* as "not the first great book of critical theory, but the last great book of political economy",[444] and a theory of praxis which stressed the material praxis of men. We have no evidence that Gramsci espoused the same errors of emphasis in 1917 but being limited in his sources, any neo-Hegelian reading of Marx must have led him to accept most of the positions of Labriola.

Labriola's notion of praxis was, of course, the opposite of that of Gentile, stressing not the thinking process but the doing process in the sense of material construction. Rodolfo Mondolfo would continue Gentile's notion into his interpretation of the starting point of Marxism as the voluntarism of praxis. We have no evidence that Gramsci knew his work before 1917, though he certainly read it when the Russian Revolution took place.

It remains, before returning to Gramsci's political activity, which took him beyond this point in his intellectual development, to consider the allegations of Bergsonianism made against him at the Florence conference of 1917. Despite Bergson's affinity the whole idealist movement, and his attack on Spencer and other positivists, and despite the fact that Gramsci appears to have read him, Bergson was not one of Gramsci's sources of inspiration in 1917. He laughed when Treves accused him and his followers of espousing *L'Évolution créatrice*.[445] Indeed, while Gramsci had considerable respect for Bergson, he could not have found the work as intellectually satisfying as Croce, since it struggled unsuccessfully to escape from positivism and biological explanations for men's behaviour.[446]

Girded with all this intellectual paraphernalia, Gramsci threw himself into the now-famous factory council experiment.

II

The Italian nation came out of the First World War in dire economic straits. In 1915 the country was still backward industrially, agricultural production was still all-important to the economy, and it had been ill-prepared for the huge expense of fighting a war. During the war-years state expenditure had risen enormously from 2,287 million to 30,857 million lire per annum. Simultaneously the mobilisation of vast numbers of peasants had resulted in drastic falls in agricultural production and consequently in national income from that important sector. In 1915-19 the grain crop had fallen from 52 to 46 million quintals; the maize crop from 25 to 22 million quintals, and the beet sugar crop from 21 to 15 million quintals.[447] In 1919 the result was, as one post-war prime minister, Giolitti, put it, that "the public debt had risen from 13 to 94 billions", and there was an annual deficit of four thousand million lire.[448] If immediate steps of extreme urgency were not taken, this would conduct the country to ruination. He concluded that the Italians would have to pay their debts themselves, or make their country ever-more indebted to countries like the United States.

Most Italians had suffered economically from the war. The rapid increase in State expenditure had created corresponding inflation. While their money bought less the cost of living index had risen from 100 in 1914 to 248 in 1918.[449] Wages had not risen commensurately. Even what money there was did not mean corresponding food to buy, and on occasions the staple, bread and pasta, ran out completely.[450] The result was a populace made poorer by the war and less in a position to pay any national debts than it had been in 1915.

The working-class had been subjected to martial discipline in the factories during the war to ensure that production was unimpaired. In cities like Turin this mean that a traditionally militant working-class was obliged to forgo practially all its claims for improvements in its conditions precisely at a time when they were most needed to offset increases in prices. Strikes were illegal and the unions, which were led by "reformists," many of whom favoured the war effort, could do little to defend the workers' interests. Even organisations like the metalworkers' *commissioni interne* feared to protest about conditions to the military delegates who ran the factories, as the slightest suggestion of independence could mean the withdrawal of a man from inclusion on the list of reserved occupations, and dispatch to the front.[451] The result was a working-class boiling with resentment, which sometimes exploded into rebellion, when, for example, the bread ran out in Turin in August 1917. Like Gramsci, the workers believed that the bourgeoisie was responsible for the war and the miseries it had brought upon them, and was determined that it would pay.[452] In Turin, in particular, it was very militant, and the local authorities were fearful that its resentment would spill over into rebellion.

The only class in the community which had benefited from the war had been the capitalist class, both in banking and industry. There had been a hot-house growth in industry because of the need for war material. The production of cars had gone from 9,200 units in 1914 to 20,000 in 1918 and the production of aeroplanes from 606 in 1915 to 14,820 in 1918. The profits in the automobile industry had increased from 8.20% to 30.51% in two years and the value of fixed capital from 17 million *lire* in 1914 to 200 million in 1919.[453] Vast fortunes had been made in industry, and much had been made by the speculation of war profiteers, the *pesce cani* whom Gramsci attacked so often in *Sotto la Mole* in 1916-17. To extend and consolidate their interests the capitalist class had strengthened links between themselves and engaged in mergers throughout the war. But they too faced the post-war period ill-prepared to pay national debts. Their plant was old and out-of-date and it had to be reconverted to peace-time production, profits were bound to fall, and the industries which could not survive except in the hot-house conditions of war would have to be scrapped. To modernise, the capitalists needed huge investments of capital. The steel and heavy machine industries were particularly affected by this problem.[454] None were prepared to tolerate industrial trouble. So, while the attitude of the government was that Italy should pay her debts herself, the mass of the people could not and would not do so, and the capitalist class would not do so.

In the last year of the war the *commissione interna* had become the primary organisation through which the Turin metal-workers expressed their resentment at the conditions the "capitalists'" war had brought them to. In April 1918 it was agreed by the FIOM and the Automobile Consortium that the *commissione interna* would decide disputes over piece-work rates in certain cases, and the leaders of the factory organisations spoke together with the union leaders to explain this to the masses.[455] In November 1918, Emilio Colombino, a leading Turin trade unionist, stated to the National Conference of the FIOM that the *commissione interna* had a leading role to play in defending workers' interests.[456] As soon as the war was ended the FIOM secured the owners' acceptance of the right of the *commissione interna* to exist in all metallurgical works. The *commissioni* themselves considered the owners' proposals before the FIOM accepted them. In March 1919 the agreement was implemented throughout the industry.

At the beginning of 1918 these *commissioni* were little different from the collaborationist organisations which they had been before the war, when the owners used them to resolve labour disputes in the interests of maintaining production, and the union leaders looked on them as transmission belts keeping them in touch with first with the organised workers and then with the unorganised. The union leaders selected their members from among union members only.[457] On the whole, both sides, capitalist and unionist, saw them as a means of smoothing over difficulties of a minor nature, and regarded matters of substance as something to be decided at a higher level in negotiations between their respective bureaucracies.

What must be grasped is that the nature of the *commissione interna* was changing throughout 1918 as a result of the real pressures placed on the working class economically and socially, and because of the inability of their own union leaders to defend their interests successfully. This change implied a critique of traditional trade union methods including the role in the movement of the grass-roots workers' organisations and of existing trade union leadership.

The union leaders' attitude towards the masses was summed up in a speech made by Bruno Buozzi in 1916 in which he stated that the trade union organiser "must see higher and further than the masses" and sometimes use any means to get the masses to do what they did not want.[458] It was innately élitist, dividing the trade union movement into those who were capable of knowing the true interests of the workers and those who were not. It had as a corollary a bitter resentment of any attempt to poach on its preserves, or to challenge its methods.[459]

The élitism was reflected in the lack of popular participation in the central organisations of the labour movement.

"A tiny minority of members take part in the life of the Leagues and Camera del Lavoro; the majority is regularly absent, though this does not preclude its intervening at decisive moments with a vote which displays the lack of thought ... of men who are not responsible for their acts.... The leaders acquire an authority and importance which they should not have according to the egalitarian and essentially democratic spirit of those organisations. The leaders make decisions, much, much too often, when they should be purely and simply executive and administrative officers."

wrote Gramsci in October 1918.[460]

The oligarchy of trade union leaders was quite complacent about this state of affairs. In February 1918, at a local union conference, Emilio Colombino complimented himself and his fellow

110

"reformists" with a report about the good relationships the FIOM had maintained with the bosses in the factories and remarked upon the favourable financial balance of the union.

The militants from the factories did not feel the same. After hearing Colombino's speech, Maurizio Garino, an anarchist of long standing and a member of the "rigids"

"attacked the report of Colombino, which was, according to him, too mild, stating that it was time to finish with the bourgeoisie, with the industrialists, and that the moment was right to act revolutionarily."

The union leaders reply was to hold a tiny assembly, as was common, and replaced the "rigids" by a firmly "reformist" leadership comprised of Bruno Buozzi, Mario Guarnieri, Gino Castagno and Alessandro Uberti. The "rigids", Garino, Fassone, Boero and Parodi were in a tiny minority for the rest of the year.[461]

As far as the "reformists" were concerned, they were proud of their "reformism", like Buozzi, who stated late in 1918: "I am not ashamed of being a 'reformist' — nor a coward about it — I've never hid it", [462] and they saw the *commissione interna* in a "reformist" fashion, as an organisation to be run from the top by them. They were not going to have anarchists and syndicalists challenge their line. They represented the workers and that was that. Throughout 1918 they frustrated several efforts of the "rigids" and their anarchist and syndicalist allies to make a comeback in the FIOM.[463]

They thus placed themselves completely out of touch with a workforce which agreed less and less with their conception of the *commissioni*. Symptomatic of the workers' new attitude, which was represented best by the ignored minority on the FIOM executive in Turin, were the letters which started to be published in *Avanti* in September 1918. Workers at the Farina coach builders asked: "should the *commissioni interne* represent the working class or the union?", and the members of the *commissioni* replied: "We represent the masses in the Farina plant and the union does not, because we were nominated by the masses and the union was not."[464]

By the beginning of 1919 the union leaders were thus facing a democratic upsurge which challenged their traditional mode of rule. If they were aware of it, they dismissed it as the masses not knowing their best interests. In a vague and inarticulate fashion the workers were groping towards a notion in which the *commissioni*, as the organisations which had best survived the war, and which had parallels throughout Europe and in the Soviets in Russia, whose revolution they applauded, could be used to impose their will on the employers.[465]

Some, like Giovanni Boero, drew strength from the commitment of the PSI in December 1918 to the Bolsheviks' methods and saw the *commissioni* as potentially revolutionary organs. In March 1919 he wrote to *Avanti* asking with characteristic blunt fervour how the hell the PSI was implementing its commitment to make a revolution and suggesting that it concentrate on developing councils of workers, peasants and soldiers, and stop wasting money on electoral campaigns.[466] At this time few would have shared his advanced views. Most were concerned with obtaining a decent wage after several years when wages had fallen behind price rises.

III

Gramsci was a stranger to these concerns of the humble and the meek and had been regarded as a maverick by the working-class leaders since his *faux pas* in supporting Mussolini in 1914. He, too, cordially hated some of the "rigids" for the way they had treated him in 1914-15.[467]

However, he was not blind to the implications of the last year of the war and early 1919. His understanding of the October revolution led him to contemplate with interest what was going on in the factories, both outside and inside Italy.

In the article *Utopia Russa* which he published in July 1918 he pointed out that the "war was the economic fact, the practical reality of life which determined the emergence of the new (Soviet) State, which had made the dictatorship of the proletariat necessary", because on the one hand it had concentrated power in the hands of a tiny minority, and, on the other, it had created a sense of solidarity among vast numbers of people against that minority which would not have occurred in peasant countries without the war.[468] Before the year was out he was writing in almost exactly the same terms about the effects of the war on his own country. In November he wrote:

"Four years of war have rapidly changed the economic and

spiritual ambience. Huge work-forces have suddenly sprung up, and the violence innate in the relations between wage-earners and owners appears so striking that it is recognised by even the dimmest minds.... The growth of industry has been made miraculous by this saturation of class violence. But the bourgeoisie has not been able to avoid offering the exploited a terrible practical lesson in revolutionary socialism. A new class consciousness has arisen: not only in the workshop, but in the trenches which have many conditions in common with that of the workshop. The proletarian movement must absorb this mass ... must educate each individual who composes it to become permanently and organically united with his fellows.''[469]

To this speculation that the war compelled the establishment of a new State power, Gramsci added a renewed interest in the role of spontaneous workers organisations, stimulated by both the example of the Russian Soviets and the development of similar organisations elsewhere in Europe. His passing interest in these institutions dated back before the war, when he and Togliatti had started to collect material on their history and development.[470] In either 1916 or 1917 he asked Togliatti to start collecting material on the English shop-stewards and on the theories of Daniel de Leon.[471] When the I.W.W. *Liberator* appeared in March 1918 he started reading it both for the accounts of the Bolshevik revolution and its leaders and for the extensive material on the de Leonite I.W.W. De Leon became of particular interest to him.[472] He also became *au fait* with the developments of the shop-stewards committees in the English trade union movement, publishing a long article on their evolution in *Il Grido del Popolo* on 27 April 1918. To this article he appended the decisions of the November 1916 Leeds' Conference of shop stewards' committees. He indicated in this article how he understood the import of these committees in England. They were necessary for the class struggle at a specific conjuncture; and implied that "the working-class must win complete control over production to defend its interests, and must eliminate capital" and they would be the organs of socialist control after the revolution. They were a progression beyond the trade union, which was characterised by an absolute centralised bureaucracy, and which was corporativist in its practice and traditional and conservative.[473]

These items of information were put together in a proposal in March 1919.

"We have seen that the Workers' Councils are the best organisation; the most sure guarantee of progress towards socialism and its
realisation. Well, let us create our own workers' councils, let us
create our own Soviets, in the limits allowed to us."

One of his followers, casting his attention around at the "limits"
in the article entitled "The Dawn of Ordine Nuovo",[474]
concluded that the existing union organisations were too
bureaucratised to be much use while, on the other hand, the
commissioni interne which had just been extended to all metal works
in Turin, offered possibilities.

In the same month, Gramsci and his friends, including Togliatti,
Terracini and Tasca, who had returned from the war, started to hold
meetings aimed at the formation of a new paper. Gramsci recalled
"The sole feeling which united us, in our meetings was a vague
passion for a vague proletarian culture", but his other accounts
indicate that there was already some other basis for unity with the
workers who attended the meetings.[475] Tasca and Gramsci were
both still in the thrall of the élitist cultural policies they had held in
earlier years and Gramsci was without doubt still influenced by
"Croceanism". Doubtless, both Togliatti and Terracini were
dominated by Gramsci, because he was now so important in the
Turin section of the Socialist Party while they had been *hors de
combat* for some years. *But* it is a mistake to think that the
relationship between Gramsci and Tasca was what was significant.
Rather it was his relationship with the workers whom he had got to
know since 1916 and who put him in touch with the working class
reality and the men who had tenuous contacts with bolshevism, for
which he was so enthusiastic.

Aron Wizner, a Polish refugee, a revolutionary socialist of
working class extraction, who used to write about Russian and
Polish events for *Il Grido del Popolo* in 1918 under the pseudonyms
Ez-Dek and Murzyn, had asked one of the people who attended the
preliminary meetings of the newspaper why there had been no
congress of the *commissioni interne* in Italy. When a technician
suggested that one of the matters the newspaper should study was
"the organisation of the factory as a means of production and we
must work to make the working class and the party concentrate on
that object", concluding that they should seek to discover whether
the Soviets had parallels in Italy, Wizner's interlocutor remembered
the question and replied: "Yes, in Turin there exists the germ of a
workers' government, of the Soviet, it is the *commissione interna*;

let's study this working class institution, let's have an enquiry, and let's study the capitalist factory too, but not as an organisation for material production in order to have a specialised knowledge which we don't have; let's study the capitalist factory as something the worker needs, as a political organism, as the 'national territory' of workers' self-government.''[476]

Real concerns were impinging on the idealist schemes of the four leaders. Not until after the paper *Ordine Nuovo* first saw the light of day on May 1 did they become dominant. Tasca, who had found the 6000 lire to finance the paper, and naturally had some influence, pooh-poohed the suggestion that they concentrate on the factory councils and filled the newspaper with his articles and editorials of a cultural nature. Gramsci later described it as ''... nothing but a rag-bag anthology — a collection of abstract cultural items and a strong leaning towards nasty stories and well-intentioned wood-cuts.''[477]

He and Togliatti, in daily contact with the ''rigid'' leaders in factories, began to believe that this propaganda of Tasca's was futile and together with Terracini plotted an editorial *coup d'état*. This took the form of publishing the article *Democrazia operaia* on 21 June 1919 without Tasca having any knowledge of it in advance. After that date Gramsci and Togliatti replaced Tasca as the editors of the journal and by the end of the year Tasca had virtually withdrawn from the journal.[478] The contents alone reveal why a single article represented an editorial *coup d'état*.

It asked:

''How can the immense social forces loosed by the war be dominated? How can they be disciplined and given a political form which has the virtue of developing normally, of continually integrating itself, until it becomes the skeleton of a socialist state in which the dictatorship of the proletariat is incarnate?

''This article is intended as a stimulus to thought and action; as an invitation to the best and most conscious workers to reflect upon this problem, and, each in his own sphere of competency and action, to collaborate in solving it, making their comrades and their associations concentrate their attention upon it. Only through this common, solid work of clarification, persuasion and reciprocal education will be born the concrete action of construction.''

The article claimed that the socialist state already existed potentially in the social institutions of the proletariat, and that a true workers' democracy could be counterposed to the bourgeois state if these institutions were organised hierarchically and centrally. This democracy would then be ready to take over from the bourgeoisie.

Socialists should therefore work directly in the "centres of proletarian life": the workshops with their *commissioni interne*, the Socialist clubs, and the peasant communities.

The main aim should be to free the *commissioni interne* from the limitations imposed on them by the employers, to give them new life and energy because they were already limiting capitalist power in the factories — "Developed and enriched, tomorrow they will become the organs of the proletarian power which replaces capitalism in all its useful functions of administration and leadership ...".

The first step was to organise a congress of the most advanced and class-conscious workers with the slogan: "All power in the workshop to the workshop committees": to which should be linked another slogan: "All state power to the workers' and peasants' Councils."

The Socialist Clubs should become the coordinating centres for the factory councils in each area, and be composed of elected delegates from all industries in the area. Thus the area committees of the workers would become the "emanation of the whole working-class" and as such able to assume the power spontaneously entrusted to them, to maintain discipline, and, consequently, to bring all work in their area to a halt.

These area committees would grow into city-wide organisations, which would be controlled and disciplined by the PSI and the trade union federations.

Such a system of workers' democracy would be a tremendous educational force, teaching the workers to think of themselves as a homogeneous group capable of political and administrative leadership. Meeting continually, the workers would elect all their leaders and exert influence on their more backward comrades "causing a radical transformation in working-class psychology, making the working-class better prepared to exercise power, and, through spontaneously generated common historical experience, spreading an awareness of the rights and duties of comrades and workers."

Concrete practical problems would only be solved in practice: "The dictatorship of the proletariat should stop being a mere phrase", the means to attaining it should be actively implemented.

"The dictatorship of the proletariat is the creation of a new state, which is typically proletarian, in which the institutional experiences of the oppressed class flow together, in which the social life of the working and peasant classes become strongly organised and widespread. This state does not pop up by magic: the Bolsheviks worked for eight months to spread and make their slogans concrete: all power to the Soviets, and the Soviets were already known to the Russian workers in 1905. Italian communists must treasure the Russian experience and save on time and labour: the work of reconstruction will alone demand so much time and work that every act, every day must be directed towards it."

While Gramsci specifically indicated that these new organisations were not intended to replace the traditional organisations, and, on the contrary, gave the latter pride of place in the movement, as the "educators", the "focus of faith", the depositary of doctrine, and the "supreme power", his novel proposals implicitly attacked the PSI and the unions as they were, and explicitly postponed their leading role to a later time, claiming that they could not afford to open their doors immediately to an "invasion of new members who are unaccustomed to the exercise of power and discipline."[479]

In the context of the Turin labour movement, his proposals could only be seen as an attack on what trade unionism was. Both Tasca, long associated with the trade unions, and the "reformist" leaders, must have seen the article in terms of the speech Gramsci gave only days later at the Assembly of the Turin section of the Socialist Party. He had then urged the local socialists to give up their past stupidity and concentrate on direct power; to learn from the Russian and Hungarian revolutions and from "the revolutionary experience of the English and American working-class masses who, through the practice of their factory councils, have begun that education in revolution and that change in psychology, which according to Karl Marx, must be considered the most promising symptom of the incipient realisation of communism."[480] Always fearful of a challenge to their authority, the "reformists" replied with accusations that developing the *commissioni interne* would split the ranks of the proletariat, and suggested that it was a "revolutionary-syndicalist" deviation. Despite Gramsci's reply that they would in fact give a stronger basis to unionism and the PSI, the Turin labour leaders saw its implicit critique of their practice and started the opposition which compelled Gramsci down a path of ever increasing intransigency. On the other hand, Tasca, who had hoped that the *Ordine Nuovo* would work with the unions, could not avoid seeing the critique of his position in *"Democrazia operaia"*, and tacitly acknowledged the editorial *coup d'état*.[481]

So the new line of Gramsci, his friends, and *Ordine Nuovo* at one and the same time brought them into alliance with the workers in the factories and into opposition to the traditional methods of the union and socialist movement. Among the first and most ardent of the supporters of Gramsci's theories was Giovanni Parodi, who had known Gramsci for some time, and was on the "rigid" minority in the FIOM.[482] Parodi organised the first factory meeting after verbal propaganda and started to spread the ideas of *Democrazia operaia*, bringing Gramsci and his friends to give a series of lectures on the factory floor. In this ceaseless contact with the workers, and in the mutual exchange of education, lay the secret of Gramsci's success. Years later he wrote to Togliatti that he had succeeded in linking his position with that of the workers by "never taking action without first sounding out the opinion of the worker in various ways ... so that our actions always had an almost immediate and wide success, and seemed like the interpretation of a diffuse deeply felt need, never as the cold application of an intellectual scheme."[483] Sometimes he would speak three times in an afternoon, and his staunch followers from the Youth Federation emulated him.[484] Parodi said simply that he completely "proletarianised" himself. [485] On the other hand, the union officials, faced by a cadres' crisis due to the huge growth in union members during the war, unused to consulting the democratic mass, and preferring to play a "double game" through their inefficient corporals, lost contact and control.

Ordine Nuovo and its followers found an increasingly militant workforce in which to evolve its ideas. The cost of living continued to rocket upwards in 1919, going from 248 to 300.6 from the 1914 base of 100. At the same time unemployment figures rose as demobilised soldiers returned and hot-house industry collapsed. There were two million unemployed in November 1919. Starvation threatened thousands and bread queues were matched by unemployment queues. The workers had started striking again to make up ground lost during the war and the need to defend themselves compelled them to continue. Strikes in 1919 totalled 1663 in industry and 208 in agriculture. Clashes between strikers and the police were frequent. When some workers were killed in a clash in Milan, the PSI conducted a general strike in April. This was accompanied and followed by a strike of the technicians employed in the metal-working industry, and a general lock-out throughout Turin which put 30,000 workers out of work. Such efforts by the employers to create dissension among the working-class by penalising the whole workforce in the industry for the strike action of 3000 proved a total failure. Faced by common problems, solidarity was spreading among the workers. This strike was followed in June and July by riots throughout Italy against the cost of living. In Emilia and Romagna improvised soviets arose as a result of these riots. In Tuscany and the Marches one could speak of a real popular insurrection. The PSI proposed a further general strike for 20-21 July, after meeting with other European labour parties in England.[486]

While the wave of unrest died down temporarily in other parts of Italy after June, in Turin the struggle did not let up. In August-September, the Turin workforce were again on strike "after long months of patient and exasperating negotiations between the Federation and the owners resulted in no improvement in workers' conditions", while prices zoomed upwards.[487]

The unrest was spontaneous and usually directed to attaining immediate improvement in economic conditions. It did, however, take on political dimensions of greater and greater import. The Italian political leaders showed no sign of giving Italy the political leadership the country needed. Orlando made a miserable and Italianate hash of affairs at Versailles, returning with a humiliating peace. The bulk of soldiers felt that they had been fighting for nothing. Rumours of a right-wing coup to save the nation spread, and the first fascist outrages started.

The desire among the workers to resolve their difficulties by following the Russian example showed more and more clearly as they flocked into the PSI, which had stated that it would introduce a dictatorship of the proletariat in Italy. Union membership rose from 321,000 in 1914 to 2,300,000 in 1919 and PSI membership from 50,000 to 200,000. In Turin the membership of the FIOM reached over 20,000 in 1919 and the Camera del Lavoro had 90,000 members in early 1920. Local socialist party membership tripled in 1919.[488]

Despite this remarkable increase in organised militancy, both in Italy and Turin, the bulk of the increasingly militant workforce was unorganised. It was to these unorganised workers that Gramsci's programme first appealed, precisely because he laid down none of the exclusive demands that the union leaders did that all members of the *commissioni interne* be enrolled union members. He met some opposition at grass roots level, and bitter opposition in the bureaucracy among the organised socialists — except in some factories where he and his followers already had an advantage because of their contacts with the "rigids", like Parodi, Boero and Garino. Parodi, who was very popular and respected by both the workers and employers for his integrity, was most important to Gramsci despite his lack of culture. One worker recalled him as "the heart" of the movement for factory councils, while Gramsci was "the brains".[489] Parodi put Gramsci in touch with the organised workers in Fiat, where he worked.

Gramsci slowly won their trust, exhausting himself and his followers by endless meetings, speeches and agitation in the factories. The workers in turn taught him what their needs were and what they aspired to. Together a theory of Italy's post-war situation was elaborated and constructive proposals about what to do put forward. These were the substance of *Ordine Nuovo's* articles in June-August 1919. For young socialists the paper became what *La Voce* was for the bourgeoisie.[490]

Some of the fundamental themes emerging were: 1) Capitalism tended to atomise the working-class, who sold themselves as commodities on the labour market, creating "citizen-individuals" and destroying all the "collective links" which constituted society. Under capitalism all men, and particularly wage-earners were terribly alienated from each other: "Every citizen is a gladiator, who sees in others enemies to be destroyed or to be subjugated to his will. All the higher links of solidarity and love are dissolved, from the artisans' corporations and classes to religion and the family. Competition is installed as the practical foundation of human association: the citizen-individual is the cell of the social nebula, an uneasy and inorganic element which belongs to no organism." It was precisely on this lack of social cohesion and disunity and uneasiness that the concept of the sovereignty of the law, a purely abstract concept, rested, as a potential deception of popular innocence and good faith. This sovereignty of the law was an anti-social concept "because it envisages the 'citizen' as eternally at war with the State," and saw men as the eternal unrelenting enemies of the State, which is "the living plastic body of society", and thus saw men as the enemies of themselves.

2) This whole tendency was countervailed by the workers' tendency to organise, which was itself "the reaction of society which seeks to recompose itself as a solid harmonious organ, sustained by love and compassion". The workers spontaneously opposed the

"comrade" to capitalism's "citizen", and expressed this in organised form. On the basis of these organisations "begins the process of historical development which leads to communism". Therefore "associating men together can and must be assumed to be the essential fact of the proletarian revolution."

3) During the war, and especially in the post-war period, the real naked class oppression disguised by the rule of law had become obvious to all, as the State had emerged as "arbiter of all our destinies" and, correspondingly, the huge solid mass of workers had found new forms to express their need to realise themselves as social beings, and to supplant the trade unions which they had evolved earlier as the expression of the working class conceived of as "a function of capitalist free enterprise", determined from outside the working-class rather than from within it, and subject to the laws of the outsiders.

4) The emergence of these new organisations showed the inadequacies of both trade unionism and the Socialist Party itself. Both had accepted the terms of the capitalist state rather than acted antithetically to it. Socialists had "let themselves be absorbed by reality rather than dominated it". They had "believed in the perpetuity of the institutions of the democratic state, in their fundamental perfection". So the "traditional institutions of the movement had become incapable of expressing the exuberant growth of revolutionary vitality", which Italy and the world was demonstrating.

"We are convinced after the revolutionary experience of Russia, Hungary and Germany, that the socialist state cannot continue the forms of the capitalist state, but is a creation which is fundamentally new with respect to these, if not with respect to the history of the proletariat."

This was not an augury, or a prediction, since history was not "predictable", but, following the "maieutic" method, it meant working through new organisations which expressed real needs to grasp possibilities; in particular, working through the organisations which tended to replace the capitalist in the administration of industry and thus to make the producer truly autonomous.

"Never has there been a more fervent drive and revolutionary enthusiasm in the proletariat of Western Europe, but, it seems to us that a lucid and exact awareness of ends desired has not been accompanied by an equivalently lucid and exact awareness of the means suitable to attaining that end. The masses are now convinced that the proletarian state is incarnated in a system of workers', peasants' and soldiers' councils. We have not yet formed a tactical conception which can objectively ensure the creation of that state. It is therefore necessary right now to create a net of proletarian institutions, rooted in the consciousness of the great mass.... It is certain that today, in present conditions of proletarian organisation, if a mass movement of a revolutionary nature took place, the results would be a purely formal correction of the democratic state and would end in increasing the power of the House of Deputies (through a Constituent Assembly) and in the assumption of power by bungling anti-communist socialists. The German and Austrian experience should teach us something. The forces of the democratic state and the capitalist class are still immense: we need not hide that capitalism is sustained especially by the work of its sycophants and its lackeys, and the progeny of that genius has not yet disappeared.

"The creation of the proletarian state is not, in sum, a thaumaturgic act: it too is a construction, a process of development. It presupposes a preparatory work of propaganda and organisation. We must give the greatest power and the greatest development to the proletarian organisations which already exist in the factories and see to it that others emerge in the villages, and ensure that the men who make them up are communists aware of the revolutionary mission that the institutions must fulfil. Otherwise all our efforts, all the faith of the masses will not succeed in preventing the revolution ending miserably in a new rogues' Parliament of irresponsible ninnies, and making necessary new and more terrible sacrifices for the advent of the proletarian state."[491]

As the theoretical expression of workers' needs and desires, these proposals did not call for an immediate revolution, but emphasised that the first steps in organising for that end by taken. No blueprints were laid down for the future, and it was specifically stated that problems would be resolved by the workers as they came to them. As such their appeal was much wider than to the communists whom Gramsci hoped would eventually become the leaders in the councils. Two thousand workers, anxious to do something, to impose themselves on the chaos and lack of leadership characteristic of Turin and Italy in 1919, met in the Fiat Brevetti works in September and elected thirty-two commissars, representing eleven sections of the works, as their factory council, in an election which was a model of democratic procedure. Despite "reformist" warnings that the wrong men would be chosen to lead the workers, the elected commissars were all chosen from acknowledged leaders in the organised labour movement. Indicating, on the other hand, that the factory council was not only a new version of the old *commissioni interne*, was the statement by one Brevetti worker that the establishment of the factory council was the "first step in the revolution".[492]

It was, indeed, the first step in the spread of the factory councils, as other workforces were inspired by the action of the Brevetti-Fiat workers and within a month the councils had spread to each of Fiats' forty-two divisions, and elsewhere.[493] In the middle of October the first assembly of the executive committees of the *consigli di fabbrica* met. It represented thirty thousand workers. A long programme of action was drawn up, declaring itself more than a programme but an exposition of the concepts which informed the new organisations, and a coming to terms with the other institutions of the labour movement.

It started by asserting that the very existence of the councils was a negation of the trade union leaders' assertion that the trade union was the sole organisation giving expression to the social life of the workers. The councils were concerned with administering the means of production and the men who worked them and not with fixing the price of labour; they had the "potential aim of preparing men, organism and concepts through a continuous pre-revolutionary work of control, to ready them to replace the bosses authority in the workplace, and to place social life within a new framework."

Consequently, in the declaration of principles it was asserted that

1) "The factory commissars are the sole true social (political and economic) representatives of the proletarian class, because they are elected by the universal suffrage of all the workers at the place of work."

2) The electors recognised the role of the trade unions and expected that all workers would become unionists.

3) *But*, the final power in the working-class movement should lie with the factory councils.

4) And, they would therefore only obey the union in its traditional role only when the commissars endorsed trade union directives.

5) And, they would resist any attempt to oust them from control of their organisations on the factory floor.

6) They would support the establishment of a single national trade union federation directed to working along the lines of the class struggle, for the communist revolution.

7) And, they asserted, the constitution of the councils marked the first step in the communist revolution in Italy.

The council's long list of rules can be broken down into the following thematic contents:

1) The commissars, who had to work in the factories, would be nominated from each factory division in proportions to be decided. Only men who were union members and committed to the class struggle could stand, but all workers could vote in elections. Instant recall of a commissar was possible when a majority wished.

2) The commissars would have two tasks: to represent the unionists of his division by controlling the union; and to defend the economic and social interests of all workers of the division.

3) They would submit any union agreement with the employers to the workers for ratification, and generally control such agreements.

4) They would encourage the workers to educate themselves to the realisation of their responsibility to work together as social beings.

5) All decisions would be carried out by an executive committee nominated by each factory council.[494]

The Assembly resolved to express the will of the masses and called for the extension of the movement throughout Italy.

Gramsci and his followers inside the outside factories were the authors of this programme, and as such it represented the point of view of the most politically advanced sections of councils only.[495] Moreover the councils were at first composed by a majority who were not followers of *Ordine Nuovo*.[496]

Gramsci was not disconcerted and applauded the rapid spread in the councils. He noted particularly what he had anticipated, the increase in militancy as the councils forced the removal of all "the agents of capitalism" from the factories, and the magnificent discipline which enabled them to bring the work of 16,000 men to a halt in five minutes in December.[497] These experiences brought the mass of the workers closer to the views of the more advanced members. Meanwhile, he and his followers engaged in intensive propaganda and education through their School of Culture and Social Propaganda, which brought their ideas about the transformation of the councils into the organs of the proletarian state before the workers.[498] Tasca recalled the intensity of his work in the last three months of 1919 in these words: "We must note the intense activity of Gramsci.... *Avanti*, the Central Executive of the Party, *Ordine Nuovo, Sotto la Mole*, lectures for the factory councils, ... prodigious activity, a sickly body and a steely will ... he is a leader."

The events which worked for the triumph of his group in the councils and in the Turin labour movement as a whole, in part were willed by him. On 1 November the "rigids" who headed the councils ousted the "reformists" from their controlling position in the FIOM. Ottavio Pastore, editor of the new Turinese edition of *Avanti*, practically turned the newspaper over to Gramsci and his supporters, giving him the apparent support of the PSI.[499] Consequently in December the local PSI accepted the councils and set up a study group under Togliatti to examine how they could be further developed and the Camera del Lavoro voted full support of the movement announcing that:

"the movement which started spontaneously in the Turin workshops has shown that the majority of the workers are profoundly convinced of the need to begin concrete work for the communist transformation of the productive organism and affirms that it is a sign of the political maturity of the masses."

As the representative of 100,000 workers it demanded the extension of the councils throughout Italy, and affirmed that they should be used for the revolutionary transformation of society.[500]

These triumphs of the *ordinovisti* only redoubled the hatred and opposition of the "reformist" trade union leaders, who saw in the movement their own disappearance from preeminence. The CGL newspaper started a determined campaign against the councils in December, accusing Gramsci of anarcho-syndicalism and adventurism. Nasty reminders of his mistake in 1914 started to circulate. Embittered by the pettiness of the bureaucrats who controlled the paper, Gramsci replied shortly that any discussion with them was impossible.[501] He was forced to take an ever more anti-unionist stand, where he had always been particularly careful to acknowledge the contributions of unions to the labour movement.[502]

The main object of his attack was the "bureaucratic spirit" which characterised the trade union officials and prevented their recognising that there was a crisis in the labour movement which paralleled that in the whole country. This crisis he typified as one of "power and sovereignty" — who should rule — and it determined developments in the whole socialist movement.

In this situation, where the question was one of where ultimate power lay, the workers felt that "'their' organisational complex has become such an enormous apparatus that it has ended up obeying laws of its own, internal to its structure and its complicated functioning, but external to the mass, which has acquired consciousness of its historical mission as a revolutionary class."

This real feeling was rooted in real circumstances and produced real new institutional and organisational forms to give it expression. The factory council was the primary form of this reality and would culminate in the dictatorship of the proletariat. The union, on the other hand, despite its historical achievements, was, "the type of proletarian organisation specific to the period of history dominated by capital", and directed by technical expertise subordinated to a bourgeois overview.

This did not mean that the unions themselves had no role in the coming revolution. In fact, they would carry out the socialisation of industry after it occurred.

But to do this the bureaucratic mentality of the leaders, jealous of their power, would have to be replaced by a sentiment of solidarity. (Here Gramsci made specific reference to the disastrous experience in Hungary, where the lack of support from union leaders had been one reason for the fall of the short-lived Soviet regime).

In sum, unions of the old sort belonged to the past, and a new sort, based on factory councils, would have to emerge. The main difference would be that the "reformist" leadership would be replaced not by other individualists but by representatives chosen by the workers themselves through the councils which were their class expression.

Mindful of the attacks made by the "reformists" that this made him a syndicalist, Gramsci also made it quite clear that he supported neither "reformist" nor revolutionary syndicalists. He claimed that the first were concerned only with bread and butter issues and could rise to no more than this, and the second thought that they could make the unions a revolutionary weapon when they were not suitable for such a task.

His position of intransigent hostility towards the union bureaucracy was not merely a question of personalities, though there was personal animus on both sides. Nor was it merely a negative estimation of the unions potential role in the existing, and worsening social situation in Italy. It was based on the belief that hierarchy of the sort unionism typified was innately anti-revolutionary. He believed that through making decisions for himself in the factory council, the worker obtained a consciousness of his own worth and ability to control his destinies and a feeling of interdependence with his fellows which he could not otherwise obtain.

"Even the most ignorant and backward of the workers, even the most vain and 'cultured' of engineers, ends up being convinced of this truth in the experience of the factory council."[503]

By 1920 Gramsci had thrown down the gauntlet before the trade union officials and their time-honoured methods, and, by implication, before all the traditional methods of the Italian socialist movement. This meant that he had an uphill battle and had to find suitable allies where he could, without troubling himself about traditional hatreds and enmities. Most of the allies he found were therefore either outside the PSI or had adopted positions which conflicted with traditional PSI activity.

Among the first group were a large number of anarchists, who either belonged to the anarchist Unione Sindacale Italiane (U.S.I.) or were unattached. He associated himself with these people because he believed that common experience in the struggle would bring them over to the communist position. For this reason he did not include anarchist intellectuals among possible allies. Typical of his allies was Garino, Parodi's comrade in the intransigent leadership of the FIOM.[504]

Among the second group were the "abstentionists" of the PSI, like Parodi and Boero, who took seriously the anti-parliamentary quality of Leninism as propounded by Bordiga, and demanded that the PSI give up participating in elections and concentrate on a revolutionary path to power.

Both groups were firmly established in the factory councils, and though Gramsci did not at first share their opinions at all, he was influenced by working in unity with them, and because the triumph of his group in the councils was by allying himself with them. Their influence became ever clearer in 1920, as they helped him become the acknowledged intellectual leader of the conciliar movement, and loved and respected by the masses, whose attitudes these anarchist and 'abstentionist' leaders embodied — attitudes which were increasingly in favour of a solution which was extra-parliamentary and typified by participatory democracy. Each time there was a dispute or strike in Turin, Gramsci and his followers were the first to know about it and to develop its theoretical implications — which became increasingly anti-party.

His discovery, when in 1920 the councils started to concentrate and build up their attacks on capitalism, that capitalism had allies within the PSI only encouraged this "anti-Jacobinism".

IV

The capitalists had never looked favourably on the *commissioni* and were even more dubious about the development of these organisations into factory councils. At first they tried to compromise the factory councils' leaders by barely hidden bribes and presents. When they had no success with men like Parodi, who won their grudging respect, they realised that the new conciliar movement would not be incorporated into the system like earlier institutions.[505] They realised that these organisations were, as Gramsci stated, concerned not only with economic gains but with making social revolution and decided that they were not to be tolerated. Having emerged from the war stronger and more united, and soon to establish their own nation-side confederation, (the Confindustria) the capitalists prepared to take offensive measures to crush the movement. Impelling them to immediate action was the occupation, near Turin, of factories by factory workforces in February 1920. On 7 March, Gino Olivetti, secretary general of the new employers' federation, pronounced that two different powers could not exist in the factories. On the 20 March he and de Benedetti, president of the Industrial League and Giovanni Agnelli, head of the Fiat works, informed the prefect of Turin that they proposed to conduct a general lockout to smash the movement as soon as the time was opportune.[506] Their opportunity came a few days later. The workers were opposed to the proposed daylight saving change in hours, from which they expected to lose, and upset by the reduction in the wages of some commissars. A factory council altered some of the time clocks in protest and the management reacted by dismissing three commissars. Immediately the local FIOM and PSI sections lent support. A general withdrawal and lockout ensued at FIAT.

Both sides were quite aware that it was a struggle between proletarian and capitalist power.[507] Gramsci had set the scene on the day the dispute began with his article, "The end of a power". He described Agnelli as a "hero" of capitalism who ruled like an autocrat in a little capitalist state of fifteen thousand men. But he warned Agnelli that it was a difficult state to rule autocratically because of its size, and because it created its own antithesis in its working-class, who found unity in the factory councils and who had sixty thousand mouths to feed.

Within days the other workers' organisations of Turin had started to galvanise support for the locked-out men. The owners retaliated and by April 3, 90,000 men were idle. The will of both sides hardened, as they saw that what was at stake was a crucial moral victory. Early hopes of moderation were dashed. Rumours started to fly around the city, as first the province, and then the whole of Piedmont, were involved: "fifty thousand soldiers, on the hills around a battery of artillery, reinforcements in the surrounding countryside, armoured cars in the city, and machine guns trained on private houses". Indeed, troops were moved into the vicinity of the city until railway workers in other cities prevented further dispatches.

Gramsci sarcastically thanked "the industrial lords for making clear to everybody, even though it wasn't needed, what the terms of relative strength were"; and he warned that there could be no favourable resolution for the Turin workers if they did not extend the strike throughout Italy. On April 13 a general strike was declared in Turin and the province and 500,000 workers stopped work.

Gramsci and the Turinese leaders then turned to the "fire-breathing" maximalist leaders of the Socialist Party, and to their rivals in the General Confederation of Labour, with an appeal to extend the strike; this was essential to the success of the Turinese workforce. The Party and the CGL refused to support the extension of the movement and ten days later the workers returned to the factories on the owners' terms. It was a disaster.

Gramsci had learnt a further lesson about the PSI and the CGL and he wrote: "The Turinese working class has been defeated. Among the conditions determining this defeat ... was the limitedness of the minds of the leaders of the Italian working class movement. Among the second level conditions determining the defeat is thus the lack of revolutionary cohesion of the entire Italian proletariat, which cannot bring forth ... a trade union hierarchy which reflects its interests and its revolutionary spirit. Among the first level conditions which determined the defeat we must therefore place the general state of Italian society, the conditions of life in every province and every region in which the Confederation of Labour has a branch. And it is certain that the Turinese working-class was defeated because in Italy there do not exist, or have not yet matured, the necessary and sufficient conditions for an organic and disciplined movement of the *working class and peasants together* [my emphasis AD] This immaturity, this inadequacy of the Italian working people is undoubted evidence of the 'superstition' and mental limitedness of the leaders responsible for the Italian working people."

Though the capitalists had made minute and extensive preparations to crush the working class from the time of the Milan conference of the Confindustria, the leaders of the Socialist party had done nothing to oppose them, placing the workers at a tremendous disadvantage.

The solidarity of workers both inside and outside Turin after the general strike had been declared had led to a belief in "the possibility of a general insurrection of the Italian proletariat against the State" but it was thought bound to fail because of inadequate preparation.

Forced, and still forced after the defeat, into specific forms of organisation by the objective conditions, the workers were also forced into their action — something little understood by the "cold unenthusiastic bureaucrats" who ran the workers' organisations, who had been placed there by nepotism and bureaucracy and not by the workers themselves.

Gramsci concluded that the PSI leaders who could have, if not secured the success of the strike, at least maintained and secured the gains the workers had made in the factories, had done nothing, and the Turin workforce would now have to fight on two fronts: for the conquest of industrial power and for the conquest of the trade unions and proletarian unity.[508]

V

Gramsci and his friends had been forced into a position of opposition to the maximalist leaders of the PSI like that towards the trade union leaders. It was not the first time that Gramsci and his followers had taken a position of criticism vis-à-vis the maximalist leaders of the party. In January he had called on them to "renew the party" if they did not wish to be left behind by events. On 11-13 January at a PSI conference in Florence, Terracini had criticised Serrati for advancing a "maximalism" which is no more than a "literary exercise and a theoretical proposal", and told him to work in the factories or return to the "melting-pot" of "centrism."[509]

But it was with their lack of support for the locked-out workers in April that Gramsci moved into a position of more extreme criticism, and an everwidening rift developed between him and the party leaders.

The party leaders had done nothing to implement the decisions of December 1918 despite a worsening in conditions among the working-class. The first step in this implementation should have been the expulsion of the "reformists" from the party after the leadership had decided in favour of creating a dictatorship of the proletariat in Italy. The "reformists," who openly supported the reconstruction of capitalism in Italy decided, at a meeting held on 22-23 December 1918, to oppose the leadership's commitment to the Russian revolution. Their leaders, Turati and Treves, wrote and spoke in denigration of the revolution and Lenin, and denied the appropriateness of Bolshevik methods in Italy[510] throughout early 1919, but Serrati tended to be affected by their vigour and his campaign against them was weak. Though the reformists themselves challenged him to expel them, he and his supporters made no attempt to do so. It appears that Serrati was so fearful of splitting the party he had united five years before that he was prepared to advance views little different from those of Treves in *Critica sociale*, and which blantantly ignored the party's commitment to revolution. Indeed, in January 1919 Serrati said that: "The fact that we won the war has made impossible in Italy the methods used in Russia and Germany — in Italy the consequences of the war have created a 'reformist' and democratic situation."[511]

This policy of concessions to the anti-revolutionaries did not correspond with the increasing class consciousness among the workers and the obviously imminent frontal clash between capitalism and the proletariat, which the party leaders ignored in the interests of maintaining unity with the reformists.

As a consequence of their wilful blindness to reality, the maximalists made no preparations for the revolution to which they were committed. No increased expenditure was made on organisation and propaganda. Even the most intransigent of the maximalists, those of Turin, suffered from a form of fatalism and waited for the revolution to happen as the result of one of the many revolts, strikes and killings of the first half of 1919. Nenni himself was forced to admit: "Nobody placed himself at the head of the mass, nobody tried to provide a political outlet to the malcontent."[512] The masses, when they fought, therefore fought for petty-bourgeois objectives.[513]

After July the first post-war wave of unrest died down, and the various sections of the party started to prepare for the party congress in Bologna in October, and the Italian general elections in November. The polemic between the maximalists and the reformists continued without resolution. The first had now committed themselves to the Third International, which was formed at Moscow in January 1919 and whose aim was to destroy social-democracy and conduct the world revolution. The second replied by attacking the maximalist programme for Italy as "the complete destruction of the party".[514] Even now Serrati's response was limited to words. He reproved Turati for "anti-revolutionary" activity when "he well knows that almost all of the party maintains that Bolshevism is the purest expression of its doctrine"[515] and called for "a sharp turn of the helm to the left". He even started a new journal, *Il Comunismo*, to propagate the ideas of the Third International.

In its first number he specifically called for the expulsion of the reformists and a complete centralisation of the party as necessary so that the PSI could " ... gather with all its forces, in a fully conscious manner, the collapsing bourgeois regime" in a revolution.[516]

Yet he never got beyond verbal attacks. Although at the Bologna congress the party accepted Bolshevism and adhesion to the Third International by an overwhelming vote of 48, 411 to the reformists' opposing 14,880, Turati and his followers were not expelled and rushed off to tell their electors that these new views would be opposed. Turati publicly stated that he and his followers would stay in the party to temper the "foreign influence". He denied that there was any revolutionary situation in Italy, or that there was any possibility of one developing.[517] He referred to the dictatorship of the proletariat as "a mean ideal of brutal and armed violence".

Serrati, despite Lenin's urging that he expel the "open and masked opportunists — and there are many of them in the Italian parliamentary group", still only engaged in verbal polemics with Turati. He denied that his group had thought of making "a systematic doctrinal defence of violence, to found on violence the new order of communism" but recognised "our practical and contingent adhesion to the use of violence."[518] "The regime of the Soviets, of the councils of workers, is already a fact, not only in Russia, but everywhere". So Turati's defence of the traditional methods of the PSI in their stead was a "puerile illusion."[519]

This lip service to the conciliar system hid the truth that Serrati had not approved of the factory councils of Turin. He did not believe that they should be elected democratically, and thus include anarchists and syndicalists. In November 1919 he called them an "aberration".[520] Thinking like a Blanquist, he did not believe in the revolutionary potential of the "amorphous mass" and thus thought that the councils could be only "technical" organisations, leaving making revolution to the party.[521]

Gramsci had bitterly opposed the reformists and supported the maximalists through 1918-19, but this hostility of Serrati caused him to reprove:

"The Socialist Party hasn't even attempted to get out of the realm

132

of verbal affirmations, it has not given the workers and peasants the concrete guide to make real institutional innovations. For the Third International, 'making' the revolution means 'giving' power to the soviets, means struggling to attain a communist majority in the soviets; for the Third International being revolutionary means getting out of the realm of trade union corporativism and party sectarian activity and seeing the movement in masses of human beings which is seeking a form, and working so that that form is the system of councils.

Lenin's letter (in support of maximalism) sanctions a rather unhappy and unreassuring situation; we totter between catastrophe ... and a worse catastrophe — a Constituent Assembly."[522]

A month after, in January, he called for a renewal of the Socialist party because it had not organised the masses whom it had aroused with its revolutionary speeches, when its task was to prepare conditions favourable for a proletarian democracy.[523] In particular, he wanted the party to expel the reformists. When this desire was coupled with his association in Turin with "abstentionists" like Parodi and Boero, he found himself very close to the position and members of the "abstentionist" group in the party, which was led by Bordiga.

Bordiga had been greatly disconcerted by Serrati's refusal to take concrete action against the reformists. Through the journal he and his followers had set up in December 1918 he engaged in savage condemnation of the reformists and opposed all maximalist compromises with them.[524]

In February 1919 he came out openly in favour of violent revolutionary action and eschewal of all parliamentary activity, earning the denomination "abstentionist". When the maximalist leaders refused to consider this policy, despite their adhesion to the Third International, which demanded similar action, Bordiga condemned them, as Gramsci did later in the year, for lack of "precise directives".[525] By the middle of 1919 his group had won many regional sections of the PSI to their intransigent position.[526] At the Bologna conference, Bordiga expressed the position of himself and many of his followers clearly:

"We, comrades, have been badly misunderstood: people in many quarters have spoken of anarchist and syndicalism. Instead we are — and we will be — marxist socialists; we hope to show that our

133

present position corresponds completely with what are the basic doctrines of the party, laid down by the classic *Manifesto* of 1848. Socialism was elaborated as a doctrine substantially through a critique of bourgeois idealist and utopian conceptions, an interpretation of history which made the emancipation of the proletariat no longer a problem of ideal Justice but a complex historical development which was studied in all its developments, from which was deduced the origins in history of societies which have preceded us, and in the organism of contemporary society, and thus could be foreseen its coming end."[527]

He went on that as Marxists, he and his followers believed that parliamentary democracy was a bourgeois sham, though "social-democrats" had ignored this fundamental Marxist tenet. The Russian revolution had belied parliamentary practice by showing what methods Marxists should use. He concluded by demanding the expulsion of any socialist who would not accept Bolshevism, adding that he feared that the maximalists would not do this as they were too concerned with electoral success to split the party.[528]

Bordiga's dark expectations were fulfilled. Serrati did nothing to expel the reformists, as we have seen, and despite disclaimers that he was interested in success in the November elections, started to gather parliamentary aspirants around him after October.

By 1920 Bordiga was so bitterly hostile to the reformists and maximalists that *Il Soviet* printed these words: "in our view, nothing does so much good as a split. The first thing must be to put everyone in his proper place. One will know in this way exactly who is a communist and who is not: there will be no more confusion on this score.... A good split clears the air. Communists to one side, reformists of all persuasions and gradations to the other."[529]

This general convergence of Gramsci's and Bordiga's views should not mislead us about their differences. Despite the leading role played in the factory councils by "abstentionists", Bordiga was as opposed to them as Serrati. Misunderstanding Gramsci's notion of their role, and, perhaps chagrined by the Turinese support for electoral activity in November 1919 (even the local "abstentionists" supported this), support which spelled defeat for his group in early 1920, Bordiga attacked the councils as a concession to gradualism, based on the error that fundamental gains could be made on an economic terrain rather than in a frontal assault.[530] Despite such abiding differences, by April Gramsci had come over to Bordiga's position on the party. Faced by the blatant PSI opposition to the councils during the lockout, Gramsci expressed a sneering hostility at the party's meeting in Milan, when it had planned to meet in Turin. He demanded that the party clean itself up. Except in Moscow, where Lenin read his report with approval some time later, his attacks were ignored.[531]

The defeat of the strike, the disastrous setback to the councils, and the negative role of the party, symbolized in the shifting of the venue of the party meeting from Turin to Milan, brought home to Gramsci the all-important role the party could play in the success or failure of a revolutionary movement. Henceforth, he directed as much attention to the party as to the councils. At the time of the lockout he had indicated that the efficiency of the councils would be nil if the party did not play a positive role in extending them to other areas and supporting their activity. Henceforth, while keeping the councils going, the foremost immediate task was to renew the party. The party he proposed in May 1920 was something fundamentally and radically new, and a complete departure from previous PSI traditions.

VI

Gramsci first outlined how he envisaged this party in a scathing critique of the PSI which he wrote in April. He had intended to deliver it at the Turin conference of the party, but when the venue was shifted to Milan, Palmiro Togliatti, as Turinese delegate, read the bitter denunciation by his friend.

The critique was in the form of three linked propositions: first, that Italy was in a revolutionary situation — a crucial time of conflict — which precluded either a victorious socialist revolution or a "tremendous reaction"; second, that the PSI had "understood nothing of the present state of development" either on a national or an international level and done nothing to organize, educate and lead the workers towards a socialist revolution; and third, this inactivity and lack of understanding stemmed from the fact that its leaders did not "live immersed in the reality of the working class struggles" but, as part of a merely "bureaucratic" organization, only observed events. The critique warned that the mass would tend to drift away from the party because of its unawareness of their needs and aspirations and that it could only avoid this fate if it changed itself into a "homogeneous and cohesive" communist party "with its own doctrine, tactics and a rigid and implacable discipline." The conclusion read; "The existence of a strongly disciplined and cohesive communist party, which through its nuclei in the factory, union and cooperative coordinates and controls through its executive committee all revolutionary actions of the proletariat, is the fundamental and indispensable condition for attempting any Soviet experiment."[532]

In this critique the germs of Gramsci's future views on the party were already present. He believed that the party could not be separate from — and above — mass action, but had to be involved in it — and, on the other hand, that its role was confined to leading "revolutionary actions" of the proletariat. The presupposition was that class-consciousness had already been created through the councils. It was a much more restrictive view of the role of the party than that which socialists had been used to. Consequently his proposals were rejected out-of-hand by the maximalists of Milan, who countered that all hope of "an immediate revolution [was] liquidated", though they confusingly and contradictorily declared that "the way was open for a preparation for revolution". They also refused the direct appeal of the Turinese socialists for support in the lockout, claiming that the lockout had been provoked by the Turinese who "ran around at the last minute to ask help from people who were weaker and less prepared than they were, and while negotiating with Casalini, Frola and Buozzi, led people to believe it was the eve of an insurrection."[533]

This rebuff made Togliatti's suggestion that all interested comrades come together in an *entente* to discuss the Turinese proposals — and to call for an extraordinary congress to consider what Socialist tactics and organization should be — much more significant than it would otherwise have been. It put the Turinese and the maximalist leaders in opposition to one another and extended the long-standing alliance between *ordinovisti* and *astensionisti* in Turin to a national level at a time when the "abstentionists" were already calling for an immediate split with the PSI.[534]

In May a still-bitter Gramsci attended the Florence conference of the "abstentionist" fraction of the party. Both had long agreed that the revolution was "actual". At Florence the differences between the *ordinovisti* and *astentionisti* emerged. Gramsci argued that the "abstentionists" should not boycott elections as this had a restricting effect on their membership. They should extend the right to membership to all revolutionary communist forces in the party and the working class.[535] Bordiga's blunt refusal to consider

Gramsci's proposal showed that the principal stumbling-block was their different assessment of the importance of the factory councils. Bordiga maintained that they did not have a primary role in the making of a successful socialist revolution, while Gramsci took the contrary position.[536]

Conversely, what was also at stake between them was the role of the party in making the revolution. Gramsci recognized that the existing party would have to be replaced, but he had a much more restricted view of the role the new party would play than Bordiga, for whom the party was everything. So while he and his followers started to set up "communist groups" in Turin after his return from Florence, he did not adopt so radical a position as Bordiga vis-à-vis the PSI. He did not call for a separate new party but argued that "the party is undergoing a process of organic transformation and the elements of the neo-formation are the communist groups in the factory."[537] He also stressed again and again the two key points of his critique at Milan: first, that the party would be changed from an assembly expressing the "psychology of the mob" into a homogeneous, disciplined *association* controlled by delegates from the factories who had imperative mandates.[538] In July he made clear this meant a party which was controlled from the bottom, not "a party which uses the masses in heroic imitations of the French Jacobins",[539] and second, that the party's role was limited to the seizure of political power — it was in the factory that the revolution was made, and the party existed to give political expression to the desire for worker's control.[540] It was not to regard itself as the "tutor", but as the "agent" of the factory councils.[541]

Contemporaneously with Gramsci's writing these lines, the *ordinovista* group and their Turinese working-class following started to break up. The lockout had been a bitter defeat. Tasca had drawn the conclusion from it that the factory council experiment was discredited and reaffirmed in the Camera del Lavoro the value of working through the traditional organizations of the Italian working-class. Gramsci replied that this was "fostering equivocations and illusions, and favouring intrigues and opportunistic maneouvres". Once again he made an accusation which we have met before: Tasca's erroneous views flowed from his failure to "immerse" himself in working-class life and his consequent failure to realize the vitality of the councils or their nature — a nature which prevented their being subordinated to the traditional organizations of the movement.[542] He argued that the "felt needs" of the working class pushed them towards the factory councils — the

137

necessary beginning for the revolution — and in them they spontaneously found their "unity of theory and practice".[543]

Togliatti and Terracini preferred Tasca's view to that of Gramsci. Consequently they proposed that the Turinese section participate in forthcoming communal elections.[544] The "abstentionist" secretary of the section resigned in protest, and in August 1920 new elections for the leadership of the section took place. Togliatti's group, forming a centre between the "abstentionists" and Tasca, emerged the clear winners, gaining 466 votes to the "abstentionists'" 186. Togliatti became secretary of the section.[545] Gramsci sided with neither group. He led a seventeen-member group fo⁻ "communist education" which refused to vote in the elections:

"Our group wishes to remain separate from the two factions in order to try to break out of the magic circle in which the best energies of the proletariat are being wasted. By continuing to remain separate, by not participating in the struggle for power within the section, we intend to begin work for the organization of a disinterested group, which can offer the proletariat for its emancipation neither communal councils, not union leaders, but work in the field of mass action: for communist groups in the factory and union, for the Workers' Council, for proletarian unity in the face of menace to its cohesion. The method for carrying out this goal of clarification and healing can be nothing else but this:1) to impose discussion of the fundamental questions of the working class and the communist revolution on the party with patient and relentless force; 2) to ensure that the choice of leaders for the section is not made on the muddy, smelly ground of artificial programmes ...; 3) to ensure that the section works usefully to prepare the cadres of the revolution and the social organization which will be its concrete expression, and thus, pushed on by the masses, give precise leadership to the unions and the Camera del Lavoro."[546]

Gramsci's programme was a two-edged rebuke to the "abstentionists" who menaced working-class cohesion and to the majority who were retreating to the traditional methods of working within the system, of which the unions and Camera were a party. Significantly, his small group was of entirely working-class origin, except for one engineer, Vittorio di Biasi. The programme showed that Gramsci still saw the factory council as the main force in the preparation for the revolution and not the party — though the latter obviously needed renewal. Indeed, it was precisely because an unorganised working class was limited ideologically to *campanilismo*, to the petty parochial view, that the premise for the renewal of the party was the organisation of factory councils.[547] These would educate the workers through their own struggles.

The programme also emphasized that the wasteful "magic circle" revolutionaries had caught themselves in was precisely being too much concerned with the issue of political leadership, or who the leaders were, and neglecting the links between the leaders and the masses. Before either the leaders or the masses could be revolutionarily effective, their links had to be organic, that is, the leaders had to be "immersed" in working-class practice.

One inference is clear. Even in August 1920 Gramsci envisaged a renovation of the party which did away with its leading role.[548] This followed from the fact that his party was not posited on the inability of the masses to raise themselves to class-consciousness without a party. As far as he was concerned the problem of raising consciousness was already solved in conciliar activity. The implications for the organisational structure and political activity of the party were considerable. It would be controlled from the bottom and act as the coordinator of revolutionary assaults on a national level.[549] His implicit denial that the revolution could be made by striking a single decisive blow at the heart of the capitalist system, did not reveal a lack of awareness of the ramifications and implications of finance capital for socialist revolution. On the contrary in an exchange with Tasca, he specifically denied that the growth of finance capital had shifted the battle with capitalism to another arena.[550]

Such a view completely bypassed what is usually thought to be the Leninist problematic — where revolutionary consciousness is one with class consciousness and is brought to the masses by a party, whose organizational structure and activity is posited on the inability of the workers to raise themselves to the level of consciousness without the party. Thus the eminent *communist* historian Spriano writes: "We cannot identify leninism with a conception of *revolution from below,* with a *molecular process* of the formation of the workers' State, which Gramsci places at the base of his theory of power...."[551] The "abstentionists" on the other hand, did attribute a similar "leading role" to the party, and they were organised nationally, where Gramsci had failed to organise because he feared accusations of "careerism", because he was politically ingenuous, and because his "forces were too slender for the

Antonio Gramsci

task".[552] He would pay for this failure in the months to come.

VII

While Gramsci was engaged in all these activities between May and August 1920, the PSI delegation to the second Comintern congress left in dribs and drabs for Russia. The delegation was overwhelmingly maximalist, centrist and right-wing — only two of its members would become foundation members of the communist party, and one of these, Bombacci, became a fascist soon after. There was no spokesman for *Ordine Nuovo* on it and certainly no spokesman for the line that Gramsci was following in Turin at that time. On the other hand, Bordiga and his wife Ortensia had made their way to Russia privately to put the "abstentionist" point of view.[553]

Lenin and the Bolsheviks had followed Italian developments from afar and had little knowledge of what had been going on in the PSI. Lenin's speeches at this time were sprinkled with admissions that "I have had too little opportunity to get to know 'left' communism in Italy". What information he had about Gramsci and the factory councils he had obtained from Zinoviev, whose informant was a Comintern delegate, V. Degott, who had been favourably impressed by the activities of the Turinese and had sent the critique "Per un rinnovamento del PSI" to Zinoviev.

This general lack of information among the Russians was evident from the way they received the PSI delegation, some of whom had been attacking Bolshevism savagely back in Italy. The same men whom Gramsci and Bordiga regarded as the worst enemies of the Italian revolution were hoisted as heroes on the shoulders of the Russian workers. Serrati, whose poster covered the walls of Leningrad, was affectionately greeted by Lenin, who really liked him "through affinity of temperament".[554] Both then, and later, Lenin and Zinoviev expressed their belief that Serrati and the maximalists would accept the Twenty-One conditions of membership in the Comintern, some of which demanded a complete break with all "reformists" and the expulsion from the party of all those who would not accept the Twenty-One conditions. Lenin thought that it was as "clear as the sun" that "reformists" like Turati were class traitors and would have to be expelled from the party if it was to conduct a revolution. Soon after Serrati arrived he made clear that their expulsion was matter of urgency. Serrati quickly belied Lenin's "complete trust" in him. First he manoeuvred Bordiga, who agreed with Lenin, into the position of an "observer" without a vote, thus ensuring that the official PSI representatives were men like himself. Then, at the congress, he defended Turati's right to stay in the party until he wished to leave it, thus flatly rejecting Lenin's demand that Turati be expelled. In reply Lenin revealed that "the II Congress of the Third International regards the criticisms of the party, and the practical proposals put before the national congress of the Italian Socialist Party by the Turin section of the party in *Ordine Nuovo* of 8 May 1920 as substantially correct. They correspond fully to the fundamental principles of the Third International."[555]

The Italians were flabbergasted — Bordiga not least. Serrati must have been surprised since he had had the ear of the Comintern delegate Niccolini and always fed the Comintern with his adverse assessments of the factory councils and the April lockout. Graziadei replied that Lenin was sanctioning precisely the sort of undisciplined activity which the Twenty-One conditions condemned. Bombacci warned against the dangers of over-valuing the "syndicalist" tendencies of *Ordine Nuovo*. Bordiga claimed that Lenin's support of the Gramscian position could be a source of future theoretical and political ambiguity, and Polano chimed in that Lenin was being contradictory in endorsing the predominantly "abstentionist" Turin executive committee and simultaneously condemning them for their refusal to participate in elections.[556]

Faced with this spate of objections, which revealed new information about the nuances of Gramsci's position, Lenin withdrew his blanket approval of the activities of *Ordine Nuovo*, but reaffirmed his support of Gramsci's critique of the PSI.[557] The delegates carried back this news of Gramsci's hollow victory at Moscow. Lenin's endorsement was too late to make any difference to the course of events.

VIII

In Italy developments had already taken place which would throw Gramsci, the "abstentionists", and the Tasca-Togliatti majority back together and begin a joint commitment to split the PSI and create the sort of Communist Party for which Bordiga and not Gramsci had argued. These developments marked the beginning of a period when, Gramsci wrote: "Without wanting to, we were ... overwhelmed by events, we were one aspect of the general collapse of

141

Italian society,"[558] words which indicate beyond doubt that his actions in the following months should not be regarded as representing his real desires because he was no longer able to make his own destiny.

For some time the nation-wide Metal Workers' Federation (FIOM) had been negotiating with the employers and the National Metal Industry Federation for an increase in wages for its members to offset the astronomical rise in the cost of living. The employers were adamant in their refusal to grant an increase because they needed to hold down wages to enable them to accumulate capital for a take-off on a renewed phase of growth from the low point reached in production after the war.[559] Their counter-proposal offering cooperative stores and other minor concessions did not satisfy even the firmly "reformist" CGL. After August there was a deadlock in negotiations and the union began a deliberate "go-slow" in production to force an increase in wages. The employers, on the offensive after their success in April in Turin, decided to take aggressive action in reply and crush the working-class movement once and for all. They started to lock workers out. The FIOM replied by occupying factories as a defensive tactic. Tasca recalls that the FIOM thought "... that the occupation of the factories would make the government intervene ..." and that a few hoped "... that the occupation would have the political outcome of getting the Socialists a share in government ...", although none confessed this wish openly.

The occupations soon spread to Turin, where 100,000 workers joined 500,000 others throughout Italy who had occupied their factories and enterprises. In Turin the occupations were orderly and systematic, unlike these in other cities. Gramsci viewed the occupations with mixed feelings, because he believed that the occupations were ill-timed and that the moment of conflict had really been chosen by capitalism. "The men in government have decided that the proletarian steed should be allowed to run on a slack rein until it falls on its knees, worn-out, hungry and completely degraded ..."[560] He also felt that it could raise false hopes among ill-prepared workers that a socialist revolution was imminent: "Not for a moment must the workers think that making a communist revolution is so easy and smooth as entering an undefended factory"[561] But, even if the decisive battle he forecast in April was to be fought under conditions which favoured capitalism, the fact remained that the factories had been occupied and that there was little point in bewailing the continuing ineptitude and irresponsibility of the leaders of the working-class. Instead, he and his friends closed down *Ordine Nuovo* and started to live in the factories, engaging in an endless round of organizational work, agitation, and propaganda.

This work had two purposes: first, to encourage the men to continue production so that the workers could see that they were capable of running the factories. This goal seems to have been partly dictated by a desire to save some chestnuts from the fire. Gramsci expressed his objects in these words; "The occupation of the factories by the working-class is a historical event of first-level importance: it is a necessary moment in the development of the revolution and the class war; however, it is necessary to establish with precision its meaning and importance and to get from it all the elements for raising the masses politically and to reinforce their revolutionary spirit."[562]

The second goal was to train a workers' armed militia which could protect worker gains and which could allow at least some hope of attaining the essential prerequisite for *"an experiment in communist society"* — the overthrow of the existing State power. Gramsci seemed to think of this militia as an auxiliary force and that overthrowing the State power was the responsibility of the PSI itself: "how could the workers come into the workshops or the streets to defend their interests if a State organization did not control an armed force which can meet all needs and events."[563]

The bourgeoisie who were sceptical or contemptuous of the workers' ability to run the factories were soon cured of these attitudes.[564] Gramsci's proposal that production be continued and that the movement be radicalised caught on gradually: first the the smaller factories and workshops and later in the huge central complexes of Fiat which had remained more under the aegis of the "reformists" and his other rivals. The councils were able to enforce their directive that all workers continue production and the factories actually raised production levels above those of the "go-slow" period which had preceded the occupation. With the help of railway workers, trucks of raw materials were commandeered and the finished articles returned to the railway yards. One telephone conversation showed what handwringing concern this caused the authorities at the railway yards: "What is really happening here ... is the taking over of the railways, you understand."[565]

A Red Guard was also formed and military training began: some 130 firearms were in the hands of the workers.[566]

Gramsci's initial cautious estimate of the possibilities of the occupation certainly fitted in with his belief that the intellect should be "pessimistic". In accord with this inclination he had erred, perhaps deliberately, in believing that the bourgeoisie was really in command of the situation because it had chosen the time for a decisive struggle against badly-organised workers. In fact, from the beginning of the occupation, the government felt that it did not have "sufficient forces to protect all establishments at the same time" and that the aggressive policy of the owners could have "incalculable consequences".[567] As early as late August, the Prime Minister, Giovanni Giolitti, saw that a collision path had been set and that "...it would be wise if government action were as little evident as possible" so that the political implications of the "economic" dispute would be as little evident as possible. The industrialists certainly started confidently, apparently with the view that "the proletarian steed (which God the Father Almighty very conveniently created for the use of the bourgeois rider) should be allowed to run on a slack rein until it [fell] on its knees."[568] *But*, as the occupations by workers increased in number, the slack-reined steed started to carry the owners they knew not where, like latter-day Mazeppas. From Milan, the headquarters of the unions and the party to which the workers looked for leadership, an alarmed Prefect reported to Corradini, the Undersecretary of State of Internal Affairs,: "... the occupiers have machine guns, are reported to have a tank ... there is speculation beginning that strong contingents of armed workers may invade the city for criminal purposes ... please send another 400 police or 500 *Guardie regie* urgently", and then, on September 7, "... have available 3000 troops and 1200 police and *Guardie regie*. With these we could hold along the Naviglio line ... which contains only a fifth of the city." He needed another 5000 men. "We need more armoured cars, having only six, and grenades: it would also be useful to have tanks ..." if the city was to fall in a revolt.[569] In Turin the Prefect, Taddei, also grew more and more alarmed as the occupiers grew more confident and radical with the production of vehicles, and in response to his own defensiveness.

Gramsci was not insensitive to this change of climate. He wrote: "If in the struggle the workers occupy the factories and wish to continue to produce, the moral position of the mass takes on a different appearance and value; the union leaders can no longer lead, the union leaders disappear in the immensity of the scene, the mass must solve the problems of the factory with its own means

144

and its own men", and argued that since every factory then became an illegal State, the fundamental issue became the question of a "military defence" of that State. Moreover, by the logic of events, each little state was driven to unite with the next and set up an urban soviet.[570] Gramsci was not so sanguine as to believe that he and the Turinese workers would be able to carry out a revolution by themselves, but Taddei hastily appealed for another 500 police to defend the city. By the second week of September the occupation had become a national issue and made revolution the order of the day. Again, all faces turned towards the leaders of the working-class movement.

The "reformist" union leaders had not expected events to develop as they had: from the outset they had expected the government to step in and settle the dispute in favour of the unionists. Consequently they were in close contact with the government from the beginning of the occupation and had continued to negotiate with the owners. Indeed, the government responded by regarding the unionists — and their political colleagues, Turati, Treves and D'Aragona — as their allies in settling a dispute in which the owners were being stubborn. Even as the occupations began the Milan Prefect reported: "During the day I spoke with Albertini, Turati, Treves and D'Aragona to avail myself of their help in reaching a solution."[571] Overall, the "reformists" opposed any politicisation of what they regarded as a dispute over wages and, pressed through the "reformist" daily, *Il Lavoro* of Genoa, for a peaceful solution to the dispute. They urged the Prime Minister to step in and compose matters. When the situation started to become critical, Buozzi also began to work more and more closely with the owners with a view to bringing about a peaceful settlement and confidential information reported Treves as saying that "helped by Turati, Storchi and his other colleagues and co-religionaries [he] would try to compose the conflict peacefully and legally."[572] Treves even advised the government to use force against the work-forces occupying the factories.

Gramsci knew in broad lines about these negotiations, and he stigmatised them as a desertion of "the most elementary principles of class action." He realized that the loyalty and support of the union leaders would be essential if any assault on the State was contemplated. On 5 September he published a bitter denunciation of the PSI for allowing such vacillation at a critical time. The PSI was "no different from the English Labour Party and revolutionary only in the general claims of its programme." It was a conglomerate of parties; it moved, and could only move, lazily and tardily; it was continually exposed — an easy territory to be conquered by adventurers, careerists, and ambitious men, who were neither responsible nor politically capable. Because it was so heterogeneous, had so many frictions in its machinery, which was worn-out and sabotaged by the bosses' lackeys, it was never capable of assuming the weight of responsibility for the revolutionary actions which ongoing events incessantly imposed upon it. This explained the historical paradox that in Italy it was the masses who pushed forward and "educated" the party of the working-class and not the party which guided and educated the masses.[573]

This assessment of the capabilities of the PSI led him to be even more alarmed when, on the same day that he published the article, the union leaders, the Trades Hall leaders, and the Socialist Party leaders, feeling themselves *overwhelmed by the events*, declared that they had given up their earlier limited goals in favour of the goal of seeking general control of all the means of production. The maximalists confirmed that they, too, were completely irresponsible on the 6 September. Without having taken any practical steps to prepare the masses for military combat against State forces, they launched a "pre-insurrectionary" manifesto to the soldiers and peasants which blared:

"If the decisive hour of battle against the bosses, against all exploiters, sounds tomorrow, you will heed the call. Take the towns and the land, disarm the *carabinieri*, join your battalions with the workers, march towards the city to help the people, who will fight against the paid agents of the bourgeoisie. Because, the day of freedom and justice is perhaps nigh."[574]

Such demagoguery encouraged the real flesh and blood workers — who were, however, not organized — to go into streets already covered by the State's machine-guns. In 1924 Gramsci recalled how each faced this nightmarish possibility — and how in such a situation men and women tend to depend greatly on decisions "higher up".[575]

"I still remember vividly a scene in Turin, during the occupation of the factories; they all seemed drunk, and about to come to blows among themselves; their responsibility overcame them, ground them to the marrow. One got to his feet — he had fought during the war for five years as a pilot, and had had a hundred brushes with death — he reeled and threatened to fall over. With an enormous nervous effort I intervened and made them smile with a wisecrack, bringing them back to normality and to useful work. Today I couldn't do it.''[576]

The men who led the unions and the party also knew that in a moment of crisis like that in the second week of September 1920 firm and united leadership was absolutely necessary — but no one was prepared to grasp the nettle firmly. On 9 September Togliatti and Nino Benso attended a CGL meeting in Milan which was held to decide what to do next. The CGL asked the Turinese to "act" first. Remembering April, and fearing a trap which could destroy the factory council movement, Togliatti refused. He argued that the movement was not prepared sufficiently for armed combat: "You should not rely on an action carried out by Turin alone. We will not attack alone; to do it a simultaneous action of the country, and above all nation-wide action, is needed.''[577]

The CGL used the Turinese warning to draw the conclusion that the occupation should end at most with a system of co-gestion. The PSI leaders, on the other hand, ignored the warning about lack of preparation, and voted at another meeting to extend the movement. In the circumstances this was tantamount to loosing the horde: ex-servicemen who had faced machine-guns could hardly have been happy about such tactics.

On 10 September the CGL and PSI met together to decide future policy. This meeting revealed the bankruptcy of the Italian socialist leadership. They showed a complete lack of will and unity in time of crisis. The unionists stated that the PSI policy of extending the movement would lead to "disaster" and offered to resign, on the grounds that the PSI policy made the further development of the occupation a "political" matter, which by party statute did not involve them.[578] Terracini and other "communists" on the Executive of the party stated that such an offer was tantamount to sabotage, as Buozzi, D'Aragona and Dugoni were "unsubstitutable leaders of the masses" who could not be replaced at the eleventh hour.[579] Even the maximalists realized how disastrous such an attitude was at a crucial moment when the issue might be that of assault on the State, and refused to accept the notion that there were "two parties". They too were not prepared to allow the unions to evade their responsibility if the unprepared mass were instructed to start an insurrection.[580] To resolve the deadlock the issue of what to do was put to the vote — that ultimate fetish of the irresolute — and revolution "was rejected by a majority". The maximalists were able to blame the unionists — and avoid complete responsibility for this final failure. In fact they had all "fled forward" and the occupation had already passed into history as the *"rivoluzione mancata"*.

We can gauge how much had depended on their leadership, and will, rather than the "concrete distribution of forces", by considering the State's contemporary belief about its own ability to defeat a socialist insurrection. Giolitti simply did not believe that he had the military force to do much if the workers came out into the streets to overthrow the State. He even cabled these words to Lusignoli: "You must make clear to the industrialists that no government in Italy will use force which will certainly provoke a revolution to save them some money. The use of force would mean that the factories would be reduced to ruins at least."[581] It is at least plausible, even given the state of unpreparedness of the socialist workers, that firm leadership by the PSI would have meant a successful transfer of State power to socialism because Giolitti *believed* that he did not have the power to oppose them. The Socialist decision on 10 September not to act permitted the astute Prime Minister to step in with a scheme for co-gestion in the factories. The workers were tired; they had been without pay since August; most, though not all of the owners were apprehensive; and so both sides came hurriedly to the conference table.[582] Within six hours of negotiation the pay rises had been granted; an indemnity promised to all those involved in the occupation; and most minor differences solved. All that was left was to draw up plans about turning over the factories to the owners. The Italian State had survived the greatest crisis it had ever faced. Capitalism had triumphed and a "tremendous reaction" was soon to follow.

When Giovanni Agnelli returned to triumph to Fiat he scarcely hid his contempt for the workers. "He was mild and insinuating. He spoke of the agreement which had been reached and complimented himself on it. Then he sang paeans of praise to work, and, in the name of work, to the collaboration of the boss and the worker for social peace and peace in the workshop."[583] The working-class leaders in Turin realized that the socialist movement had met a severe setback, but they replied with defiant words: "Tomorrow we will be like yesterday. We will work, but we will work ... in and out of here for the establishment of a better society; for the maintenance of that society, and to fight for our aspirations. Today everybody takes up his position again, and it is a position of war." After this reply the elaborate ceremony of handing over the factory could not be continued and final courtesies were immediately exchanged: "Agnelli and Fornaca accepted as a memento one of the medallions struck by the Fiat workers with the Soviet emblem and the inscription: *'Fiat-Soviet Gestione operaia 1920'*. Then the workers withdrew."[584]

From the beginning of the occupation Gramsci had been thrown back together with the workers, and thus with their "abstentionist" and "anarchist" leaders, and they had sunk their theoretical differences in a united practice. Together they had laboured tirelessly to organize the workers for the possible trials ahead and together they had observed the incompetence of the PSI — an incompetence which had possibly cost the Italian working-class a socialist society. They almost certainly all agreed with the assessment of the PSI made by the man who had moved an extension of the occupation on 10 September at Milan — Schiavello argued that the failure was not to be laid solely at the door of the open traitors and "reformists", but that on 10 September the maximalists had "repeated what they had done for ten years. Thus we were all victims of a condition wished by ourselves. We lacked an organism, we lacked a party which had the mind of the crowd under control. We lacked a party which was not of two minds: we lacked a hand of steel. Perhaps we lacked a communist party."[585] The Turin "abstentionists" and their followers and allies were in no way placated by the agreement orchestrated by Giolitti — it meant only a 4 lire increase in pay and an unreliable promise of indemnity. They called for the immediate creation of a communist party to retrieve something from the wreckage and a few days before the occupation ended Gramsci and Togliatti were summoned urgently to the Fiat factory where Parodi, their "abstentionist" friend, was prominent. "Here there came together the members of the factory council and a group of working-class leaders from the workshops, all socialists. It was proposed and decided that they proceed immediately to form a communist party and launch an appeal to the workers to join it."[586]

Although the demand conflicted with Gramsci's position before the occupation, he felt that it was no time for indecision and finally committed himself to forming a communist party to retrieve something from the "collapse and chaos" of Italian socialism.[587]

About two weeks later, in mid October, Gramsci and Terracini went to Milan to meet Bordiga, his closest associate, Ruggiero Grieco, and three extreme left socialists, Bombacci, Luigi Repossi and Bruno Fortichiari to form the national fraction of communists. Representatives of the Youth Federation were also at the meeting. They were all united by their hatred of the inhuman superficiality of men who thought that revolutions were slogans, but Bordiga, who had been calling for a separate party longest, was dominant in the proceedings. He worked indefatigably for a decision to split "to the left", with Serrati and the maximalists the main targets, and called with Neapolitan warmth for "harsher sanctions than those proposed by Moscow" in the Twenty-One conditions, which had been known to all the party since 29 September.[588]

Accepting Bordiga's proposal meant tacitly lending support to his view that the revolution in Italy could only be made by a party with an iron discipline, which maintained a clear separation from the mass, and was directed to a political assault on the State. This was not quite the "abstract ideal that a handful of men alone could guarantee the success of the revolution in Italy", but it certainly stressed the importance of political leadership.[589] It was a view which could not find undistorted echoes in the *Ordine Nuovo* group which had always emphasized the importance of immersion in the mass and organic links with it, but Gramsci was at this time disillusioned, as he saw the failure of leadership as dialectically connected with the failure of the masses to bring forth the right leaders, and he was therefore prepared to support Bordiga's view.

> "The communist party is the instrument and the historical form of that process of intimate liberation through which the worker from *executor* becomes *initiator*, from being the *mass* becomes *the leader* and guide, from being an arm becomes *will and a brain*; in the formation of the communist party a seed of liberty must be picked which will have its development and full expression after the workers' State has organized the necessary material conditions."[590]

were words he wrote on 4 September, indicating that he was even prepared to abandon to some extent his notion of the pre-formation of a workers' State on the factory floor in favour of a precedent political overthrow of the bourgeois State after which the workers' State would be formed.

Moreover, when Serrati, who refused to heed the directions of the Second Congress of the Comintern and expel the "reformists" whose treachery was clear during the occupation, visited Turin in late November, Gramsci used almost exactly the same arguments which Bordiga had already used against the maximalist leader. "Joining the Third International must be done without conditions or reservations.... The constitution of a communist party which obeys an international discipline is necessary. We don't have to be many. Thirty thousand members of the Russian CP were sufficient to bring the revolution victory, because that party was united and knew what it wanted."[591]

Yet his support for Bordiga was ambivalent. It certainly was a departure from his previous views. The ambivalence was manifest among the other editors of *Ordine Nuovo* as well. When Terracini had been called upon to decide for either a split "to the left" or "to the right" after the Comintern's Twenty-One conditions arrived on 29 September, he had suggested that neither was satisfactory as a split "to the left" would turn many away from the party and have profound repercussions because so many followed the PSI because of its extremist tactics and programme, and a split "to the right" would have little effect among the masses.[592] In Turin unity between the "abstentionists", the Tasca, Togliatti, Terracini "right", and Gramsci's education group by mid-November ended on the basis of the compromise programme that:

1) the difference between social-democrats and communists was that the first thought that they could come to power through alliances with the bourgeois class;

2) the process of forming a communist party started in the workshops and the councils;

3) a party was essential, and anarchist opposition to it should be strongly fought; and

4) that "education clubs" should the the headquarters for communist groups and the commissars.

With singular catholicity, the Turinese elected Gramsci, Terracini and Parodi to the national committee of the communist fraction.[593] Without doubt this unity of endeavour with its emphasis on a mass based party in the councils represented what Gramsci had wanted till September — and it will emerge that this was his concept of the party again later — *but*, when Bordiga threatened to "go it alone" at the Imola conference of the national fraction of 28 November, Gramsci quietly accepted Bordiga's policy of a small party of professional revolutionaries. Bordiga made quite clear that he was going to force a split "to the left" at the forthcoming conference of the PSI and "took up a knotty club and beat terribly on the table with it" when the unitary faction attempted to put the conciliatory view.[594] The Comintern delegate, Haller, (Chiarini) was so disturbed by the possibility of a separate view emerging that he approached Parodi and Berti to smooth the troubled water which could emerge if Gramsci favoured a less radical line than Bordiga. Consequently the conference resolved that at the next congress of the PSI it would "... change the name of the party into that of the Communist Party of Italy (Section of the Third Communist International).... Affirm incompatible the presence in the Party of all those who are against the principles and conditions of the Communist International, declaring that a) all adherents of the so-called concentrationist fraction [reformist] and those who attended its meetings; b) all members of the party who at the next congress vote against the communist programme for the party and against the undertaking to observe the Twenty-One conditions completely ... have placed themselves and are placing themselves in such an incompatible position."[595] A strongly abstentionist Central Committee was elected: Bordiga, Fortichiari, Grieco, Repossi, Misiano, Bombacci, Polano, Gramsci and Terracini. The only sign that the Turinese, who were the only group with a large mass following, had participated in drawing up the programme, was the statement that the proletarian State would be one of workers' and peasants' councils, like that in the Soviet Union.[596]

Gramsci did nothing in the six weeks between the Imola meeting and the congress at Leghorn to reverse his self-effacing position. The few articles he wrote were directed against Serrati and the centre. As far as he was concerned a communist party was essential, and no party could be made without Bordiga and the "abstentionists". He revealed how much his mind was made up with these lines:

"It is useless lamenting what has happened and cannot be undone. The communists are and must be calmly and coldly rational; if everything is in collapse we must remake everything, we must remake the Party; we must from today consider and love the Communist Party of Italy, which wins disciples, organises them solidly, educates them, makes them active cells for the new organization which will develop until it becomes the mind and the will of the whole working people."[597]

In conformity with this decision to support the CP he turned

Ordine Nuovo into a communist daily on 1 January. He had obviously decided that Leghorn would be only a formality, and was no doubt comforted in his decision by the unswerving support of the Comintern for the communists.[598]

When Kabakchiev, the Comintern delegate to the Leghorn conference arrived in Italy, he called on Gramsci, whom Lenin had repeatedly singled out as the proponent of the correct line in Italy, and together they drew up Kabakchiev's speech for the congress.[599] Gramsci attended the congress but did not speak, allowing Pastore and Leonetti to show the flag for the Turinese. We may assume that Kabakchiev presented Gramsci's views when he said that "the economic and financial crisis is making the class struggle more acute in Italy and creating a revolutionary situation"; that the growth of finance capital made control of production by workers no longer sufficient for revolution; and that the lessons of the Russian revolution about how to organise in this situation should be learnt; and that he gave Gramsci's views national content when he proclaimed that Serrati simply denied that the revolution was actual; therefore could not see that the occupation of the factories was "a revolutionary act *par excellence*", and had not organised properly. He blamed the failure of the revolution in Italy on the PSI: "It is perfectly clear that the declared reformists, headed by Turati, and the semi-reformists ... headed by Serrati, are in contradiction with and opposition to the principles of the CI; they are against its programme and tactics". He concluded that the second would have to break with the "reformists" if the PSI was to stay in the Communist International.[600]

Significantly, Bordiga's speech for the communist fraction differed very little in substance except for the absence of concern about a mass base. He declared that the alternatives were "proletarian dictatorship or bourgeois dictatorship"; that power could only be taken violently and that socialists who denied this were holding up the revolution; "... today the party is what it was on the eve of the war, the best party of the Second International, but not yet a party of the Third International;" and that the communists on the other hand were committed without reservations to the "doctrine, method, tactics and action of the Twenty-One conditions."

Bordiga obviously had a somewhat ominous intuition that Gramsci's quiescence was dictated by tactics and spelt no real community of principle because he said "... there can be

153

disagreements among us. Gramsci can be on a false track, can follow a wrong line, when I am on the true one, but we all struggle equally for the final result, we all make the same effort which makes up a programme, a method.''[601]

Indeed, it was inexorable unity that the communists pushed towards the split, while the other groups beat their breasts, engaged in melodrama, and slander of Gramsci. With Dives, and not Lazarus, waiting at the gate for the crumbs from the banquet table, the communists and the Youth Federation finally trooped out of the hall. The vote had been 98,028 for the unitary (maximalist) position; 58,783 for the communist decision for a split "to the left", and 14,965 for the "reformist" position.

Bordiga consolidated his victory at the inaugural congress of the PCI held the next day in the Teatro Goldoni. Three of the five man party executive, which he headed, were under his aegis: Grieco, Repossi and Fortichiari, and Terracini was soon to become devoted to him. Gramsci was only elected to the Central Committee after some opposition led by the Roman d'Amato, who recalled his 'interventionism'. This drove Gramsci back into his shell for some time. *Ordine Nuovo* was passed over as the party newspaper in favour of *Il Comunista* and the party seat was Milan, not Turin. Despite some of his friends' pleas, Gramsci, stung by d'Amato's attacks, did nothing to oppose Bordiga's pre-eminence. The party was consequently organized on a rigidly disciplined centralist basis and expressed Bordiga's attitudes towards those closest to the PCI but not in it, the "unitary communists". These were now "the worst sort of opportunists" whose action at Leghorn "had prepared this logical consequence: the expulsion of the PSI from the Communist International".[602]

He preluded his future expectations that the PCI would be the "Only Italian section of the Communist International".

Gramsci had helped form a new party, which he wanted, but it was not *the* party he wanted. He wrote in 1924 that from Imola to Leghorn the communist fraction had limited itself "to formal questions, purely logical questions, matters of pure coherence, and afterwards, having created the new party, did not know how to continue on its specific mission, that of winning the majority of the proletariat." Even with hindsight he felt that the only explanation he could give for his actions and those of the party after Leghorn was that they were compelled to take them as matters of life and death. After Leghorn "we entered the realm of necessity". Events had overwhelmed the man who had once said that the real utopians were those who did not see history as free development. This is crucial in understanding the development of Gramsci's thought from this time on.

IX

The years 1919-1920 had been of *crucial* importance in Gramsci's intellectual and theoretical development. We can distinguish two distinct, consecutive states of development in these years. First, a period when he was concerned with the factory councils, and then a period when he was concerned with the councils and the party. In the first period his experience with the factory councils taught him once and for all that the fundamental mode of creating *class-consciousness* was through the practical activity of organizing the workers in a "conciliar activity", through which their possibilities would become "visible", and theory "realized". This acquisition in his understanding marked a break from the "Crocean" position he had held before the practical experience of 1919-1920, where he had believed that the fundamental task was to inculcate a *class-consciousness* (in the wide sense) into the workers through an educative activity, which, by itself, was futile, since it sought to make "visible" a society which did not yet exist and left theory "unreal". By grasping the notion that it is in changing the world practically that class-consciousness is created, he became a revolutionary socialist — on truly marxist ground — for the first time. Henceforth, the *Theses on Feuerbach*, these brilliant germs of a new world view, became favourite references with Gramsci. More importantly, after 1920 he devoted himself to political practice, organizing for the overthrow of the capitalist state as a communist leading cadre.

Even in early 1920 he *may* have believed that the creation of class-consciousness through conciliar activity was all that there was to making a revolution,[603] though there is much evidence that he always believed that the existing State power would have to be overthrown by force. It is certain that his political practice in the factories brought him face to face with the problem of the party and the crucial role it would have to play in the overthrow of the State. Consequently the second stage of his theoretical development in these years was towards the realization that there is no single aboriginal practice which will bring capitalism tumbling down. By late 1920 the party had become just as important as the

155

factory council for Gramsci's world view.

Since the primacy of revolutionizing practice like that carried on through the councils is simply a marxist fundamental, many writers have argued that Gramsci's theory really starts when he started to consider the role of the party. A similar argument in the case of Lenin or Mao Tse-tung would be that their theory starts only where the contribution of Marx himself in their workings ends. Though in one sense true, in practice such an argument obscures more than it enlightens — especially if its culmination is that Gramsci is concerned theoretically only with the party after 1920. We can readily concede that Gramsci's interests moved from the issue of how class-consciousness is raised through a proletarian practice to a concern with the role of the party. What we cannot concede is that the concern with class-consciousnesss — conciliar activity — is left behind when he starts to interest himself in the party. The break with earlier concerns comes between his "Crocean" period and his "factory council" period. After that his theory is made up of a combination of his experiences, and concerns the lessons learnt in 1919-1920 both about raising mass consciousness and about the role of the party.

We have shown that he held two views about the party in 1920: that it was no more than the agent of the masses without whom no revolution could be made, and that the party could conduct the revolution almost by itself. These views corresponded with a rejection of the "abstentionist" position before September 1920, and an acceptance of the same position for reasons of *force majeure* after September. He makes quite clear that only the first view was really *his* view and, as we will see, it re-emerged later, when left unity was not apparently the overriding consideration. [604]

Viewed only in its first formulation the role of the party is quite different from that ascribed to it by Lenin in *What is to be Done?* and in Bordiga's many statements.[605] Gramsci believed, though he had not articulated this belief in a coherent fashion, that the role of the party was limited to leading the assault on the State, for which it was indispensable. It would never convert the workers to socialism through propaganda. Such "class-consciousness' was raised in a separate, though linked, practice of direct organization of the mass at the place of work. Gramsci, of course, was not thinking of a mindless activism or organization — socialists with concrete theory and goals would be encouraging the organisation. Later — much later — he was simply to deny that there was any such thing as "spontaneous" activity, at any place in any time. The party's educative role, in the traditional sense of propaganda, was therefore limited to the complementary creation of "revolutionary consciousness" among those who already believed that they could make their own destinies but found it quite another matter to assault the State's armed might in a decisive battle. Trotsky and Lenin had also realized this practical distinction in 1917.

Gramsci's failure in 1919-1920 — and that of the Italian socialist movement — was that he had realized the importance of each practice in a chronological order where they should have accompanied each other contemporaneously from the beginning, so that not only were the workers ready to run the new socialist society, but also so that the party was united in its determination to smash the bourgeois State when the possibility of occupation arose. He realized that this was his failure by 1924, if not earlier, because he bewailed his failure to organize to win the party until such activity was too late: "In 1919-1920 we made bad mistakes which we are paying for at present. We did not create a fraction, nor try to organize it throughout Italy for fear of being called *arrivistes* and careerists. We were not willing to give the sort of autonomous leadership to the Turin factory councils which would have been capable of exerting enormous influence throughout the country because we feared that there would be a split in the unions — that we would be expelled too soon from the PSI. We should, or at least I should, publicly admit having made mistakes whose repercussions have been far from light. In truth, if after the April split we had taken up positions which I thought necessary even then, we might perhaps have arrived at a situation different from that of the factory occupation and could have put it off until a more suitable time.[606]

1920-24 were years of practical activity which confirmed in Gramsci the views of council and party which he had started to develop before the factory occupation, years when the lessons of the *rivoluzione mancata* were maturing in him, though he had no time to write about those lessons in a thematic form.

CHAPTER IV

"...an International Figure?"

I

To his belief that history was men making their own destinies, and his realisation that making history the right way could not be achieved through "cultural messianism" or reliance on the spontaneous development of revolutionary consciousness in the proletariat, but only in a united revolutionary practice of changing the world, Gramsci had added a new ingredient to his world view. By 1921 he realised that the autonomous activity of the mass was not sufficient on its own for the overthrow of capitalism; there had to be a party acting on a national level to coordinate and organise the activity in the workplaces of the proletariat. Moreover, the addition of the idea of the party coincided with his being brought face to face with the obduracy of the objective world: with the realm of necessity. As a consequence the new theme of the party in Gramsci's writings is thought not only in terms of the subjective agent of change but also as an objective factor in an objective world. Rather than the new ingredient, the party, it is his new way of looking at the world which is important. We have come face to face in 1920-21 with the beginnings of a new as yet untheorised, unconscious, problematic in Gramsci's work. The "philosopher of praxis" begins to leave that issue behind as a truism of Marxism as defeat forces him to concern himself with the question: "Why can men not make their own destinies?" rather than how they can, and this leads to a concern with the sociology of praxis and a concern with historical materialism. In sum, Gramsci starts to come to terms with his "erstwhile philosophical conscience".

We can typify the stages in this new development as follows. The concern with the party started in 1920 as a concern with the issue of leadership in a revolutionary situation and epoch, and consequently with the coordination and organisation of all the impulses

158

towards liberation taken partially and isolatedly by men caught up in the contradictions of capitalism, but it developed in 1921 in its objective aspect into a concern with the problem of the complex structures whereby such initiatives were articulated into a national action.[607] This concern directed Gramsci's attention to the following questions, though in no unified or integrated fashion; 1) what was it in the structures of bourgeois societies which defeated initiatives by the working class, that is, what is it in the multiple articulation of different initiatives which turns attempts at history as free development into a foregone conclusion of defeat? How is the desire to be free annulled by forces outside the actors?[608] 2) what is the main locus of cohesion in a society which is threatening to break apart because of its contradictions? and 3) where, therefore, should the main blow be struck in addition to acting on the principle that "...in revolutionary action, what counts more than any oral or written propaganda is the direct experience of the mass, the spontaneity of initiatives of the mass itself?"[609] We cannot understand the full impact of these questions unless we remember that they were based on two assumptions already established in 1919-20 underlying the answers he gave to these questions in 1921, which explain the answers themselves. First, while he was very critical of the PSI leadership, he did not regard the leaders as solely responsible for PSI failure — he also regarded the conditions of the mass at the base as responsible for the leadership itself. He explained the state of the leadership by the whole structure of the party and the society, and thus dialectically regarded the masses as partly responsible for their leaders' shortcomings.[610] We cannot ascribe this global condemnation of Italian socialism merely to Gramsci's Crocean morality, or to some personal disillusion which had no base in fact, or to lack of feeling for the proletariat itself.[611] The failure of the occupation in September was similarly analysed by Klara Zetkin, who wrote: "I see something more, comrades, that is, that the masses who had risen in Italy had made no greater progress than their leaders, otherwise, had the masses been truly animated with revolutionary feeling, had they been conscious, they would that day have taken no notice of the decisions of the existing party leadership and the trade union officials and would have engaged in political struggle."[612] Gramsci's first assumption was rooted in the theoretical assumption that only the whole could explain the part and that separate issues like the problem of leadership could only be explained by the whole ensemble of social relationships.

Second, he assumed that in Italy State power had collapsed to the degree that it played an insignificant part in holding the society together and that what held the society together should be sought on the level of civil society rather than the State.[613]

Given these assumptions, we realise that the answers he gives to the questions provoked by the issue of leadership, were limited at this stage to answers on the level of civil society alone, and do not concern the issue of the State and the relationship of the revolutionary party to the State. We will attempt to make clear in the account of the beginnings of a new problematic in Gramsci that it is not a new factor which is of importance nor that he has given up his old views but that he is looking at all his concerns, old and new, in a new way.

Readers will recall that Gramsci saw the main problem of the PSI in May 1920 as owing to lack of contact, or "immersion" of the leadership in the life of the working-class. Conversely he saw the salvation of the party as something which came about when that immersion took place and in a united praxis the masses and the leadership purged each other of their respective failings. Gramsci was then writing of the party in the dimension of the subjective agent of change only, while this was apparently still considered possible by him. By late 1920 and early 1921 the PSI was completely discredited — finished in all senses — and it became possible for him to view it in terms of the structural reasons for its failure. Thus where in mid-1920 he repeatedly pointed to the "lackeys" of capitalism in its ranks who made it the agent of capitalism[614] with a view to having them expelled, he was now concerned in 1921 to explain how they had managed to avoid that fate in structural terms. This meant considering the bureaucracy of the party, in its static (composition) rather than its dynamic aspects (function). It was the bureaucracy of the party which had remained isolated "from the life and activities of the branches, organisms and individual members", and therefore provoked the lack of homogeneity in the party (an "assembly" not an "association"). Who or what, then, was this bureaucracy? Gramsci had already decided that "parties were no more than the nomenclature of the social classes", and this meant that to answer the question about the bureaucracy, he went outside the mere issue of names and positions and decided they were: "those degenerate currents of socialism who have become rotten through their parasitism on the State",[615] who believed in advancing an aristocracy of Northern workers against the interests of the South.

They were the proletariat's "petty bourgeoisie", whose ideology was no different from that of the "petty-bourgeoisie" who worked for capitalism. "We find the same element of unbridled vanity (the proletariat is the greatest force, the proletariat is invincible, nothing can stop the proletariat in its fatal march forward) and the same element of international ambition without an exact understanding of the historical forces which dominate the life of the world, without the capacity to identify their own role and function in the world system."[616]

Having identified the bureaucracy with the petty-bourgeoisie Gramsci went on soon after to further indicate what petty-bourgeoisie meant for him. It was "a purely political class" which specialised in "parliamentary cretinism". Originally it was called 'the coming to power of the left', it became *giolittismo*, ... swelled into socialist reformism [and most recently had become fascism]. "The petty-bourgeoisie is enmeshed in parliamentary institutions, ... parliament becomes a shop for scandals and gossip, becomes a means for parasitism.... *After having corrupted and ruined the institution of parliament, the petty-bourgeoisie corrupts and ruins the other institutions as well, the fundamental pillars of state: the army, the police and the magistracy."*[617]

At first, he identified fascism, of which more will be said, "as the last 'show' offered by the urban petty-bourgeoisie in the theatre of national life", but by March 1921 he identified the rural bourgeoisie as the backbone of fascism. This is important, whether it is right or wrong, because the rural petty-bourgeoisie were also widely known as "intellectuals" and Gramsci had used the term interchangeably.[618]

For the first time Gramsci had identified, if only in passing, the "intellectuals" as a "purely political class" divorced from production and specialising in compromises, deals and fixing matters up (*sistemazione, combinazione*). They provided the cadres not only for the State machine but for all institutions in that State and were clearly the cohesive element who kept the whole of capitalism functioning.

How? There is no substantial evidence at this time that Gramsci had considered deeply the mode of their activity or asked himself how they had such influence. Moreover he usually saw their role as entirely negative, and stated time and time again in 1920 and early 1921 that the failure of the PSI was due to its two (or more) class basis and that the PCI would be entirely working-class. But we can at least infer further that he thought that the petty-bourgeoisie was able to function in this fashion because the mass let them do so. Each explained the other in an unresolved, untranscendent relationship. We can further indicate that he thought the most important aspect of the masses' activity which allowed this intellectual dominance, was what he called *sovversismo*. *Sovversismo* had two linked qualities: on the one hand it was a tendency to mindless violence or use of force to solve problems, and on the other, a tendency in the working-class to see "everything rosily" and to like "songs and fanfares more than sacrifices".[619] It first had found expression in Bakuninism, and in Mussolini's and the PSI's readiness to "loose the horde". It was the mindless, disorganised violence of the romantic which Gramsci had condemned continually since *Democrazia operaia* was written. Although these themes were not drawn together systematically by Gramsci, we find evidence in these words that he was drawing positive conclusions about where the main blow should be struck by revolutionaries: "It is necessary to substitute a communist personnel for the bourgeois personnel in all the vital and dynamic functions of national life organised in the State". He wondered whether the working-class had the people to do this, and warned that because it was not something done in a day through forming a communist party, the working-class should concentrate on training such cadres.[620]

It has been argued by Togliatti that these views have strong similarities with those of Lenin,[621] and so we now turn to look at what influence the work of Lenin had on Gramsci in 1919-21. This is a particularly important issue because the PCI orthodoxy is that Gramsci became a Leninist in these years, and that he retained of his earlier ideas only a disdain for facility and a love of precision in reasoning after espousing the Russian's theory.[622] Since it is sometimes argued that all Lenin's work constitutes Lenin's theory without any weight given to particular parts, we point out that Togliatti meant by Leninism the following works: *What is to be Done? One Step Forward Two Steps Back, Two Tactics of Social Democracy; Imperialism, the Highest Stage of Capitalism; The State and Revolution; The Proletarian Revolution and the Renegade Kautsky; The Development of Capitalism in Russia* and *Materialism and Empirio-Criticism*, all of which Gramsci had read by 1922 according to Togliatti.[623] What of it is correct?

There is little doubt that by 1919 Lenin had an unparalleled stature among Marxists and that Gramsci, like the rest of Turin's socialists, anxiously sought for accounts about him and for his writings.[624] Yet these were particularly difficult to find in Italian. Gramsci himself rebuked the PSI in May 1920 for not translating Lenin's work although it was available in French, English and German by this time. So bad were the available translations, Gramsci claimed, that they were almost incomprehensible in many cases.[625] It was this that prompted him to arrange for Leonetti and Togliatti to translate the first edition of Lenin's work available in Italy. This appeared in July 1920.[626]

So until 1921 what Lenin Gramsci knew did not come from Italy, or Italian sources. He and his friends themselves translated what there was in Italian from French sources. Pia Carena spent much of her time on *Ordine Nuovo* engaged in these translations.[627] We have a precise list of the major sources. *La Vie Ouvrière* (1919-1920); *Le Phare* (1919-1920); *Demain* (1919-1920); *La Nouvelle Internationale* (1919-1920; *Le Bulletin Communiste* (1920); *La Revue Communiste* (1920) and *Clarté* (1920).[628] According to Leonetti, *Vie Ouvrière* was the most important source of his information. This journal started to reappear on 30 April 1919, a month before the first issue of *Communist International*, the official journal of the Comintern, which we can dismiss as a source of Lenin's major writings in these years.[629] It bore the face of Pierre Monatte, again one of those men of conscience so dear to Gramsci.[630] But "the thought of our groups is a combination of syndicalism and Bolshevism" and what it received of Leninism it adapted in a revolutionary-syndicalist fashion. Moreover, it received scant news of Leninism, or matters Russian before May 1920, when Monatte himself proclaimed that he had only had one letter from Russia to that time.[631]

This is indeed the crux of the problem with Gramsci's reputed Leninism in 1919-1920. Contacts with Russia were so bad until late in 1920 that very little information reached even Gramsci's French sources in those years. Of course, the situation started to improve in 1921.[632]

We turn to *Clarté*, which was supposedly the second most important source for Gramsci's Leninism. *Clarté*, the journal of Henri Barbusse, one of Gramsci's favourite authors and personally known to him in 1920, only started to appear in 1920, and carried its first significant writings on Russia in the August issue.[633] These did not include the major writings of Lenin. By March 1921 works like Lenin's *Right-wing and Counter-Revolutionary Socialism* were being published as communication with the USSR improved.

The only other journals on the list which we need pay attention to as sources for understanding Lenin in 1919-20 are Henri Guilbeaux' *Demain* and Boris Souvarine's *Bulletin Communiste* since Henrietta Rolland-Holst who had known and corresponded with Lenin for years wrote for them. She was also one of the main "letter-boxes" for communications between the Bolsheviks and the West. Amsterdam was, however, to become discredited by early 1920.[634] She, and these journals, presumably became no better informed than the others after that date.

In sum, the French "sources" of Gramsci's Leninism only provided scrappy and occasional information about the thought of the Russian leader in 1919-1920. Indeed, there is some evidence that Lenin did not approve or approved only halfheartedly of the position of either *Vie Ouvrière*, *Clarté*, or the journals Holst was associated with. If the first was associated with any figure in Russia it was with Trotsky.[635] Of course, it can be argued quite tenably, (but a departure from Togliatti's meaning), that the other Bolshevik leaders held the same views as Lenin or transmitted them to the West unintentionally.[636] This is important since the main spokesmen and writers for the Comintern were Zinoviev and Trotsky. For Gramsci Leninism thus becomes the unconscious readaptation of Lenin's thought by these men, a Leninism reduced to the manifestoes and slogans of the Communist International, or the cultural politics of Lunacharsky. Significantly, the crucial text on the role of the party and the intellectuals, *What is to be Done?* is reduced to an unimportant role in this scenario. The main picture of the Russian Revolution and "Leninism" is that of a "sovietist" theory. This was most clearly *the* view reaching Gramsci through these journals and the *Communist International*, until September 1921 and he indicated that it came through quite clearly.[637] The *New Communist Manifesto* of March 1919, which was written by Trotsky, indicated the pattern of material which would come through to Italy in 1919-1920. (It was translated into Italian.) It ran *inter alia*: "In this realm of destruction [the post-war period] where not only the means of production and exchange but also the institutions of political democracy lie in bloody ruins, the proletariat must create its own apparatus, designed first and foremost to bind together the working class and to ensure the possibility of its revolutionary intervention in the further development of mankind. This apparatus is the workers' Soviets. The old parties, the old trade unions, have in the persons of their leaders proved incapable of carrying out, even of understanding, the tasks presented by the new epoch. The proletariat has created a new kind of apparatus, which embraces the entire working-class regardless of occupation or political maturity, a flexible apparatus capable of continual renewal and extension, of drawing broader and broader strata into its orbit, opening its doors to the working people in town and country who stand close to the proletariat. This irreplaceable organisation of working-class government, of its struggle, and later of its conquest of State power has been tested in the experience of various countries and represents the greatest achievement and mightiest weapon of the proletariat of our time...."[638]

This was the sort of view reinforced by the many eye-witness accounts which *Ordine Nuovo* published and which Gramsci frequently referred to in the next eighteen months. John Reed's *Ten Days that Shook the World* was published in its entirety, and so were reports from Rapaport, Droz, Zetkin, Pankhurst and Ransome. Sometimes they were prefaced by approving or explanatory notes by one of the editors. Although there were many hostile views available by late 1920 which stressed the autocratic methods used by the USSR, Gramsci always defended the USSR as a true step forward in democratic liberties.[639] So much did he see the Soviet Union in "conciliar" terms in 1919-1920 that he equated the view of Lenin, Luxemburg, Pannekoek [and Gorter]. We read for example very late in 1920, these lines

"The syndicalist tendencies of *Ordine Nuovo* are also a myth: we simply make the mistake of believing that only the masses can make the revolution, that a party secretary or a president cannot make it through decrees; it seems that this was the opinion of Karl Marx and Rosa Luxemburg, and the opinion of Lenin."[640]

He defended the activities of *Ordine Nuovo* as the expression of Bolshevik theory, although the party had no place in this theory for him, and referred to Zinoviev and Bukharin and Radek's work.[641] To reinforce this notion of Gramsci's "Leninism" as a "sovietist" theory, in which the importance of the party was negligible, is the fact that the only work he had clearly mastered by the middle of 1920 and endorsed (whence he appears to have obtained those notions of affinity) was the famous *State and Revolution*. This work is a "sovietist" interpretation of how revolution is made *par excellence*. It is so different in tone from other writings of Lenin, that it has even been claimed as "libertarian",[642] to some extent. While the main theme is that the bourgeois state must be seized and destroyed and then replaced by a proletarian semi-state" in which "cooks would rule the state" since the only real task would be one of administration and accounting which even the inexpert could do, the document stresses heavily its inspiration in Marx's writings on the Commune and on the necessity of a mass involvement in overthrowing the State and running the new "semi-state".[643] Moreover, Togliatti, and Paggi argues, Gramsci too, understood it as being the *State and Liberty*, as Togliatti's preface makes clear, thus connecting it with the Hegelian notion that each state would mark a further stage in the development of liberty.[644]

Yet there was one new dimension to this "sovietism" which came through with greater and greater force in Gramsci's writings in 1919-1920: imperialism. Nearly all his French sources shared the sort of orientation expressed by Rosmer: "The new International has deep roots. In it we found all of those who have formed a resistance since the great weakness of 1914, and whom we later met at Zimmerwald and Kienthal".[645] It was therefore an anti-imperialist, anti-war Leninism which they advanced, laying especial emphasis on imperialism as the cause of war. Gramsci tended to confuse Lenin's view on the nature of imperialism with those of Hilferding, and did not believe that the era of monopoly bank capital meant that the revolution would have to be fought outside the factories, but by early 1921 he was tending more and more to insert national problems into the wider-context of international and supranational links.[646] This idea was also something he had been evolving autonomously.

We can only conclude that in 1919-1920 Gramsci saw the Russian Revolution and what he imagined its theory to be as a confirmation of his own attitudes. It thus followed that his Lenin was still the man who wrote "against *Capital*", and that Togliatti's admission that matters were "neither simple nor clear" in those days, is only too true. The Lenin Gramsci knew advanced no real role for the party until at least the arrival of the letter of August 1920 in late September.[647] Even this letter suggested that revolutionary movements started from below, and the party's task was to "generalise, and give watchwords". Moreover, Gramsci lumped Lenin together with the men Lenin was already condemning because they did not realise the importance of the political assault on the State and therefore the importance of the Party. Indeed, we can only assume that Gramsci took only what suited him from Lenin, seeing him as the practical revolutionary, and not a leading theoretician. How else could we explain Gramsci's assertion that Lenin had taken over the theories of Rosa Luxemburg and Hilferding, or agreed with Pannekoek *after* he had read the *State and Revolution*?[648]

Before proceeding with our tale, it is perhaps worthwhile noting that many of the French journals which Gramsci read were cultural in orientation, and associated with earlier heroes like Rolland and Barbusse.[649] *Clarté*, for example, saw the task of intellectuals this way: "The struggle of ideas has replaced the struggle of material forces. It is no less fiery. It takes on the same bloody forms little by little. But it is more important, more profound, because it goes back to the cause of all existing institutions."[650] Presumably the reason Gramsci read them was because they confirmed his already developed views, and that these were a continuing theme in his thought.[651] In turn, his novel ideas about the role of "intellectuals" had nothing to do with those in Lenin's *What is to be Done?*, at this early stage of their development. When he was again able to take them up explicitly some few years later, he, of course, knew Leninism well. In the intervening years, the demands of practical work prevented his examining these ideas further.

II

Gramsci certainly understood Lenin as the practitioner of revolution *par excellence* by the beginning of 1921, and must certainly have agreed with the letter sent by the Comintern to rebuke the PSI which said: "In Italy there are at hand all the most important conditions for a *genuinely popular great proletarian revolution*. This must be understood. This must be the starting point. This is the contention of the Communist International. The Italian comrades must themselves determine the next step." The Comintern then went on to distinguish between this generalisation and the particularity, stating that since Bologna the situation was not optimal in any immediate sense, and that by September 1920 "the Italian bourgeoisie are already not quite so helpless as they were a year ago".[652] These views corresponded closely with those Gramsci had expressed at the beginning of the occupation. They are worth noting as they establish a fundamental distinction in

Gramsci's thought as well as the Comintern's between a revolutionary *epoch* and a revolutionary *situation*. Both would continue to agree that the epoch was revolutionary, but differ in their assessment of the situation.

When Gramsci returned to Turin after the foundation of the PCI to work in the new communist branch, he still claimed that the period was one of "a regime in collapse", still blamed the PSI's failures on its "blind belief" in the mass, and still argued that the main task in winning the revolution was that of organisation as he had beforehand.[653] This meant that he was still not completely pessimistic about the revolutionary situation. Moreover he still thought that the factory council would be the main mode of organising the masses. In February 1921 he wrote:

"Through the struggle for control — a struggle which is not coordinated in Parliament but is a revolutionary struggle of the masses and a propagandist and organisational activity of the historical party of the working-class, the Communist Party, — the working class must acquire, spiritually and as an organisation, an awareness of its autonomy and its historical personality. That is why the first stage presents itself as a struggle for a particular form of organisation. This form or organisation can be nothing else but the factory council, the nationally-centralised organisation of the factory councils. This struggle must have as its result a national council of the working-class which is elected at all levels, from factory council to urban council to national council with procedures and a system decided by the workers themselves not by the National Parliament, and not by the power of the bourgeoisie. This struggle must be conducted so as to show the great mass of the population that all the problems of existence in the present historical period, the problems of bread, housing, light, clothing, can only be solved when all economic power, and therefore all political power, has passed into the hands of the working-class, that is, must be conducted so as to organise around the working-class all the popular forces in revolt against the capitalist regime; so that the working-class becomes the effective ruling class and can guide all productive forces to freedom through the implementation of the communist programme. This struggle must serve to make the working-class capable of choosing from its midst the most capable and energetic elements and to make them the new industrial leaders, its new guides in the work of economic reconstruction."[654]

The prospects of this optimistic programme already looked dim in Turin. Since November 1920 a recession had been taking place in industry and several large national firms would soon collapse, unable to support the problems of peacetime production. Despite the undertakings given that militants would not be sacked as a result of their activity in the September occupation, many were already being sacked. As unemployment grew rapidly militancy died down and Giolitti's proposal for co-gestion gained favour. Faced with Gramsci's insistence that the solution still lay in the factory councils and in "vast assemblies" of working people to discuss what to do about the cost of living, the factory councils continued to survive with difficulty. To carry out aggressive policies then proved too much. In March, Fiat dismissed 14 thousand workers, including nearly all the militants working in the factories. They were "thrown out into the darkness and lack of certainty about the morrow". The government filled the factories with troops, revealing that the days of occupations were over, and the workers were obliged to surrender unconditionally.[655] Gramsci recognised then that this marked the end of the dreams of 1918-20 that a revolution would soon start in the factory. He pointed back to the criticism he had made of the PSI in May 1920, blaming that party for the end of revolution in Italy, and excusing the men for their submission in moving and compassionate terms which some of them never forgot.[656]

Like all men who had internalised the ethics of Croce's *Filosofia della pratica*, he also blamed himself. "...it is our fault for not having understood for two years what the development of the movement would be; it is our fault for having let too much time go by and for not having put an audacious stop to the fatal *andare delle cose*."[657] Although the *commissioni interne* struggled on for two more years, never quite smashed even under Mussolini, [658] Gramsci recognised that their situation had changed. The main problem was henceforth one of survival in face of the style of violent activity which characterised Italy, and for which the PSI emphasis on *sovversismo* was partly responsible.[659] In an analysis of the trade unions prepared for the Second Congress of the PCI in 1922 he indicated that: "The events which took place in Italy after September 1920 had nothing unexpected or exceptional about them: they were prepared by the whole preceding period so that it was not the events which destroyed the masses, but rather the latter and through it the political party which failed the events".[660] After the defeat in Turin in April fascism triumphed in that city too despite the workers' moral superiority, and Gramsci had to be accompanied everywhere by a giant bodyguard, Giacomo Bernolfo.[661] Even *Ordine Nuovo* became, like other party offices, heavily guarded.

Gramsci's forced admission that the situation was no longer revolutionary, whatever the character of the epoch, did not throw him back onto a position of seeking an alliance with the socialists. Rather, it redoubled his hatred of the PSI and its leaders, on whom he blamed the whole defeat of the labour movement. He made his position quite clear in his speeches at the first regional PCI congress at the Teatro Chiaberra, Savona, on 20-26 March, 1921. His strongly "anti-socialist" speech was reported like this:

"In Italy we had an example of a 'revolutionary' party which had cut itself off from the International and this fact had immediately been exploited by the Russian counter-revolutionaries to make the working masses believe that henceforth the power of the Soviets was abandoned and disowned by those people who were the first to recognise and extol them. The gravity of the situation was such that it should drive Communists to the greatest fervour, discipline and spirit of sacrifice. The task of the Ligurian Communists was particularly onerous, especially in Genoa, where, before anywhere else, there the counter-revolutionary and petty-bourgeois tendencies of social-democracy had developed, which created worker aristo-cracies and did not lead the struggle for the overthrow of capitalist society."[662]

By the middle of the year his attacks on "Barnum's Circus" (the PSI) and its leaders had become particularly savage as they responded by malicious and untrue personalities, even asserting that Gramsci had volunteered and fought for the *Arditi* in the First World War. Serrati, in particular, whom Gramsci had formerly respected and to whom he had felt beholden, felt Gramsci's venom. Gramsci, whom observers noted was not over-concerned with dress and cleanliness, made much of the fact that Serrati "stupidly, though not dishonestly" had borrowed money through a police spy and set himself up in bourgeois style with fine furniture and drapes.[663] If anything, Gramsci although now relegated to the role of a "regional leader" loyal to the leader Bordiga, was the most subtle and bitter communist critic of the PSI, and continually pointed out the affinities between socialism and fascism.

This hostility towards the other working class party was accompanied by public professions of belief in the PCI, though his private feelings about the party were not unmixed.[664] He extolled the party as the only solution to the chaos and defeat which faced the working-class, and despite the unexpected smallness of its membership he continued to demand that it remain a pure party of the proletariat providing the leadership necessary for the only solution possible: the revolutionary overthrow of the bourgeois state. He typified the situation as "catastrophic" and publicly proclaimed that a "miraculous" victory of the proletarian party like that of Garibaldi's thousand might be possible.[665] However, we may doubt that he really expected this, despite his claims that the class struggle was not a matter of numbers.[666] Both the masses and the man himself needed some sort of reassurance in times which called for "sacrifice".

This ambivalence towards the PCI in 1921 was what would eventually separate him from Bordiga for though in 1921 both considered the PSI was the worst enemy of the revolution, they differed over how to best cope with the situation politically and organisationally. This difference depended in turn on their differing assessments of fascism. So we turn first to Gramsci's experience of the party, and then to his experience of fascism.

III

The PCI had won 58,000 votes at Leghorn. It started its life, if not with the support of the greatest part of Italian socialists, as Zinoviev had anticipated, at least with reports that there had been unexpected support from all over the country.[667] But it emerged fairly quickly as the new party faced numerous fascist attacks on its members and offices,[668] that nothing like the mass of former socialists were going to join it, and that it was grossly optimistic to hope for even 58,000 members. Moreover, even those who did nominally become communists, often left the party soon after, causing a decline in the first quarter of 1921 in the numerical strength of the PCI much like that being experienced by the PSI. This decline in members was paralleled by a communist collapse in the factory councils and trade unions as well.[669] Most alarming were the defections either to the PSI or the fascist PNF. When Gramsci's own brother Mario joined the *fasci* of Varese Gramsci even paid him a visit to see if he could dissuade him from taking this course.[670] This decline in support was matched by a decline in the circulation of the newspapers throughout 1921. The newspapers also lost their verve as Gramsci and his group were dispersed around the country.

In the face of this decline, quite marked and obvious after the disastrous results for the communists in the elections in May 1921,[671] Bordiga maintained a firm commitment to the political position he was to expound in the celebrated Rome theses of 1922. In practice this meant that he did little to countervail the decline through organising the party so that the defections would fall off and recruiting improve. In a somewhat symbolic way the various party offices became forts in which the "true faith" remained cut off from the masses. While Gramsci constantly wrote explanations and excuses for these failures, he was not happy about the failure to maintain contact with the masses because he still believed in spite of the defeats of April and May that the factory councils were essential to revolution and he and Tasca were involved in trade union and press work.[672] He was able to take advantage of the sensible decision of the PCI's foundation conference not to split the unions, to advance the idea of a united front "from below", in particular with the anarchist USI. This meant that he was not following so "purist" a line as Bordiga for whom the "true faith" were the only people who mattered.

Bordiga was developing more and more into the theoretician *par excellence* — a man with a vision — while Gramsci was tending to become an organiser. This experience had its effects. While Gramsci's targets were various: the PSI, Mussolini, the masses; he started to repeat certain arguments again and again after the middle of 1921. First, that no revolution could be made without extensive organisational preparation for the post-revolutionary society and state. Second, that the idea that small groups could take power without such preliminary work (*Blanquism*), was the obverse of *sovversismo*. Third, that the *sovversismo* of the masses was therefore to be deprecated rather than lauded.[673]

Yet it must be admitted that these arguments only become important when seen in the light of later developments. They did not derogate from his "leftism" in 1921, which was the direct opposite of the policy then being laid down by the Communist International on party and tactical matters.

The Communist International had been revising its policies since the failure of the 1921 March action in Germany. At that time it had expelled Paul Levi for claiming that the attempt to take power was no more than a "leftist" putsch.[674] But it could not escape the judgment he had made as the German party immediately divided into a "left" and a "right" on the issue, showing that the issue was not finished. Faced with the problems of the triumph of reaction in the West and allied problems for the new Soviet State, Lenin and Radek started to speak guardedly in favour of the "right" of the German party, which now included Zetkin, Lenin's close friend. Some of the International, in particular Zinoviev, appear to have taken a more "left" position. The debate was particularly important for the PCI as Levi had attended the Leghorn conference and opposed a "split to the left". The German "left" on the other hand had supported Bordiga and Gramsci, and they were now out of step with Lenin, no matter how popular they had been with him in 1919-20. The issue would obviously be debated at the Third Comintern Congress, due to start at the end of June.

The implications were not fully realised when the Italian delegation of Bordigans left on their twelve day journey to the USSR.[675] Terracini recalls the journey as a pilgrimage with "a shoemaker from Naples who jealously guarded in his little trunk two pairs of shoes of his own make which he refused to show to anyone — one man's, one lady's — which he intended to present to Lenin and Krupskaya; a barber from Caserta who had his own definite opinion of Lenin's beard, and lastly a farm-hand from Tuscany, who, having learned from Niccolini [the Comintern delegate accompanying the delegation] that Lenin presumably liked Chianti, had bought a bottle of this wine in an Italian shop in Berlin."[676] Terracini, typified as a combative politician by Gobetti,[677] certainly came full of respect for Lenin but not *dona ferens*. In a statement which again suggests that the PCI claim that Gramsci was a Leninist by 1921 is anachronistic, Terracini wrote of Lenin: "Until then I knew little of him and his activities. He was known more as a revolutionary than a Marxist theoretician".[678] Although Lenin greeted them warmly, his disapproval of their "leftism" was clear. The delegation faced the immediate practical consequence that the PSI delegation, which hoped to persuade the Comintern that PSI should not be expelled, might be successful. They quickly made common cause with the Germans to oppose the theses of Radek which would argue that the revolutionary wave was receding and that therefore the main object of communists should be to avoid isolation from the masses and seek a united front.[679] Knowing that Lenin would disapprove Terracini started his speech at the congress with some trepidation but gradually grew more and more forceful:

"In our opinion the theses of comrade Radek can serve only as a basis for discussion. It is necessary to reverse them immediately. ...We are of the opinion that we should not fight radical groups first, but that we should strike with more force against the right [...] We are of the opinion that the assertion regarding the need to win the greatest part of the working-class to communist principles can arouse misunderstanding in the parties [...] We think that we should not expect the bulk of the proletariat to be organised and accept communist principles as a prerequisite for taking revolutionary action [...] We think, on the contrary, that the working-class will only be educated by action of the party [...] In my opinion, a communist party will always be, and can only be, composed of the most active workers, until the moment that the struggle begins, or, rather, until the moment when it is almost won."[680]

After opening gently (in French) Lenin lashed the young Italian for his lack of realism, for his "leftist rubbish", pointing out that in the Soviet Union the majority of the soviets was with the party. It was infantile to think that anyone could make a revolution with a minority. What was necessary was "mass" support and by "mass" he meant the majority of the exploited in this case.[681] The perturbed Terracini watched the PSI delegation smile, sure after this rebuke that the PSI would be readmitted to the Comintern. "For a fleeting moment it even occurred to me that it would have been better if I had not gone to Gorki a few days before". "At the end of the session I found myself face to face with Lenin, 'Comrade Terracini' he said to me in French with a friendly and calm smile, 'we must be shrewd and wise'."[682] Terracini's confusion did not overcome his stubbornness. This contributed to a compromise solution, though Zinoviev may also not have wanted to admit that his decision to split the movement at Leghorn was wrong.[683] The Comintern finally agreed that the split was the correct action to take vis-à-vis the PSI, and that that party had continued to move to the right. It also told Maffi, Riboldi and Lazzari that the PSI would not be readmitted to the Comintern until the "reformists" were expelled from its ranks. Chastened, the delegation of Socialists announced that they would fight for the position of the Comintern in their party.

The result was that the "turn" to the right in Comintern policy was not made officially applicable to Italy. At most we can say with certainty that the whole of the Bordigan group and Gramsci were out of step with the opinions of the leaders of the Soviet Union, Lenin, Trotsky and others.[684]

By September the Socialist delegation was back in Italy and news of the new line arrived with them: it was understood to be an offer of a second chance to the "unitary" communist group of the PSI whom Gramsci, Bordiga and all and sundry in the PCI had been attacking savagely and personally, and whom they blamed for the misery of the working class condition in Italy. On 19 September Bordiga sent off a tart letter to the Comintern to the effect that it was a waste of time to assume that any real communists were left in the PSI or that there would be any reunification.[685]

We can find no evidence whatsoever that Gramsci disagreed with Bordiga on this issue, though there were continuing disagreements in other areas. All through August and September Gramsci continued to attack the "centrists" of the PSI, "the demagogic parrot" Serrati,[686] and to blame all defeats of the PCI on the PSI:" "the socialist party is responsible for what is happening because its idiotic, blind tactics are solely responsible."[687] Its intransigents were working under a "lying label",[688] and its leaders were not even honest.[689] Gramsci also poured out articles arguing that numbers and figures did not matter but that the PCI was in fact growing while the maximalists declined in strength.[690]

When the PSI started to prepare for its congress to be held in Milan between 10-15 October 1921, Gramsci wrote a particularly scathing article in which he pointed out that there were only 18,000 in the PSI who had nothing to lose by a split — the rest, all 62,000 of them, had jobs of some sort through the party. Only this explained the party's continuing mass base. The PSI was thus to be compared with the Bourbon regime described by Gladstone as the "Negation of God"; or with the bureaucracies of Tsarist Russia or Austro-Hungary. He was therefore extremely sceptical that anything would come from the meeting at Milan; at best Maffi and Riboldi might persuade some 10,000 to split off from the party. "The truth is that the socialist party is already dead and stinking."[691]

What the communists should concentrate on rather than concern about the mass, no matter how unpalatable the idea was to young members, was the substitution of counter-revolutionary officials by officials tightly disciplined by the Central Committee. Reality was a rebellious thing which had to be disciplined correctly.[692]

At the Milan congress of the PSI the efforts of Maffi had come to nought because nothing had been done organisationally by the *terzinternazionalista* group. When Serrati and Baratono declared flatly that they had nothing to add to their position at Leghorn: conditions in Italy were too different from those in Russia for the methods of revolution to be the same they had overwhelming support.[693] Zetkin and Walecki, who attended the Congress for the Comintern, though against the wishes of the PCI, merely repeated the Comintern's position but did not emphasise it.[694] Gramsci concluded that the whole party had been poisoned by social-reformism and that Lazzari was the *only* honourable man left in it.[695] As if to emphasise that Gramsci's position was not without reason, Zetkin also felt, after her observation of the goings-on at Milan, that the PSI was dead and that the PCI should be given full support in its efforts to build up its own strength.[696]

So strong was Gramsci's agreement with Bordiga on issues like this that he refused point blank a suggestion made in early October by Chiarini, the Comintern delegate, that he join the party leadership to control Bordiga and take his place. He was not going to take part in such backstairs intrigues.[697]

On 21 December this position put both Gramsci and Bordiga in direct disobedience towards the Comintern, which introduced a general policy of a united front for all parties. In Moscow Terracini stuck tenaciously to his guns in opposition to the new policy, which was justified by pious hopes like that of Radek that the "reformists were even moving a bit to the left".[698] (In fact they were soon to provoke a split in the PSI by half-offering to form a coalition government). Jules Humbert-Droz recalls that at the meeting of the enlarged EKKI in February 1922 Terracini spoke up strongly against the united front, asking "...should we abandon our principles to win the masses? We think that it would be possible for parties to win the masses by the methods advised by the Executive, but then we would not be Communist Parties, but only parties which in all senses are the same as the old social-democratic parties...." He opposed partial actions and called for generalised struggles. "Each time the socialist leaders try to start a partial action for a special claim, we oppose it and remind them of the need to generalise the struggle",[699] he went on. He concluded that to conduct joint action with the Socialists the Communists would have to give up part of their programme, and that the *joint* interests of the worker should be defended only in the unions.

Despite bitter criticism from Trotsky and Lunacharsky, which ensured that his motion was lost, Terracini was obdurate and refused to give the same undertaking to abide by Comintern discipline that the French delegates gave.[700]

Immediately after the meeting Droz, the new "rightwing" Comintern secretary[701] left for Italy, where the PCI had been preparing for its Second congress since October. The central isue at the congress would be the tactics which the party should adopt given the attitude of Lenin and others at the Third Comintern congress. The news of the enlarged EKKI meeting had not yet reached Italy but Gramsci almost certainly knew of the attitude of Lenin by the time the "Rome theses" began to be circulated in the party in late December, even though few of the rest of the party did.[702] Indeed, so long and thoughtful are Gramsci's and Tasca's theses on the trade union question which depended on the Rome theses that we are inclined to think that he must have seen the Rome theses already in October. The "Rome theses" were drawn up by Bordiga and Terracini and corresponded with the position Terracini took at the Moscow meeting. After a long speech in their favour by Gramsci they were adopted by the Turin section of the party.[703] Their substance is very important as they show, when put together with Gramsci's own theses on the trade unions, Gramsci's position in December 1921-April 1922.

The Rome theses stated that they took as their starting point the programme adopted at Leghorn that the proletariat could only take power violently through its political class party, which had emerged as an organic development of the proletariat at a particular stage of its history. This party, in its normal state, was completely homogeneous, disciplined and unchanging in the programme it presented to the masses, as this was essential to win them. It followed that bringing different views into the party was harmful even if it increased the members. This did not mean that the party should not be involved in the struggles of the proletariat. Rather it meant that it should have a dialectical and generalising relation to the everyday interests of the workers in their organisations. However, here a sharp distinction should be drawn between leaders and organisations on the one hand and the masses and individuals on the other. The party should only attempt to win support on the level of mass and individual and avoid attracting other organisations or boring from within them. As a party of formed revolutionaries it should intervene at moments of revolutionary *floridezza* to make the most of them.

Certain tactical principles followed from this view of the party. "The essential task of the Communist Party in the ideological and practical preparation of the proletariat for the revolutionary struggle for the dictatorship of the proletariat is pitiless criticism of the programme of the bourgeois left and of every programme which wishes to find the solution to social problems in bourgeois-democratic parliamentary institutions." The party should avoid like the plague concern for partial reforms, support for, or participation in, coalitions of the left, as this would retard the inevitable development of disillusion with parliamentary solutions. It should not defend any such coalition from the attacks of reaction. Not only should any united front be "from below" only but the party should not even preclude actions designed to harm its rivals.

Practically, since there were no more communists in the PSI, it followed that any adhesion to the PCI should be individual and not in a group.[704]

On the whole these theses reflected much more Bordiga's Mazzinian view of the party as a collection of "do or die" converts who had scant interest in the mass except as sacrificial victims (who would be carried to the revolution by social conditions anyway), than Gramsci's notion of the party as an "association" immersed in the masses. However, there were sections which argued in favour of working from the practical issues upwards and these provided the link with the theses which he and Tasca drew up. Although it is sometimes argued that the theses on trade union work were drawn up by Tasca, many of the themes in the Gramsci of 1921 reemerged clearly in the document. "Reformist" socialism was blamed for all the ills which had fallen upon the working-class movement and "reformism" was typified as a manifestation of the petty-bourgeoisie who serve capitalism.

What is important is how Gramsci expanded on the briefly touched-on links with the masses in the "Rome theses". He stressed that union work should be linked with that of the factory council which would be the main "critical" organ of working class He also indicated that as "the unification of the action of the great masses" was the fundamental problem of the party, the factory council was most important. Its importance was emphasised by the wave of reaction in 1920-1 when unity on basic interests in the working-class was essential in the face of the disunity petty bourgeois office-holders fostered. So, despite the immense difficulties posed by the existing situation: "The struggle for control represents for the councils the specific ground on which the working-class places itself at the head of the other oppressed classes of the population and succeeds in obtaining their consensus in its own dictatorship." In sum, only through the councils could the social collapse of the time be overcome.[705]

We have no record whether Droz spoke to Gramsci before the Congress at which these theses would be discussed, but he certainly found Bordiga and others he talked to even more intransigent than Terracini. Only when Terracini arrived from Moscow was he able to persuade the Italians that the "Rome theses" should only be the basis for tactics to be drawn up by the incoming Central Committee rather than adopted *sine die* as party policy.[706] As it was Droz faced a party united in support of the theses when the congress opened, though he blamed this on a deliberate policy of Bordiga that the membership not be informed of the new Comintern line.[707] Droz decided not to interfere although it became clear to the delegates that there was conflict between the party and the Comintern, causing some confusion in the minds of those present. The Rome theses were carried, and the same executive, which Droz typified "as entirely Bordigan in tendency" re-elected. A more moderate motion put by Tasca and Graziadei, suggesting a compromise between the party position and that of the Comintern, was lost. Significantly for this book, Gramsci was not one of those present moved by the Comintern delegates' speeches. He got up to say that he agreed with the theses presented by comrades Bordiga and Terracini and wanted to raise a problem for the consideration of the congress:[708] "the problem was that the Comintern's directions could cause the misunderstanding that the united front should extend to the PP [the Catholic Popular Party] where he thought that the PP and part of the PSI should not be included in any united front as both were bourgeois". He pointed out that what was done in Germany was irrelevant to Italy where conditions were different. Germany was an advanced capitalist country where the Socialist Party was based on the proletariat, where in Italy the PSI was two-class, drawing support from the proletariat and the peasants. The united front was only applicable in countries like Germany where a parliamentary majority could act as a defender of the more backward workers but "...with us the situation is different. If we launched the slogan of a workers' government and tried to put it into effect, we will go back to the old ambiguities of socialism, when the party was condemned to inactivity because it could not decide whether to be a party of the proletariat only or a

179

party of the peasantry only." It followed from this and from the cultural backwardness and confusion of the Italian situation, and the probability that the left of the PSI would oppose a united front anyway, that "general slogans about a united front should be avoided."[709]

Furthermore, after his return to Turin Gramsci reported on the congress in terms hostile to the postponement of a firm commitment to the "Rome theses". He pointed out: "the inconsistency of the principal objection raised by the opposers [of the theses] according to whom the theses presented by the Central Committee should not have been discussed or voted upon solely because there were points of divergence between them and those voted at the Executive meeting in Moscow..." and he explained why it was impractical to apply the united front in Italy in the same way as it had been applied in other countries, insisting that a united front could exist only *within the proletariat*, and, since the PCI was the only proletarian party in Italy, only within the PCI. Only the working-class proper could become communists as a class, though individual converts could, of course, be made among the peasantry. "The speaker ended by inviting the meeting to approve the position of the Central Committee, which at the congress maintained that the theses should be discussed and voted upon to show that the new Central Committee effectively represents the great majority of party members."[710]

It was doubtless this practical unity of view with the "left" which explained why the incoming Central Committee chose Gramsci as the new PCI representative on IKKI in Moscow.[711] Gramsci had opposed the line of Lenin and the Comintern throughout 1921-April 1922 as much as they had and there was no reason for anyone to expect that Gramsci would suddenly change his mind, even had one of his main characteristics not been "inertia".

IV

They had forgotten the man who lurked behind the politician. This was partly Gramsci's fault, since he himself had effaced his personality in 1919-22, crushing it with steely determination as he devoted himself to politics. If our account of these years has lost sight of the real, sensuous Gramsci, it is not because of some contempt for the trivialities of humanity, or because we have equated the man with his work in a fetishistic devotion to mind, but because Gramsci himself deliberately led a disciplined ritualised existence in these years, living like some robot worker. He was so much the professional revolutionary merged with his work that he even showed careless disregard for personal cleanliness and lived on cigarettes and coffee rather than on food.[712]

Yet behind the Crocean morality which dictated that men should be governed by the intellect and the will only, there still lay the man who had chosen this path partly because he had decided that he would never have a normal life because of his hunchback. "How many times I have asked myself if it was possible to tie myself to the mass of men when I have never loved anyone, not even my own family, if it were possible to love a collectivity if I had never been loved deeply myself by individual human beings?" "Wouldn't it have reflected on my life as a militant, wouldn't it have made my revolutionary qualities sterile and reduced them to merely intellectual matters, purely mathematical calculations?" were words he wrote in early 1924.[713]

As he himself intimated, this mortification of the flesh, this denial of his own feelings, was distorting his judgement and by 1921 it was becoming too much to take emotionally. His nervous tension showed through in irascibility and illness. "I saw him, small, diaphanous, two black, penetrating eyes which stared at me without moving. He spoke slowly as if weighing his words, while over his face there passed signs of anger, pain, sarcasm, and the greatest love of life. After chewing the end of his cigarette nervously during a short silence, he turned to a young editor and chided him sharply for a dull report."[714] Leonetti also recalls his outbursts at *Ordine Nuovo*: "This isn't a newspaper, its a sack of potatoes. Tomorrow Agnelli can call all his workers together and say: 'Look, you see! This lot can't even put a newspaper together, yet they want to run the State!' We've got to stop his saying this, but how can we if we turn out a paper which looks like a sack of potatoes."[715] In 1921 men again walked gently when they were near Gramsci, much as they had when he first arrived in Turin, for the more miserable he became the more demanding he became. Once again we saw the desperately insecure man peeping out from his "cave".

1921 was a particularly miserable year for him. Not only was the movement he set up defeated, but he himself felt the sting of personal defeat and dislike. The malignity of d'Amato at the foundation congress of the party dogged him to Turin, where once again he became the butt of socialist abuse,[716] and was so discredited and isolated by May that he received only a paltry vote in the elections. The other two communist candidates, though much less able and well-known, were elected.[717] Stung by the accusations of incompetence and treachery, he lost his confidence. In 1920 he had seemed "to have grasped all the problems of the universe" and to be in command.[718] Now he again started to feel that the world was "great and terrible" and he was desperately lonely.

Perhaps this loneliness explains why he visited Umberto Cosmo at the stately Italian Embassy in Berlin as he passed through on his way to the USSR in May 1922. It is tempting to see in their reconciliation the first step in Gramsci's pilgrimage to Canossa. Cosmo rushed down the stairs and threw himself weeping in Gramsci's arms, crying through his beard: "You understand why."[719] Afterwards, when the tears were dry, they talked about Machiavelli. It was the first of many instances in the future when Gramsci would turn for help to friends who came out of the same pre-war Crocean mould.

Eventually, exhausted, he reached the Hotel Lux in Moscow. In no time the other guests were eyeing him askance as he ground his teeth and threw fits, like those which had beset him the year before in Turin. Later he flippantly recalled that they thought that as a rather black looking Sard he might whip out a knife and stab someone.[720] However, we can assume that it was from kindness and concern that Zinoviev suggested that he take a rest-cure near the Black Sea. A miserable, withdrawn "bear in a cave" Gramsci entered the Sanatorium with the magical name Silvery Wood to convalesce.

He soon got to know another patient, a woman somewhat older than him, Eugenia Schucht, who was confined to a wheel-chair as a result of some psychiatric illness. She had spent some time in Italy and spoke the language well, which helped Gramsci avoid his limping French. One day Gramsci hovered nervously in her doorway, as she had a visitor, who made him shy and tongue-tied.[721] It was her younger sister, Giulia, whose beautiful oval face and sorrowing musicians' eyes greatly disturbed Gramsci.[722] Soon the common bond of the Italian language, and Giulia's nostalgia for Italy where she had studied music for many years, made them bosom companions, and they spent long hours talking or walking through a countryside which Tolstoy has made synonymous with a place of sun, bees and peace. The relationship for Gramsci became one of torment for he fell ever more deeply in love with the young Russian musician. He was "poisoned" with self-hatred because he felt that his physical deformity precluded any requite. The "sewer of his past" welled up each time he thought of declaring his love: "I laughed at myself, I thought terrible thoughts."[723] He was not only troubled that he would be refused because he was a "monster" (his letters use the word too often for it to be merely a figure of speech), but he was afraid of letting slip the mask he had presented for so many years to the world. So great was his torment that he sometimes found it difficult even to be civil to the young woman, and a feature of his future correspondence was apologies to his "evilness", which often reduced her to tears. What thoughts he had when he accompanied her one day to the road as she left the Silvery Wood: "I stood motionless there for so long watching you grow smaller and smaller down that road, carrying a bundle across your shoulders on your way back to the great and terrible world outside."[724]

We are not surprised to learn that on his return to Moscow later in June after six weeks rest-cure, he still suffered from amnesia and pains and paralysis in the legs.[725] He was also desperate to see the young woman again. One of his first plaintive letters, written in August 1922, runs:

Dear comrade,
Did you come to Moscow on 5 August as you said you would to me. I waited three days. I didn't move from my room for fear that what happened the last time would happen again. I waited because I felt and still feel a little demoralised by the nerve-racking waiting to leave and I would have been (and would still be) very happy to see you again. You didn't come to Moscow, right? Or you would certainly have visited me for at least a minute or two. I wanted to write immediately but I waited so that you could let me know. Will you be coming again soon? Will I be able to see you again? I remember too well that you are taking leave in September. I am waiting ... perhaps I will be in Moscow for a week or a fortnight more, maybe a month, perhaps we could talk together for a few more hours and even take a few long walks together. Please write. Everything you say really makes me happy and makes me stronger (you see, I am not as strong as I thought and led others to think).
Affectionately

He was still writing these letters, so transparent in their meaning, and so obvious in their desire to provoke sympathy, at the end of the year. Reading them, we forget momentarily that it is not an eighteen-year-old who is writing but a skilled and mentally-mature man in his thirties.[726]

Like an eighteen-year-old he used all the time-honoured wiles to win her. He borrowed a motor car to carry her around; he paraded his compassion for her crippled sister, he wrote to her about his job, which was very important by Soviet standards and he joined with her in the intellectual enterprise of translation.[727] He was amazed to discover that he enjoyed the pursuit which, watered his dry and parched spirit as if "by a tiny spring ... of sadness and moonlight with surrounds of blue."[728]

Eventually Giulia gave in to his importunings. It is a great pity that we cannot read her letters to decide why she did. Was it the sensitive spirit she saw behind Gramsci's staring eyes (looking outwards to hide the torment within), or was it his moral strength, or was it merely her nostalgia for Italy? We do not know. It is perhaps wise to remember that she was a romantic. Certainly Gramsci was enormously happy, grateful, and touchingly innocent in the first flushes of the affair, changing, as he put it, from the bear in the cavern which he had been into a "sentimental wolf". He wrote that the world seemed fresh and new again, and he certainly saw it anew: the sleighs in the snow and the first flowers. Yet there were soon contradictions in the relationship for which Gramsci was not entirely responsible. It seems that he felt more deeply than her, perhaps because she was a romantic and therefore not quite as capable of talking out her emotions. He too could not always put his feelings into words: "I would like to tell you many things. But will I be able to? I often ask myself about it, draw up plans for long conversations. But when you are close to me I forget everything ..." and this troubled him greatly though: "I love you and I am certain that you love me. It is true that for many years I have been accustomed to think that it was fatally, absolutely impossible, that anyone could love me. This belief has been a defence against myself for too long for it not sometimes to return to needle me and make me gloomy."[729] Such psychological encrustations could only be overcome by the most direct, even brutal, frankness and the tragedy lay in the fact that she, more romantically inclined, refused to help him overcome misunderstandings in so cold-blooded a style: "I have been a brute really. There is much in me which still has to be destroyed. You will help me won't you? Because there are some scars which still hurt and maybe even some bleeding wounds which date from my childhood," was the way he wrote to her, but she (regretting her liaison or being coy?) used to reply in circumlocutions about it being too "soon to know". The words are disastrously reminiscent of contemporary pop-songs, and preluded a widening rift between them in later years.

But this was all in a then distant future. In 1922 and 1923 his happiness outweighed any tugging at the heart strings. He joked, sang snatches of song, gathered flowers and found sexual fulfilment. He crept away from the Lux at night time to trysts where in his new fresh world they talked about Dante, poetry and love. He was again able to work without that feeling of being cut-off from other men which had beset him in 1921-22. No longer was he the "misunderstood genius" who was so harsh with others, because he had rediscovered that political life "must be lighted by a moral force: human sympathy."[730] While he was "peaceful and serene" he began to reassess his situation and those of his fellows and this brought him to consider fascism which further developed his ideas about the petty-bourgeois intellectuals who constituted the traditional political class. It led to a break with Bordiga.

While he was working for the Comintern Gramsci published at least two articles on fascism for the Comintern press.[731] In these articles he made clear the gap between him and Bordiga in their assessment of fascism, which, after the tragicomic march on Rome on 28 October 1922, became the concrete expression of the "realm of necessity" into which Italian socialists had entered in September 1920. On the differing assessment of fascism, which was the political question of life and death importance for all communists in Italy, hinged what action each man would take in the future.

Gramsci, of course, experienced the rise of fascism at first hand and it would be fatuous to expect that he should realise immediately the novelty or the import of the new movement. In his day-to-day journalism he noted the phenomenon as it grew, only gradually realising what it was or what it signified for him, for the communist movement, and for society generally. Moreover, unlike historians commenting on fascism after the event, he was faced with contradictory developments in the movement, and did not always forecast correctly which trend would become dominant, though his account captures the "what if" complexity better than commentaries after the event. Finally, he was a political actor who acted on his analysis of any particular development, throwing in his political weight on the side he wished to win. Each article was a political act. However, while Gramsci's account naturally does not

185

have the consistency of a historical account written after the event,
and it therefore does not seem worthwhile to argue that Gramsci
was never mistaken about the significance of fascism,[732] what is
important is that he appears to have grasped the novelty and
significance of fascism before other writers in or out of the socialist
camp.

At first, in the early days of fascism as a political force, and
before *squadrismo* had started to become widespread in the first
quarter of 1921, Gramsci did not notice its novelty as a movement
— as something distinct from earlier authoritarian movements —
because these were the days when a socialist revolution still seemed
possible. Gramsci felt much more the master of events than he
would feel later. In response to the clamour of papers like *La
Stampa* for a strong man who could control the Bolshevik menace
which had so alarmed Italian leaders in September 1920, he wrote
curtly that communism was not responsible for reaction:
"Reaction has always existed in Italy". It was the result of the
perennial failure of the Italian State, which again could not cope
with the failure of the economy and production, and the fact that
"Italy has been reduced to a war wound, whose blood runs from its
hacked body." Unable to save the nation from chaos, the state had
turned to distracting national attention from the internal problems
it could not solve with vainglorious episodes like that of the
occupation of Fiume. Socialism and communism was a response to
reaction, rather than vice versa.[733] Indeed, reaction was merely a
form of capitalist violence which sought to solve the crisis of the
bourgeois State *in order* to restore the State. Capitalist violence
thus expressed itself in two forms, legally through the State and
illegally through movements like fascism.[734] In 1920 Gramsci's
attitude towards fascism was, then, that it was merely a form of
capitalist coercion of a particularly violent sort which could even be
seen as an illegal, unofficial arm of the State. In his own words:

"Giolitti is powerless against d'Annunzio because in Bologna,
Milan, Turin and Florence his officials support fascism, arm
fascism, and mix with the fascists; because in all these centres
fascism is mixed up with the military hierarchy, because in all
these centres the judiciary leaves fascism unpunished. Fascism,
as a national phenomenon, cannot found its own State, cannot
make itself the central authority, because it is already mixed up
with the State, because it is already centralised in the present
Government of Giolitti; fascism, as the d'Annunzian

phenomenon, is a contradiction, it is not an antithesis, it is one face of the Giolitti government itself, it is in no sense revolutionary, because it is not capable of going beyond its apparent adversary dialectically, because it is unable to replace it."[735]

Even a consideration of fascism on a "world-wide" scale did not make him change this estimation.[736]

Perhaps the isolation of Turin from fascism before the end of 1920, because it was the working-class bastion of Italy, was responsible for this rather limited view. However, fascism was already committing outrages at an increased rate by the time the PCI was formed at Leghorn, where Misiano, one of the delegates, had to be accompanied by a bodyguard each time he left the conference hall.[737] Delegates made repeated references to the phenomenon, and it was widely known that the congress was only being held at Leghorn because the previously chosen venue was infested with fascists. Gramsci's interest and concern grew with the increased number of assaults on socialists and their offices. From this came the first important step in his understanding of fascism in the article already discussed in another context, the "Monkey People", which started "Fascism is the last 'show' put on by the urban petty-bourgeoisie in the theatre of national political life. The miserable end of the Fiume adventure is the last scene in the play" and went on to describe the petty-bourgeoisie as a "purely political class" which, since it no longer had any role in production, had specialised in "parliamentary cretinism", and when parliament started to decline before 1914 had tried "in every way to retain a position of historical leadership: it aped the working-class by coming onto the streets".

It met checks through working-class action on 2-3 December 1919 despite its programme of national imperialism, national syndicalism, and "revolution" and "from that moment ... sought to organise the group itself around stronger and richer patrons than the official State." The movement then split into two wings: the romantic wing which engaged in activities like those of d'Annunzio; and the wing which defended private property against the threat of the revolutionary working class. The latter was Fascism. Both posed as "revolutionary" and therefore anti-State, but the second attempted to control the main arms of the State: the army, police and judiciary. In thinking they could defend themselves better against the revolutionary class "by abandoning the institutions of its State to the hysterical caprice of the 'monkey people', the petty-bourgeoisie'', the property owners "repeated vis-à-vis the executive the same mistake they had made vis-à-vis Parliament''. It was becoming ever clearer that fascism served property, and ruined a State it could not replace.[738]

Already we observe some interesting themes beginning in Gramsci's understanding of fascism: 1) fascism is a movement of the petty-bourgeoisie reacting to a loss of political importance in society; 2) it has two faces, a revolutionary and a conservative face; 3) it starts by emphasising the first face but soon becomes allied with capitalism and turns on its revolutionary wing, and 4) it is unable to set up a State of its own or to prevent the collapse of the bourgeois State. The first three qualities are basically the same as the celebrated thesis of Salvatorelli[739] which has become the orthodoxy in Italian scholarship, and which Gramsci's view preceded by some years. The fourth assertion was premature and soon revised. Yet it was a miscalculation which vitiated much of his other insight for a few more months, despite the increase in fascist violence and its spread even into Turin, where he too had to be accompanied at all times by a bodyguard.

Early in 1921 fascism started to spread into Tuscany in a big way.[740] Then, following the classic tactics described by Tasca, of roaring into villages fully armed and greatly outnumbering the local socialists, burning their offices and beating them up, the fascists finally started to move into Piedmont, and then Turin, in the months of March and April.

"...from Alessandria the fascists are attacking in force towards Turin. Punitive expeditions are moving on Bra, Casale etc. Challenges and threats are being made against the Turinese working class.''[741]

Gramsci at first dismissed local fascists as "shop keepers'' who were certainly "not famous for sublime warlike victories'', where the Turinese workers were tried veterans of war and the class struggle. He claimed that because the Turin workers had a "spirit of initiative'' through their experience in the factory councils they would not be defeated like the workers in other cities who lost all initiative after the local Camera del Lavoro was burnt down. He urged the Turinese workers to be tough and not to forget the lessons of Hungary where the revolutionary government had been too gentle with its opponents. He called for a hundred deaths for every working-class death.[742] As the *razzia* became more

formidable, he noted gloomily that fascism observed on an
international scale was an "attempt to solve the problems of
production and exchange with machine-guns and revolver shots",
but he clearly did not think that this was possible — the
petty-bourgeoisie and middle-class had learnt nothing from
history: "Illusion is the most tenacious weed in the collective
consciousness, history teaches but it has no students": working-
class tears and suffering could not be wiped away by machine-gun
blasts.[743] Moreover, the help the police gave fascists did not
encourage him to give up his view that it was an arm of the State.
The only new item in his analysis we discover before fascism took
over Turin definitively (marked on April 28 by the successful
assault on the Camera del Lavoro), was his observation, quite true
in Italy, that fascism started as a rural phenomenon and spread to
the city.[764]

This led him to a very significant development in his
understanding which coincided with a recognition that fascism was
something more than a manifestation of State power, intent on
shoring up the old order. Fascism, he observed on 26 April was
rooted in "elemental forces", and explained by Italian national
history. We reproduce *in extenso* a fascinating analysis.

"It has now become evident that fascism can only partly be
assumed to be a class phenomenon, a movement of political
forces which are conscious of having a real goal: it has over-
flowed, has broken out of every organisational framework, is
superior to the will and intention of every regional and central
committee, it has become an unleashing of elemental forces
within the bourgeois system of economic and political government, which cannot be braked: fascism is the name for the
profound decay of Italian society, which could not but
accompany the decay of the State, and can today be explained
only by the low level of culture (civilisation) which the Italian
nation has reached in sixty years of unitary 'administration'.

Fascism has portrayed itself as an anti-party, has opened its
doors to all comers, has, by promises of impunity, provided a
means for a confused multitude to cloak a savage overflow of
passions, hates and desires with a veneer of vague and nebulous
political idealism. Fascism has become a matter of national
habit (*costume*) and has become identified with the anti-social
and barbaric psychology of certain strata of the Italian people,
which has not yet been modified either by traditions or by

schooling, or by living together in a well-administered and ordered State. To understand fully the meaning of these assertions we need only recall that Italy has the highest number of homicides and killings; that Italy is the country where mothers bring up their children by beating them about the head with a clog; that Italy is the country where the younger generation is least respected and protected; that in some regions of Italy it seemed natural until a few years ago to muzzle the wine harvesters so that they would not eat the grapes; that in some regions the owners locked up their employees in the stables after they returned from work so that they could not attend meetings or night-school.

The class struggle has always taken on a very bitter character in Italy because of the 'human' immaturity of some strata of the population. Cruelty and absence of understanding (*simpatia*) are two characteristics of the Italian people, who pass from childish sentimentality to the most bloody and brutal ferocity, from impassioned anger to cold contemplation of the evil-doing of others. On this barbaric soil, which a still-weakly articulated and uncertain State has only managed to cultivate with great difficulty, today when the State has decayed, there bubble all the poisonous gases. There is much that is true in the claim of fascist newspapers that not all those who call themselves fascists or act in the name of the *fasci* belong to the organisation; but what can we say of an organisation whose symbol can be used to cloak actions which each day besmirch Italy? Besides, this claim gives the events a much graver and more decisive character than the writers in bourgeois papers want to give them. Who can control them, if the State cannot and private organisations are powerless?

And thus we find justification for the communist thesis that fascism as a general phenomenon, a scourge which overrides the discipline and will of its exponents with its violence, its monstrous arbitrariness, with destructiveness which is as irrational as it is systematic, can only be extirpated by a new State power, a 'restored' State as the communists understand it, that is, a State whose power is in proletarian hands, the sole class capable of reorganising production and thus all the social relations which depend on the relations of production".[745]

Already in April 1921 Gramsci had started to typify fascism in terms which remind us of the analyses of many of the "mass psychological" or "cultural" historians of fascism.[746] Because he had now realised that fascism was tending to become uncontrollable because of its "decadent" qualities, and therefore could not be viewed as part of the bourgeois State and lumped together with it for political purposes, Gramsci started to evolve practical policies towards it. First, on the basis of analyses which went back to the time of Fiume, which he regarded as a threat to the bourgeois State rather than a support of it, but a threat of a radical nature, he attempted to drive a wedge between the revolutionary and conservative wings of fascism.[747]

Gramsci had already identified the attractiveness of d'Annunzio for young men because of his "real elements of populism" and because he aroused "ingenuous and fanatical admiration for the ... intelligent man as such, which corresponds with the cultural nationalism of the Italians, perhaps the only form of popular chauvinism in Italy."[748] Though his feelings for d'Annunzio were not unmixed he too may have shared the general overemphasis on the revolutionary potential of the poet's legionaries.[748] Certainly the same poetry appealed to the young legionary and the working-class.[750] One of the legionaries who was regularly at *Ordine Nuovo* in early 1921 was Mario Giordano, remembered by Togliatti as "a strange but pleasant fellow. He must have been wounded in the head during the war, because he sometimes fell asleep on his feet while he was talking. He had long talks with Gramsci and with us; there was, moreover, a period when he was in the office and Gramsci's room every evening. He called himself a communist but his ideas were confused like many of the ex-servicemen and Fiuman legionaries oriented towards the left."[751] It is not clear whether he or Gramsci suggested a meeting with d'Annunzio but the purpose was broadly that "Gramsci thought that it might be possible to have an organised armed mass resistance to fascism's offensive, and thought it wise to reinforce, extend and increase the influence of this resistance by making contact with the Fiuman legionaries, or at least part of them."[752]

However, Gramsci had acted prematurely. D'Annunzio took Giordano's telegram that they were arriving badly, and Gramsci, on meeting Nino Danieli, his contact at Como, was distressed at his hastiness in engaging, without party authority,[753] in so delicate a mission. D'Annunzio had as house guest Mario Martini, a member of the extreme right of the legionary movement, who showed supercilious scorn about the proposed meeting, and swayed the scented and shallow Comandante. Gramsci was ill and worried about the consequences if news of his mission got out. Danieli therefore asked him to spend a few days with him to recover at an empty hotel on the lake. There he was greatly impressed by Gramsci, who he claims hid neither his support for patriotic war in 1914, nor his admiration for d'Annunzio. "Throughout our conversations he recognised the revolutionary and disinterested spirit of the legionaires which he distinguished sharply from the pragmatic and reactionary spirit of the fascists."

Gramsci's absence had hardly been noticed, and despite its failure, he continued to press to some sort of *entente* with the populist wing of the mass movement which he had now recognised fascism was. This again became clear when there emerged in June throughout the country the movement known as *Arditi del Popolo*. The *arditi* were groups of much the same composition as the legionaries, though perhaps even more to the left, who emerged not only with an anti-State programme but with a strongly anti-fascist bent. They received enormous support from the rank and file of both the PSI and the PCI, but the first, then arranging a pact of peace with the fascists, denounced them, and the Central Executive of the PCI, after some suspicious investigation of the "d'Annunzian" qualities of the movement also directed its members not to join the *arditi*. Significantly, Gramsci disagreed publicly with the Central Executive despite the anarchist and d'Annunzian overtones of the *arditi*, stating that the communists were not against the *arditi*.[754] In fact he felt that their anti-fascism was rather too limited and should be expanded as much as possible and include the State among their enemies.[755]

There is no record that he was reproved directly for this stance, but soon after the party threatened expulsion of members who joined the *arditi* and announced that it would set up its own protection squads. The *arditi*, which might have saved Italy from fascism, collapsed soon after for lack of leadership.

Gramsci now concentrated on the notion of a mass opposition as the only way to combat the triumph of fascism, only giving up his hope of splitting the reaction when Mussolini and Dino Grandi were reconciled at the Rome congress of the PNF in October. He became less and less optimistic as time went by. In April he still denied that the present period was reactionary,[756] but as it became clearer and clearer that even for the ruling élite Mussolini was a "new monster" and after the beginning of a terrible onslaught of the *squadre* in June and July in Treviso, Viterbo and

Grosseto,[757] he began to speculate that a *coup d'état* by the fascists might be possible.[758]

He was not always consistent, living too close to the ups and downs of a movement which was then very undecided about what it should do. Sometimes, fastening hopefully on a movement of mass resistance he wrote hopefully that fascism was in crisis and that it had too many internal contradictions to survive.[759] We must, however, remember that Gramsci was a political leader whose duty it was to write such supportive articles, especially when it was Socialist policy to seek peace *à l'outrance*.

We may state with considerable surety that by the beginning of 1922 Gramsci had realised that fascism was a movement with mass, cross-class support, in which the petty-bourgeoisie from country and town was predominant. Fascism was confused and romantic ideologically, but directed to the maintenance of the former eminence of the petty-bourgeoisie in a society that had made it anachronistic. Since it was prepared to rule by violence of any sort whatsoever, it had built up close links with traditional army conservatives. Moreover, since it had in fact established its rule in Italy *de facto*, the ruling capitalists would soon compel the government to admit it to rule *de jure*, in the hope of taming it. Gramsci claimed later that he even had theses 51 and 52 of the "Rome theses" changed because they precluded the possibility of a fascist *coup d'état*, which he now felt was imminent. Since the masses were the only possible opposition and they were being killed in their thousands, Gramsci forecast gloomily shortly before he left Italy for the USSR that the country faced "the gravest crisis in its history since unity."[760]

After the march on Rome confirmed his worst expectations, Gramsci wrote his articles for the Comintern. They were designed for foreign audiences and therefore projected the factual material he thought important and gave background to his analysis. In the first he typified the elements of Italy's crisis, which had brought fascism to power. The key was the backwardness of Italy and the consequent artificiality and weakness of its bourgeois State. This State was set up because international conditions favoured its establishment. It had to face a predominantly feudal country and fight it off by allying the northern urban bourgeoisie with the agricultural day labourers. This policy, whose main author was Giolitti, failed with the First World War, and the peasants grouped themselves around the PSI — with "more than a million agricultural labourers and sharefarmers from the centre and north"; the Catholic Popular Party which numbered the slightly better-off middle peasants and small proprietors of the same area; and the ex-servicemen's leagues which the peasants of the backward South joined. Together they assaulted the feudal landowners of the country, occupying land and forcing the owners to move to the towns. After 1919 the owners started to organise civilian battalions to fight against this "peasant tyranny". The PSI, whose membership was 60% peasant, could have led the peasant movement and given it a concrete policy. But instead, because 110 of its 156 members of parliament were from peasant electorates, because 2000 of the 2500 municipalities it controlled were peasant, and because four-fifths of its cooperatives were agricultural cooperatives, it merely reflected "the chaos in ideas and programmes which ruled in the country". In March 1920 the "owning classes" started to prepare the counter-offensive through the new Conference of Italian Industrialists. Giolitti formed a compromise ministry with the High Command, represented by the Minister for War, Bonomi. A month later, in July, Bonomi started the demobilisation of 60,000 officers on the following conditions: "the officers were demobilised on 4/5 pay; the greatest part was sent to the most important political centres, with the obligation that they join the *"Fasci di combattimento"*, which had until this time been a little organisation of socialists, anarchists, syndicalists and republicans in favour of Italian participation on the side of the *Entente*." Giolitti also attempted to ally the industrialists and the landowners of the centre and north together, and "... the first armed teams of fascists appeared and conducted the first terrorist activities."[761]

Gramsci's next article, which continued the analyses, appeared just after Xmas 1922, and thus immediately after the House of Deputies had risen. Gramsci now noted how far the House had declined and speculated that what would happen next would depend on the fascist party: "Never in any of the bourgeois States, have we seen a legislative assembly sink so low. Born to suffocate under an avalanche of voting slips the civil war which was unleashed with extreme violence throughout Italy in May 1921, it has only shown the complete ineffectuality of democracy before fascism. It has not even managed to avoid lending ... fascism the appearance of legality.... Giolitti had hoped to treat the fascist illness with the same homeopathic method which had succeeded in September 1920 against the workers." But despite the desire of the bourgeois democrats to control fascism, Giolitti, opposed by the reactionary right, failed. Bonomi, his successor, was even more determined, machine-gunning fascists at Sarazana when they tried to take over from the legal authorities, but he, too, was forced to give in when the general of the *guardia regie*, Amelio, suicided and there was a general reaction. He, too, with the help of Nitti's men and reformists like Modigliani, then fostered the *arditi del popolo* which, in turn, also failed to contain fascism. Finally, Facta, an insignificant "country lawyer", was supposed, backed by the big bankers and industrialists of the North, to crush fascism with the help of the army.

"But it was obviously too late, and the forces which democracy could deploy were insufficient. Towards the middle of 1922, the Facta government tried to reduce the strength of the *carabinieri* — which were then under the direct control of the Minister for War, the agrarian fascist Prince of Scalea — to have half (about 30,000) transferred to the *guardie regie* under the general control of the police then in the hands of the giolittians. In the middle of October general Badoglio still thought it possible to say that fascism could be liquidated in a fortnight with the ordinary methods of the police and the army."

But, the fascists, faced with the possibility of an anti-fascist action on 4 November by the d'Annunzians, with whom Giolitti had been flirting for some time, tricked the government into believing that a new government with only three or four fascists in it would be the solution to the crisis,

"The parliamentary majority which had favoured Giolitti's anti-fascist policy and even, if necessary, the formation of a 'left' government which was openly and decidedly anti-fascist, suddenly fell on its knees before Mussolini's bludgeon. They gave him the full powers which he had taken; they did not make the slightest gesture of protest against the personal vendettas and intimidatory methods of the new government; they took it all from the victors without flinching."

Even communist members of parliament like Bombacci were conciliatory.[762]

In his next article Gramsci drew up a plan of the relative strengths and weaknesses of fascism and the probable developments in the movement. The main theme was that fascism was very successful in the countryside, but not among the industrial workers, and that this success was revealed in the failure of its union movement in the city. To a considerable degree the failure stemmed from the petty-bourgeoisie's inability to realise that the class struggle was not fomented by communists and socialists, but caused by the contradictions of capitalist production, and that an integral corporative union structure conflicted with the life experience of the workers. But, it was also due to the opposition of the industrialists to their control. Mussolini had recognised that "integral unionism" was possible only in the country and this marked the beginning of the end of fascist unionism. Communists should and would work further to discredit fascist unionism.[763]

Gramsci believed that this would not only break up fascism, but would also build up revolutionary forces. However, by now he saw the removal of fascism as something only possible if armed force was used and denied that a peaceful change of government to another bourgeois party was possible.[764] He noted in his comment on the Italian elections of 1924 that they had revealed what was essential in Italy: "the disorganisation of the masses, the impossibility of holding meetings, and the small circulation of opposition newspapers...." They had also shown that all hopes of a bourgeois "anti-fascist revolution" were fatuous and that the principal source of opposition in the future would be the "revolutionary opposition". Yet, while fascism was strong in country, the communists' strength was in the cities. It followed that the PCI should not only seek alliances with the PSI, but "elaborate a programme for a worker and peasant government which can satisfy the mass of peasants who have experienced fascist terror the most".[765]

So by mid-1924, Gramsci's analysis of fascism had turned his attention to the problem of the peasants and the South, and, we note, to the Catholic Church as well,[766] and was driving him away from a purist position where the exclusively proletarian party kept itself isolated from the corrupting groups of "non-believers". It was this which finally started to separate him from Bordiga, and confirmed the decisive turn in his theoretical outlook which had been implicit since 1920.

V

Bordiga continued to think of fascism as the ultimate system of violent rule by capital, which signified its imminent collapse. He did not realize that it was a cross-class popular phenomenon because of his isolation from the people and because of an exceptionally doctrinaire approach to the problem. When Lenin asked him in 1922 what the masses felt about fascism he was unable to reply adequately.[767] He underestimated its strength and durability, and from this underestimation flowed his policy of refusing to deal with the socialists, whom he considered an equal, if not a worse threat, to the working-class in a situation of incipient revolutionary crisis. Without understanding this estimation of Italy's main political problem, we cannot understand his unrelenting opposition to the united front.

Gramsci, too, shared Bordiga's hostility to uniting with the socialists when he first came to the USSR. He was sent there to represent it and not because Bordiga wished to get rid of him or break up the former *Ordine Nuovo* group.[768] He told Radek soon after arriving "Serrati hasn't a single worker behind him.... Serrati can't make an open speech ... he'd be howled down by all the workers, not only the communists".[769] Moreover, a few days after his return from Serebriani Bor, he sent Radek off with a flea in his ear when the latter abruptly proposed that he replace Bordiga as party leader, because "I didn't think that Amadeo could be replaced in any way (least so by me) without considerable work in the party", and because he thought Amadeo was worth any three others.[770] We should beware thinking that the first was the more forceful reason. When Bordiga and the rest of the delegation arrived for the Fourth congress of the Comintern, Gramsci immediately contacted him. Camilla Ravera recalls the conversations they had: "Gramsci wanted ... to have talks with Bordiga on Italian and international problems: talks ... exchanges of opinion to mutually clarify each other's thought, with the desire, even within this formal framework, of excluding any idea of opposition, open disagreement, of a break. Between Gramsci and Bordiga there existed close friendly relations. Bordiga felt, and showed, a deep concern for Gramsci's health and a profound admiration for his knowledge and intelligence. Gramsci admired in Bordiga a vigorous personality and his general ability and capacity for work, and appreciated the positive role he had played in difficult circumstances in building and organising the party in early days."[771]

So much did Gramsci share a community of view with Bordiga on the error of uniting with the socialists that he was horrified by the "shameful and politically disgusting" tendency of some members of the majority, who when approached individually, showed themselves potentially members of the minority in favour of unity.[772]

The minority, represented in Moscow by Tasca and Graziadei, Vota, Berti, Presutti, and others, took an open stand against Bordiga at pre-congress discussions. It was the first time the PCI leader had been challenged. Graziadei accused him of indiscipline dating back to the Rome Congress in March because of his refusal to implement the slogan of the Comintern for a "workers' government". Gramsci was as suspicious of the personal probity of Graziadei as he had always been of that of Tasca. Later he assessed Graziadei as: "...one of the cleverest opportunists in the party — a real liquidator". Moreover, Graziadei was a reviser of Marx' economic theories and Gramsci could only explain why so open a revisionist had joined the PCI by a "curious psychological phenomenon found among intellectuals ... persuaded of the intellectual foolishness of political reformism, he gave it up and opposed it."[773] It was this disbelief in the probity of the minority leaders, and the way they understood their policies, rather than the policies themselves, which kept him firmly with Bordiga all through the pre-congress discussions about the possibility of reuniting with the Third International fraction of the PSI (*terzini*). Though the minority had the backing of the Comintern, Gramsci was as firmly opposed to them as Bordiga. On 15 November he repeated Bordiga's refusal to accept the fusion the Comintern desired in terms almost identical with those voiced by Bordiga two days earlier — "no fusion except by individual maximalists joining the PCI — and stated flatly that the PCI would be fusing with nothing as the "maximalists" had no support left. Zinoviev, who was fostering the fusion, replied curtly that this position of Gramsci was "a joke" and Trotsky also condemned him: "We have reached the maximum point of disagreement between the PCI and the Communist International. Any further and we split. Gramsci wants the privilege of intransigency for Italy. On the question of the united front you formed a bloc with France and Spain. The others have recognised their mistakes, but you haven't...."[774] These words emphasised the seriousness and degree of Gramsci's opposition to the Comintern. It took a letter from the CPSU signed by Lenin, Trotsky, Zinoviev, Bukharin and Radek to get Bordiga and Gramsci to step down. It was half-threat and half-advice, warning them that a public expression of their view would have

disastrous consequences and asking them to state at the Fourth
Congress only that because the Comintern commission had decided
on fusion, they would conscientiously carry out that policy.
Bordiga replied for all his group: "After your request, your
fraternal advice, we will tell you that the PCI majority will remain
silent. It will not advance the opinions which you know it has, and
of whose correctness it is still convinced."[775] Indeed, he had
known he would reach this foregone imposed conclusion from the
day he arrived in Moscow.

The iron unity between Bordiga and Gramsci then began to
break. Bordiga refused absolutely to engage in the negotiations
with the PSI delegation about the terms of the fusion the Russians
had imposed on the PCI. Gramsci, Scoccimarro, and Tasca for the
minority, attended the talks. Gramsci felt that if he did not the
terms would be decided by default by the minority. He certainly felt
no more readiness than before to compromise when he found
Serrati, Maffi and Tonetti facing him across the table with all the
past bad blood and suspicions about their probity lying between
them. As far as Droz, the Comintern secretary overseeing the
fusion, was concerned, both Gramsci and Bordiga were still seeking
to wreck plans for fusion in their different ways.[776] Gramsci's
terms appeared impossible. He demanded the exclusion of the Vella
majority from the new party. He demanded that the PCI be
allowed to draw up a list of PSI members to be excluded because of
their "personal unworthiness" together with all ex-communists
who had joined the PSI. He demanded that many PSI communal
and parliamentary members be recalled. He demanded that the new
Central Committee be 2/3 communist and that all party
newspapers have communist editors, and finally, he demanded that
the PCI (in agreement with EKKI) have the right to veto
membership on leading bodies of anyone it wished.[777] Naturally
the negotiations were long and torrid. For example, the point about
newspaper editors was indubitably directed against Serrati.
Eventually Gramsci's adamancy won him many of these demands,
which the socialists were too divided to oppose. They were told that
Vella and his followers could not become members of the new party
and that Gramsci and Serrati would be joint editors of the party
newspaper. What was even more significant, it was decided that the
details on which agreement could not be reached, would be decided
in Italy by mixed committees of two communists and two
socialists.[778]

Given Italian realities these terms precluded the possibility of fusion. Vella and Pietro Nenni immediately started to organise their majority following to prevent any decision in favour of fusion at the next PSI congress. Bordiga may well have already realised this when he quietly agreed at the Fourth Congress to Zinoviev's "wish of the Comintern to see a rapid reunion of both parties in the near future".[779] Certainly fusion was going to be very difficult to achieve. However, he must have been stung by the rest of Zinoviev's words, and scarcely emotionally prepared to honour his undertaking to "accept the decision of the Congress without any further discussion and ... carry it out as loyal and disciplined members." Zinoviev practically blamed the success of fascism on the failure of the creators of the PCI. "Nowhere has it been more palpably demonstrated than in Italy how great is the historical role of a communist party for the world revolution. It has shown how the absence of such a party can turn the course of history in favour of the bourgeoisie."[780] To the attendant Droz, Zinoviev was saying that the Comintern was no longer concerned whether people came from the "old party or the new" but "where they stood at that time".[781] Lenin also joined in by admonishing the Italians who should "understand what we have written about the organisational structure of communist parties."[782]

Gramsci, too, must have been aware that private agreements reached in the negotiations would make great practical difficulties for those in favour of fusion, even though for 21 December he signed the manifesto of the Comintern to the Italian proletariat which called on all workers to join the united PCI after it was formed in March.

Bordiga returned to an Italy where the majority of the PSI was already actively organising an opposition to the fusion proposed by the *terzini*. Vella and Nenni had set up a "National Committee for the Defence of Socialism", and were cleverly uniting great numbers of party members around the defence of the party's name, which under the terms of the agreement would become the United Communist Party of Italy. Serrati, who might have opposed this successfully, had remained in Moscow where he had little influence over events in Italy. Droz claims the PCI deliberately engineered this so the fusion would fail.[783] When Droz arrived in Milan a few days before the PSI conference, he discovered that it was a foregone conclusion of defeat for the *terzini*. Indeed the motion of the anti-fusionist faction received 5361 votes to 3968 in favour of fusion. The agreement had been that in this event the minority would immediately secede and join the United Communist Party, but Droz proposed that they stay in the PSI to try to win a majority by the next congress.[784] When Zinoviev agreed, the PCI majority rebelled. Grieco wrote a letter to Zinoviev which effectively constituted a letter of resignation from the majority to the Comintern: "We cannot write what we don't feel and in favour of what we are not convinced. We cannot maintain three positions at the same time...."[785] Droz also claimed that all minority leaders were being systematically removed and that the situation was such that "it is necessary for the International to intervene in the Communist Party to ... place in leading positions at least some comrades who agree with us."[786] In Moscow Gramsci declared to the EKKI in April: "that we are fully disposed to struggle to safeguard in Italy the traditions and the healthy basis of the Communist Party because we believe that it is the destiny of the Italian revolution which is at stake when the organisational bases of a party are being laid." He claimed that the same sort of situation existed in Italy that had existed in Hungary and it brought the same dangers. It was wrong then to pursue fusion at all costs. "After the period of fascist government we will enter the phase of the decisive struggle for the power of the proletariat. This period will be reached at some undefined time in the future. It is difficult to say, to prophesy how the situation will develop in Italy up to the conquest of power. But we can state that the decomposition of fascism will mark the beginning of the decisive struggle for power of the proletariat."[787]

A collision course with the Comintern was averted by the great anti-communist purge which the fascists unleashed in early 1923, when "in the space of a week the police arrested more than 5000 comrades among whom there are all the Federation secretaries, all communist union organisers, and all our provincial and municipal councillors. Furthermore, it has succeeded in laying its hands on all our funds, striking what is perhaps a mortal blow to our press...."[788] Among those captured were Bordiga, Grieco and most of their most intimate followers. The Comintern was able to coopt an interim Central Committee of Scoccimarro, Togliatti, Tasca, Graziadei and Ravera, creating an uneasy balance between members of the former Communist minority and the former majority. This uneasy balance was left with the wreckage of a party to put together. Even though Togliatti knew that Gramsci could not come back to Italy as there was a warrant out for his arrest, Togliatti asked him to come back close to Italy to provide the needed leadership for the majority.[798] A formal request to the

Comintern was made soon after.

It was in this situation of starting anew that Gramsci first started to intimate that he would not be Bordiga's *alter ego* if he returned to such chaos. He agreed, as his April speech in Moscow indicated, that the party's starting point was the preparation for a revolution, but he disagreed that the revolutionary crisis was necessarily very close or that the party should hold itself in readiness for that crisis. Togliatti maintained that they could only obey the Comintern if the party was loyal to its *raison d'être*, which had been expressed in the Rome theses.[790] Gramsci wrote to Togliatti that he was "too optimistic" given the facts, and that a "vast and minute political action" was needed to break the hold of social-democracy in Italy. The three years which culminated in the Milan conference of the PSI showed this.

The party should give up the dry doctrinaire position which separated it from the masses, and seek to immerse itself in the masses as he once had. "We shouldn't be too concerned about our leading role: we must go forward carrying out our political action, without glancing in the mirror too much. If we can work properly we will absorb the socialist party and we will resolve the first and fundamental revolutionary problem: to unify the proletarian vanguard and destroy the demogogic populist tradition."[791]

He wrote a month later that the problem of the united front was one of "deficiency in leadership", and the greater problem that of "the revolution in Italy" and not the purity of the past in the PCI. His milder tone in these reconsiderations did not mean that he felt any more well-disposed towards the Comintern. He wrote: "The attitude of the Comintern and its agents is breaking up and corrupting communist ranks. We have decided to fight against the liquidationist and corrupt elements in our party. The situation of illegality and emigration impose this. We don't want what happened in Hungary and Yugoslavia to happen in Italy. If, in this struggle to regain our feet, the Comintern is hurt, we should not be blamed ... we should not be associated with untrustworthy elements."[792] In sum, his new position was one of going beyond Bordiga without giving up his critique of the minority or the PSI.

Shortly afterwards he started to take positive steps to that end. He wrote to his former associates in Turin that the solution to the impasse with the Comintern was to go beyond both Bordiga and the minority by shifting the discussion from formal and organisational questions to issues of effectively working in the Italian environment. Fundamental to such a reorientation of their work was a recognition that Leghorn had proved the "greatest triumph of the reaction", and that now the foremost need was for unity in face of fascism, which he typified as "tending to become the integral movement of a new class, which in Italy has never been independent before — the agrarian bourgeoisie, allied with the great landed proprietors." [793]

The formal request that he be allowed to return closer to Italy to coordinate activity there, permitted a further development in his programme, as a crucial proposal was for the re-establishment of *Ordine Nuovo*. This, and the decision in September to set up a new newspaper since *Avanti* would now remain in the hands of Nenni, allowed him to formulate his view of the role of the press.

"I propose that the paper be called *L'Unità*, both because it means something to the workers, and more generally because I believe after the decision of the Enlarged EKKI [in June—A.D.] in favour of a 'worker and peasant government' that we must lay special stress on the Southern Question, that is, on the question in which the problem of worker/peasant relations is not only a problem of class relations, but is also a special territorial question, that is, is one of the aspects of the national question. Personally, I think that the slogan of 'worker and peasant government' should be readapted in Italy as the 'Federal republic of workers and peasants'. I don't know whether the present time is favourable to that, I do believe however that the situation that fascism is creating ... will make our party adopt this slogan." [794]

And finally, from his assessment of fascism and the type of political action it made possible, Gramsci returned to the essentiality of the workplace, shop-stewards, and factory councils in any action for working-class unity against fascism. "In what way do we intend to keep in contact with the great proletarian masses, to interpret their needs, to gather these together and to make them concrete in will....? [when] A great part, practically all, the revolutionary elements who in past years acquired the capacity to organise and lead and to work systematically, have been massacred, have emigrated or have been scattered?" He went on: "The working class is like a great army which has been deprived of all its subalterns at one blow; in such an army it would be impossible to maintain the discipline, unity, the spirit for the struggle, and singleness of policy if there were only a high command.

"The worker is naturally strong in the factory where he is concentrated and organised. He is, on the other hand, isolated, scattered, and weak outside the factory." And, in the factory, where capitalism needed organisation and discipline to ensure effective production, it had allowed the *commissioni interne* to continue operating even while it destroyed working-class unity outside. So, he concluded: "It is clear what our tactics should be: 1) to work to create revolutionary groups in the factories, groups which could win control of the CI and spur them on to extend their sphere of action more and more; 2) to work to create links between factories, to impress on the present situation a movement which will progress naturally in its development from CI to factory council."[795]

Gramsci's policy for the party would clearly be the same policy as that practiced by the *Ordine Nuovo* group in 1919-1920. He revealed his intentions to Zinoviev shortly before leaving for Vienna on December 4, 1923. We know that they took cordial leave of one another and assume that this showed that Zinoviev approved.[796] It remained to be seen if his former supporters would.

VI

Men do make their own destinies, but they do not do so "just as they please". Gramsci had a given material with which to realise his programme; the PCI and its members. On 9 August 1923, the PCI had met at the villa d'Angera to discuss the directives of the June meeting of the EKKI that a new leadership be established which contained members of the minority on it and that the policy of the PCI be to work for a "workers and peasants" government in unity with socialists. At this meeting a duel had developed between Terracini, Bordiga's most loyal surviving spokesman, and Tasca. Terracini argued that the Comintern was ignoring the opinion of the majority and making a grave mistake in proposing that the imprisoned Bordiga be removed from the Executive. Tasca replied by accusing him of making "sentimental appeals" which might work in Moscow, but which he had not dare voice in Moscow when it was decided that a new coopted leadership be set up. He also accused Terracini of plotting secretly against the implementation of the Moscow decisions on June in favour of a "worker and peasant government" even after Togliatti and other former members of the majority had agreed to work for that goal. Graziadei then chimed in, implicitly blaming the majority for Mussolini's advent to power, by claiming that the split at Leghorn had been too much "to the left". This was too much for Togliatti, who replied by blaming Italy's troubles on the PSI.

It was clear at the end of the meeting that, back in their Italian environment, the two groups were going to find it very difficult to work together. The main bone of contention was still over what policy they should adopt towards the PSI. The minority, supported by Droz, favoured fusion even after past failures, and the former majority, backed by Manuilsky, were firmly opposed to further attempts at fusion.[797] The advantage went first to the majority. Manuilsky returned to Moscow and convinced Zinoviev that further hopes for fusion were forlorn. In late October the Comintern issued a manifesto which made a violent attack on Vella and Nenni and the PSI generally and called on all *terzini* to join the PCI as individuals.[798] Humbert-Droz meanwhile worked on a policy more agreeable to the *terzini* and the minority, neither of whom approved of the principle of individuals joining the PCI. On 26 December 1923 he sent a report to Zinoviev from Paris, straight after returning from Italy. This stated:

"The talks which I had at Rome and Milan with communist comrades show that Bordiga's mjaority is very far from being homogeneous and that a good number of his partisans consider that the party has made political mistakes. They trust Bordiga but deplore his intransigency on certain points. In the discussion which is going to start on the policy of the party I will pressure certain comrades to express their thoughts in an independent fashion so that Bordiga will understand that the majority of the party does not approve of his political line in its entirety."

He went on to report that the *terzini* did not like the policy that each should join the PCI individually, and they had suggested instead that they call a special congress and try to force a split again. Droz favoured this second policy, as it would save face for the *terzini*. He requested the Comintern to act on his views, and to give up the idea of appointing Bordiga to the Comintern or resolving problems through a PCI congress.[799]

The importance of this endless bickering can only be realised if it is grasped that the party had almost collapsed as a result of the fascist purge and desperately needed leadership when:

"The conditions of life imposed on communists by the conquest of the State by fascism were very harsh but they also constituted the touchstone for some of their political theses and the opportunity to develop a type of organisation which suited their mentality.... So, for some years, I too, got used to living like a foreigner in my own land. I had to change my name, give up associating with my family, change my habits, take up residence in a province I had never been in before, and live a life which would arouse no suspicion that I was a conspirator. The party became family, school, church and barracks, the whole world outside existed only to be destroyed...."[800]

Bordiga had been acquitted in October after a brave and brilliant speech in his own defence, and he symbolised this style for the members. It was therefore an arduous task for Gramsci to pull the party together so that it became more than a sect characterised by the psychology of a religious order. The first hurdle to be overcome was the charisma of Bordiga.

Gramsci had hated leaving the USSR. "You experience great distaste when you leave proletarian for bourgeois territory", he wrote to his wife soon after arriving in Austria. He felt lonely, it had started to snow, everything was going slowly and he had to put up with the anti-communist talk of the Jewish wife of the party official with whom he was staying. She "curses the party continuously". His first distasteful task was to obtain a residence permit. To do this he had to turn for help to the embittered Angelica Balabanoff, who had *entrée* with the Austrian socialists and was surrounded by a retinue of equally embittered Italian socialists. The old woman, who does not recall the episode in *My Life as a Rebel*, made him pay for her services by berating him about the Comintern, with which she was completely disillusioned. Gramsci listened with an ironical smile: "She is a jeremiad, a lament, a complaint embodied. Everything is wrong, the world is on the edge of a precipice, the roots of humanity itself are decaying.... I was given dirty looks because I was one of those who had wanted the split at Leghorn...."[801] Eventually, no doubt after much gritting of teeth he was introduced to Dr Pollak of the Austrian police as "Professor" Gramsci. Pollak realised who he was, but being a gentlemanly man, indicated that since Gramsci had been introduced as "Professor" he would not ask him to sign the customary document promising to refrain from all political activity.[802] Finally, he established himself in a *pension*, in a room covered with religious motifs, where he had to wear slippers in order not to mark the highly waxed floors. He started to settle into the pattern of withdrawn life we have met many times before. His "secretary" who had accompanied him to Vienna, Mario Codevilla, was not much help. "I am always alone. My companion isn't really able to engage in anything but banal conversation." [803] He fitted awkwardly into the humdrum day to day existence "losing his way at night in familiar streets, taking the wrong train, indifferent to the comfort of his lodgings and the quality of his means...." The pattern of getting up late and retiring late to bed, enormous labour, and going out only for meals, rapidly reduced his spirits and gave him nightmares and headaches. Intellectually, however, he remained absolutely alive, and started to answer the "many letters from Italian comrades" who wanted "faith, enthusiasm, will and strength" from him as if he were an "inexhaustible spring". While he privately felt that this was too much for him, he also felt that the parlous state of the party and Bordiga's Olympian stance called for great efforts from him.[804]

The first issue he had to face was whether to sign the manifesto which Bordiga had issued from prison in October and whose first draft he had seen in Moscow before he left. He had then discussed it with Terracini, though both received different impressions of the conversation. Togliatti, Scoccimarro and others had signed it and now he faced a letter from Togliatti asking him if he would sign. The manifesto has been lost but it appears that it merely reaffirmed the old positions of Bordiga, which Gramsci no longer thought good enough. For example, Togliatti stressed that it was a backward-looking document intent on establishing the line of succession in the party. Scoccimarro, however, claimed that it suggested the "present tactics of the party and the action which should be taken in the future."[805] Gramsci refused point blank to sign it and broke openly with Bordiga. He made clear that his reasons were simply that: "I have another concept of the party."[806] He told Togliatti, and the other recipients of his letter, that he would use his position as a member of the Central Committee and EKKI to fight both the right and the left as both were to blame for the state of the party by their concentration on the relations with the PSI and would draw up "a programme of action for the future from the doctrine and tactics of the Comintern", whose prestige was all that was holding the PCI together. This meant, he went on, that there would be no compromise with Bordiga, given the man he was.

He indicated that his concept of the party was that which he had held before August 1920: "We have not thought of the party as the result of a dialectical process in which the spontaneous movement of the revolutionary masses and the organisational and directive will of the centre converge, but only as something floating in the air which develops in itself and for itself, and which the masses will reach when the situation is favourable and the revolutionary wave has reached its height, or when the party centre thinks that it must start an offensive and lowers itself to the masses to stimulate them and carry them into action."[807]

His independent line, which reverted back to the policies of *Ordine Nuovo*, was not what the struggling survivors in Italy had expected. Those closest to Bordiga began to accuse Gramsci of double-dealing and of being the Comintern's man.[808] Grieco even published articles in papers making unfavourable comparisons between the "studious" Gramsci, who was struggling to escape his idealist heritage, and the practical political Bordiga who has "never seen the cover of a book by Gentile or Croce".[809] Gramsci single-mindedly ignored the abuse and replied curtly that since they faced *the* great change of direction in the Italian communist movement what mattered was complete clarity in choosing the new basis on which the party should be organised.

At such a distance all he could do was persuade others that his policy was correct and conduct propaganda through new newspapers and journals. He proposed to EKKI and his correspondents that a journal based on Croce's *Critica* be set up, but it never appeared. In March the first issue of a new series of *Ordine Nuovo* came out under Gramsci's editorship. It proclaimed itself a journal of proletarian culture and politics and took as its starting point the belief that "...fascism has faced Italy with a crude and cutting dilemma: that of a permanent revolutionary situation, and the impossibility not only of changing the form of State, but also of changing the government, other than with armed force."[810] In the editorial Gramsci wrote: "*Ordine Nuovo* takes up publication in the same format and with the same orientation it had when it started publication in Turin on 1 May 1919. The activities of the weekly of 1919-20 and the daily of 1921-1922 have left on the history of the Italian working-class and especially the Turinese proletariat traces which are broad and deep,... The situation seems much changed since those years but it has in fact changed more superficially than substantially. The problems to solve are the same, though they have become more difficult and complicated ... if the working-class seems disorganised and dispersed, it retains even so a strength which is perhaps even greater than it was in those days, if we consider it from the point of view of political education, clarity of ideas, and greater historical experience ... *Ordine Nuovo* takes up its battle to deepen this education, to organise and give more life to this experience."[811]

In March Gramsci also made his disagreement with Bordiga known to the party at large through the columns of *Ordine Nuovo* when he examined "the little we have done and the immense work yet to be done" in an article significantly entitled *Contro il pessimismo*. Readers will recall the motto of *Ordine Nuovo*: "Pessimism of the intelligence, optimism of the will." His object was to decide what the party should do when the existing situation drove its members to the deepest pessimism. Clearly, he proceeded, Bordiga's position should not be espoused because "what difference would there be between us and the socialist party if we too, even starting from other considerations, from other points of view, even having a greater sense of responsibility which we demonstrate by trying actively to prepare organised forces and suitable material to meet any event, give ourselves up to fatalism, lull ourselves with the sweet illusion that events cannot but unfold according to a determined linear development, which we have foreseen, in which those events will inevitably find their way into the channels and canals prepared by us, taking on a historical force and strength in them." It was due to such doctrinaire attitudes that the terrible mistake of the split at Leghorn had taken place and the communists had not only been unable to win the masses, but had not developed the experience of 1919-1920 into a language understood by the mass of workers.

The most pressing task was to turn the "Caporetto" of Leghorn into a "Piave" by winning a great army of supporters for future battles. He concluded that:

"We must react energetically against the pessimism of some groups in our party, even the most highly qualified and responsible, as it represents the greatest danger at present..."

One of the central tasks was thus theoretical, and on this level Gramsci's main criticisms of Bordiga became that he was too deterministic in his views. He explained in letters that Bordiga thought that the "voluntarism" which was so successful in Russia owed its success to the exceptional circumstances of that country, but "...that for the more developed countries of central and western Europe these tactics were inadequate, or outright useless. In these countries historical mechanisms worked according to all the Marxist canons: there [was] the element of determinism which Russia lacked and therefore the main problem [had to be] that of organising the party in and for itself." Gramsci maintained a different position, posited on an imperialism which on the one hand determined that the revolution would take place in Russia and on the other, because "it had created an upper stratum, the worker-aristocracy, and its associated union bureaucracy and social-democratic groups", demanded, "a slower and more patient action of the masses and therefore demanded from a revolutionary party tactics and strategy which were of much greater complexity and duration than those needed by the Bolsheviks in March-November 1917."[813]

In later issues of *Ordine Nuovo* he returned again and again to the notion that such fatalistic modes of thought would be replaced in the activity of factory councils.[814]

Naturally, after his open declaration of disagreement, there were bitter replies from communists for whom Bordiga was the leader. Even Gramsci's closest friends felt at first that the "turn" was too much, perhaps because it was so similar to the position of the minority.[815] This poor reaction (one old communist, Oberti even accused him of deserting his position of 1919-1920) made him less sure about his policy. Perhaps, because his information was so poor he was in fact making miscalculations when he urged such a policy?[816]

In Italy his correspondents were still to vexed by the issue of relations with the PSI, too under Bordiga's spell, or too cautious to engage in more than slow and agonising reappraisal of their position which they lived each day. Droz had returned from France at the beginning of the year determined to oppose the Comintern policy that only individuals could now join the PCI from the PSI and, once established on the Gianicolo, began long talks to this end with all the interested parties. He was somewhat surprised at the "cordial relations" between the *terzini* and the communists, who were preparing a joint list for the April elections. The proposed list included Gramsci, Bordiga, Graziadei and Maffi, Riboldi and perhaps Lazzari.[817]

However, Bordiga soon threw a spoke in the wheels by refusing to run on the list, on the grounds that in parliament he would have to speak in favour of a policy he did not support. Droz was afraid that his attitude would spread to the middle cadres of the PCI, and, indeed, it did so soon after. The Comintern had considered and adopted Droz' proposals of December that there be another attempt to fuse the parties. This was a reversal of previous policy and bitterly resented in Rome, where some of the leaders began to oppose and even sabotage the policy as soon as they heard of it. Droz' policy of detaching "Bordiga from Gramsci's group" because of what he thought were differences which went back to the Rome congress, was only slowly to bear fruit, as more and more leaders verbally committed themselves to Gramsci and a polarisation began around the "ultra-left" and Gramsci's "centre".[818]

The new "centre" was not the same as the old *Ordine Nuovo* group, as some former members of that group, notably Terracini, stuck closely to Bordiga at first. In fact it was now a loose alliance of various personal friends and backed by the Comintern. Naturally, in this "molecular process" of winning support for Gramsci's "centre" the Comintern delegate fell out with Bordiga who took the position that:

"...in June [1923] the International maintained that I should be removed from the leadership for political reasons. I therefore passed into the left both in my party and in the International. I observe discipline when it is a question of not speaking out in the interests of the International's tactics, but you can't force me to take up an important job again. In particular I would have to speak about my disagreement with the party I represent, unless the party itself writes my speeches. In that case they should choose another gramophone."[819]

This intransigency gained rather than lost Bordiga friends in the party. Grieco told Droz privately: "The International and the Party have an anti-communist line, and it is the duty of some leaders, when they note such grave deviations, to refuse to observe discipline. Some comrades are, in a manner of speaking, predestined to be leaders. Bordiga, like Lenin, is one of these. Such men cannot be disciplined like other members of the party: their historical mission is to apply discipline to others, not to observe it."[820]

Given the fact that the mass of party members were loyal to

Bordiga, Droz, and Gramsci's friends, faced the possibility of mass defections if he were forced out, as many suspected he would be, and they were slow to take any action which would alienate him. Droz saw all his plans going up in smoke and drew savage and undeserved analogies between Mussolini and Bordiga. He reported:

"[Bordiga's] ... attitude has had grave effects on the Executive of the party. The Executive when confronted with Bordiga's indiscipline is faced with this dilemma: either to ignore the refusal of Bordiga without insisting, or to take disciplinary measures against him. The first solution would be the best for a normal Executive but in the present delicate situation where the Executive was imposed by the International ... [where] it is frequently chided in veiled or open manner because it was not elected by the party and therefore has no authority over it, to let the indiscipline of Bordiga go by would open the door to the indiscipline of all the little Bordigas and would be to give up the leadership of the party.

To take measures against Bordiga when the majority [of the rank and file—A.D.] still doesn't know that he is no longer one of the leaders, and why he is no longer one of the leaders would provoke grave crisis in the party."[821]

Some of Gramsci's "centre" even adopted "Machiavellian" tactics, deliberately sabotaging the electoral policy by allowing a confidential circular which condemned the past policy of the *terzini* to be leaked to *Avanti*. This provoked a major rupture, and discredited Tasca in the eyes of the *terzini* as he had condemned them in the circular.[822] Togliatti reported this action as an attempt to force Tasca in "our direction". Togliatti also wrote to Gramsci informing him that he did not want to form a fraction which did not include Bordiga.[823]

Gramsci's firm reply that no compromise was possible with Amadeo might have completely isolated him again, had he not been elected for the Veneto electorate on 13 April.[824] This allowed him parliamentary immunity from prosecution and on the 4 May he returned to Italy to take up the battle to overcome the immense problems which still faced the party.[825]

VII

Shortly before Gramsci returned to Italy a Central Committee meeting was held which technically marked the coming to power of his "centre" group but which in fact revealed that the party was still riddled with factionalism. Although the "centre" declared that any examination of the past must be designed to overcome strife within the party, its members showed a tendency to defer to the "left" around Bordiga in a way which led the "right" around Tasca to accuse them of being motivated only by a desire for power and position and not by a desire to establish a distinct political line from that of the past.[826] So strongly did the "right" feel this suspicion that immediately after the meeting their leaders resigned from the Central Committee. Bordiga did not attend the meeting but he indicated on the other hand in a note that despite the deference shown him by half-hearted members of the "centre" like Scoccimarro, he did not feel that they shared a common position and proposed to do battle against them for the principles of the Rome Theses.[827]

Shortly after Gramsci returned he attended a secret meeting of the still disunited party at Como. Sixty-seven communist officials attended including 46 secretaries of the regional federations and sundry others, who could indicate how the party felt about its new leadership. The meetings were held in mountain valleys full of blooming narcissus, and at night the representatives of the "Milan firm", supposedly on "retreat", engaged in the tomfoolery of fascist anthems and speeches to delude the other guests at the inn.[828] The daytime meetings quickly revealed that the new leadership had practically no support among the middle cadres of the party, who supported Bordiga overwhelmingly. Even the "right" had more supporters than Gramsci's laboriously constructed "centre" with its commitment to patient organisational work in the proletariat.[829] The sharp exchanges between Gramsci and Bordiga highlighted their differences. Bordiga, confident that history was on his side, remarked that he was in no hurry to start work among the masses, provoking a tirade from Gramsci whose sense was probably close to Montagnana's recollection: "You are in no hurry, Bordiga, but those of us who feel close ties with the working-class and the people are in a hell of a hurry, just as the workers are in a hurry, just as the mass of people who suffer bodily from the fascist dictatorship and capitalist exploitation are in a hurry."[830] He argued forcefully that there

213

were situations in which to be slow spelt defeat.[831]

The Como meeting made clear that Gramsci's major task in the immediate future would consist of winning over to his view the middle cadres and the members of the party. Winning the party through constant inner-party activity was, however, still merely an essential preliminary to what he considered the fundamental prerequisite for making a revolution, organising the masses through factory councils. He had again made the object of his inner-party activity clear in April in an exchange of letters with Piero Sraffa, a friend of *Ordine Nuovo* days (1919-20) and in 1924 a university teacher in England. Sraffa urged that existing conditions in Italy necessitated a support of democratic and liberal parties and goals, and that a "bourgeois revolution" would be necessary before the party could think of positive political activity.[832] Gramsci replied shortly that this was "liquidationism", and that an "organised party" could not remain "passive" as Sraffa urged. "...Only concrete activity, unbroken work, continuously keeping up with developing historical reality" kept a party, like an individual, preeminent and made it a leader. To deny such concrete work was to deny that it was a revolutionary epoch, which nobody, not even Sraffa, believed. The result of allowing the "constitutional parties" to monopolise the organisation of the social classes who were historical allies of the proletariat, would be to make the working class "absent" from politics. Gramsci countered with the assertion that the main tasks of the PCI were not only to create an awareness in the party that the main activity should be to spread the slogan of revolution as the order of the day among ever wider sectors of the community, but also to make the slogan "for a workers' and peasants' government" a national question. This could only be done by concentrating attention on the Southern Question.[833] So he started his campaign to win the party by widening his organisational objectives in the masses rather than limiting them.

The forces opposing him were rather less united than the vote at Como suggested, as the rank and file of the party, who suffered directly from fascist oppression, were rather readier than the local and regional leaders to accept his views. Even Tasca conceded in a letter to Rákosi that the "centre" would soon win the majority in the party because of this, and Scoccimarro argued encouragingly for the rather out-of-touch Gramsci that it was really a matter of making manifest the latent support in the party for the "centre" position.[834]

Gramsci started an endless round of travelling between cities, dodging the police, speaking at meetings, and organising the party around his views. Bordiga, from a fast disappearing Mount Olympus, did nothing concrete to oppose him at first. From his digs with a German family near the via Nomentana, Gramsci's letters told a tale of enormous organisational work in the second half of 1924: "...enormous work is taking place in the country" (21 July 1924); "I've got to keep an eye on everything. Tomorrow I'm leaving for Milan and Turin to see how our two largest organisations are working" (18 August 1924); "I have been out of Rome for more than two weeks, without being able to read your letters, which I so anxiously await" (8 September 1924); "I've been in Turin, where I attended three meetings" (8 September 1924); "Every week I have to speak at three or four meetings at either a leadership level, or to local groups of comrades." (18 September 1924); "Last week I was at Naples for the congress of the local federation." (6 October 1924); "In a few days I am off to Sardinia and will not be able to write." (20 October 1924); "In a few days I am leaving again and will spend at least a fortnight in Milan" (26 November 1924).[835]

What he said at these interminable meetings has been recorded by some of his listeners (including the police spies present). He pressed two linked themes as the basis on which the party should be organised. First, it would have to include the peasantry in any effective revolutionary movement, and thus would have to study the Southern Question closely. Second, it followed that it would have to view itself as an educator or intellectual. Both these themes explicitly presumed that the revolution could be prepared immediately. He held one particular important meeting in Sardinia on 26 October 1924, where his supporters were organising the local branch in favour of the "centre". At the meeting, held under the trees at Is Arenas, he addressed his audience of seventeen or eighteen on the "left" and the problems of reorganising in Sardinia. An interviewee recalled: "Gramsci spoke first about the situation of the party, underlining the leap forward which the party had made, the possibility of advancing even in Sardinia, and on the difference between his line and that of the Bordigan minority. He emphasised the need in Sardinia for the party to be established in as many inland villages as possible, and that it make closer contact with the peasants, shepherds and fishermen." The delegate from Sassari, who favoured Bordiga, spoke against this policy but he remained isolated.[836] After the meeting Gramsci went to spend a few days with his parents where he played with his niece and spoke to the peasants in his easy and engaging manner. He reported:

"The members of the local co-operative of artisans, workers and peasants came to see me, pushing forward their president, who didn't want to compromise the a-political nature of the organisation. They asked me many questions about Russia, the way the soviets work, about communism, about the meaning of capital and capitalism, about our tactics towards fascism, and so on. This meeting was very interesting because, if it enabled me to assess the backwardness and prejudice spread through the peasantry, it also proved to me their readiness to resist the state of things and the immense influence Russia had among them. 'Everybody wants to be Russian'. Even the president ended up agreeing after much humming and hawing."[837]

At another "secret" meeting, this time with the young communists of Liguria, Gramsci began by emphasising "that we still lacked a history of the Italian socialist movement, Angiolini having intended only to write a simple uncritical chronicle, and Michels not having been capable of examining and judging the action of the Socialist Party within a general framework of national history ..." He went on to make two interesting points: first, that the Risorgimento should be understood as a failed "national popular" revolution, and second, that the incorporation of the mass of the populace into the nation had gone hand in hand with the revival of Marxism among the Turinese workers, to which revival corresponded their desire to build unity between the northern proletariat and the southern peasantry.[838]

VIII

While Gramsci was engaged in the exhausting labour of winning the party to his views, the Fifth Comintern congress of June-July 1924 abruptly declared what is usually termed a move to the "left". The new line was primarily explained by Zinoviev's desire to worst Trotsky in the struggle for the succession to Lenin within the CPSU(B). He had to appear more "left" than the young eagle himself, especially since Lenin had condemned him as being too faint-hearted to be a leader. So, despite the defeat in Germany in 1923 of an insurrection which Trotsky had supported —

and despite the relative stabilisation of capitalism throughout Europe — Zinoviev declared that insurrections still showed some chance of success. It followed that the social-democrats should be seen as the most "left" force of the bourgeoisie and not as potential allies. Commentators have mistakenly seen the new policy as either a confirmation of what Gramsci was already doing in Italy or as "definitively healing the rift between the Italian party and the International."[839] Gramsci was not so misled by labels like "right" and "left".[840]

All this "leftism" was merely window-dressing. Zinoviev, like Trotsky himself, had realised that there had been a relative stabilisation of capitalism throughout the West and therefore advised practical policies which frequently, if not always, were in contradiction with the programmatic statements of the Fifth Congress, and with the policies Gramsci was following in Italy.

Bordiga was one of the many misled by appearances. He had come to the Congress prepared to do battle against the errors of the policy of the united front. On hearing Zinoviev state that revolution was imminent and that a united front should be conducted from "below" rather than from "above" he declared: "The Italian 'left' will vote despite everything for Zinoviev's programme, which, beside the resolutions of the IV Congress is much closer to the theses we have always sustained. We are completely in agreement with the greater part of Zinoviev's programme.... We can even accept the formulation in the paragraphs against so-called 'left deviations' because these have nothing in common with the ideas which the Italian 'left' has really defended."[841] He quickly learnt that a wide gap existed between the Fifth Congress' theory and its practice when he tried to apply the logic of Zinoviev's programmatic "leftism" to the practical issues of the international movement. Bordiga assumed that the new policies were a condemnation of the preceding policy of the united front and therefore argued that such lapses from the revolutionary path should be forestalled in the future by the establishment of a "left" throughout the international communist movement. This suggestion tended to support the temporarily worsted Trotsky and was therefore impermissible. He was warned that his views encouraged factionalism and none of his supporters were elected to the PCI Central Executive.

Togliatti, representing Gramsci's "centre", had not been so gullible as Bordiga. He had noted ambiguities in Zinoviev's position from the outset although, diplomatic as always, he had voted for it. He noted that the new line tended to favour Bordiga in principle, if not substantially. However, the only half-explanation he gave was that the "leftism" was uncritical. He did not note how Zinoviev's formulations depended more on the inner-party struggle in Russia than on objective assessments of the possibilities of revolution in the West.[842] Thus Bordiga came home from the Fifth Congress feeling morally vindicated but without any real power in the party and Gramsci, whose group retained the majority in the Central Executive, did not in fact enjoy the support of the Comintern. The dispute between Gramsci and Bordiga therefore became much worse late in 1924. It took the form of a debate over the views and treatment of Trotsky. Bordiga had half-indicated his support for Trotsky in talks held after the congress and on his return to Italy went onto the offensive against the "centre" and the Comintern, posing as *the* supporter of Trotsky in Italy. He managed to unite some middle cadres of the party around the slogan of a defence of Trotsky. Gramsci had a marathon fourteen-hour discussion with Bordiga at the congress of the Naples section of the party — one of the few which Gramsci did not win to his position. Droz reported that Gramsci thought "...that Bordiga led the opposition in a demagogic way ... according to him he put the Comintern on trial, claiming that it had eliminated Trotsky, and playing on the popularity of the latter in order to meet easy success, without examining the Russian crisis in depth."[843] Gramsci was thus compelled to take up a position on the "Trotsky question".

Only at a Central Committee meeting of 6 February 1925 did Gramsci and the party clearly state their disagreement with Trotsky. The main topic of debate was Trotsky's view that there had been a relative stabilisation of capitalism in Western Europe under the aegis of United States imperialism. Gramsci refused to agree with this view, or that the revolutionary wave had subsided, or with the practical policies which flowed from these views. Bordiga, on the other hand presented a motion in which he agreed with Trotsky's position, but denied that it led to "pessimism" about the possibility of revolution. He argued that Lenin and Trotsky had always agreed that the revolution was permanent and that Trotsky's views should be openly debated within the communist movement.[844]

Gramsci's open criticism of Trotsky did not mean that he was parrotting the Comintern's position, or have no reserves about the treatment of the leader of the Russian "left". This was clear from the nature of the debate in the Central Committee and the conclusions it reached. The Central Committee certainly resolved that: "The measures taken [by the CPSU] against Trotsky are necessary actions for the defence of the fundamental problems of communist doctrine", but also argued that Trotsky's political position was linked to the theoretical views in his *Permanent Revolution*. The Central Committee typified these views as "...a pessimistic view of the development of world revolution and a conception of the revolutionary process which ignores correct relationships between the workers and peasants ... considering the defeat and degeneration of the proletarian revolution in a predominantly petty-bourgeois country inevitable if the victory of the working-class in the West does not ensure within a brief term the help of proletarian state power from the most advanced industrial countries."[845] And it warned that the strength of a party depended on its unity on the basis of the "principles and methods" of Leninism; that any cult of an individual was detrimental to revolutionary leadership; and that "only in the Russian party's history have there been created to date the conditions which warrant regarding a leading group as 'Leninist' and as a real headquarters of the proletarian revolution". It concluded: "The trust that the militants of the Comintern place in the Russian party and its leaders, is not therefore given to any single person but because it continues a historical process and a revolutionary tradition."

In accord with this views, Bordiga was instructed not to make his motion public knowledge (it was only published in July 1925). Gramsci had, on the other hand, condemned the cult of personalities and warned that PCI support for the CPSU and the Comintern depended on their continuing the tradition of "Leninism" as he understood it, which can be summed up as a policy favouring mass work and unity.[846] Since the Comintern was starting to move away from such "Leninism" at an accelerating pace an ever-widening gap grew between it and Gramsci in 1924-5.

The logic of Gramsci's ideas also drove him to a practice far removed from the real positions of the USSR and the Comintern. He still believed that capitalism was collapsing in Italy and that a revolution was possible if sufficient mass support for communism were organised in the meantime but he doggedly pursued his organisational policy even after the Fifth Congress of the Comintern. This belief had some justification. After the assassination by fascists of the socialist deputy Matteotti in May 1924, there was a wave of anti-fascist feeling throughout the country. Gramsci really thought that the regime was in danger of collapse — Italy was an "erupting volcano" — and he talked openly with constitutionalists like Amendola and Bencivenga about the possibility of an armed insurrection.[847] Most of the other parties on the left of the Italian House were more in favour of a "moral" withdrawal from Parliament than the practical measures Gramsci proposed and they had the mass of the people with them. Gramsci quickly realised that "we are going through a wave of fanatical devotion to democracy, which reacts against us although the party is getting stronger and more people are joining it,"[848] and that lack of party organisation meant that any independent insurrection would fail.

So he had to formulate some policy towards those parties who had withdrawn to set up an "anti-parliament" on the Aventine Hill. Despite the fact that the workers felt that it was too risky to follow the PCI, Gramsci continued to call at a Central Committee meeting in July 1924 for preparations for the "violent" struggle necessary to overthrow fascism and predicted that "worse events" would follow the assassination. He argued that the party should work to prevent the mass from "consolidating itself permanently" in support of the Aventine parties, because "armed insurrection" would still be the order of the day if the fascists and the democrats could not come to some sort of *modus vivendi*.

This hostility of Gramsci towards the other opposition parties was mirrored in the PCI, which left the "opposition committee" and started to attack it. Gramsci counterposed to any democratic solution to the Matteotti crisis in the normal sense a solution which called for a "molecular transformation of the bases of the democratic state", again reaffirming the conciliar policy which dated back to 1919-1920.[849] Given the rapid change of events in the Matteotti crisis, this policy was too belated. It was certainly not one shared by the Comintern, which disagreed with Gramsci's stress on autonomous activity by the PCI, and his tendency to drift towards the recalcitrant "left" at times of crisis. The Comintern objected strongly to the views which he presented to the Central Committee on 11 August, which stated that it was evident: "...that for the next few months the prospect will be catastrophic" and which went on to argue against supporting any democratic coalition when the fascist government fell.[850] Droz was obliged to "insist" before Gramsci and his fellows would carry out the

Comintern policy of approaching the Aventine parties with a proposal for a counter-parliament. Even the careful Togliatti wrote to Moscow defending Gramsci against the Comintern criticism on the ground that in the circumstances Gramsci's was the right policy.[851]

Thus it was an independent Gramsci, little more in line with the Comintern than Bordiga — despite the Italians' differences over Trotsky — who finally went to the Soviet Union in February 1925 to attend the meetings of the EKKI between March 21 and April 5. Once in Moscow he installed himself with his in-laws. Matters were more than a little strained on the domestic front, as Delio had the whooping cough, and Eugenia, whose mental deterioration was quite obvious, insisted that she was the boy's mother. It was not a good beginning to meetings whose main theme was to be the issue of indiscipline in communist parties, and, inferentially, the "indiscipline" of Trotsky in the CPSU.

Gramsci did not speak at the EKKI meetings, leaving Scoccimarro to speak for the PCI in terms which revealed an indelibly Gramscian imprint. The main point of Scoccimarro's argument was that there were affinities between the theoretical positions of Trotsky and those of Bordiga, though there were differences as well, in particular over the extent of the Comintern's responsibility for the failure of revolution outside the USSR. Both shared a mechanical view of Marxist dialectics which neglected the real processes taking place, the specific explanation how there was a change from one position to another. Their affinities thus lay "in the fact that they neglect and ignore the essential and characteristic element of every situation as *the* factor which determines the tactics of the party;[and] in their concept of the relationship between the function of the party and the spontaneous movement of the masses, which while it raises a party voluntarism as against a determinism of the masses, also diminishes and undervalues the task of the party in relation to that of the leaders...."

Scoccimarro went on on lines that were almost identical with Gramsci's earlier comments on Bordiga, that in Trotskyism "...could be perceived quite clearly a certain disbelief in the adaptability of Bolshevism, that is the revolutionary method formed during the Russian revolution, to the revolutionary movements of Western countries. It thinks that in Russia, given the backward conditions of the economy, the Party had to seek a remedy for the insufficient pressure of economic forces in particular tactics. In Western countries where capitalism had reached a high level of development, where the concentration and centralisation of capital are more advanced than in Russia, it is assumed that the contradiction of the capitalist system will exert a much more active pressure in determining the raising up and the insurrection of the proletarian masses and that in consequence the tactic of the party should be different. From this derives a particular conception and revaluation of the party, of the spontaneity of the masses, which is behind that political fatalism which we observe in the tactics advanced by Bordiga.'' Scoccimarro typified these tactics as laying most stress on opposing the slogan of the united front and a workers' government, when because of the pernicious past influence of social-democracy in the West, the united front offered the ''specific tactical means'' for freeing the proletariat from its degeneration.

While the Comintern leaders applauded the conclusion that: ''In reality, Bolshevism has supplied us with political and tactical methods of universal value''[852] they could have wished for more. There was a clear attempt in Scoccimarro's speech to separate Trotsky's own position from the practical views which Bordiga and others attributed to him. This separation was tantamount to a defence in terms which ran against the trend in the Comintern. Scoccimarro denied that Trotsky thought that the Comintern should have primacy over member parties. He denied that the Russian opposed the united front or thought that it was a failure, and he argued strenuously that he had become the rallying point for opposition in the international communist movement because he ''appeared to be left''.

Moreover, while it was true that Trotsky's theories had mechanistic overtones, so did those of the CPSU(B) and the Comintern as a whole. The speech was thus also an implicit criticism of all that was common between the Comintern and Trotsky. It also hinted that Gramsci was not going to give up his own line, based on the specific interests of the Italian proletariat and its situation. This did not necessarily include the expulsion of the undisciplined ''left''. Gramsci disagreed with Bordiga, he also respected him, and he had already guaranteed a year before that there would be no expulsion of ''leftists'' from the party.[853]

Not even the nuances of Gramsci's views changed after his return from Moscow. He had stated just before leaving Italy that ''just as in Russia, we must create a centralised organisation of factory councils which will replace the existing union organisation in the mobilisation and the action of the mass.''[854] He had also affirmed that his estimate of the situation after the Matteotti crisis had been correct. On his return he continued to "translate into Italian" all the slogans of the Comintern. Before the Fifth Congress the policy had been to call for a "workers' government" and after to call for "committees of workers and peasants". Gramsci translated both into renewed calls for factory councils.

The intricacy of this translation did not hide its substance. Even the demand for "Bolshevisation" of the party was given a "Gramscian" interpretation.

IX

The most important decision of the Fifth Congress of the Comintern had been its decision to "Bolshevise" all member parties. "Bolshevisation" meant the reorganisation of the Communist International on the "democratic centralist" model, so that not only the formal structure but the style of activity of all parties corresponded to that of the CPSU(B). The Comintern was to become a true "world party" in which the interests of each particular section were subordinate to that of the whole. In fact this meant subordination to the conception of the whole held by the Russian leaders of the Comintern. After 1924 this conception became more and more that the foreign parties were adjuncts to the CPSU(B) and subordinate to its interests. Gramsci had never had the same view of the Comintern and in February 1925 had reiterated in Moscow the view that PCI practice could not be subordinate to the interests of either general developments, like "world revolution", or the CPSU(B): praxis always started from the particular. Trotsky's error was to hold a contrary view about the primacy of "world revolution". So the "Bolshevisation" Gramsci initiated took on a different overall character from that envisaged by the Comintern although they coincided on particular points.

In April 1925 Gramsci called for the establishment of a party school so that as part of the "world party" the Italian party could become "communist, Bolshevik and Leninist". He agreed that "without the weapon [of theoretical consciousness] a Party did not exist" and that "without a Party no victory is possible". It was therefore reasonable to expect all party members to assimilate Leninism, which was contemporary Marxism, though this theory alone would not enable them to make a revolution. He warned a month later that it was "unmarxist" to believe that actions by small groups of men however equipped, would make the revolution. The object of this inner-party education was not to provide communists with final, infallible knowledge of how the world worked. It was not "objective study" which was "value-free". It had the "character of impassioned militancy". "Study and culture are for us nothing but the theoretical awareness of our own immediate and supreme ends, and the way we can succeed in transforming them into action."

It was a spur as well as a guide to action, but the truth of that practice did not lie in the theory, or "first principles", even if the party had to strive for the maximum theoretical correctness. Rather the party had to start its practice from the "practical application" of its overall orientation. Precisely because: "...the party represents not only the working-class, but also a doctrine, the doctrine of socialism, [it] therefore struggles to unite the wills of the masses in the direction of socialism, sticking to what really exists, but exists as movement and development." Sticking to what really existed did not mean preaching at the worker, precisely because the individual proletarian could not be expected to develop class consciousness until "...the life style of the class itself is changed", that is, his consciousness would only change in the process of making the revolution itself. A full proletarian class consciousness could only come through the establishment of factory cells as the Comintern demanded and by following the practice urged by *Ordine Nuovo* in 1919-1920.[855] Gramsci concluded that organisation was first of all a political question of organising a leadership for the masses which could develop the *commissione interna* in a revolutionary direction.[856]

A particular understanding of "centralisation" depended on this continuing commitment to a conciliar practice. Centralisation was understood as no more than fitting all members of the party to be leaders of the mass so that they could always work no matter what the situation.[857] In turn, the capacity to work — to conduct a massive ideological campaign — had been thwarted when the party was regarded wrongly as an "army", confused with its own central organisation, when nothing was ever discussed and when the main concern was to prevent its becoming contaminated by petty-bourgeois views. This, Gramsci alleged, was the case when Bordiga had led it. Many Russian leaders and the Comintern also held similar views to those of Bordiga but Gramsci did not allude to that.

224

Gramsci did not engage in a witch-hunt against the "left" who espoused the view of the party as an "army". His moderation also depended on his overall view, in which it was unity itself which provided safeguards against incorrect policies. Rather, to neutralise Bordiga, Gramsci concentrated on building up the practical links with the masses as he had in the past.

The party had grown immensely in 1924 and 1925. From 9,000 members in 1923 it reached 25,000 at the end of 1924 and continued to grow in 1925. About 3000 of these members were *terzini* who had joined *en masse* late in 1924, but many others were being won by Gramsci's policies. 70-75% were proletarians, although only in cities like Turin were they predominantly factory workers. Since the party slogan had been "a communist group in every village" there was also a widespread, but sparse, peasant membership totalling about 20% of membership by 1926.

These members were not well-organised. Throughout 1925 Tasca was able to tax Gramsci with the fact that his policy was not working well in practice. There was a real reason — the bulk of the former tested activists in the factory had either emigrated, been imprisoned, or been killed.[858] So Gramsci was not put off, merely drawing the conclusion that more effort would have to be made among the newcomers. In an important report about the "situation in 1926", he indicated his abiding belief that the way to revolution was through the type of activity formerly pursued by *Ordine Nuovo*, and he denied that there was no possibility of success: the organisations dominated by the bourgeoisie were susceptible to conversion to socialism. He argued that "...old reformist and maximalist workers who have great influence in the factories ... the most advanced members of the rural villages, [and] small urban intellectuals ..." were being attracted to communism by his type of united front "from below". The immediate practical lesson was that the party should work to develop new Agitational Committees, which were, in his estimation, the latest version of 1919-1920's councils: "Technically it is a problem of slogans, and forms of organisation too. If I hadn't a certain fear of being called an *ordinovista*, I would say that today one of the most important problems which affect especially the great capitalist countries is that of factory councils and workers' control, as the basis for a new regrouping of the proletariat which would permit a better struggle against the union bureaucracy and permit the organisation of the huge masses who are disorganised not only in France but also in Germany and England." His only concession that Italy did not fit exactly into this scheme lay in his admission that the technical preparation for insurrection was more on the order of the day in Italy than in more advanced countries.[859] It is interesting in the light of his still extremely intransigent revolutionary stance and his demand for conciliar activity despite the difficulty imposed on that policy by objective conditions, that Togliatti expressed the view that he was asking too much of the workers in times of repression, and thus moved implicitly much closer to the positions of Tasca, beginning that departure of the erstwhile "centre" from Gramsci's "leftism" which was both to coincide with Gramsci's arrest and his removal from the political activity of the PCI.

X

Of all the Comintern slogans which Gramsci was able to incorporate in this conciliar theory, the most significant in 1925 and early 1926 was that calling for "committees of workers and peasants". Gramsci had always been particularly interested in the way the peasants fitted into his general theory of how a revolution was made.

In 1919-1920 he had argued over-optimistically that these traditional forces of reaction would no longer serve capitalism after the dreadful experience of the war. He had also believed that the revolution in the North would simultaneously free the peasantry from their oppression. Both expectations were belied by events. By 1922 as we have seen, Gramsci explained the success of fascism by the hegemony that the bourgeois of the villages exercised over the peasants and therefore started to think about the ways this hegemony could be broken. Obviously the party would have to go forth into the villages and convert the peasants, and, as best it could, it did so after 1923. How would it convert these people? On reflection Gramsci decided that even if the whole system of rule rested on the peasants (as his earliest mentors suggested and as his experience confirmed) the method of raising of proletarian consciousness through councils was still the first step in breaking reaction's hold over the peasants but this process would have to extend to the peasants as well. After breaking down class corporativism, the councils, which swept away all the distinctions between "better qualified" and "less qualified", would have to extend to the countryside. This view became a keystone of Gramsci's policies in the documents he drafted together with

Togliatti in August 1925 for the Third Party Congress.[869]

The starting point of these theses was still that the conditions for revolution were actual, but that no revolution could be made without direct party work among the masses. The theses argued that the correct way to work could be discovered in an analysis of Italian history. This analysis showed that the dominating force in Italian history, the bulk of the population, were peasants, as in Russia. This "relative backwardness" made Italy another of the "weakest links" in the chain of imperialism, but this favourable situation was complicated by the lack of unity between the industrial North and the peasant South. As the main revolutionary force in the country the proletariat's main task was therefore to build up its hegemony over the peasants, whose great revolutionary potential was deviated by the rural magnates and petty-bourgeoisie who dominated them socially and politically. This domination would have to be broken. What characterised the domination was that "...the Southern peasants ... as a whole ... don't have any autonomous experience of organising themselves." To break them out of the "traditional schemas of bourgeois society", they suggested that the party make the key-point of its activity the development of self-educatory organisations: "Associations for the defence of the peasantry."[861]

This practical desire to win the peasants to an alliance with the proletariat prompted Gramsci to examine closely how the petty-bourgeoisie had managed in the past to nullify the revolutionary potential of the Southern peasant. As a result in 1926 he took up the analysis of the way hegemony was secured and developed further on the ideas he had already touched on five years earlier. He never completed his long and important essay on the Southern Question, but it is still invaluable as Gramsci indicated that the themes of his famous *Prison Notebooks* continued those in the Southern Question.[862]

In the Southern Question Gramsci typified the system of rule in the South as a "great social disunity", with three social classes; the peasants, the little intellectuals of the petty-and-middle-bourgeoisie of the villages, and the great intellectuals and landowners. The first were incapable of autonomous centralised action, and were represented by the second group in a myriad of ways. It was the last group which "centralised and dominated" this myriad representation by the second. "As is natural, it is in the ideological field that this centralisation is carried out with the greatest efficiency and precision. Giustino Fortunato and Benedetto Croce are therefore

227

the master keys of the Southern system and, in a certain sense, are the two greatest personalities of the Italian reaction."

Thus the key to Italy's politics — to the failure of the revolution — lay with its Southern intellectuals, who, Gramsci noted, also dominated its state machinery. Who and what were these intellectuals? Gramsci recognised that they were the "old type" who organised in a peasant and artisan society, and that since intellectuals were "radically changed by the development of capitalism" the old type were being replaced in more advanced countries by the "technical organiser, the specialist in applied science". The "corrupt, untrustworthy, political" intellectual of the old type was in fact very close to the peasant and therefore skilled at manipulating him. At the same time he was intent on keeping him in thrall and exploiting him. Thus through these little village intellectuals and their organisations the great landowners were able to control the peasants. In turn, the agrarian bloc constituted for mutual interest functioned in the South as an intermediary for Northern capitalism and banking.

To disintegrate this structure of domination it was necessary to start from the fact that the intellectuals themselves were not united culturally and had no homogeneity. In the past, many had wished to break out of the system and had gone to the North to provide the inspiration for *La Voce, L'Unità* (Salvemini's paper) and other journals which attacked the Southern system of oppression. It was here that Croce and Fortunato had become very important. They had seen to it that these journals never became revolutionary in their criticism by inculcating a modality of response — the "serene, classical" *via media*, which they advanced in their philosophy. Viewed in this light, the "national" function of Croce in particular had been to pull the revolutionary teeth of the dissident Southern intellectuals by *separating them from the peasants*, and thus turning them once more into servants of the system of the South and of Italy.

Ordine Nuovo had tended to counteract this effect of Croceanism by redirecting the intention of these internal emigrés to the reality of the Italian proletariat, and thus to its possible role as the subject of modern Italian history. Gobetti, although not a communist, was archetypal of these new intellectuals and "represented a movement which should not be opposed, at least in principle", as he provided a link with left intellectuals from both the North and the South.

These new intellectuals, who constituted the key to breaking the ruling hegemony, could not, however, be converted as quckly to communism as other social groups, as they represented "...the cultural tradition of a nation, and wish to take up and synthesise its entire history."

The essay concluded abruptly, but significantly for any understanding of Gramsci's further intellectual development:

"Now, we are interested in the intellectuals as a mass, not solely as single individuals. It is certainly important and useful for the proletariat that one or more individual intellectuals take up its programme and doctrine, mix with the proletariat and become and feel that they have become an integral part of it. As a class the proletariat is poor in organisational elements, has no, and can only form, an intellectual stratum of its own very slowly, with much effort and only after the conquest of state power. But it is also useful and important that there be an organic split in the intellectuals as a mass — a split of a historical character, which forms a left tendency in the modern sense of the words, that is, oriented towards the revolutionary proletariat."[863]

Gramsci won the party to these views, or, at least, to the policies which depended on them, at the Lyons congress, which was held in January 1926. In winning the party, he also worsted Bordiga and the "left", who for some time had been conducting last ditch factional activity against Gramsci's line. The "left" hurled their last taunt at Gramsci shortly before the Congress met, pointing out that Gramsci was bringing petty-bourgeois ideology into the party through his emphasis on mass work, and that his "Leninism" was no more than "Leninism *alla moda*". In sum, Gramsci and his supporters were unreconstructed "idealists", whose policies would cause party fortunes to decline. Gramsci replied scathingly that the purism of Bordiga's line was responsible for the ease with which Mussolini had come to power, that the "Rome theses" rather than the policies of his group were "inspired by Crocean philosophy", and that the Bordigan line was unrealistic, "pre-Hegelian" and "pre-Marxist" in its lack of concern with real conditions. Had Bordiga directed his strictures against Gramsci's followers rather than Gramsci himself he would have been showing considerable perceptiveness. Togliatti's reply to Bordiga's attacks was merely that there was no better way to come to Marx than through a study of Hegel, indicating an interesting divergence between himself and Gramsci.[864] Within a few years he and others were to start stripping Gramsci's line of its revolutionary teeth.[865]

Gramsci made clear both the fatuity of arguing that he was an "idealist", and how much he was against "rightism" in his attacks on Tasca at the congress. He condemned the "right" for believing that there was a "solution to the bourgeois crisis outside that of revolution", because he disagreed with their estimate of how the existing State could be used, stating specifically that if he were to accept that the social-democrats were the right-wing of the proletariat, as Tasca urged, he would have to accept that he could not take up arms against them, an untenable position if they came to power.[866] Clearly he believed that the capitalist State would have to be destroyed, not that consciousness raising in the factories was all there was to revolution. Moreover, his invitation to Bordiga to join the Central Committee at a time when Droz was warning the Neapolitan that he would be expelled if he continued his factional activity, showed his continued affinity with "leftism".

His triumph in the party was short-lived. Ever since his maiden speech in Parliament in May 1924, he had humiliated the fascists and the fascist leader in public and private exchanges. The cruel mockery (*"parla Rigoletto"*) with which they replied to his fearless challenge — "... the revolutionary forces of the nation will never let themselves be shattered, and your dark dream will never be turned into a reality" — did not hide their awareness of the danger presented to the regime by Gramsci's moral courage and civic duty. Their problem was to find a way in which to shut up a man who enjoyed parliamentary immunity without the risky business of a second Matteotti case.[867]

Their police, of course, kept a close eye on Gramsci, followed him everywhere, and built up their dossier on his political activity whenever possible. The most significant of his activities seemed to them to be his activities among the Southern peasantry — perhaps because they agreed with Gramsci that the Southern peasant provided the mass support and power behind the "only historically national" class, the petty-bourgeoisie, who constituted the backbone of fascism, and that therefore the main battle to overthrow fascism lay among the peasantry.

Ultimately they succeeded in gathering sufficient "evidence" to frame him and arrest him. Gramsci believed that Sardinia was least under the control of fascism and had therefore built up contacts with Emilio Lussu, the leader of the Sard Action Party. From 1924 onwards they used to meet regularly in Parliament and at Gramsci's home in via Morgagni. Gramsci decided that the PS d'A provided a "concrete socialist reality" and in July 1926 sent Lussu a questionnaire about the Sard peasant and Sardinian problems which fell into the hands of the police.[868]

The capture of these documents coincided with the arrest of two secret PCI couriers in Bologna. Among the documents in their possession were letters signed by Gramsci and others, money, subversive literature directed at soldiers, and, as a reminder of the debate in the party, a copy of Trotsky's *Europe and America*. At the subsequent trial the military court decided that the PCI was an "opponent of the national order". In September other communists whose names had come to light at the trial were arrested. Gramsci chose not to leave the country, although he knew that moves were also afoot to arrest him.[869] On 8 November he was finally arrested and deported to the tiny island of Ustica with its "Saracen citadel" to await his trial. He found the populace "very polite" and reported to his wife that he was treated "very correctly".

The first trial hearing was held in Milan on 9 February 1927, after a terrible journey back from the South. Gramsci argued that he did not know what the couriers were carrying and was innocent of any charges in relation to that "crime". So the fascist regime, which was determined to stop his "mind functioning" for twenty years, brought new charges a few days later, and although they had been unable to obtain any evidence against Gramsci from the spies they had put in his cell, another trial was held in May in Rome. They relied on the police report of his activity at Is Arenas two years earlier, with the questionnaire to Lussu supposedly providing the link with the charges laid. The police report claimed, without any truth, that Gramsci had stated at the Is Arenas meeting: "... that if the Italian situation did not change Italian communists and political refugees would be found, ready, armed and waiting on the French frontier."[870] The charge was therefore that he had encouraged mayhem, civil war and looting within the realm.

Gramsci's defence was simply that the PCI did not intend to take power by armed force in the sense intended in the laws under which he was charged; that it had no hidden armed caches, nor had it made preparations for such violent action. This was only half-true, as communist military specialists had visited the party and talked about insurrection.[871] His lawyer was rather inept, and, in any event the conviction was a foregone conclusion. On 4 June 1927 Gramsci was convicted to 20 years, 5 months and 5 days in prison.[872] His active political practice had finished. He now had four and a half thousand days to think on its theoretical implications for Marxism and revolutionary socialism.

CHAPTER V

"A Revolutionary Theory"

I

It was during his years of revolutionary activity in the PCI that Gramsci was able to read the work of Lenin, first at the Comintern, and then after his return to Italy in 1924. He was also able to read the work of the other luminaries of the Russian revolution. What is striking is how little they are cited or appear in his writings. It is worthwhile to make a general point here. Any acquaintance with the comparative history of communist movements reveals that it was only with the rise to pre-eminence of Stalin, — which can be dated as early as the Sixth Congress of the Comintern in 1928 but is usually dated from the early thirties — that the works of the Soviet leaders became gospel for communists. Before that date there prevailed an undoubted respect for these leaders, but a respect not untinged with a feeling that they too were disciples of Marx and not really to be ranked with him in the way the famous Soviet image does. Lenin was *not* well-known outside the Russian movement before the Russian revolution, and certainly did not enjoy the unreserved adoration which was already his unsought lot in the Soviet Party after 1917.

Gramsci did not have any direct personal contact with Lenin, and when he met Trotsky it was to oppose him bitterly on some matter of policy. Of course, he was able to learn many ways in which the Russian revolutionary movement worked directly from his experience at the Comintern. But again, the Comintern he knew after 1922 was a body from which Lenin had practically withdrawn due to his illness and it is impossible to argue that Gramsci imbibed a Leninist practice directly from his work on its various organs.[873]

To understand Lenin and Leninism he had to turn to books as he had with Marx, and much as any of us would have to do today.

232

Since he knew little Russian despite valiant efforts to learn it, and since the complete works were not in translation in 1926,[874] he had to put together what was available in French and Italian. Without doubt he tried to do this as best he could since he was enthusiastic about the Russian revolution and intent on learning from its methods. Through his regular reading of *Communist International* he had been able to read the following titles in 1921-April 1922: *Notes from a Publicist; Theses on the National and Colonial Questions* and *Speeches* by Lenin to the Second and Third Congresses of the Communist International. After 1923 no further writings by Lenin appeared in the journal. After his arrival in Russia and up to his imprisonment four years later, by collecting his references and quotations together we can ascertain that he read or knew the contents of: *Marxism and Revolutionism, Karl Marx, Two Tactics, What is to be Done?*, and *Imperialism*. He did not read either *Materialism and Empirio-Criticism* or the *Philosophical Notebooks*, but when all these titles are put together with those he had already read before 1921, we see that he had a good knowledge of Lenin's work by 1926. What did he get from this knowledge?

Two months after the Russian leader's death he wrote an obituary for Lenin. This began with the assertion that while there were states there would be dictatorship and that meant the dictatorship of a leader. He went on: "The essential problem of the dictatorship of the proletariat is not the physical personification of the function of command.... The essential problem lies in the nature of the relations that the leader or leaders have with the party of the working class, and in the relations which exist between this party and the working class: are they purely hierarchical, of the military sort, or are they organic and historic in character. Are the leader and the party working-class elements, are they a part of the working-class, do they represent its most vital and deepest interests and aspirations, or are they an excrescence, merely a violent superimposition? How was this party formed, how did it develop, according to what processes were its leaders selected? Why did it become the party of the working class? Through chance? The problem becomes that of the historical development of the working class, which slowly constitutes itself in the struggle with the bourgeoisie, wins some victories and is defeated many times. It is not only a problem of the proletariat in one country alone, but of the whole world working-class with its superficial and yet so important differences taken at particular moments, and yet its substantial unity and homogeneity."

"The problem becomes that of the vitality of Marxism, whether it is or is not the most sure and precise interpretation of Nature and history — of its possibilities — whether it becomes an infallible method through the intuitional genius of a politician, an instrument of extreme precision for exploring the future, for foreseeing what will happen in the masses, for guiding and thus leading them.

"The international proletariat had and still has a living example of a revolutionary party which exercises a class dictatorship; it had, but unluckily no longer has, a living example, who best characterises and expresses what it is to be a revolutionary leader, comrade Lenin." If Lenin's theoretical importance lay in his practice as a revolutionary leader, what did Gramsci think this practice was? For Gramsci Lenin was the "initiator of a new process in historical development" because he was the most individualised "moment" of all past history. But he was this expression not through some automatic endowment but as a result of thirty years struggle to emerge as such, a struggle which often took on the strangest and most absurd forms. It was a struggle of great complexity on several levels to "understand, foresee and provide". But it was a struggle conducted together with the Russian proletariat, without whom Lenin could never have remained in power, and conversely which could never have retained power without him as leader. This organic unity between the mass and the leaders was what made the dictatorship of the proletariat a liberating and not a repressive force. "A continuous coming and going on all social levels (*capillarità*); a continuous circulation of men. The leader whom we mourn found a society in a state of decomposition ... everything has been put into order and reconstructed, from the factory to the government, under the leadership and control of the proletariat, with the means of a new class in government and in history."[875]

These lines reveal that reading Lenin had not changed Gramsci's view of how a revolution was made, or what he thought Leninism was, from that which he had held even in 1920 before he knew much about Lenin's theory. Leninism in practice was not the history of a party but of the relations between that party and the masses. Gramsci still held an anti-Jacobin view of the Russian revolution, and while recognising the important role of the party as educator, denied its leading, or, to use his words, "hierarchical" role. In the same month he wrote these words confirming this analysis: "The circulation reached in the first two numbers could not but depend on the position which *Ordine Nuovo* took in the first years of its publication, and which consisted essentially of this: 1) of having been able to translate the principle postulates of the doctrine and tactics of the Communist International into an historically appropriate Italian language. In the years 1919-1920 that meant the slogan of factory councils and control over production, that is, the organisation of the mass of all producers for the expropriation of the expropriators, for the substitution of the proletariat for the bourgeoisie in the running of industry, and therefore, of necessity, in the government of the State." He even cited Lenin's approval of his theses on the "Renewal of the Socialist Party" as evidence of a total, rather than a limited approval for such a line.[876]

Given this continuity in his overall view, and his interpretation of Lenin despite his reading of Lenin, a continuity which we have already observed in his practice, it is interesting to remark on the impact on his understanding of "Leninism" of the Bolshevisation policy introduced by the Fifth Comintern Congress in 1924. This policy was designed to rid the International of vestiges of socialism and introduce a party organisation along Russian lines, that is, with a rigid hierarchy of command. This policy was, of course, presented as Leninist: technically the parties were being made "Leninist". Gramsci was quite happy for the PCI to become Leninist, but he again defined Leninism in a very particular way. He stated that Lenin laid down five fundamental qualities for an efficient communist party "in the period of preparation for the revolution". First, that every communist should be a Marxist (or contemporarily "a Marxist-Leninist", which begged the question); second, that every communist should be in the front line in the proletarian struggle; third that every revolutionary should be a political realist; fourth that every communist "must feel that he is always subordinate to the will of the party and must judge everything from the point of view of the party, that is, he must be a sectarian in the best sense of the word"; fifth, that every communist must be an internationalist. It is the fourth requirement which is interesting since the fourth requirement is obviously capable of being understood as "Leninist" in the sense applied to that word by the post-Leninist communist world. However, Gramsci understood the fulfilment of this demand as dependent on an adequate theoretical level in the party and therefore argued that the campaign to attain it should therefore be "ideological", rather than political, as Bordiga would have it. Citing directly from

235

Left-Wing Communism, which proved to be one of his most frequent references in these years, Gramsci indicated that he regarded Bolshevisation as a work of suasion rather than expulsion. This view conformed to his contemporary and past practice. Even with Bordiga "we think it is possible to reach some agreement ... and we think that comrade Bordiga believes this too."[877] For Gramsci the process of obtaining discipline, of "Bolshevisation" meant no more than organising the workers in the factories from below, and "subjecting intellectual elements to a rigorous process of selection and to a rigid, unmerciful trial of their practical work, in action."

So even when Bolshevisation was the policy of the Comintern, Gramsci did not give up his technique of seeking unity around policies of action rather than through splits and inner-party activity. This moderate interpretation was frequently legitimated by reference to *Left-Wing Communism*[878] and denials that Lenin took a sectarian attitude towards fusions with other parties or alliances with other classes. Significantly, Gramsci demanded a study of the tactics of the Russian party between 1905-1922 in Lenin's writings (note the first date) and the history of the Russian revolution.[879] What is crucial is that he regarded not the early years of the Bolshevik party as important, that is, not the years of *What is to be Done?* but the years 1907-9. He showed a good knowledge of this history which consisted essentially of a defeat of the left-wing who wished to continue past methods, which were those in *What is to be Done?* It was in the context of this struggle against "leftism" that, and here he quoted Zinoviev[880] "The Bolshevik party acquired its definite character..." In June 1925, when we meet his first clear reference to *What is to be Done?*, which he cites to support the proposition that the masses' wishes should not be followed at all times, as often they are bourgeois, he is again considering the relation between the party and the non-revolutionary working-class, and not inner party relationships or relationships within the revolutionary movement.[881]

The criticisms which Bordiga levelled at this sort of interpretation only provoked the response from Gramsci that his views were "Leninist" and that there had been no right-wing degeneration in "Leninist" theory since Lenin's death.[882] The differences in their understanding of the Russian's theory highlighted what Gramsci considered important. Bordiga wished to stress the leading role of the party and to deny that the fundamental emphasis of Leninism was on the links with the working class. Again we point out that in 1925, as in 1919-20, Gramsci stressed the contrary position. In 1925 he maintained with copious references to Lenin's speeches at the Second Comintern Congress that even when the twenty-one conditions of membership were the central issue in the Comintern, Lenin still regarded the links between the party and the mass as what were at stake in discussing the "leading role" of the party. Gramsci argued that the theses on the party at the Third Congress were no more than a translation into "European" of Lenin's views at the Second Congress.[883] He made his point even clearer in a succeeding article on the basic organisation of the party, in which he argued that: "One of the most marked characteristics of Leninism is its remarkable coherence and way it hangs together logically: Leninism is a unitary system of thought and practical action, in which everything explains the everything else, from the general view of the world to the smallest problems of organisation. The fundamental nucleus of Leninism in practical action is the dictatorship of the proletariat, and all tactical and organisational problems in Leninism are tied to the question of the preparation for, and organisation of the dictatorship of the proletariat." This meant that the organisation by cell was no discovery of the third congress. Indeed, if he had been it would have marked a dangerous "right" deviation of Lenin's theory in the direction of social-democracy. Rather, this apparently technical problem was in fact a political problem related to Lenin's overall concern with the preparation of the dictatorship of the proletariat, that is, "the leadership of the masses". The way in which the matter had been discussed so far (whether it was better to organise by district or factory) was therefore only of secondary importance. The fundamental issue was that which Gramsci himself had indicated in July to the Central Committee of the PCI: He argued that independent communist leadership of all levels of struggle was necessary, and the only way to achieve this and avoid social democratic errors was through the factory cell, the *commissione interna* and their development into "mass bodies ... not only for the union struggle but for the general struggle against capitalism and its political regime". This was what "Leninist criteria" were when translated to western Europe.[884]

His formulation made clear that for Gramsci "Leninism" was still the "conciliar" policy of 1919-20 where the issue was not that of the party but how this party was related to the masses in a specific form: that of councils. This did not mean that he thought that Lenin was no more than Marx. On the contrary he asserted specifically that this was not so, indicating that the fundamental novelty of Lenin's contribution was the theory of imperialism and the national and agrarian question.[885]

If Gramsci denied that "Leninism" had degenerated after the death of Lenin, he also denied that there had been any deviation from Communist policies with the introduction of NEP. He maintained, again with copious quotations from Lenin's speeches after 1917, that it had never been maintained that Russia would pass immediately to socialism after the revolution, but that steps to control production and distribution would be taken, through the development of a peasant revolution which would allow the development of proletarian soviets. Quoting from the *April Theses'* eighth paragraph, he went on to stress Lenin's words: "...The introduction of socialism is not our immediate end". This analysis he linked up with Lenin's theories of national problems and imperialism, on which it depended.[886]

Gramsci typified Lenin's theory of imperialism as "definitive" and as indicating the impossibility of returning to individualism from the era of monopoly capitalism. His conclusion that revolutions which were socialist could certainly be started, but not be concluded in one country, necessarily presumed an attitude towards Trotsky's theory.

Certainly, from 1919-20 Gramsci figures among the grouping normally regarded as close to Trotsky. He had cut his teeth on the papers of the French anarcho-syndicalists, with whom Trotsky had been associated before the war and who respected Trotsky more than Lenin, when Lenin appeared to them to be moving "right".[887] Alfred Rosmer recalls Gramsci with an affection which leaves no doubt about where the rest of the "left" thought that he stood.[888] However, as we have seen, Gramsci's position was too undisciplined even for Trotsky and their public relations at the Comintern from 1922 onwards were hostile. Obviously there were fundamental differences despite the similarities. Gramsci was able to read much of Trotsky's work in translation during the same years in which he read Lenin's work. In the works of a historical nature Gramsci was able to discern what he called the "mechanist" Marxism of Trotsky. In particular, he disliked Trotsky's books on Lenin and on the history of the Russian Revolution (1917). In reviewing the last book, he noted that it instituted a revision of Marxism, and he approved of its censorship by the Soviet government.[889] Naturally, his assertion that there had not been a departure from "Leninism" after 1923 impelled him into an ever greater disagreement with Trotsky, who maintained the contrary. In 1924 he disagreed completely with Trotsky's estimate of the influence of United States imperialism in Europe (*Europe and America*) (*The Permanent Revolution*) because it was too mechanist.

However, his very stress on the notion that it was the links between the party and the masses, rather than the party itself, with which Lenin was concerned, which enabled him to avoid support for Stalin's policies, and to maintain a continuing belief in Trotsky's importance as a revolutionary practitioner. Already late in 1923 he shared the disapproval over the trends in the Russian party shown by Trotsky in the *New Course*. He spoke in Vienna to Victor Serge, one of Trotsky's supporters, in these terms: "Once, we consulted together about the quarter million workers who had been admitted at one stroke into the Russian Communist Party, on the day after Lenin's death. How much were these proletarians worth, if they had had to wait for the death of Vladimir Ilyich before coming to the party?"[890] While his overall analysis led him much closer to the theory of socialism in one country advanced by Stalin than the mechanistic doctrine of world revolution maintained by Trotsky, he stressed on a number of occasions that the leading role of the Soviet party depended on its maintaining the traditions of "Leninism" in the sense which he had described "Leninism". This led to an every-widening breach with Stalin, whom he only defended personally once in the period before he was jailed. The developments in the Soviet Union in 1925 and, especially, 1926, when it became clear that Trotsky was going to be expelled for his opposition, thus splitting the party — a solution which Gramsci never believed in — finally drove him to make clear that his support of the Bolshevik Party and condemnation of Trotsky for indiscipline was not unreserved. He wrote a letter to Togliatti in Moscow which was technically from the Political Committee of the PCI to the Central Committee of the Russian party. This said that today "we are no longer so sure as in the past" that unity of the CPSU would be maintained, and feared grave repercussions if the leading group of Leninists split. He warned that the Western masses accorded a leading role to the CPSU "only insofar as its government showed a united fighting" spirit. He warned that the whole process of consolidation of the PCI since 1924 was being jeopardised by the tendency of the Russians to forget that their obligations were to the world proletariat and to immerse themselves in their personal struggles for power. While the Italian party was prepared to support the majority of the Russian party in its line, if this became necessary, he pinned his hope on unity based on "convictions". "We wanted to tell you this in a fraternal spirit, dear comrades, even if we are younger brothers. Comrades Zinoviev, Kamenev and Trotsky have contributed greatly to our education in revolution, sometimes they have corrected us energetically and severely, they have been among our teachers. It is especially to them that we address ourselves as they are mainly responsible for the present situation, because we want to be sure that the majority of the CC of the USSR does not intend to exploit its victory too much in the struggle and is disposed to avoid excessive measures."[891]

Togliatti's reply was that the main issue was whether the position of Stalin was correct, not whether unity should be maintained. Moreover, he inferred that Gramsci did not really know what was going on, which Gramsci had half-admitted when he first started to take sides against Stalin two years earlier.[892] Togliatti warned that the leading group of Bolsheviks was not likely to remain united after the death of Lenin. He also made clear that Gramsci's letter was considered by him to be hostile to the majority, and that the way to get over the crisis was to come out in its favour without reservations.[893]

Gramsci's reply clarified his position even further by flatly rejecting Togliatti's point of view. "The question of unity, not only in the Russian party but in the Leninist nucleus, is of the greatest importance in the international field, and, *from the point of view of the masses* (Gramsci's emphasis), is the most important question in this historical period which is one of intensified and contradictory progress towards unity." He indicated that he was very unhappy about Togliatti's way of looking at things, and insisted that the "Leninist line consisted in fighting for unity within the party, and not only the appearance of unity ..." Togliatti's view of the concrete needs of Russia imposing themselves "was without value."[894]

The bitter exchange concluded with Togliatti consigning Gramsci's second letter to the waste-paper basket.[895] We do not know whether Gramsci was aware of this deceit, but from this time on all contact between him and Togliatti was broken off and, we may mark his spiritual disassociation with Stalinism and therefore from the new trends of international communism from this date. Less than two weeks after writing the second letter he was arrested.

If his view of Leninism had not changed even after reading Lenin's work, and if he never agreed with Trotsky or Stalin's theoretical views, what also had not changed was his overall view of Marxism, even after contact with these new influences.

While in Vienna in 1924 he embarked on the translation of Ryazanoff's edition of the *Communist Manifesto* because, he stated, it corresponded directly with his opinions, and he thought it would be very useful.[896] Ryazanoff's edition of the *Manifesto* contained a long introduction to Marxism in which the following views were expounded: First, that the *Manifesto* had to be situated in the historical context in which it was written if sense was to be made of it. This meant situating it, as Marx and Engels intended, in the context of the political evolution of the French bourgeoisie, and its antithesis. Developing on this historicising of the *Manifesto*, Ryazanoff proceeded to make the following points at various stages of his introduction: "In *Capital*, Marx shows that the value of labour power, as of all other commodities, is determined by the labour time necessary for the production of the means of subsistence wherewith the worker satisfied his need for food, clothing, shelter, etc. But the dimensions of these fundamental needs, the extent to which they can be satisfied and the ability to satisfy them, are the outcome of historical determinants. They depend on large measure upon the cultural development of the country with which we are concerned, and among other things, upon the conditions under which the class of free labourers came into being, upon the habits this class formed, and upon the standard of life which it claimed for itself. Thus, in contrast with other commodities, the determination of the value of labour power depends partly upon historical and moral factors." This shifting of the prime object of Marxist analysis from Marx's works to the specific historical reality led Ryazanoff to a theory of revolution very close to that of Gramsci: "The fact that the proletariat is enslaved or not is not therefore, the thing of prime importance. Other classes are likewise enslaved. What is of importance is the manner of the enslavement, the form it assumes; for, by changing the form we also change the minds of the enslaved, the thoughts which are born or may be born in the brains of the enslaved." There was no automatic emergence of an awareness, — as this new "philosophy of history" argued that the working class was dominated by the "ideas of the ruling class", which conflicted with its own real, psychologically-lived, reality. One of the problems of the proletariat was that no bourgeois intellectuals were prepared to

241

join the ranks of the fighting proletariat. The first step in breaking out of this determination was to establish a real democracy — "the sovereignty and self-government of the people" — which destroyed all bureaucracy.[897]

Clearly, such views had much in common, first, with the Marxism of Labriola, and, then, with the liberating "conciliar" activities Gramsci had developed in 1919-20. Equally clearly, Ryazanoff does not present an identical view, maintaining a rather more mechanist position than either of the Italians. However, what is important is that on the eve of his imprisonment Gramsci maintained much the same view of Marxism as he always had, even *after* making contact with the ideas of the Russian leaders. In particular, his typification of Lenin's contribution as the theory of imperialism and the national and agrarian problem, did not mean that he had given up the implication that the proletariat "must deal with the bourgeoisie of its own country first."[898] There had certainly been no stupendous rupture in Gramsci's intellectual development since 1919-20.

II

When first in prison Gramsci felt the deprivation of his liberty so strongly that he even wondered whether he should sink into oblivion — "like a stone into the sea" — and cut off all contact with the outside world. Yet, with characteristic strength of will his first letter from prison spoke of his optimism that he would survive even the murderous Fascist prison sentence.[899] Indeed, in the early days of his imprisonment, especially at Ustica, he survived better than his companions, who came down with terrible stomach upsets. Gramsci was living on his nerves in these early days. By April 1927 his travail was beginning: he admitted that he was unable to sleep and that he had toothaches. By the end of 1927 he was beginning to consume a large number of medicines and he had reached his fiftieth self-administered injection by March 1928.[900] The outlook was grim. Gramsci had always been physically weak as a result of his deformity, but he had overcome his disabilities by enormous strength of will and determination.[901] This very repression of his weaknesses created an enormous tension in his organism, which had not always been able to survive intact. Gramsci's life had, as he said, not been marked by many illnesses, but on occasions his body had rebelled and he had needed a rest cure.[902] To survive the terrible regimen of prison life he had to call on even more strength of will than usual and this took an ever heavier toll on his body, initiating a process of disintegration which was evident even after one year in prison. It is against the background of this physical collapse, which we will touch on again and again, that he read, thought, and wrote in prison. Naturally there was a dialectical relation between how he felt and what he wrote at the time.

The object of this imprisonment had been to stop his "...mind working for twenty years." It was precisely this activity which it could not stop, although it was able to prevent the products of Gramsci's mind from becoming public for almost exactly the time it proposed. Cut off from activity, Gramsci turned immediately to reading to fill in his time. In February 1927 he wrote; "I am reading all the time." And two months later he had already consumed eighty two of the most "bizarre and extravagant" titles from the prison library.[903] Naturally, the sort of books in a prison library were not the most stimulating for a man of his intellect and culture, but, "I believe that a political prisoner could get blood out of a stone. It is all a matter of giving an end to one's reading and knowing how to take notes (if you are allowed to write).... Well, I have found that even Sue, Montépin, Ponson du Terrail etc. are enough if you read from this point of view; why is this literature always the most read and the most widely published; what needs is it satisfying; what aspirations is it responding to; what feelings and points of view are expressed in this sort of literature to make it so popular?"[904] And by March 1927, taking up the gauntlet cast down by fascism, he announced that far from stopping mental work he would start collecting material to a contribution to theory "für ewig". This work itself, precisely because it was undertaken systematically and intensely, would sustain him in prison through providing a "centre" for "his inner life".

It was thus his emotional needs as a prisoner which first made him decide "to study some subjects" in prison. These he listed in March 1927 as 1) research into the formation of the public mind in Italy in the last century; in other words, a research into the Italian intellectuals, their origins, their grouping according to cultural streams, their different modes of thought etc.... "An impressive subject of the highest order, that I can naturally only sketch in broad outlines, given that it is absolutely impossible for me to obtain the immense quantity of material necessary. Do you remember the rapid and superficial thing I wrote on Southern Italy

243

and the importance of Benedetto Croce? Well, I would like to fill in the thesis which I touched on there, from a 'disinterested' and 'für ewig'. 2) A study of comparative linguistics, no less! But what could be more 'disinterested' and 'für ewig' than that? It would be, naturally, only a question of dealing with the purely theoretical and methodological part of the subject, which has never been dealt with completely and systematically from the new point of view of the neo-linguists, as against the neo-grammarians.... 3) A study of the theatre of Pirandello and the transformation of Italian taste in theatre represented by Pirandello and which he contributed to creating.... 4) An essay on serials on popular taste in literature. This idea came to me while reading the death of Serafino Renzi.... when I remembered how entertained I was when I went to see him, because there was a double play on: the restlessness, the uncontained passions, the participation of the popular audience was certainly not the less interesting play.

What do you think of all this? At bottom, for those who see clearly, a homogeneity exists between these four subjects: the creative popular mind, in its various phases and levels of development, is at the base of them all in equal measure."[905] We see that in his initial plan of study of ambitious scope — Gramsci was proposing to go over in thought the activity he had lived before his imprisonment: to continue theoretically his more practical investigations of the relationships between the masses and their leaders. He had to supplement his somewhat meagre sources with different books, because he equated the problem of mass consciousness with a study of the intellectuals.[906] The first book he requested was Croce's *Teoria della storia della storiografia.* He wrote that the book "contains, not only a synthesis of the entire Crocean philosophical system, but a real, true revision of that system, and can provide deep food for thought (whence its specific 'jailhouse' usefulness)."[907] It is too tempting not to recall that this book had constituted Gramsci's self-admitted "starting-point" of 1916, but it is also important not to infer a systematic return to the study of Croce at this stage. Gramsci certainly also asked for Croce's *History of Italy from 1871-1915* and Roberto Michels' recent work soon after, but he discovered in jail in Milan (as his trial dragged on and on) that there were "technical and pscyhological reasons" why it was difficult to study in prison. Not only was there the cavalier indifference of the doctors to his ailments, which got worse and worse with every frustration he met, but there was also the deliberate way in which the prison officials refused his requests for ink, pen and paper, which had been officially approved by the military judge who was trying him.[908] Moreover, his few "learned" books were either still at Ustica, or always getting lost in the mail. In sum, he did not examine Croce or any other writers work with much care in 1927-28 and was forced into the sort of idleness which frayed his nerves and was not conducive to any sort of systematic study at all. Even after his trial was over and he had been shifted from Milan to the prison of Turi di Bari he did not summon up the enthusiasm and material necessary to research for some time. In November 1928 he wrote: "After leaving Milan I got terribly tired. I felt prison more.... I am reading a lot of books and journals: a great many relative to the intellectual life that we can lead in prison. But I have lost my taste for reading. Books and journals give only general ideas, rough accounts of the general development of life in the world (which succeed more or less well) but they can't give an immediate, direct, living impression of the life of Tom, Dick, Harry, of real individuals. And unless we know their lives we cannot understand what has been generalised and universalised."[909]

Gramsci was facing the first weapon in the hands of his opponent in the duel: his isolation. Solitude had always harmed him emotionally and productively while the very active years of his life (1919-20) (1922-26) had released an enormous creative energy. He had to come to terms with prison and solitude without being overwhelmed by it. To his struggle against physical adversity, he had to add a struggle against spiritual adversity.

He had the strength to do this. Early in 1929, well after his transfer to Turi, and after two years in jail, he finally obtained six exercise books and permission to write and settled down "to follow up certain questions rather than devour books." It is a comment on his character that he deliberately chose to start by translating and the study of language to accustom himself to methodical work and to discipline the mind.[910] His first four exercise books (about 450 pages) are full of translations from German and Russian, and a fifth, begun between 1930-31 is a translation of the Reclam (Leipzig) edition of Marx, including the *Theses on Feuerbach* excerpts from the *Manifesto*, from *Wage Labour and Capital*, from the *Holy Family*, from the *Jewish Question* and from other writings of the young Marx. The sixth, almost empty, contains the beginnings of translations of children's fairy tales which Gramsci had promised to do for his children. These six exercise books are those numbered in the Einaudi edition of Gramsci's Works as XIV,

XV, XIX, XXVI, VII, XXXI.

This systematic work of translation did not mean that he had given up his original plan of work. In February 1929 he restated his aims, amplifying them into sixteen points for investigation.[911] He also sent a letter to his sister-in-law early in 1929 stating that he had decided to take notes about three main questions: 1) the history of Italy in the nineteenth century with special emphasis on the formation and development of intellectual groups; 2) the theory of history and historiography; and 3) Americanism and Fordism. Again he sent off a letter asking for several of Croce's and Michels' works "which I would like to have as soon as possible." He also announced that he had the "most important relevant works of Croce already". Moreover he indicated that he would read them as a history of philosophy, by stating that he would have to go back to Hegel.[912]

His mind was working on at least two levels in 1929-30, especially in the latter year when his work rhythm started to accelerate rapidly. First, he translated the collected notes regularly and almost mechanically. This constituted the seed bed for his thought. Second, he ruminated about the implications for method and substance of his overall plan to investigate mass consciousness.

We can reconstitute the thoughts he was developing about method from his letters. He stated that he could not consider the issue of mass consciousness without considering the intellectuals as early as March 1927. Both considerations drove him back to Croce: to an anti-Croce in which there were elements of acceptance and of rejection. By July 1929 he had reread the *Teoria della storia* and sent it back as he was required to do by prison regulations. He had thus been back to his "starting point" of 1916 to understand his end-point in 1930. Among the early ideas he reaffirmed in his letters is an emphasis on the importance of will. In 19 December 1929 he wrote: "My state of mind synthesises these two feelings [pessimism and optimism] and goes beyond them. I am a pessimist intellectually and an optimist from the point of view of will. In any situation I think of the worst outcome, to put into action all my reserves of will and overcome the obstacle. I have never had any illusions and I have never been disillusioned. I have armed myself on purpose with limitless patience, not a passive or inert patience, but a patience enlivened by perseverance...."[913] On this level then, Gramsci makes clear that his overall view had not changed since 1916 except in details. Indeed, it is useful to compare these views with those in Croce's *Filosofia della pratica*. But, if he still emphasised the capacity of men to make their own destinies, we are not entitled therefore to assume that he had cancelled out all the other refinements of this idea which he acquired between 1916-1930. On the contrary his very words show that he still subscribes to the view of 1919-20, when *Ordine Nuovo* carried the caption "Pessimism of the intellect, optimism of the will", apparently taken from Rolland. This indicated a fundamental difference between his understanding of the dialectic, and that of Croce, for whom the dialectic was a fundamental and simple contradiction. To borrow from Marx *Theses on Feuerbach*, so often cited by Gramsci when he wrote his notes, Croce believed in a human essence, that of the Mind (or was at least tending that way by 1916) where Gramsci had grasped and internalised the proposition that "...the human essence is no abstraction inherent in each individual. In its reality it is the ensemble of the social relations" (Thesis VI) Gramsci made. this completely clear in another letter of December 1929, to his wife Giulia: "...I have the impression that your conception, and that of the rest of the family is too metaphysical, that is, it presupposes in the child the potential of the man and that it is necessary to help and develop what is already latent, without coercion, leaving all to the spontaneous forces of nature or something. I, on the other hand, think that man is formed completely by history, through coercion (though this should not be understood only as external violence or brutality) and I believe only that. To believe otherwise would be to fall into a sort of transcendence or immanence. What we think is a latent force is no more than the formless and indistinct complexity of images and feelings of the first days, months and years of life, images and feelings which are not always the best one could hope for. This fashion of thinking of education as the unravelling of a pre-existing thread was very important when it was counterposed to that of the Jesuit school, that is, when it was the negation of a worse philosophy but today it too has been passed up. If we refuse to educate the child we are only allowing his personality to develop chaotically as he receives all the impulses in life from his general environment. It is strange and interesting that the psycho-analysis of Freud is creating, especially in Germany, ... similar currents to those in France in the eighteenth century. He is creating a new type of 'noble savage' corrupted by society, that is, by history. From this is born a new sort of intellectual disorder which is very interesting."[914]

There could be no clearer refutation of the celebrated thesis of Louis Althusser that in his notes Gramsci remained a "Hegelian" idealist, committed to the *theoretical* notion that Marxism is a "humanism", and that he never broke away from the core notion of "former religions" in his concept of the dialectic.[915] Gramsci's Marxism certainly does not start from an original innocence which had been lost in alienation and must be re-appropriated. It therefore is not capable of reduction to an implicit determinism, or to an evolutionary or passive theory of history, as Croce's serene dialectic is. Present at all times in Gramsci's thought in 1929-30 is the notion of social coercion and social contradictions and therefore a primary interest in politics and not theory. This became particularly important when he started to write his notebooks on particular subjects, with their emphasis on the role of ideology and the intellectuals. This we will discuss below.

Some lines which indicate his sense of the social contradictions in life run "...it seems that all life is a struggle to adjust to our surroundings and especially to dominate them and not be crushed by them."[916] He stressed his "practicality", by which he meant that he knew "that to beat one's head against the wall is to break one's head and not the wall."[917] Finally, he typified his Marxism as a philosophy of praxis.

In conformity with these ruminations at some time in 1930 he extended his plan of study to include "Notes on philosophy. Materialism and Idealism. First Series" (No XIII in Einaudi). This title was taken up again in the exercise book which is numbered VII in the Einaudi edition and as the "Third Series" in 1931, towards the end of the year.[918]

While he was making these translations, reading the young Marx, and ruminating about his general plan of work in a fashion leading to general principles of method, Gramsci's health continued to decline. He was in a state of continual crisis all through 1929 and 1930. His teeth fell out, he suffered from terrible skin complaints as the result of a blood complaint, and the result was frequent pain and ensuing lethargy. Ceresa recalled that on his arrival at Bari in 1929 he was already "...afflicted with a skin complaint of urecemic origin, his digestive system was completely upset, he was breathing with great difficulty and he could not walk more than a step at a time without leaning on someone."[919] He made little of his complaints and was at first the leader in the occasional joke sessions in the exercise yard.[920] The prison regime, which Mussolini personally ordered, was mainly respon-sible for this decline.[921] In 1930 a contributory factor was the hostility and misunderstanding of many of his political comrades in prison with him.

In 1929, after Gramsci's "links with the world had been cut" one by one, the entire international communist movement embarked on the policies of the "Third Period". The central thesis was that in the immediate future the imperialist world would go into a new period of crisis and economic collapse like that of 1917-20 and that these conditions would lead automatically to a renewed series of revolutions in the West. In this period the social-democrats would play the main part in shoring up a system which was collapsing through its own contradictions and they were therefore the worst enemies of socialism, against whom the "main blow" should be directed. The theory, for which Stalin was mainly responsible, reeked of fatalism and dogmatically ignored concrete historical realities. It was, however, duly taken up by the PCI, by 1930 under the leadership of Palmiro Togliatti. The party started to talk of the imminent collapse of fascism. As the news of this new policy began to seep through into the prison in 1930 as new inmates arrived, the political prisoners naturally began to discuss it at exercise periods, the only times that they ever saw each other before returning to their lonely cells. In July 1930 Gramsci's brother came to visit him to discuss the new line and, in particular, the recent expulsion of Alfonso Leonetti, Paolo Ravazzoli and Pietro Tresso for opposing it. "The Three' had objected profoundly to the Politburo's decision that it was radically wrong to believe that: "The very pressure which fascism brings to bear tends to create the opinion among certain sections of the workers that, given the impossibility of the workers' overthrowing fascism quickly, the best tactics would be to support a movement of the bourgeoisie and petty-bourgeoisie who propose to overthrow fascism in Italy without a proletarian revolution."[922] Gramsci indicated that he disagreed completely with the new policy with such unequivocal force that his brother hid his disagreement from Togliatti when he returned to Paris stating that "Nino is completely in agreement with you."[923]

Instead Gramsci started a series of discussions in the exercise yard in which he developed his thought about the role of the intellectuals. "The intellectuals present an absolute necessity for the proletariat both in the period when it is only a class-in-itself, and in the period when it is a class-for-itself. Without intellectuals the proletariat cannot conquer power, nor consolidate that power or develop it.... on which intellectuals should the party concentrate its activity?... He said that the intellectuals of the working-class are the elements who make up the vanguard of the proletariat, the Party ... among the intellectuals we can number all those people in the field of production who are entrusted with the task of realising the plans for work laid down on general lines by the high command, by the boss of the enterprise, like the engineers, the office bosses etc ... among the semi-intellectuals we can number those to whom is entrusted the task of overseeing the technical and administrative problems of ensuring satisfactory work, like section heads, workshop foremen, foremen, lesser employees...." This definition made clear Gramsci's desire to avoid any confusion of his "intellectuals" with bourgeois intellectuals, but he also made clear, in defiance of current Party policy, that the Party should extend its influence gradually among the peasantry and petty-bourgeoisie.[924]

He extended this defiance of the policy of "class against class" laid down by the Comintern, by explaining that the conditions for revolution had existed for fifty years, that hunger and misery alone would not cause a revolution, and that in fact fascism had pushed the Italian proletariat back into positions which far from favouring an imminent revolution and a frontal assault on the State, called rather for the "reconquest of the liberties destroyed by fascism".[925] This added up in the minds of his listeners to the suggestion that communists should work for the re-establishment of the Constituent Assembly rather than seek the overthrow of the fascist State.[926] After ten days of patient explanation only two of his listeners opposed him but soon his disobedience vis-à-vis the Party awoke old resentments. Some recalled his excessive observance of regulations — something he had found necessary if he was to use the system to obtain his books and permission to write.[927] The exercise-yard discussions descended to the level of petty personalities, and Scucchia, in particular, started a whispering campaign that he was a Crocean idealist and a social-democrat.[928] When Garuglieri reported these grumblings: "You know, Gramsci, that certain comrades think you are a Crocean", he replied, "Another stupidity being spread about me: you can add it to the accusation that I was a captain in the Arditi (his brother was), where it belongs.... I respect Croce as we should respect men who are high intellectuals (*di alto pensiero*); Croce is a serious scholar; in his historical criticism he proves how solid his thought is and how profound his culture. As a philosopher he marks the highest development in Italian thought, but as a politician he is the latest expression of a liberal dcotrine which defends a society which is at the end of its day. My comrades will realist how 'Crocean' I am when they see the work about Croce that

I am going to produce."[929] However, he was sufficiently upset by their campaign against him to stop arguing. Henceforth, the prison was divided into two groups: those for and those against Gramsci. Gramsci showed no readiness to break off contact with the Socialist, Pertini, with whom he had cordial relations, much as he had refused to be anything but friendly with Bordiga when they were confined at Ustica three years earlier.

In sum, in 1930 he was brought face to face with the problem of the central dispute in the international communist movement: that between Trotsky and Stalin, which posed the question whether the CPSU(B) was still continuing the traditions which entitled it to the support and respect of revolutionaries. In particular he had to start to come to terms with Trotsky, whom he had defended against the measures proposed against him in 1926, who had been expelled from the USSR in 1927, and who by 1931 was bitterly critical of the policies adopted by the international communist movement. The problem was first political: to what extent did he really share the positions of the Three who by 1932 were part of the Trotskyite opposition.[930] The Opposition, citing its own document on the "Prospects of the Italian revolution and the tactical tasks of the Communist Party" claims that although there were no direct contacts, "...we can assert with certainty that there was contact in the realm of ideas",[931] even by 1930. More important for Gramsci were the theoretical implications, since the support of both Gramsci and the Trotskyites for a policy of a united front against fascism stemmed from a basic agreement on the nature of fascism in the writings of Trotsky and Gramsci. In a work published from Prinkipo in January 1932 Trotsky singled out Gramsci as the only man in the PSI who had an attitude towards fascism which was sufficiently undogmatic to admit the possibility that fascism might take power. Moreover, in Trotsky's recognition that there was a little bit of Hitler in every petty-bourgeois German, we can see similarities with Gramsci's view that fascism could not be understood without taking into account the reasons for its mass support.[932]

Because of the evident affinities between his position and that of the exiled Russian revolutionary, whose theoretical views he had always decried, while sharing a similar passion for the role of councils in making a revolution, Gramsci now turned to studying him late in 1930. He asked for permission to read *The Revolution Betrayed, Towards Capitalism or Socialism* and *My Life*. He received permission to see the last only. With evident reference to the contemporary conjuncture, and the political problem facing him, he wrote: "Transition from the war of manoeuvre (and frontal attack) to the war of position even in the political field. This appears the most important problem in political theory, and the most difficult to solve correctly posed by the post-war period. It is tied to the questions raised by Bernstein, who in one way or another can be regarded as the political theorist of the frontal assault in the period in which it only caused defeats."[933] Gramsci went on to say that the mode of exerting hegemony through greater State intervention indicated that the war of position had reached a culmination, illustrating that the ruling classes were really besieged. However, in his overall judgements about the respective positions of Trotsky and Stalin which were at stake in 1930-31, he clearly rejected the positions of Trotsky. That he did not share Trotsky's view is evident from a note of 1933. "Certainly the development is towards internationalism, but the point of departure is 'national' and it is from this point of departure that we must begin."[934] He went on that "non-national" conceptions were wrong, and had led to passivity and inertia in two distinct stages: "1) in the first phase, nobody thought that they should start, that is, they thought that they would find themselves isolated; through waiting for everyone to move together, nobody moved or organised in the meantime; the second phase (that of Trotsky to 1924, while the first referred to the Second International) is perhaps worse, because what is being awaited is an anachronistic and anti-national form of 'Napoleonism' (since not all historical phases repeat themselves in the same form). The theoretical weaknesses of this modern form of the old mechanicism are masked by the general theory of permanent revolution, which is nothing but a generic forecast presented as a dogma, and which demolishes itself by not in fact coming true."[935]

It is clear then that despite conjunctural agreements between Trotsky and Gramsci in 1930-31, hinging on their similar assessments of fascism, and their disbelief in the imminent collapse of that movement, as well as the dependent policies of the Comintern, there was no common theoretical ground. Gramsci still felt, as he had in 1924, that Trotsky was a mechanist, and theoretically on the same ground as the Second International. Moreover, in reaching these conclusions, Gramsci re-evaluated precisely what had most reconciled him with the left as early as 1919: the common interest in the Soviets. In particular, he rejected the analyses Trotsky had made in 1905 in favour of what he regarded as the concrete realism of a Lenin who never allowed abstract theory to dominate him.[936]

However, despite such a rejection of the theory of Trotsky, which revealed Gramsci's continuing commitment to an overall view of Marxism in which the total outlook was all-important in determining practical successes or failures, and which laid primacy on practice, he was obliged to reexamine his relationship with the PCI. Since there is no value in establishing his "objective" alienation from the party — it is possible to show that he was still "revolutionary" when the party was tending towards "compromise" — we will only inquire into his own subjective opinions at the time. Certainly he ruminated long over the history of the party and his experience in it, and drew long-term lessons from that experience. This is not, however, what concerns us here. Rather it is his immediate comments on its activity, and hence on the Comintern and the Russian party as well. We may speculate that this rumination about his short-term relations with the party started in 1930 when the issue of the Constituente came up but that it only became more important in 1931-32 when Gramsci had isolated himself from many of his comrades in prison.[937] Then the issue of discipline, and the exact obligations he had to assume, were posed. This must have been a terrible internal struggle for him, as he had always insisted that the unity of a Communist Party had to come through "concrete individual efforts". "If there must be polemics and scissions, we mustn't be afraid of facing them and overcoming them: they are inevitable in this process of development and to avoid them only means putting them off till they become dangerous and even catastrophic etc..."[938] Moreover, with implicit reference to the social-fascist period, he denied the need for "automatic obedience" when this meant no discussion of the matter under consideration. Rather the gut reaction of the mass to an inappropriate order "was most important".[939] Later such affirmations of the right to autonomy were to take him further, but at this juncture they were merely a new reflection to feed the ensemble of his views, and certainly did not mark any rupture with the PCI.

In 1931 his health declined even further under these increased pressures. He reported that he was again very ill with stomach upsets in March, and in July he admitted that he was so debilitated that he was suffering from lack of memory. This was disastrous, since he relied a great deal on his memory to cope with the paucity of books allowed him, especially those by communists. On 3

August 1931 he started spitting up blood: "It began like this: at one in the morning on 3 August.... I coughed up blood suddenly. It was not really a proper continuous haemorrhage of the sort I have heard others describe; I felt a gurgle while breathing, the sort you have with catarrh, followed by a bout of coughing and my mouth filled with blood. The coughing wasn't violent and not even strong: just the sort of coughing you have when something sticks in your throat, isolated coughs, not fits or spasms of coughing. It lasted until about four and in the meantime I threw up about 250-300 grams of blood. After that there was no more blood, but I coughed catarrh with streaks of blood in it. Dr Cisternin prescribed 'calcium chloride with a thousandth part of adrenalin' and told me that he would see the illness through. On Wednesday, 5 August, the doctor listened to my chest and excluded the possibility that it was a bronchial infection: he suggested that the fever which had now developed could be the result of a stomach upset. The catarrh with the streaks of blood, lasted until a few days ago although there wasn't very much and it didn't occur often: a few days ago the streaks disappeared entirely: even if I had some relatively strong bouts of coughing I did not spit up catarrh; it must have been chance nervous coughing ... there is nothing to worry about, but, as the doctor says, it must be watched."[940]

Gramsci's state of mind, as well as his health, was not improved when he heard that his wife had suffered a nervous breakdown, after a long nervous illness. This illness explained to some extent why she had not written to him at all between July 1929 and July 1930, but was of course, no compensation for his feeling in that year that he had been deserted by a family already far-distant.[941]

The combination of worsening health, and isolation both from the world outside and from his fellows inside, made him bitter, less ready to laugh, and short and extravagant in his remarks about the people who constituted his "great and terrible world". He himself was aware of this and wrote in March 1932 "... I myself have become more bookish and I have sometimes preached or talked like a primary school teacher, which makes me laugh at myself — with the disagreeable outcome that it makes me say foolish things."[942] His words were occasionally trenchant enough to make his continuing concerns, which, as we will see, were more and more with philosophy and the intellectuals, appear élitist. "One day I expressed my point of view on the notion of 'democracy' in an incorrect manner, and he, who made a religion of true democracy, would not overlook my mistake, and said: 'Dear

Mario, all the plebs think that they are democratic: people who want to be equal usually call themselves democrats; everyone who desires the well-being and government of the people normally calls himself a democrat, but this is not the same as having a democratic view of life. To obtain that something has to take place inside you, you have to try to improve your mind, and feel inside you that it is necessary for all your fellows to reach the level you have reached, regardless of whether you reach your goal or not. You must lend them a hand, reach down to them if necessary, and raise them up to yourself. A democratic mind must set the highest standards for the human 'personality', because, when there is no respect for that, there is no real idea of democracy, and the human personality is limited in his development to 'democratic liberties'.''[943] And, as if ruminating to himself, he wrote in May 1931: "... I always avoid judging anybody on the basis of what is normally called 'intelligence', 'natural goodness', 'quick-mindedness' etc. because I know that such judgments are of limited range and tend to mislead. More than all these things what seems important to me is 'strength of will', love of discipline and work, constancy in opinion, and in this judgment I take into account more than the child itself. I take into account those who bring him up and have the duty of making him acquire such habits without crushing its spontaneity. It is clear that my observations were directed not at Mea, but at the people who educate her and bring her up: in this case more than ever it seems that the educator must be educated.''[944]

We must bear in mind this over-élitist quality when we consider his writings after 1930 since 1931 was a particularly important year, because it was in that year that all his thoughts and material synthesised into some sort of overall pattern and the direction of his research changed entirely. Gramsci suddenly renumbered the notebook containing his third series of notes on philosophy, or method, I (formerly XXVIII and appearing as such in the Einaudi edition). However, under the original title he included the heading *Note sparse e appunti per una storia degli intellettuali italiani*. His new list ran: "General introduction — development of the Italian intellectuals to 1870: different periods: popular serial literature — folklore and common sense — the question of literary language and dialects; the grandsons (offspring) of father Bresciani — Reformation and Renaissance — Machiavelli — schooling and national education — the position of Benedetto Croce in Italian culture up to the world war — the Risorgimento and the Action

Party — Ugo Foscolo in the formation of national rhetoric — the Italian theatre — the history of Catholic Action — integral Catholics, Jesuits, Modernists — the medieval commune, the economic-corporative stage of the State — the cosmopolitan function of the Italian intellectuals up to the XVIIIth century — the reaction to the absence of a national-popular culture in Italy: futurists — the single school and what it means for the whole of the organisation of national culture — 'Lorianism' as one of the characteristics of the Italian intellectuals — the absence of 'Jacobins' in the Italian intellectuals — the absence of 'Jacobins' in the Italian Risorgimento — Machiavelli as political technician and as the total or active politician — Appendix Americanism and Fordism."[945]

Two minimum inferences are that he had reached conclusions about his method, and in accordance with that method was going to put his sparse and unsystematic research into a preliminary pattern. Moreover this order remained the same until his death. Necessarily the most important items were those on method. Indeed, in 1931 and 1932 he renumbered existing notebooks and added notebooks II and III which are directly on Crocean philosophy.[946] His method was going to be that of an "anti-Croce", which meant considering Croce's thought not solely as a system of ideas (philosophically or speculatively) but as it functioned socially and hegemonically (historically or "practically"). He considered Croce one of the two most important figures of the Italian reaction precisely because his theory was the most advanced possible. It was therefore the necessary starting point for any Marxist method.[947] This method followed from his understanding of the dialectic as a complexity in which the starting point was to realise that there was no aboriginal essential quality in men, who were no more than their social relations, and that it was not in terms of the Subject of history that he thought.[948] We cannot, however, ignore as another reason for this choice his feeling that he was so cut off from life that only the past had any meaning for him.

Examining Croce as a function of intellectual dominance, also depended on his historical study of the intellectuals, which he started on systematically late in 1930, but which had concerned him as far back as 1920 when he had written an essay "on the question of language in Manzoni." The main thrust of this research would be, he announced to his correspondent, at first to see how from the Roman Empire onwards two languages had developed, the written, which was the preserve of the intellectuals, and the spoken, which was the preserve of the people. In sum, he was going to examine the failure of the national intellectuals to give a form to the realisation in the popular language of everyday practice.[949] In other words, he was going to try to explain mass consciousness in terms of the absence, both structural and intellectual, of the "cultured" classes from popular reality, not only as it was lived, but as it was thought. He already indicated that the two great divisions he would study would be up to the eighteenth century, and after. Or, as he put it, the Renaissance and Machiavelli, and the Risorgimento.

But as he proceeded with the new list in 1931 he decided that the task he had set himself was an impossible one because of the lack of sources. He wrote: "To give you an example — one of the subjects which has interested me most in recent years was to establish the general features of the history of the Italian intellectuals. This interest was born, on the one hand, of the desire to deepen the concept of the State, and on the other hand, to understand certain aspects of the historical development of the Italian people. Even when limited to the central issue, this research remains formidable. It is necessary to go back to the Roman Empire and the first concentration of 'cosmopolitan' ('imperial') intellectuals it created: thus to a study of the Christian-Papal clerical organisation which gave the imperial cosmopolitan heritage the form of a European caste etc. etc.... Only thus, I believe, can we explain how after 1700, that is, after the beginning of the initial struggle between the Church and State over their jurisdictions, can we speak of 'national' Italian intellectuals: up to that time, Italian intellectuals were cosmopolitan, they exercised a universal jurisdiction (either for the Church, or for the Empire). Being supranational, they contributed to the organisation of other national states as technicians and specialists, they offered 'managerial' personnel to all of Europe, and were not concentrated together as a national category.... As you see, this subject could give rise to a whole series of essays, but to do that scholarly research would be necessary — So it is with my other research. You must also realise that the demanding discipline of philosophy, which I experienced at university, has created perhaps excessive concern in me about matters of method."[950]

So, in a somewhat dilatory and preliminary fashion he started to turn over some of the problems involved in the previous two years' reading, and to concentrate particularly on the intellectuals and the State. He made clear as he started this research that he had not rejected Croce in any outright fashion as a result of coming to terms with his thought. Rather he regarded Croceanism as the main contribution of Italian intellectuals to world culture, and Croce as a man whose theory should not be lost.[951] His new projects for research were new in the sense that he was moving only from the "general" philosophical issue to that of sociology. In September 1931 he indicated that he had arrived at the definition of intellectuals which we find again and again in his notes "... I am extending the notion of intellectual greatly, and I do not confine myself to the current notion which refers to the 'great intellectuals'. This study leads to a particular view of the concept of the State, which is normally understood as political society (or dictatorship, or coercive apparatus to make people conform with the type of production or economics at a particular moment) and not as a balance between political and civil society (or hegemony of one group over the entire national society exercised through so-called private organisations, like the Church and the unions, the schools and so on) and it is precisely in civil society that the intellectuals operate (Ben. Croce is, for example, a sort of lay pope and a very efficient hegemonical instrument even if from time to time he found himself in conflict with this or that government etc...). I think that this concept of the function of the intellectuals throws light on the reason, or one of the reasons, for the fall of the medieval Communes, that is, for the fall of the government of an economic class which couldn't create its own intellectuals and thus exercise hegemony as well as rule by dictatorship; the Italian intellectuals did not have a popular-national character but were cosmopolitans after the model of the Church." Gramsci went on to argue that the Communes were thus a "syndicalist" State, which did not manage to develop into a centralized united State, despite what was implicit in the vain urgings of Machiavelli that they extend their hegemony over the countryside. He concluded by indicating that he now proposed to prepare, in a preliminary fashion a series of monographs instead of his grandiose but unfeasible *magnum opus*. These monographs would start from this analysis in terms of the role of the intellectuals.

In 1932 we remark the beginning of the ordering of his material in accord with this project into "Special Exercise books" (numbered XXXIII, XVII, XXIX, XXX in the Einaudi edition). In May he still stated that it was "too soon" to announce any definite conclusions about how the intellectuals functioned, and he warned that his views were voluntarily mutilated and incomplete, but in the process of regrouping his notes, he revised them in interesting new directions. In particular he highlighted the contemporary relevance of his historical material. For example, in transcribing his notes on Machiavelli in VII and XIII into XXX, he started to develop his theory of the contemporary role of the party, as the Modern Prince. Reading the first draft with the second becomes essential if his thought is to be understood. In the case of the party, contrary to the frequent assertion that Gramsci understood the party as no more than the class under a different name (a possible inference from the second draft, which appears in the Einaudi edition), he makes quite clear that he is not interested in the party "as a sociological category" but as a "party which wishes to create a State, and which is always a concrete reality."[952]

This *aggiornamento* of his concerns is clear in the letters in which he discussed the contemporary function of Croce and the ways it was achieved. In the first of these letters Gramsci argued that Croce had succeeded in the pre-war period in convincing his audience that because peace existed dialectically in war, the real contradictions did not exist. As a result, Italian intellectuals were not nearly so antagonistic towards German intellectuals as their French colleagues were. After the war, when the Italian government wished to secure a rapprochement with the Germans, such attitudes became useful and Croce was elevated to Minister of Education. Indeed, Gramsci even believed that because of Croce's position as leader of a world-wide cultural elite, he was able to fill the same revisionist function internationally as well.[953]

The next problems which Gramsci tackled in his letters to Tatiana was why Croce had such success in leading the intellectuals. He wrote: "It seems to me that the greatest of Croce's qualities has always been this: to have his view of the world circulated around in a succession of brief works which were not pedantic and in which philosophy was presented directly and absorbed as common sense (*buon senso*) and as a mass attitude (*senso comune*). Thus the solutions to many problems ended up circulating anonymously; got into the papers, into everyday life, so that there were a great many 'Croceans' who didn't know that that was what they were, or even that Croce existed."[954]

Gramsci continued in a later letter that the fundamental view which Croce transmitted was a belief that power was unilaterally hegemonic, or exercised through cultural leadership. Rule was through agreement. His object in this stress was to do away with the Marxist theory of rule as class coercion. However, and here

Gramsci's view is very important since he did not fall back on the traditional denial of such a view in favour of the notion that the State is only an oppressive organ: "It is even possible to affirm that present-day Marxism in its essential traits is precisely the historical-political concept of hegemony." In arguing this Gramsci was being entirely consistent with his overall view of Marxism, since the theory that social power rested only on the forceful rule of one class over the other could be easily reduced to an "economism" which was fatalist and mechanist. Instead, he argued that in attacking "economism" Croce had set up a Marxism which never existed.[955]

If both Marxism and Croceanism were theories of hegemonic rule, what then was the distinction between them? According to Gramsci the distinction lay in the fact that Croceanism was "philosophy" or "speculation", where Marxism was not. While both contained an "ethico-political" history, Croce's problem was that he was so tangled up in the language of idealism that he could not escape from its concepts. He therefore mistakenly thought that Marxism retained the concept of structure like a "hidden God", when marxism was free from every theory of the last instance, and was an absolute historicism in the sense that it had no theory of origins.[956]

The limitedness of Croce could be seen in his history, which he proclaimed a history of liberty, but which was in fact a history of the precise mechanism by which such an "ideological" concept arose and was spread among the intellectuals as a "religion" and among the masses as "superstitution" in such a fashion that the latter felt that they belonged in a particular united "historical bloc" with the former, who acted as priests.[957]

In this analysis Gramsci highlighted what really interested him in his treatment and analysis of history: how particular notions arise historically and how they are diffused concretely or *organisationally*. This concern, we again repeat, is a different concern from a history of ideas, or even a history of the intellectuals as the bearers of ideas. Gramsci's intellectuals are conceived of as organisers, though obviously not as mindless organisers — from the history it was clear that men organised for a purpose. In Croce's case the purpose was to make men conform to what existed (capitalism) by stressing not the real contradictions but their mental conciliation as "maturity" and "reasonableness".[958]

All through 1931 and 1932, Gramsci's health had declined, though there is no sign of weakness in his clear hand. In the middle of 1932 he felt that he could go on no longer. "I have reached the point where my powers of resistance are about to collapse completely, with what consequences I don't know. These days I feel worse than I ever have before..."[959] he wrote to his sister-in-law. His friends in prison noted with alarm that he zig-zagged when he walked. It was only when he reached his low point that he started to consider the various schemes put to him by his sister-in-law and his friend, Professor Piero Sraffa,[960] to get him out of prison.

These schemes dated back to the earliest days of his imprisonment. Tatiana Schucht recalled hopes for an amnesty even back in 1929, though Gramsci himself was not so sanguine about his chances of an early release from prison.[961] In 1930 and 1931, when it was clear that there was not going to be an early commutation of his sentence, Sraffa in particular undertook to secure his release. Sraffa had important connections, and also thought that his personal prestige as a teacher at Cambridge might be a help.[962] The main stumbling block was Mussolini's insistence that Gramsci appeal for mercy before he would allow him to be released (Mussolini concerned himself personally with Gramsci's file).[963] This would have been tantamount to an admission of guilt and in May 1932 Gramsci let Sraffa know that he considered this an unpermissible sign of weakness by referring in damning terms to the appeal for mercy of Silvio d'Amico to the Austrian authorities as "completely ... abject."[964] Mussolini continued to hold out the bait as Gramsci's health declined. When Sraffa proposed to visit Gramsci late in 1932, after hearing how ill he was, he was again requested to urge the prisoner to ask for a pardon. When he refused to comply he was not allowed to see Gramsci. In sum, by 1932 when Gramsci was collapsing, it had become clear that one of the weapons in the duel with Fascism was the pardon, and that Mussolini was not going to release him unless he gave in. For example, it had been hoped that Gramsci might be exchanged for prisoners held by the Soviet Union in a proposed exchange designed to secure the release of Roman Catholic priests and bishops at a time when the fascist regime was intent on developing good relations with the Vatican. Togliatti authorised Sraffa to facilitate such an exchange[965] and the deputy minister of the Vatican Foreign Office even came to Turi to see Gramsci. Yet, despite the express proposal that Gramsci be included in the exchange, Mussolini opposed it.[966]

It appears that in the second half of 1932 Gramsci's friends decided that he did not know what was good for him in insisting so strongly that he would not consider any *démarches* to secure his release. He was only informed of proposals after they had been initiated by his friends, or after they had come to nought. He was furious about such action, and berated Tatiana when he discovered that she had been so brash as to arrange a medical examination for him, without his specific authorisation.[967] He was, however, in urgent need of medical attention, and in February 1933 wrote that he was entering a catastrophic stage of his life. A crisis came on March 7, 1933. On getting out of bed Gramsci collapsed and remained unconscious for some time. The prison officials were really worried as it appeared that he was going to die through their ill-treatment and neglect, just as international left opinion was hardening against the fascist regime's treatment of communist prisoners. The prison doctor diagnosed cerebral anaemia, and a priest was called, which indicates the severity of the crisis. For days Gramsci was delirious and raved in the Sard dialect, speaking of the immortality of the soul: "... in a realistic and historicist sense, that is, as a necessary survival of our useful and necessary actions, and an incorporation of them which is beyond our control into the ongoing process of history."[968] When he came out of the crisis, Dr Arcangeli visited him, as his sister-in-law had arranged, and urged him to ask for a pardon. According to one recollection, the priest, who was also present, added his pleas, but Gramsci replied: "You, chaplain, are a keeper of souls, isn't that so? There are two lives, that of the soul and that of the body. Which one do you want me to save? A pardon would save my body, but would kill my soul. Do you understand?"[969] Tatiana also rushed to the scene to talk to him. Again pressure was placed on her to suggest that he ask for pardon. Gramsci guessed at this before she mentioned it and told her firmly, but without anger, that it would be a "form of suicide".[970]

This firm refusal to give in, which was tantamount to choosing another, more honourable, form of suicide, as Gramsci realised himself, was not made without much soul-searching. Gramsci wrote interesting words in his notebooks at this time: "How much more indulgent I have started to become with catastrophes of personality after experiencing how such disasters come about. No indulgence for people who act against their own principles 'all of a sudden' — I mean through not having thought about the fact that remaining true to one's principles is going to mean suffering which they did not foresee.... It is strange that we are usually less indulgent with changes that come 'bit by bit' than with 'sudden' changes. The 'molecular' type of change is more dangerous, because, while it demonstrates the subject's will to resist, on reflection it allows you to 'see through' to a progressive change in the morality of the person, which, at a certain point, from being 'quantitative' becomes 'qualitative'; that is, no longer is it truly a matter of the same person, but of two.... It is an established principle that a captain should not desert the sinking ship before everyone else has, when all the others have been saved.... These are less unreasonable views than they seem..." (as only by leaving last can he be sure that the ship is really lost or that the least damage has been done). But this meant, Gramsci went on, that it was not really a moral but a practical issue. "I say that it is morally more justifiable to change 'bit by bit' (through *force majeure*, of course) than to change at one go, although the contrary is usually maintained. You hear people say: 'He has resisted for five years, why not six. He could have stuck it out another year and won't. Well, sometimes this is wisdom after the event, because in the fifth year the subject did not know that 'only' one more year of suffering faced him. But apart from this, the truth is that the man is no longer the same man in the fifth year that he was in the fourth, the third, the second, the first, and so on, he is a new person, completely new, in whom the years which have gone by have destroyed the moral brakes, the strength to resist which was characteristic of him in the first year.... If someone in the full flush of his physical and moral strength were placed at the cross-roads he would probably kill himself (once he had realised that it was not a game, but something real) but this is no longer probable (if someone finds himself at the crossroads after having experienced the molecular process in which his moral and physical strength has been destroyed etc.)."

"So we see men who are normally peaceful give way to sudden fits of anger and ferocity. It is not really a 'sudden' change of character: there has been an 'invisible' molecular process in which the moral strength which made those men 'peaceful' has been dissolved.... The drama for such people consists of this: they see the process of being undone, that is, they foresee what they will become and they think that at a certain stage of the process they will kill themselves to avoid the outcome. But at exactly what 'point'? In reality everyone believes in his own strength and hopes that something will turn up to get them out of their situation. And so (with a few exceptions) the majority of them find themselves in a full process of change which has gone beyond the point where they are still capable of reacting with the alternative of suicide.

"This fact should be studied in its daily manifestations. Not that it has not occurred in the past, but it is certain that in the present it has taken on a special and voluntary form.... Against this anti-moralistic way of seeing things there exists a falsely heroic way, full of rhetoric and words..."[971]

It is evidence of his great strength of will and courage that he did not give in even after such a penetrating self-analysis. For he had surely chosen an impossible alternative, which also was suicide. Arcangeli had filed the following medical report: "Antonio Gramsci ... is suffering from Potts' disease; he has tubercular lesions of the upper lobe of the right lung, which have caused two haemorrhages, one of which was serious and followed by severe fever for some days; he also has arterio-sclerosis with hardening of the arteries. He has had fainting fits with loss of consciousness and paraphasis lasting several days. Since October 1932 he has lost seven kilos in weight; he is suffering from insomnia and can no longer write as in the past. Gramsci cannot survive much longer under present conditions; I consider it necessary to transfer him to a civil hospital or clinic, if it is not possible to release him on probation..."[972] The prison officials were not prepared to let him leave without an appeal for a pardon. Naturally his condition became worse and worse, and by May 1933 his will to survive was beginning to crack. He wrote that if he had felt that it was realistic to hope for a change in his conditions, he would have continued to be an "optimist of the will". "I don't believe that any more. That doesn't mean that I have decided to give in. But it means that I no longer see any concrete way out and can't count on any reserve of strength..."[973] Indeed, in the first half of 1933 his letters change, becoming full of schemes and comments on ways to get his sentence reduced or revoked. When Tatiana Schucht visited him on the 1 July she found a shadow of the man she had known, a man so tired that he was will-less.[974] Yet, only when "he could last out no longer" because his headaches were driving him crazy, did the prison officials even agree to shift him to a quieter cell, where his cellmate, Trombetti, could help him.

In this entire period of six months he hardly wrote at all, though he started on four exercise books with a miscellany of notes, including the beginning of his notes on politics and the political part. He stopped writing again in August.

In the meantime the *démarches* of his brother Carlo, who went to

Rome to intercede with Mussolini, a growing press campaign, and the ominous reports about his health worked to provoke a decision in September that he be shifted to a sanatorium. On the 20 November he was suddenly shifted to the Cusumano clinic at Formia, where he arrived in a state of exhaustion and neuropathy.[975] At the last minute the faithful Trombetti had slipped his twenty-one exercise books in with his luggage.[976]

By April 1934 Gramsci had recovered his strength sufficiently to start writing again. Another eleven exercise books date from the years 1934-35. They were all "special notebooks" on which Gramsci himself wrote a title: There was one on Machiavelli (XXVII in the Einaudi edition) started in 1934, there were 132 pages on the Risorgimento (X); there was one entitled "Catholic Action — integral, Jesuit and modernist Catholics" (XXV); there was another on problems of national culture (popular literature) (XVII) and yet another "Americanism and Fordism"; 75 pages of 'Literary Criticism'; and 18 pages on "Journalism". More importantly there was one (XXIII) on the history of the "subaltern classes" (XXIII) one on "culture" (XII) and dating from 1935, but much briefer, seven pages on folklore (XI) eighteen pages on "Lorianism" (III) and ten pages on a study of grammar (XXI).

Whatever he felt, he was obviously better off, though conditions were by no means ideal, what with the constant police surveillance, and the lack of sleep due to the Cusumano family tramping up and down on the floor above until the small hours of the morning. He felt, too, that he did not have sufficient money to stay long enough at the clinic to make it worthwhile. By April 1934 he was making requests to be transferred to another clinic at Fiesole and was visited by Professor Vittorio Pulcinelli of the Quisisana clinic near Rome. On July 22 he wrote to his sister-in-law that "... I am firmly decided to leave the Cusumano clinic within the shortest time possible, even if it means transferring me to Sardinia. The condition of my nervous system is becoming acute (apart from everything else) and the memory of what happened for similar reasons (lack of rest) at the end of my stay in prison obsesses me and sometimes makes me desperate. You should make clear that transferring me to Sardinia (to my village) could not solve matters for me, because the operation which I have to have and the other ills affecting me would make new requests necessary ..."[977] Although now free to see his family and walk in the garden, the omnipresent police surveillance irked him and he even encouraged Tatiana to appeal directly to the relevant official of the Secret Police to have it removed. In September he wrote directly to Mussolini in very polite terms asking for "conditional liberty" under section 176 of the Penal Code. Shortly afterwards he was notified that this would be granted to him and on October 14, 1934 he wrote to Antonio Valenti, the Inspector-General of Police, in these terms: 'I am of the opinion that the concession made to me was not made for political reasons, and for my part, I undertake not to use this decision (*provvedimento*) to engage in propaganda either in Italy or abroad."[978]

A photograph taken at about this time is alone insufficient explanation for this loss of will. It revealed a prematurely aged, puffy-faced, and very sickly man, who no longer seemed to have that determined stare in his eyes. Gramsci had been crushed by his illness. He stressed in conversations with visitors that his active days were over, and that he was now a man of study.[979] But his preparedness to withdraw from politics (perhaps a promise he would not have kept had he recovered his health) was certainly also related to a growing difference between his views and those of the party. Athos Lisa's report of his views on the Costituente had reached the party in 1933, and in 1934 his views, which were still the same, were regularly passed on to the party and the Soviet Union by Sraffa and Tatiana.[980] It may be fortuitous, but after 1934 the campaign for his release, galvanised by the communist movement, died down.[981] Gramsci's picture was certainly still on display in Gorky Park in Moscow, but he may well also have felt that he was being deserted, or shunted aside.

Finally, after many more letters, he was transferred on 24 August 1935 to the Quisisana clinic near Rome, since the doctors felt that a hernia operation might be needed. When Professor Frugoni visited him two days later to make preliminary tests, he was obliged to report that Gramsci's illnesses were all just as bad as two years earlier, if not worse. Gramsci was in fact so exhausted by the onwards march of his combined illnesses that he could no longer write, not even letters. He appealed unsuccessfully to his wife to come and be near him. After 1936 he wrote only occasionally, and then to his wife and children. Little, if anything, was added to his notebooks.[982] He still maintained a sort of equilibrium, and wrote with considerable serenity for a man for whom life had been an endless struggle to overcome contradictions. He made plans to return to Sardinia when his sentence was up on 21 April 1937, now so close in time, and in preparation for his return his family took a room for him in Santu Lussurgiu.[983] Each day resembled the previous one, and he spent most of them with the selfless Tatiana. It was on one of these days, 25 April 1937, four days after his sentence was up, that he started to die. We reproduce Tatiana's letter which describes so well his last year and days of life: "Nino had a cerebral haemorrhage on the evening of 25 April. At half-past twelve on the same day I had taken him the booklet with the signature of the Clerk of Justices at the Rome Court, with the declaration of the Office of Prisons that since the period of conditional liberty was up, all further measures to secure his imprisonment had ceased.

I don't think that Nino felt worse that day than he normally did. Indeed, I can say that he was more relaxed than usual. As always I returned to the Clinic in the afternoon at about 5.30. As usual we talked about the events of the day and, as I had intended to prepare for a class on French literature and would have liked to study a little while he read, he protested that since I had come to see him I shouldn't work, that I should not have agreed to do the work since it needed special preparation, that I was tiring myself out, and so on. However, we still looked up some words together in Larousse. He didn't want me to read Corneille to him. Then we talked until dinner. When I suggested that I take the booklet downstairs to show it to the people, or that I call the Inspector, he told me that there was no hurry — that I could do it another day.

He ate as usual: clear soup with noodles (brodo), some stewed fruit and some *pane di spagna*. He went out to the lavatory and was carried back on a chair by several people. While in the lavatory he was paralysed on his left side completely — he was speaking quite clearly and repeated several times that he had slipped down but not struck his head, dragged himself to the door and called for help. One of the patients arrived, called the nurse, who urged him to call on his strength to open the door, which he managed to do by relying on his right side. Unfortunately he expended enormous effort when he should have been avoiding all effort or emotion. When he had been put to bed one of the doctors on duty was called. First Dr Marino came, but he refused to inject any stimulant, saying that this would only make things worse although Nino demanded that he be injected, indeed asked for a double dose. He was completely in command of himself and told the doctor what had happened down to the last detail. When a hot water bottle was put on his feet he first said that it was too hot and then that he could feel it very well with his left foot. Professor Pulcinelli was expected at any moment as he was to perform an emergency operation and I asked the janitor and the operating theatre to send him to see Nino the moment he arrived. He arrived with his assistant at about nine, noted that the left side, arm and leg were completely paralysed, ordered ice compresses for the head, a saline enema and that the hot water bottle be removed. Nino told him that he didn't want the enema and what he had felt in the lavatory. He made it clear that he had not lost consciousness, but only feeling in his left side. Pulcinelli tried to get him to move his lower limbs and contented himself with repeating Nino's words 'the left leg is weak', yes it is 'weak' he said. He ordered a blood letting. Nino was still speaking perfectly, with only a few signs that he was tired, which Pulcinelli noted. He told me that Nino should have complete rest.... Unfortunately they only came to give him the blood-letting after an hour and a half had elapsed and Nino had vomited several times. I was alone but I was able to help him, he asked to urinate and did, and then again tried to vomit and then tried to blow his nose, which, of course, had become blocked with food. He spoke and then he tried to look for his handkerchief but didn't speak. He felt for it and then lay back with his eyes shut, breathing heavily. The blood-letting did not have the desired result and Dr Belock let the sister know that the patient's condition was desperate. The priest came, and other sisters, and I had to protest in the most vehement fashion before they would leave Nino alone. They wanted to ask him questions to see if there was anything he wanted. The priest even told me not to give orders etc... The next morning at about ten Frugoni arrived. The whole night had gone by without the least change in his condition.

"In reply to my question to Frugoni about the real condition of the patient, I was told that he was extremely ill and that I couldn't be told anything, just like an architect who has no opinion after the house has collapsed. However, he ordered leeches on the mastoids and certain injections. It seemed that Nino was breathing more easily in the afternoon. But twenty-four hours after the attack he started to try to vomit again, and was breathing with extreme difficulty. I watched over him all the time, doing what I could, bathing his lips, trying to get him breathing again artificially when he seemed about to stop; but then there came a last noisy breath and an unchangeable silence settled.

"I called the doctor, who confirmed my fears. It was ten past four on the 27th."[984]

In the ten years of his imprisonment his mind had "not stopped working" and he lived on in his notes, which were smuggled out of the hospital and sent to Togliatti in Moscow. On 20 May 1937 the PCI leader wrote to Sraffa "... please let me know with precision what instructions Antonio left for the eventual publication of his writings. I mean in the first place the writings in prison, but also other earlier writings.... I haven't the slightest, even approximate idea of what is in them, or what they are about. Are they in a form which will allow us to publish them within a relatively brief period?... The editing of Antonio's literary and political legacy is too important a matter to be left to the hazard of our chance encounters...."[985] So, within a month of Gramsci's death, the publication of his notes was already being mooted.

Ten years elapsed before the first volume, carefully edited, appeared. Why? Of course the notes were difficult to edit and the war intervened. We may speculate, however, that in his last conversations with Sraffa in 1936-7 his scepticism about Zinoviev's and other leaders "confessions" in the purge trials which were just beginning in the USSR, made him once again too much of a heretic.[986] His criticism of the methods of international communism would have reached impermissible levels, even for a man of his stature, and Togliatti, despite urgings from Montagnana and others that the notes be published, may have thought it prudent not to be too hasty.

The non-publication of his notes was a first confirmation of the enormous political significance of Gramsci's notes, which more than that of any Third International theoretician, were to inaugurate and inspire first, the critique of the structures of Stalinist communism by the Italian Communist Party, provoking the tendency towards "polycentrism" in the communist world, and, later to provoke an increasingly trenchant criticism of the ensemble of communist movements which characterised the period of the Comintern and Cominform.

III

The physical and spiritual life of Antonio Gramsci had lasted only forty-six years. Like the lives of all men it had been multifaceted, with a concrete personal content to each phase of suffering and thought. To some extent this book has tried to trace this life as Gramsci would have wished; as a "continuous attempt to go beyond a backward way of living and thinking" in which "his activity, his experience of a political and ethical sort have formed a dialectic, allowing us to discover what is of universal and national value in his life'', but in which strictly autobiographical details are not lacking.[987] But we have also not neglected Gorky's dictum that every man should write his own biography be it apparently ever so insignificant, and stressed, even when considering Gramsci's life as a series of transcendences of his past, the immense personal and moral struggle it involved.

The choice to stress *his* life and *his* thought rather than consider him only as a moment of greater historical forces stemmed from a realisation that his own technique had allowed other students to confuse his positions with those of movements which were contemporaneous and of which he was supposedly a moment, when he was in no way associated subjectively with such movements. Or, more usually, because he had lived through so many experiences — Croceanism and the PSI; Leninism and the PCI; Trotskyism and the moral collapse of international Communism — to confuse his own real historical association with those movements with *their* general characteristics. As a result, the perfectly legitimate method of seeking for "epistemological ruptures" in his thought in fact became the process of asserting that the real Gramsci was "Leninist", or "Crocean" or "Trotskyite" after a certain date because his thought was confused with the social theory characterising these movements. All that preceded that date was really "pre-Gramscian".[988]

There was one "real" Gramsci, whose growth away from a "threefold and fourfold Sard provincial" was always a building upon the past in such a fashion that successive influences and developments in his views could only be understood in terms of earlier ones and his life itself, only in terms of *his* history.

In this life the really significant change in his thought occurred in 1919-20. Before that date he had believed that men had to understand the world before they could change it and that the main socialist task was one of education — to teach was to lead. After that date he realised that men would have to change the world to understand it — to organise was to lead.

Thereafter the latter view remained the cornerstone of his thought, which he never changed. He summed it up in his prison notes in 1932 in these words: "... any distinction between giving leadership and organising (and by organising I also mean 'checking up on') indicates deviation and betrayal".]989] This corner-stone directed his attention to the fundamental importance of acting politically rather than philosophically if he was to help change the world. From 1919-20 onwards his concerns in action and thought were with what men did, or were doing, not with what they thought they were doing. This thought too, found culmination in the notebooks: "Let men be judged by what they do, not what they say."[990]

This "philosophy of praxis" called for no general organisation, but a very specific form. As a Marxist, starting his analyses from the reality of a world of social contradictions which called for resolution, he believed that the organisation would have to unite men to take control of their destinies first at the place of production and then elsewhere. As he wrote in 1919: "... associating men together can and must be assumed to be the fundamental fact of the proletarian revolution". Concretely this meant working through organisations which tended to replace the capitalist in the administration of industry and thus to make the producer truly autonomous.[991] This book has shown how this idea remained basic in his thought right through his life and how, in pursuing its implications, he developed his theory of the role of the intellectuals *qua organisers* in their concrete structural, rather than their ideological, role. The basic fact of language was thus understood as having an organising rather than an ideological role.

Given the basic *credo* that the mass of men only liberate themselves in a process of conciliar action, which because it alters social relations is a "revolutionising praxis", the overwhelming concern with intellectuals in the prison notes indicates no return to idealism, but a theorisation of how men have been prevented from taking steps to unite together through the structural separation capitalism imposes between "those who know" and "those who don't know". Gramsci's addition to revolutionary theory in 1929-35 thus is a complement to the basic view evolved as early as 1919-20 — a view not greatly different from that held by marxists as diverse as Lukàcs and Mao-Tse-tung. Gramsci wrote in his last years about the role of intellectuals as organisers of a revolutionary practice in which the revolution is only made by *organised,* i.e. self-conscious, masses of men.

Notes

INTRODUCTION

1 J. Cammett, *Antonio Gramsci and the Origins of Italian Communism* (Stanford University Press, Stanford, 1967).

2 G. Fiori, *Antonio Gramsci Life of a Revolutionary* (NLB, London 1970).

3 A. Gramsci, *Socialismo e fascismo, l'Ordine Nuovo 1921-22*\(Einaudi, Turin, 1967); *La Costruzione del Partito Comunista italiano, 1923-1926* (Einaudi, Turin, 1972) Henceforth *SF* and *Costruzione*.

4 P. Spriano, *Storia del Partito Comunista italiano, I, Da Bordiga a Gramsci* (Einaudi, Turin, 1967).

5 *Archives de Jules Humbert-Droz, I, Origines et débuts des partis communistes des pays latins, 1919-1921* (Dordrecht, Reidel, 1970).

6 J. Humbert-Droz, *Mémoires, De Lenine à Staline. Dix ans au service de l'Internationale Communiste 1921-1931* (La Baconnière, Neuchâtel, 1971).

7 Parts of the archives had already been published as a book in Italy in 1969: J. Humbert-Droz, *Il Constrasto tra l'Internazionale e il P.C.I. 1922-1928. Documenti inediti dall'archivio di Jules Humbert-Droz, segretario dell'Internazionale Comunista* (Feltrinelli, Milan, 1969).

8 For a useful survey of the debate see M. Salvadori, "L'attuale storiografia sul Partito Comunista (1921-1926)", in *Gramsci e il problema storico della democrazia* (Einaudi, Turin, 1970), pp. 155-185.

9 See S. White, "Gramsci and the Italian Communist Party", *Government and Opposition*, 2, 1972, pp. 186-205.

10 Fiori is, in fact, a journalist, but his book is a lesson in writing history for most historians.

11 As Marx puts it in a scathing criticism of Stirner in the *German Ideology*. See A. Davidson, "Marxism and Anarchism", *Australian Left Review*, 33, November 1971, pp. 40-41.

12 A. Davidson, "The Varying Seasons of Gramscian Studies", *Political Studies*, XX, 4, December 1972, pp. 448-461.

13 L. Paggi, *Gramsci e il Moderno Principe* (Riuniti, Rome, 1971), I.

CHAPTER I

14 The baptism certificate is reprinted in L. Russo, "Antonio Gramsci e l'educazione democratica in Italia", *Belfagor*, II, 4, 1947, p. 400n.

15 G. Fiori, "La giovinezza di Gramsci", *Rinascita sarda*, V, 7, 20 April-5 May 1967, p. 10.

16 G. Manno, *Storia di Sardegna* (Visaj, Milan, 1835), I, *passim*.

17 *Ibid.*, II, pp. 207, 211, 228-230; A. Boscolo, *Feudalesimo in Sardegna* (Fossataro, Cagliari, 1967) pp. 1-36. In 1611 the population of Cagliari was 14,000 and Sassari, 2,800. In 1728 the figures were 16,924 and 13,737 respectively and Oristano had 4,646 inhabitants. See Manno, II, pp. 234-405. Cagliari still had only 30,905 inhabitants in 1861. See SVIMEZ,

Statistiche sul Mezzogiorno d'Italia 1861-1953 (Tip. F. Failli, Rome, 1954) p. 9. Even in 1904 the average· Sardinian sharefarmer ate only 2600 calories a day when he needed 4000. SVIMEZ, p. 712. In the nineteenth century death by starvation was known. D. Mack Smith, *Italy* (University of Michigan Press, Ann Arbor, 1959), p. 189 writes: "Contemporary newspapers in 1896-7 tell of people in Sardinia eating grass and dying of hunger". More than two in every 1000 Sardinians died of malaria in 1900-02 Compiled from SVIMEZ, pp. 106-8.

18 Manno, II, pp. 193, 234, 309-322, 411-455; C. Cabitza, *Sardegna Rivolta contro la colonizzazione* (Feltrinelli, Milan, 1968), pp. 13-18 and *passim*; J. W. Tyndale, *Island of Sardinia* (Bentley, London, 1849), III, pp. 277, 296. In 1885 only 3 communes in 100 in Sardinia had hospitals and doctors were rare even after a law was passed in 1885 making it compulsory for communes to have them. See F. Nitti, "Poor Relief in Italy", in *Scritti sulla questione meridionale* (Laterza, Bari, 1958), p. 244.

19 See Cabitza, *Sardegna, passim.*

20 J-F. Coffin, "Mémoire sur la situation politique de la Sardaigne" (1798-1799) in C. Sole ed., *La Sardegna di Carlo Felice e il problema della terra* (Fossataro, Cagliari, 1968), p. 214.

21 Cabitza, p. 107.

22 *Ibid*, pp. 20-21.

23 "He who commands is the law."; "The law never binds its maker." See Gonario Pinna, *Il pastore sardo e la giustizia* (Fossataro, Cagliari, 1967), ch. II for these and many other traditional folk sayings. See also G. Spano. *Proverbi sardi* (Cagliari, 1871).

24 Coffin, in Sole, p. 226.

25 Tyndale, III, p. 278.

26 Alfredo Niceforo, *La delinquenza in Sardegna* (Remo Sandron, Palermo, 1898).

27 Giovanni Maria Angioy, "Mémoires sur la Sardaigne" (1799) in Sole p. 180.

28 Matteo Luigi Simon de Alghero, *Mémoire pour Napoléon* (Giuffré, Milan, 1967), p. 77.

29 Tyndale, III, pp. 276-77.

30 Sole, pp. 14-15; Boscolo, p. 20.

31 Sole, p. 11.

32 Giovanni Maria Angioy, *op.cit.*, p. 202 wrote: "Les habitants des villages, outre les principes généreux de liberté et de bonheur public ont des motifs très forts pour désirer le système républicain, c'est-à-dire l'abolition des droits féodaux."

33 Tyndale, III, pp. 296-303.

34 Sole, p. 55.

35 Cited in Cabitza, *Sardegna davanti ad una svolta decisiva* (Feltrinelli, Milan, 1968), pp. 8-9.

36 Pinna p. 28.

37 "Pastures enclosed by walls, taken by force, if heaven were on earth, you would enclose that too." See Cabitza, *Sardegna, Rivolta,* p. 51.

38 Tyndale, III, p. 296.

39 Sole, p. 56 n.

40 The sum later rose to 576,000 lit per annum. See P. Gobetti, "Il problema sardo" in P. Spriano ed., *Opere complete di Piero Gobetti, I, Scritti politici* (Einaudi, Turin, 1960), p. 713.

Notes

41 Tyndale, III, p. 296.
42 F. Salaris, *Atti della giunta per l'inchiesta agraria e sulle condizione della classe agricola* in Gobetti, p. 718.
43 *Ibid.*
44 Cabitza, *Sardegna, Rivolta,* p. 52.
45 Gobetti, p. 718.
46 Sole, pp. 50-55.
47 For the general content of the rest of the chapter I refer the reader to the various biographies of Gramsci listed in the Introduction as most of the material is well-known. There is a good chronological table in A. Gramsci, *Lettere dal Carcere* (Einaudi, Turin, 1965), pp. xxi-xlvi. Henceforth *Lettere.*
48 *Lettere,* p. 316. In this letter Antonio Gramsci stresses how far people can change politically in three generations.
49 Fiori, *Vita,* p. 10.
50 The standard work on Southern Italy is Friedrich Vochting, *La questione meridionale* (Instituto editoriale del Mezzogiorno, Naples, n.d.).
51 See *La Voce,* 16 March 1911, reported in G. Arfé ed., *Gaetano Salvemini Movimento socialista e questione meridionale, Opere IV,* Vol. 2, (Feltrinelli, Milan, 1968), p. 484.
52 *Lettere,* pp. 117, 548.
53 A contemporary speculated: "Perhaps, like so many mainlanders ... he then thought of staying briefly, the few years he was obliged to fill in, in an uncomfortable place after entering his career." Fiori, *Vita,* p. 9.
54 *Ibid.* This sign of respect was double-edged in the class-conscious villages of Sardinia. See G. Deledda, *Colombi e sparvieri* (Mondadori, Milan), p. 205, for the hatred of the "white-faced" bourgeois.
55 G. Bottiglioni, *Vita sarda. Note di folklore, cante e leggende* (Trevisini, Milan, 1925), p. 38. This book is particularly valuable for an understanding of the Sardinia of Gramsci's youth as it was researched before 1914. See also L. Alziator, *Il folklore sardo* (La Zattera, Bologna, 1957), pp. 63, 96-102.
56 Bottiglioni, pp. 40-45.
57 They still wore traditional dress when D. H. Lawrence visited the island in 1922. D. H. Lawrence, *Sea and Sardinia* (Martin Secker, London, 1923).
58 Bottiglioni, pp. 83-86.
59 See folktales nos 89-117 in Bottiglioni.
60 *Ibid.,* pp. 82-86.
61 *Ibid.,* p. 90.
62 Alziator, p. 105.
63 A. Anfossi, *Socialità e organizzazione in Sardegna* (Angeli, Milan, 1968), p. 56.
64 For the number of literates see Fiori, *Vita,* pp. 11, 42.
65 *Lettere,* p. vii.
66 *Ibid.,* pp. vii, xxi.
67 G. Fiori, "Gramsci e il mondo sardo" in *Gramsci e la cultura contemporanea* (Riuniti, Rome, 1969), I, pp. 444-45 indicates that the hatred was extreme when Gramsci was born.
68 Fiori, "La Giovinezza di Gramsci", p. 10; *Lettere,* p. 184, where Gramsci notes on the death of his aunt that she maintained a pose of "continental superiority".

69 Fiori, "La giovinezza di Gramsci", p. 12.
70 *Lettere,* pp. 122, 309.
71 Fiori, *Vita,* p. 11.
72 Gramsci himself regarded the years 0-2 as unimportant in development compared with later years, *Lettere,* pp. 312-13.
73 In 1891, *cav.* Nicolino Tunis, the source of the above account, was a boy of ten, who frequently held Antonio in his arms before the Gramscis shifted to Sorgono.
74 See the photographs of Gramsci in S. Romano, *Gramsci* (UTET, Turin 1965), p. 32; *Lettere,* p. 438.
75 Romano, p. 10.
76 M. Garuglieri, "Ricordo di Gramsci", *Società,* 7-8, July-December 1946, p. 700, recalls that even when in his forties Gramsci "... loved his mother so much and spoke of her often." See *Lettere,* pp. 53, 398, 696.
77 Cammett, p. 7, remarks on this. It is striking that there are no letters to his father in the *Lettere* and that the letters of youth from Cagliari are singularly devoid of affection.
78 Cammett, pp. 3-4; Romano, ch. I.
79 There are various account of this. The best is that given by Gramsci himself in a letter to Tatiana Schucht dated 23 April 1933 in C. Casucci, "Il carteggio di Antonio Gramsci conservato nel casellario politico centrale", *Rassegna degli archivi di Stato,* XXV, No 3, September-December 1965, pp. 21-23; see also *Lettere,* p. 479; Fiori, *Vita,* p. 17.
80 *Ibid.*
81 *Ibid.*
82 *Lettere,* p. 479.
83 M. Cutri, "Nella casa di Ghilarza", *L'Unita,* 27 April 1947; Nennetta Cuba's interview in Fiori, *Vita,* p. 17.
84 *Lettere,* p. 479.
85 Fiori, *Vita,* p. 17.
86 *Lettere,* p. 663; SVIMEZ, p. 772 which gives the numbers of kindergartens as 11 in 1886-87 and 15 in 1901-02.
87 *Lettere,* p. 350.
88 This was the characteristic style of politics in Southern Italy at the time. Usually the peasant was the sufferer. Often at the core of the local disputes were unresolved conflicts over the local "baron's" right to land he had enclosed in earlier years. The *Pungolo* described this in 1882 as follows:
"Usually there are two possible situations in communes which have not resolved court actions over land. Either the municipal council is controlled by the usurpers ... themselves and thus it is not really in the interest of the commune to have the case concluded; if titles and deeds are not stolen as ordinarily happens they are put to sleep on the dusty shelves of the archives. Or the head of the council is a representative of the petty-bourgeoisie who are bitter enemies of the landholders ... ; then, while the former keep the case going and stir up suspicions in the minds of the plebs, they do not care really whether the case ends or not. It is their object, rather, to keep the issue alive and frightening ... and stimulate an inexhaustible fund of lies, hates and vendettas — a real civil war which disrupts the life of our provincial communes. For Southern Italy the land question is

an inexhaustible field of corruption in which the usurpers and the powerful, the traffickers and politicians of all variety, clientless lawyers and doctors — all the people who wish to climb the ladder of power to fill their pockets; a vast field of corruption in which only the don Rodrigo's and overworked tribunes take first place, to the detriment of honest proprietors and workers of good faith." B. Finocchiaro ed., *L'Unita di Gaetano Salvemini* (Pozza, Venice, 1958), p. 129.

89 Cited in Fiori, *Vita*, p. 14.

90 *Ibid.*, pp. 13-15; Fiori, "Gramsci e il mondo sardo" in *Gramsci e la cultura contemporanea*, I, pp. 453-55.

91 *Critica sociale*, XII, 1902 in M. Spinella, A. Caracciolo, R. Amaduzzi, G. Petronio eds., *Critica sociale* (Feltrinelli, Milan, 1959), I. pp. 171-72.

92 Fiori, *Vita*, p. 24. Gennaro recalled in an interview: "I was in fourth class at *ginnasio*, living with uncle Nicolino. Uncle died about Christmas, but papa saw to it that I finished the school year at Ozieri. I went back to Ghilarza for the vacation. When school started again (dad was no longer at home) my mother told me that for the moment I could no longer go on with school, and told me why. I was then, of the seven of us, the only one to know that dad was in prison."

93 *Lettere*, p. 395.

94 Fiori, "La giovinezza di Gramsci", p. 12.

95 Fiori in *Gramsci e la cultura contemporanea*, I, pp. 455-56.

96 *Lettere*, pp. 682-83.

97 Cammett erroneously stresses this. Cammett. p. 5.

98 The house, furnished as it was, is now a museum.

99 *Lettere*, pp. 142, 395. He frequently visited his aunt, Maria Domenica Corrias, in Abbasanta to gorge himself with fruit.

100 Teresina in interview in Fiori, *Vita*, p. 27; Teresina and Grazietta in interview with M. Cutri, "Nella casa di Ghilarza", *L'Unità*, 27 June 1947.

101 *Lettere*, p. 54.

102 *Ibid.*, p. 685.

103 *Ibid.*, p. 456.

104 *Ibid.*, pp. 391-92.

105 A classic example is in Fiori, *Vita*, p. 22, where a primary school companion, Chichinnu Mameli said: "He was, as you know, of a certain build, and naturally the deformity prevented his joining in games we played. Boys, then and now, wrestle and wear themselves out: our favourite games were tests of physical power and strength, and he, Nino, at best could only stand and watch. He therefore came with us only rarely. Generally he remained at home, reading, drawing coloured figures, making models and playing in the courtyard. Or he went wandering in the countryside. I saw him a lot with Mario. Of the other brothers, Gennaro was too big, seven years older, to keep him company; and Carlo too small, six years younger."

106 Garuglieri, p. 700.

107 Fiori, *Vita*, pp. 21, 31.

108 *Lettere*, p. 108.

109 Fiori, *Vita*, pp. 21, 29, 31.

110 *Lettere*, p. 733, seems to infer this conclusion.

111 M. Cutri, "Nella casa di Ghilarza", *L'Unità*, 27 April 1947; Fiori, *Vita*, p. 20.

112 *Lettere*, p. 673.

113 G. Carbone and L. Lombardo-Radice, *Vita di Antonio Gramsci* (Critica sociale, Rome, 1957), p. 10.

114 *Lettere*, p. 893.

115 *Ibid*, pp. 904-05.

116 *Ibid.*, pp. 578-79.

117 *Ibid.*, p. 899.

118 *Ibid.*, pp. 145, 287, 561, 642, 673, 783.

119 M. Cutri, "Nella casa di Ghilarza"; Fiori, *Vita*, p. 22.

120 *Lettere*, pp. 442-43.

121 *Ibid.*

122 A. Gramsci, *L'Albero del Riccio* (Milano Sera, Milan, 1949), p. 109; *Lettere*, p. 852.

123 *Lettere*, p. 396.

124 *Ibid.*, pp. 164-65; A. Gramsci, *Scritti giovanili* (Einaudi, Turin 1958), p. 10 Henceforth *SG*.

125 For the marks see Fiori, *Vita*, pp. 29-30; Cammett, p. 6, gives the marks for the *esami di proscioglimento* which he had tried to sit before time, and which he finally sat on 24 July 1901. The originals of the examination results are held at Gramsci's home in Ghilarza and reproduced in Romano, p. 49.

126 *Lettere*, p. 381.

127 As one of his school companions recalled in an interview in Fiori, *Vita*, p. 19.

128 He swung Venetian lanterns and shouted: "Viva il leone di Caprera" with other boys when he was eight. *Lettere*, pp. 164-65. See also *Ibid.*, p. 132.

129 Fiori, *Vita*, p. 21.

130 *Lettere*, p. 525.

131 *Ibid.*, pp. 80-81.

132 *Ibid.*, pp. 99-100.

133 *Ibid.*, pp. 100, 653.

134 *Ibid.*, p. 432.

135 *Ibid.*, p. 685.

136 *Ibid.*, p. 184.

137 *Ibid.*, pp. 165, 624-25, 672.

138 *Ibid.*, p. 623.

139 Report by Dr Professor Filippo Saporito to the Director-General, Instituti di prevenzione e di pena, 21 April 1933 in Casucci, p. 443.

140 Much later he wrote à propos his niece: "... it seems to me that our whole lives are struggles to adapt ourselves to our surroundings, but also, and especially, to dominate them and not be crushed by them." *Lettere*, p. 363.

141 *Ibid.*, p. 97; G. Ferrata and N. Gallo, *Due mila pagine di Gramsci* (Il Saggiatore, Milan, 1964), II, p. 23.

142 *Ibid.*

143 *Lettere*, p. 737.

144 *Ibid.*, p. 674.

145 *Ibid.*, p. 682.

146 Fiori, *Vita*, p. 30; Ferrata and Gallo, II, p. 32.

147 Ferrata and Gallo, II, p. 33.

148 *Lettere*, p. 525.

149 *Ibid.*, p. 674

150 *Ibid.*, p. 201.

151 *Ibid.*, p. 348.

152 Fiori, *Vita*, p. 46.
153 Romano, p. 33.
154 M. Cutri, "Nella casa di Ghilarza".
155 Fiori, *Vita*, pp. 46-48.
156 Romano, p. 46.
157 *Ibid.*, pp. 33, 37.
158 *Ibid.*, p. 49.
159 Fiori, *Vita*, p. 59; *Lettere*, p. 125.
160 Several of these letters are in *Rinascita sarda*, V, 7, 20 April-5 May 1967, pp. 9, 12. The quotation is from a letter dated 31 January 1909.
161 The letter is in Fiori, *Vita*, p. 60.
162 *Ibid.*, p. 61.
163 *Lettere*, p. 125.
164 *Ibid.*
165 Fiori, *Vita*, p. 62.
166 *Ibid.*, p. 61. The inverviewee, *avv.* Dino Frau, said this: "He lived by himself. There were six or seven of us boarding at signora Doloretta Porcu's. We lived on the top floor which was reached only by one steep set of stairs. Antonio Gramsci climbed slowly and was out of breath on arrival. Then he shut himself in his room, without hobnobbing with us. I only went into his room a couple of times. There were no ornaments, but a smell of cheese, and books and papers everywhere. One day all the boarders were invited in. Songs and sounds were coming from the room. We found quite a few unknown people, mostly villagers. They were singing and someone was dancing. And in the middle there was Gramsci intently playing popular Sard dances with an accordion."
167 This letter is in *Rinascita sarda*, V, 7, 20 April-5 May 1967, p. 9, and is apparently mistakenly dated by Gramsci 31 January 1909. Fiori suggests, in my opinion correctly, that the date should be 31 January 1910.
168 P. Togliatti, *Gramsci* (Riuniti, Rome, 1967), p. 60.
169 The marks he received were as follows: Italian 7 and 7; Latin 8 and 8; history of Greek culture 9; history and historical geography 8; philosophy 7; natural history 7; physics and chemistry 7.
170 Fiori, *Vita*, p. 69.
171 For an interesting article on Gramsci's school years see A. Cajati, "Gli anni liceali di Gramsci e gli strafalcioni di alcuni suoi biografi", *Annali del liceo classico G.-M. Dettori di Cagliari*, I, 1962-3, Bari, 1963, pp. 115-120.
172 See I. Delogu, "Casa Gramsci", *Rinascita sarda*, V, 7, 20 April-5 May 1967, pp. 8-9. A. de Jaco, "Visita a Ghilarza. Lettere di A. Gramsci, studente, alla famiglia", *L'Unità*, 22 January 1966.
173 *Ibid.*
174 *Lettere*, p. 201.
175 Romano, p. 47-49; Cammett, p. 9.
176 Fiori, *Vita*, p. 79.
177 *Lettere*, p. 125.
178 *Ibid.*
179 See the interview with Renato Figari in Fiori, *Vita*, p. 65.
180 A. Gramsci, "Lettere al Grido", *SG*, p. 28.
181 Fiori, *Vita*, p. 65.
182 A. de Jaco, "Visita a Ghilarza".
183 *Ibid.*
184 *Lettere*, p. 201.

185 Cammett, pp. 4-5.
186 *Passato e presente* (Einaudi, Turin, 1966), p. 174. Henceforth *PP*.
187 "Truly, I have been used to thinking for many, many, years that it was absolutely impossible, almost Fate, that I could be loved by anybody.", he wrote in a love-letter to his wife in 1923. He traced this feeling back to the age of ten. Ferrata and Gallo, II, p. 23. See *Lettere*, p. 614 for his hatred of family life.
188 See the interview with Gennaro Gramsci in Fiori, *Vita,* p. 65.
189 Ferrata and Gallo, II, p. 24.
190 Togliatti, *Gramsci,* p. 78.
191 *Lettere*, p. 161. Gramsci makes it a joke: "Certainly it was a collection of goodtimers, who were having some fun frightening us" and not a "brigand tale".
192 *Lettere*, p. 184.
193 *Ibid.*, p. 560.
194 *Ibid.*, p. 525, where he writes contemptuously of a signor Camedda, a typical village "intellectual", and of his posturing.
195 Garuglieri, p. 700.
196 See Delogu, p. 8. *Lettere,* pp. 80, 100, 105, 132, 161, 184, 232, 363, 432, 441, 445, 485, 506, 509, 525, 551, 653, 685, 736.
197 Romano, pp. 47-48; Fiori, *Vita,* p. 59.
198 Fiori, *Vita,* p. 21.
199 Romano, p. 53.
200 *Lettere*, p. 126.

CHAPTER II

201 *Lettere*, p. 432.
202 Pirastu, p. 135, points out that every decade of Sard history was tied to the name of a particular well-known bandit. Tolu was the hero in 1858-80.
203 Ferrata and Gallo, II, p. 33.
204 Togliatti, *Gramsci,* p. 76.
205 Fiori, *Vita,* pp. 68-69.
206 *Ibid.*, p. 90; *Sotto la Mole* (Einaudi, Turin, 1960), pp. 148-150.
207 Togliatti, *Gramsci,* p. 50; G. Amoretti, "Con Gramsci sotto la Mole", in *Gramsci, Scritti di P. Togliatti ed altri* (L'Unita, Rome, 1945), p. 47; G. Spano, "Gramsci sardo" in *ibid.,* pp. 108-111.
208 "La madre dell'ucciso", A Sard folk figure. See the plate in Pinna, p. 179. One of Deledda's novels is about *La madre.*
209 Fiori, *Vita,* p. 65.
210 *Ibid.*, p. 69.
211 M. Cutri, "Nella casa di Ghilarza", *L'Unita,* 27 April 1947; Fiori, "La giovinezza di Gramsci", p. 11.
212 G. Ferrata, "Introduction" to *La Voce 1908-1916* (Landi, Rome, 1961), p. 27.
213 R. Rolland, *Jean-Christophe* (Michel, Paris, 1956), pp. 1453-54.
214 N. Bobbio, "Profilo ideologico del Novecento" in *Storia della letteratura italiana* (Garzanti, Milan, 1969), p. 132.
215 Editorial, *La Voce,* II, 1909 in *La cultura italiana del'900 attraverso le riviste, III, La Voce 1908-1914* (Einaudi, Turin, 1960), pp. 177-183.
216 Ferrata ed., *La Voce,* pp. 68-69.

217 *La Voce,* II, 44, 1909; III, 19, 1911; III, 19, 1911, in *La cultura, etc.,* pp. 241-52, 329, 634.
218 *La Voce,* II, 28, 1910 in *ibid.,* pp. 206-210.
219 *Ibid.*
220 *La Voce,* II, 28, 1910; III, 33, 35, 36, 1911 in *ibid.,* pp. 350-367.
221 G. Contini, *L'influenza culturale di Benedetto Croce* (Ricciardi, Naples, 1957), p. 9; Ferrata ed., *La Voce,* pp. 297, 187, 205.
222 B. Croce, *La filosofia della pratica* (Laterza, Bari, 1954), *passim.*
223 Ferrata and Gallo, II, p. 33.
224 M. Cutri, "Nella casa di Ghilarza".
225 See M. Spinella, ed., *Critica sociale,* I, *passim;* L. Valiani, "Il problema delle 'grandi riforme' fra i socialisti dal 1900 al 1914" and "Filippo Turati", in *Questioni di storia del socialismo* (Einaudi, Turin, 1958); Fiori, *Vita,* p. 41.
226 G. Salvemini in *La Voce,* II, 44, 1910 in *La cultura* etc., pp. 241-250; *Avanti,* 23 March 1910.
227 *SG,* p. 28.
228 Lecture, 28 March 1910 in Rome in N. Valeri, *La lotta politica in Italia dall'unita al 1925* (Le Monnier, Florence, 1962), pp. 322-327; see also A. Labriola, *Storia di dieci anni, 1899-1909* (Milan, 1910) pp. 246-48, 250-53, 257-58.
229 Ferrata and Gallo, II, pp. 13-15.
230 Fiori, *Vita,* p. 82.
231 See the letter in *ibid.,* p. 82; *Lettere,* p. 125.
232 D. Zucàro, "Antonio Gramsci all'universita di Torino", *Società,* December 1957, pp. 1091-92.
233 Gramsci to father, 4 November 1911, in I. Delogu, "Casa Gramsci", p. 9.
234 *Lettere,* p. 125; Casucci, p. 443.
235 Zucàro, p. 1093.
236 *Ibid.*
237 Fiori, *Vita,* p. 93.
238 Delogu; Gramsci to father, 3 January 1912, in Ferrata and Gallo, II, p. 17.
239 *Lettere,* p. 125; Fiori, *Vita,* p. 85.
240 Zucàro, p. 1094.
241 *Ibid.*
242 L. Russo, p. 39n.
243 He attended both law seminars and Italian literature courses in 1912. He also attended courses on the history of art. *Lettere,* p. 491.
244 Zucàro, pp. 1094-95; for Balsamo-Crivelli see P. Spriano, *Socialismo e classe operaia a Torino 1892-1913* (Einaudi, Turin, 1958), *passim.*
245 Ferrata and Gallo, II, p. 17.
246 *Lettere,* pp. 58-59.
247 *Ibid.,* p. 467.
248 His main work on Dante was a biography on St. Francis *Con madonna poverta* (Laterza, Bari, 1940). His writings at the time Gramsci was a student are collected in *Studi-francescani* (Laterza, Bari).
249 *Lettere,* p. 412.
250 *Ibid.,* p. 466.
251 *Ibid.,* pp. 412-466, 468. Togliatti declared that "We arrived the same way as Karl Marx, that is beginning from the philosophy of Hegel." A. Garosci, "Totalitarismo e storicismo nel pensiero di Antonio Gramsci" in *Pensiero politico e storiografia moderna* (Nistri-Lischi, Pisa, 1954).

252 Zucàro, p. 1095.
253 *Avanti* (Piedmontese ed.) 10 April 1916 in Sergio Caprioglio, *Antonio Gramsci, Scritti 1915-21* ('Il Corpo', 1968), p. 7.
254 Togliatti, *Gramsci,* p. 65.
255 For example, Norberto Bobbio in "Tre maestri" in *Italia civile* (Lacaita-Manduria, Bari, Perugia, 1964), p. 129 recalls that Cosmo set his students an example of "freedom of conscience" and loyalty in his beliefs.
256 On Turin University at this time, its teachers and their views, see Paolo Spriano, "l'Universita di Torino", in *Torino operaia nella grande guerra* (1914-1918), (Einuadi, Turin, 1960), pp. 22-27 and "Le universita e la cultura: Torino" in Spriano ed., *Opere complete di Piero Gobetti,* I, pp. 908-912.
257 Casucci. In 1911, when ill, Gramsci suffered from a recurrent nightmare about a spider coming to suck out his blood, which Freudian psycho-analysts would find interesting. Gramsci to Giulia (his wife) 29 March 1924 in Ferrata and Gallo, II, p. 39.
258 Russo, p. 39n.
259 Renzo de Felice, "Un corso di glottologia di Matteo Bartoli negli appunti di Antonio Gramsci", *Rivista storica del socialismo,* VII, 2, January-April 1964, p. 219-221.
260 Cammett, p. 17. For the infrequency of Gramsci's letters see *Lettere,* p. 307 "... when I was at university I never wrote letters." For a typical letter see Ferrata and Gallo, II, p. 18.
261 Cammett, p. 18, describes Cosmo as a "political liberal". In fact he was a socialist until 1914. *Ordine Nuovo,* p. 362. Henceforth *ON.*
262 A. Leonetti, "Coerenza di Gramsci", *Paese sera,* 6 March 1964, republished in A. Leonetti, *Note su Gramsci* (Argalia, Urbino, 1971), p. 69.
263 Togliatti, *Gramsci,* p. 49.
264 In 1913 he purchased a small library of books on Sardinia from Marchese Boyl's collection. *Lettere,* p. 131.
265 M. and M. Ferrara, *Conversando con Togliatti, Note biografiche* (Edizioni di cultura sociale, Rome, 1953), p. 17 report the meeting; A. Tasca, "I primi dieci anni del Partito comunista italiano", *Il Mondo,* 18 August 1953 describes Togliatti as more interested in his studies than in anything else.
266 Leonetti, *Note su Gramsci,* p. 171.
267 Lombardo Radice and Carbone, p. 35.
268 *Il Risorgimento* (Einaudi, Turin, 1955), p. 113, nl. This notion was widespread among the Salveminian wing of the Socialist Party.
269 Gramsci's extreme anti-"continental" Sardism was still dominant in 1912, as Togliatti reports, *Gramsci,* pp. 70-79. The story, which Gramsci was fond of telling, but which could be interpreted in several ways, is reported in *ibid.*
270 Tasca, in *Il Mondo,* 13 August 1953.
271 See Battista Santhià to Leonetti in Leonetti, *Note su Gramsci,* pp. 165, 170
272 Tasca in *Il Mondo,* 14 August 1953.
273 Zucàro, p. 1102. Togliatti wrote many years later: "In 1912 and 1913 when we left the lecture hall in the morning ... we met groups of men quite different from us ..." [industrial workers AD] *Gramsci,* p. 69.
274 Zucàro, pp. 1102 ff.
275 Russo, p. 39 n.
276 *SG,* p. 22; Tasca in *Il Mondo,* 18 August 1953.
277 Togliatti, *Gramsci,* pp. 50-57, 76-77.

278 Tasca in *Il Mondo,* 18 August 1953; Spriano, *Torino operaia,* pp. 57-61; Gramsci, "Alcuni temi della questione meridionale" in F. de Felice and V. Parlato eds., *La questione meridionale Gramsci* (Rinuniti, Rome, 1969), pp. 136-38. Salvemini's account is in G. Arfe ed., *Salvemini Opere* (Feltrinelli, Milan, 1968), IV, p. 677-78.

279 See the recollections of G. Castagno and G. Benso in Zucàro, p. 1103.

280 L. Cortesi ed., *Il socialismo italiano tra riforme e rivoluzione,* 1892-1921. *Atti congressuali del PSI* (Laterza, Bari, 1969), p. 544.

281 *Ibid.,* p. 526.

282 *Ibid.,* pp. 549-551. Party numbers increased from 20,459 in 1912 to 47,724 in 1914. The Youth Federation had reached 10,000 by 1914.

283 Cortesi, p. 568. For the period 1912-14 seen from a "reformist" point of view see G. Arfe, *Storia del socialismo italiano (1892-1926)* (Einaudi, Turin, 1965), chs. 11-13.

284 M. Montagnana, *Ricordi di un operaio torinese* (Rinascita, Rome, 1949), p. 28; see also Tasca in *Il Mondo,* 18 August 1953.

285 In the rather vexed debate about this, the onus of proof is on those who assert that Gramsci did not support Mussolini. I follow Aldo Romano, "Antonio Gramsci tra guerra e rivoluzione", *Rivista storica del socialismo,* I, 1, 1958, p. 413.

286 *Avanti,* 18 October 1914.

287 *Il Grido del Popolo,* 31 October 1914 in Ferrata and Gallo, I, pp. 178-180.

288 The words are from Arfe, *Storia del socialismo,* p. 178 and sum up Mussolini's populist position succinctly.

289 In the *Popolo d'Italia,* 15 November 1914, Mussolini wrote: "Today I shout out loud, anti-war propaganda is cowards' propaganda ... anti-revolutionary propaganda ... I cry a fearful, fascinating word: war." For the allegation that Gramsci proposed to collaborate with the newspaper see G. Berti, *I primi dieci anni di vita del PCI. Documenti inediti dell'archivio Angelo Tasca* (Feltrinelli, Milan, 1967), p. 47.

290 Zucàro, p. 1108.

291 C. Negarville recalled: "When he was a student at Turin University, he used to earn his living giving lessons and exercises to others. He had among others, three pupils, rich boys, 'three superb examples of imbecility', whose homework he used to do from the first to the last word."; in "Gramsci, maestro e capo", in *Gramsci, Scritti di P. Togliatti ed altri* (L'Unita, Rome, 1945), p. 128; Berti, p. 47.

292 Zucàro, p. 1109.

293 For the influence of the Palermitan school and Gentile on Gramsci see Gioele Solari's introduction to Aldo Mautino, *La formazione della filosofia politica di Benedetto Croce* (Laterza, Bari, 1953), p. 75.

294 Ferrara and Ferrara, p.43; Spriano, *Torino operaia,* p. 100.

295 *Il Grido del Popolo,* 15 November 1915 in Caprioglio, pp. 2-3.

296 Tasca in *Il Mondo,* 18 August 1953 recalls that Gramsci used to be a brilliant teacher in the Youth Federation as early as 1914; the first outside lecture that we know he gave was entitled "Romain Rolland e la sua opera" and was delivered at the Borgo san Paolo workers' club on 26 August 1916. See Spriano, *Rinascita,* 28 March 1964. He also gave a lecture on "Karl Marx and Andrea Costa". See B. Santhià, *Con Gramsci all'Ordine Nuovo* (Riuniti, Rome, 1956), p. 43.

297 R. Montagnana, "La sua grandezza e la sua semplicità" in *Gramsci, Scritti di P. Togliatti ed altri*, p. 83.

298 Gramsci to Grazietta Gramsci (beginning of 1916?) in Ferrata and Gallo, II, p. 18.

299 *Ibid.*, p. 19.

300 *Ibid.*

301 P. Gobetti, "Storia dei comunisti torinesi scritto da un liberale", *Rivoluzione liberale*, IV, 2, 1922; *ibid.*, III, 17, 1924, p. 66.

302 G. Amoretti, "Con Gramsci sotto la Mole" in *Gramsci, Scritti di P. Togliatti ed altri*, pp. 47-48; and G. Spano in *ibid.* The cartoonist on *Ordine Nuovo*, "Cip", was a Sard. Later Gramsci's brother Gennaro started working on the newspaper.

303 *Avanti* (Piedmontese ed.), 1 January 1916 in Ferrata and Gallo, I, pp. 187-88.

304 *Avanti* (Piedmontese ed.) 22 January 1916 in *Sotto la Mole* (Einaudi, Turin, 1960), pp. 14-15. Henceforth *SM*.

305 See Amoretti, *passim* and Parodi, in *Gramsci, Scritti di P. Togliatti ed altri*.

306 See Gramsci, *Falce e Martello*, June 1921 and Spriano, "La scelta di Gramsci" in *Rinascita*, 27 July 1967.

307 Gobetti wrote: "He seemed to have come from the countryside to forget tradition, to get rid of the sick, anachronistic heritage of his island and replace it with a single-minded, inexorable drive towards modernity." P. Gobetti, *Opere complete* (Einaudi, Turin, 1960), IV, p. 1003.

308 Gramsci to Grazietta Gramsci (beginning of 1916?) in Ferrata and Gallo II, p. 18.

309 *Ibid.;* "Socialismo e cultura" in *Il Grido del Popolo*, 29 January 1916 in *SG*, pp. 22-26; *Avanti* (Piedmontese ed.) 29 August 1916 in *SM*, pp. 230-31.

310 Amoretti, *passim;* Parodi, *passim.* The mode of writing expressed his care for precision. See the article in *SG*, p. 63 and Togliatti, *Gramsci*, pp. 66-67.

311 Amoretti, *passim.*

312 *Ibid.*, p. 44.

313 Parodi, p. 67.

314 Tasca in *Il Mondo*, 18 August 1953.

315 Tasca in *Energie nuovo*, 12 March 1919, cited in Spriano, *Gramsci e l'Ordine Nuovo* (Riuniti, Rome, 1965), p. 32.

316 Tasca in *Il Mondo* 18 August 1953; Gobetti, *Opere complete*, IV, p. 1006; Romano, "Antonio Gramsci tra guerra e rivoluzione", p. 408.

317 Romano, "Antonio Gramsci tra guerra e rivoluzione", p. 408.

318 See his statement to Turin's young Socialists on 30 August 1914 in Spriano, *Torino operaia*, p. 29.

319 Tasca in *Il Mondo*, 18 August 1953; *SG*, p. 163.

320 Tasca in *Il Mondo*, 18 August 1953.

321 "Socialismo e cultura", in *Il Grido del Popolo*, 29 January 1916 in *SG*, pp. 22-26.

322 Amoretti, p. 45.

323 *Avanti* (Piedmontese ed.) 9 December 1916 in Caprioglio, *Scritti*, pp. 23-25.

324 "Storia dei comunisti ...".

325 See *Il Grido del Popolo*, 13 October 1917; *SG*. pp. 238-39.

326 G. Trombetti, "In cellula con la matricola 7047", *Rinascita*, September 1946, p. 233.

327 *MS*, p. 199.

Notes

328 *La Citta futura,* 11 February 1917. The article has been republished in Ferrata and Gallo, I, pp. 228-233.

329 *Ibid.,* pp. 233-39.

330 Gramsci to Giuseppe Lombardo Radice, March (?) 1918 in *Rinascita,* 7 March 1964; see also the interview with Pia Carena by Giovanni Bosio, now in Leonetti, pp. 105-108.

331 Spriano in *Rinascita,* 28 March 1964, p. 28.

332 *MS,* p. 199.

333 Amoretti, p. 45.

334 For Salvemini's support for Mussolini see Romano, "Antonio Gramsci etc ...", pp. 418-19.

335 For example, "Religione e serenita" which appeared in *Critica* in March 1915, pp. 153-55 and which was republished in abbrievated form in *La Citta futura.*

336 Pia Carena in Leonetti, pp. 107-108; Boccardo in Fiori, *Vita,* pp. 132-33.

337 *Ibid.* See also A. Leonetti, "Romain Rolland e Gramsci", *Rinascita,* 20 June 1969. Amoretti reports a meeting with Barbusse, Amoretti, p. 44.

338 Ferrara and Ferrara, p. 29.

339 For the contacts between Gramsci and Mondolfo before 1917 see Mondolfo to N. Bobbio, 6 May 1967, which is republished in part in Rodolfo Mondolfo, *Umanismo di Marx,* (Einaudi, Turin 1968), pxlv fn2.

340 Amoretti, p. 45.

341 See e.g. "La critica critica" in *Il Grido del Popolo,* 12 January 1918, in *SG,* pp. 153-55.

342 Leonetti, p. 70.

343 E. Garin "La formazione di Gramsci e Croce" in *Prassi rivoluzionaira e storicismo in Gramsci. Quaderni di critica marxista,* 3, p. 121 maintains that by 1919 Gramsci had read some of the pre-1848 writings of Marx.

344 Amoretti, p. 43; Santhià, *Con Gramsci,* p. 43.

345 Santhià, *Con Gramsci,* p. 41.

346 L. Paggi, "'La redazione culturale' del Grido del Popolo", in *Prassi rivoluzionaria,* pp. 158, 165ff.

347 *Il Grido del Popolo,* 29 April 1917 in Ferrata and Gallo, I, pp. 251-52.

348 *Ibid.,* pp. 251-54.

349 Cortesi, p. 635; S. Caprioglio, "Un articolo di Gramsci alla vigilia dell'Ottobre", *Rinascita,* 13 October 1917; Spriano, *Torino operaia,* p. 210.

350 *Il Grido del Popolo,* 29 September 1917 in Caprioglio, *Scritti,* pp. 35-36.

351 *Ibid.,* 29 July 1917 in *SG,* pp. 122-24.

352 *Ibid.*

353 Gobetti wrote in the "Storia dei comunisti ..." that Tasca's socialism was that of a "literary man, of a messiah who conceived of the redemption of the masses as a palingenesis of enlightenment", and who superimposed on modern civilisation a "narrow petty-bourgeois dream" of "workers' virtue" which was born of and nourished by "patriarchal habits" and who still had "something Turatian and patriarchal in his thought".

354 A. Lepre, "Bordiga e Gramsci di fronte alla guerra e alla rivoluzione d'ottobre", *Critica marxista,* V, 4-5, July-October 1967, p. 105.

355 Spriano, *Torino operaia,* pp. 272-73.

356 Spriano, *Socialismo e classe operaia a Torino dal 1892 al 1913* (Einaudi, Turin, 1958), ch 1; E. Avigdor, "Il movimento operaio torinese durante la prima guerra mondiale", in A. Caracciolo and G. Scalià eds., *La Città futura* (Feltrinelli, Milan, 1959), pp. 41-60; G. Procacci, "La classe operaia

italiana agli inizi del secolo XX", *Studi storici,* III, 1, January-March 1962, pp. 3-76.

357 Santhià, pp. 1-13; Montagnana, *Ricordi,* pp. 1-63; M. Guarnieri, *I consigli di fabbrica* (Il Solco, Citta de Castello, n.d.) for a discussion of the *commissioni.*

358 Spriano, *Torino operaia,* chs. 3-5; Avigdor, pp. 63, 72.

359 Santhià, pp. 37-40.

360 Cortesi, pp. 628-30; Arfé, *Storia del socialismo,* 214-220; See V.I. Lenin, *Sul movimento operaio italiano* (Rinascita, Rome, 1952), pp. 54-57 for the Russians estimate of the Italians at Zimmerwald and Kienthal.

361 A. Caraciolo, "Serrati, Bordiga, e la polemica gramsciana contro il 'blanquismo' e il settarismo di partito", in Caracciolo and Scalià, pp. 93-114.

362 Spriano, *Torino operaia,* chs. 9, 12.

363 *Avanguardia,* 20 October 1912. On the history of the Youth Federation see G. Arfé, *Il movimento giovanile socialista* (Avanti, Milan, 1966).

364 Lepre, p. 110; Cortesi, p. 590.

365 G. Germanetto, *Memoirs of a Barber* (Co-operative Publishing Society of Foreign Workers in the USSR, Moscow/Leningrad, 1934), p. 136; *MS,* p. 20, *PP,* p. 59.

366 Germanetto, p. 138.

367 "Il nostro Marx" in *Il Grido del Popolo,* 4 May 1918 in *SG,* pp. 217-221.

368 "La rivoluzione contro *Il Capitale*" in *Avanti* (Milanese ed.) 24 November 1917 in *SG,* pp. 149-153.

369 "Indifferenti", *La Città futura,* 11 February 1917.

370 "L'Utopia russa" in *Il Grido del Popolo,* 27 July 1918 in Ferrata and Gallo, I, p. 317.

371 *Ibid.*

372 "Wilson e i massimalisti russi" in *Il Grido del Popolo,* 2 March 1918 in Ferrata and Gallo, I, p. 278.

373 "La cultura nel movimento socialista" in *Il Grido del Popolo,* 1 June 1918, in Caprioglio, *Scritti,* p. 71.

374 "L'Opera di Lenin" in *Il Grido del Popolo,* 14 September 1918 in *SG,* p. 308.

375 *Trent'anni di vita e lotte del PCI. Quaderni di Rinascita,* II, p. 37; Ferrara and Ferrara, p. 43.

376 Ferrara and Ferrara, p. 43.

377 Spriano, *Torino operaia,* p. 329.

378 "La Russia dei Soviet", *Rivista di Milano,* 20 February 1921.

379 *Avanti,* 17 November 1917.

380 Cortesi, pp. 640, 690-95.

381 *Ibid.,* pp. 650-90.

382 P. Nenni, *Storia di quattro anni 1919-1922* (Einaudi, Rome, 1946) p. 8.

383 "Programma socialista di pace" in *Il Grido del Popolo,* 2 March 1918 in Caprioglio, *Scritti,* pp. 55-57; "Il caso Turati" in *ibid,* 3 August 1918; "Partito e Confederazione" in *ibid,* 10 August 1918 in Caprioglio, *Scritti,* pp. 77-80.

CHAPTER III

384 *Lettere,* p.466, *MS,* p.199.

385 *Ibid.*

286

Notes

386 A. Gramsci, *Sotto la Mole*, (Einaudi, Turin, 1960) pp. 145, 365. Henceforth *SM*.

387 Croce collected the essays in the book *Teoria della storia della storiografia* (Laterza, Bari, 1954) see pp. 19-52.

388 The argument behind this is in his essay of 1906, *Saggio sullo Hegel* (Laterza, Bari, 1948).

389 *Teoria della storia* ... , p. 56.

390 *Ibid.*, p. 64.

391 *Saggio sullo Hegel*, p. 31.

392 To avoid complications in later discussion the history men write or record will be capitalised as History.

393 *Teoria della storia*, p. 101.

394 Eugenio Garin, *Cronache di filosofia italiana* (1900-1943), (Laterza, Bari, 1959), p. 273.

395 *SM*, p. 365.

396 Benedetto Croce, "Intorno all'idealismo attuale", *La Voce*, V, 46, 1913, pp. 595-605.

397 *Il Grido del Popolo*, 19 January 1918, cited in Paggi, *Antonio Gramsci e il moderno principe* (Riuniti, Rome, 1970) p. 21: on this it is interesting to compare Togliatti, *Gramsci*, p. 63.

398 It first appeared in *La Critica*, XIII, 20 March 1915, pp. 153-55.

399 *La Città Futura*, February 1917.

400 *SM*, (8 March 1917) p. 296.

401 *SM*, (25 May 1917) p. 316, Paggi, p. 21.

402 Among the other works of Croce to which he makes implicit or explicit reference by 1918 are the *Aesthetics*, the *Logic* and the *Logic as the Science of the Pure Concept, Lettere*, pp. 413-14, 466-67; *SM*, pp. 447, 450.

403 Usually these were more 'practical' articles against democracy or socialism: q.v. B. Croce, "Il partito come guidizio e come pregiudizio", (1912) in Finocchiaro ed., *L'Unità di Salvemini*, pp. 28-30.

404 *SG*, pp. 271-73; Paggi, *Antonio Gramsci e il Moderno Principe*, p. 33.

405 *The French Revolution* (Cape, London, 1954).

406 *Problemi educativi e sociali d'oggi* (Batiato, Catania, 1914).

407 While the more important of the articles of the *Problemi* concerned the role of the intellectuals in the misgovernment of the South, the theme of those on education was important for Gramsci's intellectual development. Salvemini's argument was this: Freedom of education meant that all teachers must be allowed to teach what they sincerely believed to be true. This meant that free education was intolerable to Catholicism, as it had to teach what was theologically correct. Whenever the Church attempted to participate in a free education system, like that of Italy, its object was to subvert the system, and not to support it. Salvemini's anti-clericalism had made him known to the clergy of the Bitonto electorate as the "wrath of the Lord". See *L'Unità*, 28 November 1913.

408 *La Voce*, V, No. 6, 1913, pp. 1003-05; Tasca, in *Il Mondo*, 18 August 1953; Santhià, pp. 38-39.

409 Garin, "La Formazione di Gramsci e di Croce", *Critica Marxista, Quaderno* 3, p. 123.

410 *SG*, p. 33; *Avanti* (Turin edition) 6 May 1916 in Ferrata and Gallo, I, p. 204; Spriano, *Gramsci e l'Ordine nuovo*, p. 23.

411 *SM*; (19 April 1916) p. 118.

412 Ferrata and Gallo, I, p. 205.
413 Charles Péguy, *Oeuvres en prose 1909-14* (Pléiade, Paris, 1957) p. 514.
414 *Ibid.,* p. 519.
415 *Ibid.,* p. 526.
416 *Ibid.,* p. 539.
417 *Ibid.,* p. 559.
418 *Ibid.,* p. 580.
419 Compare *ibid.,* p. 341, with Ferrata and Gallo, I, pp. 203-05.
420 A. Leonetti, "Romain Rolland e Gramsci" in *Note su Gramsci,* pp. 209-221.
421 Ferrata and Gallo, I, p. 204, suggests that Gramsci had also read Rolland's *Life of Beethoven* which he had also published in the *Cahiers.* See Romain Rolland, *Jean-Christophe* (Editions Michel, Paris, 1956), p. xv.
422 Rolland dedicated the book "To the free souls of all the nations that suffer, struggle, and that will overcome."
423 Rolland, p. 221.
424 Leonetti, "Romain Rolland e Gramsci", p. 219.
425 Péguy, *op. cit.,* p. 558.
426 Leonetti, "Romain Rolland e Gramsci", p. 211.
427 Romain Rolland, *Au-dessus de la mêlée,* in *L'Esprit libre* (Michel, Paris 1953) pp. 64 and 80.
428 *Ibid.,* p. 88.
429 *Ibid.,* p. 124.
430 Eugenio Garin, *Cronache della filosofia italiana 1900-1943* (Laterza, Bari, 1959) p. 310.
431 Professor Norberto Bobbio, who was Pastore's student, and knew him well, has suggested to me that Pastore may have overstated the extent of his influence on Gramsci. Letter to author 8 December 1972. In 1916 Gramsci seems to have regarded Pastore as both "conscientious and wise". See *SM,* p. 89 or is it mockery once again?
432 For a discussion of Pastore's lectures, see p. 69 above. Gobetti described Pastore as "Having moved continuously away from his positivist origins to follow the dream of mathematical logic", P. Gobetti, *Opere complete di Piero Gobetti,* I, p. 911; Gentile's translation is in *La Filosofia di Marx* (Spoerri, Pisa, 1899), pp. 58-61, see also Togliatti, *Gramsci,* p. 65.
433 An excellent treatment of the mistranslation of Marx is given by Norberto Bobbio, in the Introduction to *Rodolfo Mondolfo, Umanismo di Marx Studii filosofici, 1908-1966* (Einaudi, Turin, 1968), p. xvii.
434 *Ibid.,* fn 1.
435 *SM* (3 April 1916) p. 101-02.
436 See B. Croce, *Come Nacque e come Mori il marxismo teorico in Italia* in A. Labriola, *La concezione materialistica della storia* (Laterza, Bari, 1953).
437 *Ibid.,* p. 31.
438 *Ibid.,* p. 151.
439 *Ibid.,* p. 73.
440 *Ibid.,* p. 155.
441 *Ibid.,* p. 18.
442 *Ibid.,* p. 76.
443 Labriola, *Discorrendo di socialismo e filosofia* (Laterza, Bari, 1947), p. 59.
444 Labriola, *La concezione materialistica* ... , p. 73.
445 Ferrata and Gallo, I, p. 502-3; *Ordine Nuovo,* 2 January 1921, in

Notes

Socialismo e Fascismo (Einaudi, Turin, 1967) pp. 13-14.
446 Henri Bergson, *L'évolution créatrice* (Alcan, Paris, 1911), *passim*.
447 R. Romeo, *Breve storia della grande industria in Italia* (Cappelli, Bologna, 1961), pp. 91-92.
448 G. Giolitti, "Discorso per le elezioni della XXV Legislatura" (12 October 1919) in *Discorsi extraparlamentari* (Einaudi, Turin, 1952), pp. 294ff.
449 Pietro Nenni, *Storia di Quattro Anni 1919-1922* (Einaudi, Turin, 1946).
450 P. Spriano, *Torino operaia,* chs. VIII-IX.
451 This information is based on a manuscript written by Tasca and republished in Berti, p. 47; see also Piero Gobetti, "Le commissioni interne", *La Rivoluzione liberale,* IV, No.22, 20 September 1925, p. 134.
452 "Il canto delle Sirene", *Avanti* (Milan), 10 October 1917 in Caprioglio pp. 41-44.
453 Romeo, pp. 85-87.
454 E. Soave, "L'occupazione delle fabbriche e i problemi del partito e della rivoluzione in Italia", p. 174.
455 Spriano, *Torino operaia,* p. 298.
456 Emilio Soave, "Appunti sulle origini teoriche e pratiche dei consigli di fabbrica a Torino", *Rivista storica del socialismo,* VII, no. 21, January-April 1964, p. 11.
457 Tasca in Berti, pp. 45-7; Gobetti, "Le Commissioni interne"; Mario Guarnieri, pp. 14-22; Spriano, *Gramsci e l'Ordine Nuovo,* pp. 48-51.
458 *Avanti,* 22 April 1916.
459 Berti, p. 46.
460 "Il Patto d'Alleanza", *Il Grido del Popolo,* 12 October 1918.
461 Spriano, *Torino operaia,* p. 297-8.
462 *Avanti,* 10 September 1918.
463 Soave, "Appunti", pp. 9-10.
464 Spriano, *Torino operaia,* p. 299.
465 Factory councils were a phenomenon common to most of Europe after 1916. Richard Müller, in "Comment nacquirent les conseils révolutionnaires d'Usine", *Spartacus,* 1 July 1921 explained the origins of the Berlin workers councils in 1916-18 as the "result of the economic repercussions of the war, of the suppression of all freedom of movement in the working class by means of a state of seige, and of the total lack of power of the trade unions and political parties".
466 *Avanti,* 13 March 1919.
467 Berti, p. 47; Gobetti "Storia dei comunisti, ..."
468 Ferrata and Gallo, I, pp. 313-19.
469 *Ibid.,* pp. 329-332.
470 Santhià, p. 41.
471 Ferrara and Ferrara, p. 44.
472 Togliatti in *Studii gramsciani,* p. 18; Gramsci, "Il programma del Ordine Nuovo", *Ordine Nuovo 1919-20* (Einaudi, Turin, 1955), p. 152. Henceforth *ON.*
473 Soave, "Appunti", pp. 3-4.
474 *Avanguardia,* 9 March 1919.
475 "Il Programma del Ordine Nuovo", in *ON,* p. 146.
476 Sergio Caprioglio, *Rinascita,* XXII, No. 11, 13 March 1965; Gramsci, "Il Programma del Ordine Nuovo", pp. 146-47.
477 *Ibid.,* p. 148.

478 *Ibid.,* Leonetti, p. 109; Amoretti, *op. cit.,* pp. 44, 53; Parodi, "Gramsci con gli operai in *ibid.,* pp. 65-68.
479 "Democrazia operaia" in *ON,* pp. 10-13.
480 Resoconto in *Avanti,* 25 June 1919, republished in A. Caracciolo, "Il movimento torinese dei consigli di fabbrica", *Mondo operaio,* 2 February 1958, pp. 16-27.
481 Ferrara and Ferrara, p. 54; Santhià, p. 70.
482 Parodi, *op. cit.*
483 Gramsci to Togliatti, 27 March 1924 in P. Togliatti ed., *La formazione del gruppo dirigente del PCI* (Riuniti, Rome, 1962), p. 257.
484 Umberto Terracini, "I Consigli di fabbrica: vicende e problemi dall' Inghilterra alla Russia, dalla Germania a Torino" *L'Almanacco socialista 1920.*
485 Parodi, p. 67.
486 Nenni, p. 47ff.
487 "Lo sciopero dei Metallurgici", 6 September 1919, in *ON,* p. 271.
488 Soave, p. 15.
489 Montagnana, *Ricordi,* pp. 148-9; Santhià, p. 63.
490 Spriano, *Gramsci e l'Ordine Nuovo,* pp. 54-5.
491 "La sovranità della legge", 1 June 1919; "La conquista dello Stato" 12 July 1919, in *ON,* pp. 3-5, 13-19.
492 *ON,* pp. 455-57.
493 Gramsci had a clear intuition that this would happen. See *ON,* pp. 31-34.
494 This declaration was promulgated on 31 October 1919. See *ON,* pp. 192-93.
495 *ON,* p. 129.
496 Santhià, p. 70.
497 *ON,* p. 184, p. 463.
498 P. Spriano, ed., *L'Ordine Nuovo* (Einaudi, Turin, 1963), p. 37 n.1., Tasca in Berti, p. 67.
499 O. Pastore, "Il problema delle commissioni interne", *ON,* I, 14, 15 August 1919. See Spriano, *Gramsci e l'Ordine Nuovo,* pp. 54-8.
500 Guarnieri, pp. 28ff.
501 *ON,* p. 386.
502 See e.g. the decisions of the Camera del Lavoro in Guarnieri, p. 28, pp. 49-50; Caracciolo in *Mondo operaio, op. cit.*
503 See "Sindacati e consigli", 11 October 1919; "Sindacati e dittatura", 25 October 1919; "Sindacalismo e consigli", 8 November 1919; in *ON,* pp. 34-48.
504 *ON,* p. 185; "Discorse agli anarchici", 3-10 April 1920, *ON,* pp. 396-401.
505 Montagnana, pp. 148-49.
506 See *ON,* p. 109 for Gramsci's description of the Milan meeting of Confindustria; Guarnieri, pp. 60-8; Spriano, *Gramsci e l'Ordine Nuovo,* p. 103.
507 See e.g. the Camera del Lavoro's motion in Guarnieri, p. 74.
508 "Superstizione e realtà", *ON,* pp. 108-114.
509 Spriano, *Gramsci e l'Ordine Nuovo,* pp. 104-5.
510 Turati wrote in a reply to an article by Antonio Labriola in support of Leninism, "that 'Viva Lenin' meant 'death to socialism'", *Critica sociale, op. cit.,* p. 435.
511 *Avanti,* 5 January 1919.
512 Nenni, p. 31.

513 Cortesi, p. 709.
514 *Critica sociale,* 1-15 September 1919.
515 *Avanti* (Rome edition), 10 October 1919.
516 *Il Comunismo,* 1 October 1920, p.2ff.
517 See *Agli elettori di Milano* (Critica sociale, Milan, 1919) *passim;* *Trent'anni di Critica sociale* in Valeri, pp. 523-530.
518 *Il Comunismo,* 1 November 1919, p. 184.
519 *Ibid.,* 1 December 1919, p. 428.
520 Spriano, *Gramsci e l'Ordine Nuovo,* p. 91.
521 *Il Comunismo,* 15-20 December 1919.
522 "Il rivoluzionario qualificato", 20 December 1919 in *ON,* pp. 387-89.
523 "Primo: Rinnovare il Partito", 24-31 January 1920 in *ON,* pp. 389-392.
524 *Il Soviet,* 2 February 1919.
525 *Ibid.,* 18 May 1919.
526 Cortesi, p. 708.
527 Cortesi, p. 735.
528 *Ibid.,* pp. 735-742.
529 Fiori, *Vita,* p. 153.
530 Guarnieri, pp. 52ff.
531 *ON,* p. 186; Tasca in *Il Mondo,* 1 September 1953.
532 "Per un rinnovamento del Partito socialista italiano" *ON,* 8 May 1920, in *ON,* pp. 116-123; see also *Cronache de Ordine Nuovo,* 21 August 1920.
533 Nenni, *op. cit.,* p. 87 citing *Avanti,* 27 April 1920.
534 See F. Ferri, "La situazione interna della sezione socialista torinese nell 'estate del 1920", *Rinascita,* April 1958, p. 259; Tasca in *Il Mondo,* 25 August 1953.
535 "Contro il pessimismo", *Ordine Nuovo,* 15 March 1924 in Spriano, *Scritti politici,* p. 545; see also Spriano, *Storia del Partito comunista italiano,* I, pp. 58-59.
536 *Ibid.,* Ferri, p. 259; *Storia della sinistra comunista* (ed. il programma comunista, Milan, 1972), pp. 362-63.
537 "I gruppi comunisti", *Ordine Nuovo* 2 July 1920 in *ON,* p. 141.
538 *Ibid.*
539 "Due rivoluzioni", Ordine Nuovo 3 July 1920, in *ON,* p. 140.
540 "Consigli di fabbrica", *Ordine Nuovo* 5 June 1920 in *ON,* p. 124.
541 *Ibid.,* p. 127.
542 "Il Programma dell *'Ordine Nuovo",* *ON,* pp. 146ff; "La relazione Tasca e il congresso camerale di Torino", *Ordine Nuovo,* 5 June 1920 in *ON* pp. 127ff.
543 "La relazione Tasca ...", p. 130.
544 Tasca in *Il Mondo,* 25 August 1953.
545 *Avanti,* 16 August 1920.
546 *Ibid.,* 12 August 1920, reprinted in Ferri, *op. cit.*
547 "Superstizioni e realtà", *Ordine Nuovo* 8 May 1920 in *ON* pp. 108-144; see also "La relazione Tasca ..." and "Il Programma dell *"Ordine Nuovo* ..." discussed in Ch. III, Pt. III of this book.
548 See A. Caracciolo, "Serrati, Bordiga e la polemica contro il blanquismo" in *La Città Futura* (Feltrinelli, Milan, 1959), p. 102.
549 Spriano, *Gramsci e l'Ordine Nuovo,* p. 118; see also "La Settimana politica, Dove va il PSI?", *Ordine Nuovo* 10 July 1920, in *ON* pp. 401ff; *Avanti,* 11 August 1920, cited in Spriano, *Gramsci e l'Ordine Nuovo,*

p. 120. Gramsci knew few Leninist writings at this time, and what he did know definitely did not include *What is to be Done*? or the directions about the party made public at the second Comintern congress. (See below, Ch. IV). The general argument so far corresponds with the account given in Berti, esp. pp. 59-65.

550 "Il programma del Ordine Nuovo", *Ordine Nuovo,* p. 146ff; "La relazione Tasca ...", pp. 127ff.

551 Spriano, *Storia del Partito comunista italiano,* I, p. 62; Readers acquainted with the contemporary debate in Italy will recognize the similarities of this conclusion with that reached by "left" critics of Gramsci. See e.g., A. de Clementi, "La politica del partito comunista d'Italia nel 1921-22 e il rapporto Bordiga-Gramsci", *Rivista storica del socialismo,* No. 28, 1966. For the "left" such a departure from "Leninism" is a form of lèse-majesté.

552 P. Togliatti ed., *La formazione del gruppo dirigente del Partito comunista italiano* (Riuniti, Rome, 1962), p. 183. Cronache dell *'Ordine Nuovo'*, "Rassegna di politica e Cultura operaia", No. 1, March 1924 cited in Spriano, *Gramsci e l'Ordine Nuovo,* p. 119.

553 The official delegation was Serrati, Vacirca, Graziadei, Rondani, Bombacci, D'Aragona, Bianchi, Colombino, Dugoni, Pozzani, Nofri, and, for the Young Socialists, Polano.

554 V. Lenin, *Sul Movimento operaio italiano* (Rinascita, Rome, 1952) p. 132. See also J. Humbert-Droz, *Il contrasto tra l'Internazionale e il P.C.I. 1922-1928. Documenti inediti dall'archivio di Jules Humbert-Droz, segretario dell'Internazionale Comunista* (Feltrinelli, Milan, 1969), p. 13 which reads "I russi furono certamente malinformati sulla reale situazione in Italia"; Berti, p. 91. In October 1920 Lenin referred to Serrati as an "excellent communist". See *Sul Movimento,* p. 156. See also Spriano, *Storia del Partito comunista,* I, p. 66 for Zinoviev. For the posters see A. Balabanoff, *Impressions of Lenin* (Ann Arbor, Michigan University Press, 1968), p. 86.

555 Lenin, *Sul Movimento,* p. 140. See *Communist International,* II, No. 13, August 1920, cols. 2487-2492 for the Comintern's republication of the critique delivered at Milan by Togliatti.

556 Spriano, *Storia del Partito comunista italiano,* I, p. 73 citing *Il Soviet,* III, No 24, 3 October 1920. Also reprinted in *Storia della sinistra comunista,* pp. 683-84.

557 *Ibid.*

558 "Contro il pessimismo" in Spriano, *Gramsci, Scritti politici,* p. 546.

559 Soave, *op. cit.*

560 See Gramsci to Zino Zini, 10 January 1924 in *Rinascita,* 25 April 1964 where he stated that he was very pessimistic about the chances of revolution in September 1920. See also "Chiaro-scuro", *Avanti,* 8 September 1920; "Cinque mesi dopo", *Avanti,* 14 September 1920; "Proletari avanti", *Avanti,* 14 October 1920 in Caprioglio, pp. 132-142. The telling quotation comes from "L'Occupazione", *Avanti,* 2 September 1920 in Caprioglio, pp. 130-2. Gramsci was quite correct in believing that the owners were choosing the time and place, as these lines from the appendices to Spriano's, *L'Occupazione delle fabbriche Settembre 1920,* show "... it seems that the industrialists consider it necessary to declare lockout ..." (under-secretary for Internal Affairs to Prefect of Milan) and "he found the

industrialists stubborn, but the workers' leaders not averse to discussing the matter to find solution" (the Undersecretary for Internal Affairs to the Prime Minister).

561 "L'Occupazione", *Avanti,* 2 September 1920.

562 "L'Occupazione", *op. cit.*

563 *Ibid.*

564 Occasionally in a very direct way: "Three gentlemen walked around the factory at about nine at night; the Red Guard approached them: 'What are you doing here?' 'We came to see how you were working': 'Oh, you want to see how we are working. Come inside'. The three resisted a bit, were carried inside, were searched, and were found to have revolvers and membership cards in the *Fasci di combattimento.* 'Well, since you want to see how we work, the best thing for you to do is to go to work with the workers.' Three overalls were put on and they were sent to the furnaces. Here they shrieked that the irons were burning them; the workers replied: 'They burn us all our lives; they burn you for one night only, when you will work.' Over the furnace was written: 'Work enobles'". Giovanni Parodi, "La Fiat Centro in mano agli operai", *Stato operaio*, No. 10, 1930, p. 638.

565 Spriano, *L'Occupazione,* pp. 192-94.

566 Santhià, pp. 92-115.

567 Spriano, *L'Occupazione,* p. 210 and *appendices, passim.*

568 *Avanti,* 2 September 1920 in Caprioglio, *Scritti 1915-1921,* pp. 130-32.

569 Spriano, *L'Occupazione, appendices,* p. 191.

570 "Domenica rossa", *Avanti,* 5 September 1920 in *ON,* pp. 163-67.

571 Spriano, *L'Occupazione, appendices,* p. 183.

572 Spriano, *L'Occupazione, appendices,* p. 188.

573 "Il partito comunista", *Ordine Nuovo,* 4-9 September 1920 in *ON,* p. 161.

574 *Avanti,* 6 September 1920.

575 See Tasca, *Nascita e avvento del fascismo,* (Nuovo Italia, Florence, 1950) p. 121; Spriano, *L'Occupazione,* p. 88 for confirmations of Gramsci's assessment.

576 Gramsci to Giulia Gramsci, 6 March 1924, in Ferrata and Gallo, II, p. 34.

577 Cited in Spriano, *L'Occupazione,* p. 103; see A. Gramsci, *Socialismo e fascismo, l'Ordine Nuovo 1921-1922* (Einaudi, Turin, 1967), p. 328. Henceforth *SF.*

578 *Livorno 1921. Resoconto stenografico del XVII Congresso nazionale del Partito Socialista Italiano* (Leghorn 15-20 January 1921) (Avanti, Milan, 1962), pp. 373-75.

579 Spriano, *L'Occupazione,* p. 110; Lenin, *Sul Movimento,* p. 158.

580 Spriano, *Ibid.,* p. 109.

581 Spriano, *L.Occupazione,* p. 118.

582 One conversation between owners in Rome and Milan expresses their sentiments well: "Well sir, I will tell you the conclusions in a few words. Well, Conti's advice and mine is this; there is the alternative of going along with the provisions of the government, or resisting to the bitter end. Both hypotheses have very grave consequences which we are not hiding from ourselves, but given our situation that the government would end by intervening against the weaker party, that is, the industrialists, you know what we think that is, that we should come to a settlement. In these conditions we say it is better to end it because we are

afraid that the situation of the industralists might be worse tomorrow than it is today." See Spriano, *L'Occupazione, appendices,* p. 210.

583 *Avanti,* 10 October 1920.

584 *Ibid.*

585 *Livorno,* p. 252; Tasca, *Nascita,* p. 122.

586 *Conversando con Togliatti,* p. 83; Santhià, p. 116.

587 *SF,* p. 53.

588 G. Berti, "Il gruppo del *Soviet* nella formazione del P.C.I.", *Stato operaio,* IX, 1, January 1935, pp. 66-67; Spriano, *Il Partito comunista,* I, p. 86.

589 A. de Clementi, p. 151 and *passim.*

590 "Il Partito comunista", *Ordine Nuovo* 4 September 1920 in *ON,* p. 157.

591 *Avanti* (Piedmontese ed.), 27 November 1920 cited by Spriano, *Storia del Partito comunista,* I, p. 88.

592 *Ibid.,* p. 84.

593 *Ibid.,* pp. 101-02.

594 Berti, "Il gruppo del *Soviet....*", p. 68.

595 Reproduced in *Livorno,* pp. 442-43.

596 *Ibid.,* p. 444.

597 "Scissione o sfacelo", *Ordine Nuovo* 11, 18 December 1920 in *ON* p. 435.

598 See *Communist International,* II, No. 13, August 1920. eds. 2487-2492 for the endorsement of the Comintern, which Gramsci knew already. See *Ordine Nuovo* (9 October 1920). p. 489.

599 See interview with Pia Carena in Leonetti, *Note su Gramsci,* p. 110.

600 *Livorno,* pp. 70-99 esp. p. 89 and p. 396.

601 *Ibid.,* pp. 271-296.

602 *Ibid.,* p. 470.

603 This position has been argued by Carraciolo, Berti and Soave and contested by Paggi as well as communist writers of earlier and less valuable vintage. It seems that the limitations of both groups are that they have grasped Gramsci one-sidedly, without taking into account how the first position led to the second. Gramsci may have started by being as anti-party as Lukács (see G. Lukács, *Political Writings 1919-1929* (New Left Books, London, 1972), pp. 27-36, 53-80) and he certainly published some of Lukács' writings of the anti-party period in *Ordine Nuovo,* but, because he was much more involved in working-class practice than Lukács, his progress was away from the anti-Jacobin position he held at first. This may also explain why, when in 1923-4 Lukács and Karl Korsch were both condemned for their erroneous "anti-party" views, Gramsci, though in opposition to the Comintern, was not numbered with them. Indeed, there is no record that he had contact with them or the Black Forest circle at any time. R. Paris speculates on rather tenuous evidence that Gramsci may have made contact with this group's ideas in Vienna in 1923 or '24. See *Gramsci e la cultura contemporanea,* II, p. 30.

604 In 1924 Gramsci was to state many times that he had been close to the "abstentionists" in the second half of 1920. These affirmations should not be understood, as some writers argue, as indicating a community of opinion which was unreserved. After all, while admitting this undeniable community of opinion vis-à-vis the PSI and "reformist" socialism, he was also condemning at the same time the split at Leghorn, which the "abstentionists" fomented. See P. Togliatti, ed., *La formazione,* pp. 65, 102, 151.

605 It is well known now that Lenin indicated that the precepts in *What is to be*

Notes

Done? were relevant at only a specific time and place and not to be understood as containing his theory of the party. He moved away from such limited views thereafter to the position where he too argued that "The history of the Russian revolution has shown precisely that no argument can convince the great masses of the working-class, the peasants and the employees, if they are not convinced by their own experience". (See Lenin, *Sul Movimento*, p. 146). I have developed the implications of this argument somewhat in "Gramsci and Lenin 1917-1921", *Socialist Register*, 1974, but the most tenchant exposition of the argument is in Antonio Carlo, *Lenin sul Partito* (Bari, 1970) which is translated by Thomas Hull in *Telos*, No. 17, Fall 1973, pp. 2-40. For Bordiga see *Storia della Sinistra comunista*, II, *passim*.

606 P. Togliatti, ed., *La Formazione*, p. 183.

CHAPTER IV

607 *Ordine Nuovo*, 3 July 1920 in *Ordine Nuovo*, p. 139; *Ordine Nuovo*, 4 September 1920 in *ibid.*, p. 466, *Avanti*, 24 September 1920 in *ibid;* p. 171; *Ordine Nuovo*, 28 January 1921 in *Socialismo e Fascismo*, p. 52.

608 For this type of objective analysis of forces see Caprioglio, pp. 140-2, where the need for such an objective analysis is made clear by the "opacity" of the structures.

609 *Ordine Nuovo*, 21 February 1920 in *ON* p. 470.

610 See above p. 129 and Caprioglio, p. 134.

611 See the famous article "Uomini di carne ed ossa", *Ordine Nuovo* 8 May 1921 in *SF*, p. 154-6; see also *ibid.*, p. 30.

612 Cited by Spriano, *Storia del partito*, I, p. 81.

613 See *ON, passim,* and e.g. "L'Occupazione", *op. cit.*, and *ON*, pp. 365-6, See "La forza dello Stato" *Avanti* (Piedmont), 11 December 1920 in Caprioglio, pp. 150-52 "Fiume", *Ordine Nuovo*, 11 January 1921 in *SF*, pp. 35-36; "Responsabilità di governo", *Ordine Nuovo*, 5 February 1921 in *SF*, p. 60; "Reazione" *Ordine Nuovo*, 23 April 1921 in *SF*, p. 146.

614 See above Ch. III esp., pp. 145-46.

615 *Ordine Nuovo*, pp. 119, 403; "Il Congresso di Livorno", *Ordine Nuovo*, 13 January 1921 in *SF*, pp. 40-1.

616 "Previsioni", *Avanti*, 19 October 1920 in Caprioglio, *Scritti*, pp. 140-1.

617 "Il Popolo delle scimmie", *Ordine Nuovo*, 2 January 1921, in *SF*, pp. 9-12.

618 "Il Parlamento italiano", *Ordine Nuovo*, 24 March 1921, in *SF*, p. 117. "Gli Avvenimenti del 2-3 dicembre [1919]" *Ordine Nuovo*, 6-13 December 1919, in *Ordine Nuovo*, p. 61.

619 Paggi, pp. 270-1 states that the notion has roots in Labriola. See letter to Zino Zini, *Rinascita*, XXI, No. 17, 25 April 1964, for the quotation about working-class attitudes.

620 *Ordine Nuovo*, 4 December 1920 in *ON*, pp. 491-2.

621 Togliatti, "Il leninismo nel pensiero e nell'azione di A. Gramsci" in *Studii gramsciani Atti del convegno tenuto a Roma nel giorni 11-13 gennaio 1958* (Riuniti, Rome, 1969), pp. 16-19.

622 For the entire thesis and its problems see Davidson, "The Varying Seasons" *op. cit.*

623 Togliatti, "Il leninismo ...", pp. 10-20.

624 "Trent'anni di vita e lotte del PCI", *Quaderni di Rinascita*, II, p. 37.

625 "Per un rinnovamento", *Ordine Nuovo*, p. 117-121.

626 Leonetti, *Note sul Gramsci*, p. 24.

627 Leonetti, *Note sul Gramsci*, p. 109. "The source was always in French". The first collection of Lenin's writings he reputedly ever saw, was provided by Alfredo Polledro in the middle of 1919. See Caprioglio, in *Rinascita*, 13 October 1967. Significantly Polledro was an "ex-syndicalist".

628 Leonetti, letter to *Rinascita*, 22 February 1964.

629 Leonetti also mentioned this journal as a source for Leninism but J. Hulse, *The Forming of the Communist International* (Stanford, California, 1964), p. 29 has done a breakdown which shows that only seven pieces by Lenin appeared in 1919, and this author finds none of Lenin's important theoretical works in the journal in 1920.

630 A. Kriegel, *Aux origines du communisme francais* (Flammarion, Paris, 1969), p. 107.

631 *Ibid.*, pp. 196, 195.

632 Hulse, p. 29, Kriegel, pp. 196-203.

633 Vladimir Brett, *Henri Barbusse, Sa marche vers la clarté, son mouvement Clarté* (Editions de l'Academie Tchecoslovaque des sciences, Prague, 1963), pp. 208, 218; *Ordine Nuovo*, pp. 493-4.

634 See Kriegel, pp. 199-206.

635 Monatte wrote, "Tandis que Merrheim était porté particulièrement vers Martov, Rosmer et moi l'étions vers Trotsky" see E. Dolleáns, *Histoire du mouvement ouvrier 1871-1920* (Colin, Paris, 1957), II, p. 234.

636 This has been the technique used to maintain the thesis that Gramsci was a 'Leninist' from 1919 in the face of mounting evidence to the contrary.

637 The sole indirect reference to *What is to Be done?* which can be found in *Ordine Nuovo* is from Charles Rapaport who briefly described Lenin's theory of the party in *Ordine Nuovo*, 10 January 1920. Gramsci dismissed it briefly as an "old thesis of Lenin's" and indicated that he had not grasped its implications correctly. See Paggi, p. 303, with whom we are in agreement. For Gramsci's statement that the day to day news of doings in the USSR was coming through by 1920 see *Ordine Nuovo*, 30 June 1921 in *SF*, pp. 218-222.

638 Reproduced in R. Daniels, *A Documentary History of Communism*, I, p. 90.

639 See *Ordine Nuovo* 23, 25 October 1919; 3-10 April 1920; see also *Ordine Nuovo* pp. 152, 406-7, 411, Caproglio, *Scritti*, p. 161; Paggi, pp. 234-6, p. 242.

640 *Ordine Nuovo*, 5 June 1920 in *Ordine Nuovo*, p. 130, 9 October 1920, in *Ordine Nuovo*, p. 489.

641 Spriano, *Gramsci e l'Ordine Nuovo*, pp.60, 75 fn 1.

642 D. Guerin, *Anarchism* (Monthly Review, London, 1970), pp. 77, 86 but see fn.38 at pp. 69-70.

643 V. I. Lenin, *The State and Revolution* (F.L.P.H. Moscow, 1949), pp. 54, 75, 123, 134, 140. A similar work of Lenin's, *The Tasks of the Proletariat in Revolution*, was translated into Italian in September 1917. See Spriano, *Gramsci e l'Ordine Nuovo*, p. 65 fn.1.

644 Paggi, pp. 234-6.

645 *La Vie Ouvrière*, 30 April 1919 cited by Dolléans, II, p. 289; see also D. Caute, *Communism and the French Intellectuals*, (Deutsch, London, 1964), ch. I.

646 *Ordine Nuovo*, p. 130, 153.

647 *Korrispondenz internationale*, No.13, 1920, col. 260 cited in Degras, I, p. 190.

Notes

648 See *Ordine Nuovo*, p. 130.
649 See L. Langevin and G. Cogniot, "Les Premiers intellectuals communistes francais", *La Pensée*, No. 136, December 1967, pp. 10-12.
650 See Brett, p. 170.
651 "To find a point of union between working class and intellectuals: that is the first aim of Clarté ... Clarté also belongs to us", *Ordine Nuovo*, 11-18 December 1920, in *ON*, p. 494.
652 Degras, I, pp. 189-190 and *Communist International*, I, No. 1, May 1919, and No.5, 1919 for the Comintern attitudes at Bologna.
653 "Negazione di Dio", *Ordine Nuovo*, 6 January 1921 in *SF*, p. 23 and "Forza e prestigio", *Ordine Nuovo*, 14 January 1921 in *ibid.*, p. 44.
654 "Controllo operaio", *Ordine Nuovo*, 10 February 1921 in *SF*, pp. 68-69.
655 "L'Avvento della democrazia industriale", *Ordine Nuovo*, 6 April 1920 in *SF, p. 128.*
656 Santhià, p. 138.
657 "Terrore e Orrore", *Ordine Nuovo* (25 March 1921) in *SF*, p. 118.
658 P. Gobetti, "Le commissione interne" *La rivoluzione liberale*, IV, No. 22, September 1925, p. 134 wrote "However, they were never reduced in these years to simple corporative organs; they were centres for contact and agitation; they were not even broken by the fascist reaction and continued to exercise a noteworthy prestige among the workers."
659 "Terrore ed orrore" in *SF*, p. 118.
660 "Il Partito comunista e i sindicati. Risoluzioni proposte dal Comitato centrale per il Il congresso del Partito comunista italiano", in *SF*, p. 508.
661 In "La guerra e la guerra", *Ordine Nuovo*, (21 January 1921) in *SF*, p. 55, where he optimistically suggested that Turin would not succumb to fascism like other cities because of the workers' 'moral superiority' and control over the city. For the bodyguard, see Fiori, p. 173.
662 *L'Ordine Nuovo*, 26 March 1921; "Gramsci al primo congresso comunista ligure", *Movimento operaio e contadino in Liguria*, III, No. 2-3, May-December 1957, pp. 35-7.
663 "La politica estera del Barnum", *Ordine Nuovo* 30 June 1921 in *SF*, pp. 217-222, 210-212.
664 For a private statement made in April 1921 that "he seemed to me not so much optimistic as critical with regard to his party" see "Un mancato incontro Gramsci D'Annunzio a Gardone nell' aprile 1920", *Rivista storica del socialismo*, V, No. 15-16, January-August 1962, p. 271.
665 "Smarvimento", *Ordine Nuovo*, 12 June 1921 in *SF*, p. 189.
666 "Linee di sviluppo", *Ordine Nuovo*, 27 May 1921 in *SF*, p. 171.
667 See *Internazionale comunista*, II, no.15 January 1921, p. 314 cited by Spriano *Storia*, I, p. 98; *Livorno*, p. 454. Only 10% was from the Mezzogiorno.
668 Eg., the sacking and burning of the Camera del Lavoro at Turin by fascists on 26 April. See "L'attacco a Torino", *Ordine Nuovo* 28 April 1921 in *SF*, pp. 152-3.
669 See Spriano, *Storia*, I, pp. 165-170; "Linee di sviluppo" in *SF*, p. 171. At the union congress after Leghorn the PSI received 1,435,873 votes and the PCI only 434,564. In the May elections the votes were 1,569,553 and 291,852 respectively.
670 Fiori, *Vita*, p. 176.
671 In "I comunisti e le elezioni", *Ordine Nuovo*, 12 April 1921 in *SF*, p. 134 Gramsci stated that electoral participation was only to discover who supported

297

the communists. In Turin, where only 30 thousand voted communist and he was not elected the message was disastrously direct.

672 See Gramsci in "Il primo congresso della comunista ligure".
673 See e.g. "Sovversismo reazionario", *Ordine Nuovo,* 22 June 1921 in *SF,* pp. 204-6 and "La politica estera del Barnum", *op. cit.,* p. 217ff.
674 Paul Levi, *Unser Weg wider den Putschismus* (Berlin, 1921).
675 The PCI delegates were Terracini, Egidio Gennari, Francesco Misiano and Montagnana.
676 Terracini, "Three Meetings with Lenin" in S. F. Bezveselny and D. Y. Grunberg, *They Knew Lenin* (Foreign Languages Publishing House, Moscow, 1968), p. 213.
677 Gobetti, "Storia dei comunisti ..." in Valeri, p. 595.
678 Terracini "Three Meetings", p. 211.
679 Droz, *Il Contrasto,* p. 28.
680 *Protokoll des Dritten Kongressen der Kommunistischen Internazionale, Moskau 21 Juin 1921, Hamburg 1921,* pp. 498-508.
681 *Sul Movimento Operaio,* pp. 171-184.
682 Terracini, "Three Meetings", pp. 258-9.
683 Spriano, *Storia,* I, p. 156.
684 Trotsky, *The New Stage,* (1922).
685 Spriano, *Storia,* I, p. 158.
686 "La'hai visto il Fez", *Ordine Nuovo,* 4 September 1921, in *SF,* p. 318.
687 "Aprile e settembre 1920", *Ordine Nuovo,* 7 September 1921, pp. 327-8. "I piu grandi responsabili", *Ordine Nuovo,* 20 September 1921 in *SF,* pp. 342-2, See also, p. 348-9.
688 "La Tattica del fallimento", *Ordine Nuovo,* 22 September 1921, in *SF,* pp. 348-9.
689 *Ibid.*
690 See e.g. "Non spaventarti, Ludovico" *Ordine Nuovo,* 14 September 1921, in *SF,* pp. 336-8.
691 "Un partito di masse" *Ordine Nuovo,* 5 October 1921, in *SF,* p. 363-6 at p. 365.
692 *Ibid.*
693 Arfé, *Storia del socialismo,* pp. 307-9.
694 Spriano, *Storia,* I, p. 159.
695 "Il Congresso socialista", *Ordine Nuovo,* 9 October 1921 in *SF,* p. 329.
696 Spriano, *Storia,* I, p. 160.
697 *La Formazione,* p. 228.
698 See *Inprekorr,* 7 January 1922.
699 Droz, *Mémoires,* pp. 44-5.
700 *Ibid.*
701 Droz himself speculates that he was chosen because he did not believe revolution was possible in the West before the mass of the workers was won, See *Il Contrasto,* p. 23.
702 Droz claims in *Il Contrasto,* p. 29 that the bulk of the party did not know about the differences at the Third Comintern Congress until the II PCI congress. The Rome theses were published starting on 3 January 1922. See Spriano, *Storia,* I, p. 178.
703 See *Il Comunista,* 19 February 1922 in *SF,* pp. 497-8.
704 The theses are reproduced in full in Droz, *Archives,* I, pp. 513-553.

Notes

705 See *SF*, pp. 499-519.
706 Droz, *Memoires*, pp. 55-56.
707 Droz, *Il Contrasto*, p. 29.
708 Droz, *Archives*, I, pp. 155-6.
709 *Ordine Nuovo*, 28 March 1922 in *SF*, pp. 520-1.
710 *Ordine Nuovo*, 6 April 1922 in *SF*, pp. 521-3.
711 Droz, *Mémoires*, p. 60; *Archives*, I, p. 157, Spriano, *Storia*, I, p. 190.
712 "Un mancato incontro a Gardone ..." p. 69, S. F. Romano, *Gramsci*, pp. 470-5.
713 Gramsci to Giulia Gramsci, 6 March 1924, in Ferrata and Gallo, II, p. 33.
714 Leonildo Tarozzi, "Ricordo di Gramsci", *Vie Nuove*, 4 May 1947; see also Romano, *Gramsci*, p. 449.
715 Fiori, *Vita*, p. 177.
716 "La ragione dei fatti", *Ordine Nuovo*, 4 March 1921, in *SF*, p. 91-2.
717 It was suggested unconvincingly that it was because his name was difficult to spell. Spriano, *Storia*, I, pp. 129-30.
718 See Romano, p. 439; See Santhià, p. 162.
719 *Lettere dal Carcere*, p. 412.
720 Fiori, *Vita*, p. 181.
721 Ferrata and Gallo, II, p. 46.
722 See the photograph in Romano, *Gramsci*, p. 481. This part of Gramsci's life which is so significant in his development is best treated in Romano's work, which was cavalierly dismissed as a "rosy romance" but which as Cammett rightly notes, shows brillant and sensitive insight into Gramsci's personality, linking the sensuous and the theoretical in a fashion which does justice to the man.
723 Did he recall his brother, Mario's heartless remark of childhood that he should become a priest as he could have no thought of women?
724 Ferrata and Gallo, II, pp. 46-7.
725 *La formazione*, p. 228.
726 In Ferrata and Gallo, II, pp. 20.
727 *Ibid.*
728 *Ibid.*
729 Gramsci to Giulia, 13 February 1923 in Ferrata and Gallo, p. 23.
730 See Romano, *Gramsci*, p. 471.
731 See "Les Origines du Cabinet Mussolini", *La Correspondance internationale*, 20 November 1922 and "Le parlementarisme et le fascisme en Italie", 20 November 1922 and "Le parlementarisme et le fascisme en Italie", in *ibid.*, 28 December 1923. The other four articles republished by A. Romano in "Antonio Gramsci. Note sulla situazione italiana 1922-24", *Rivista storica del socialismo*, IV No. 13-14, May-December 1961, pp. 625-644 were also probably written in Moscow.
732 Among the rare articles available on this issue, Alfonso Leonetti, "L'.analisi del fascismo", *Paese Sera*, 8 November 1963 tends too much in this direction. So does Togliatti in "L'Ante-fascismo di Gramsci", in *Gramsci*, pp. 81-104.
733 "Reazione", *Avanti*, 17 October 1920 in *Ordine Nuovo*, pp. 351-2. This view should be compared with that of the much debated E. Nolte, *Three Faces of Fascism* (Holt, Chicago, 1967) whose contrary assessment is posited on the uniqueness of fascism and its difference from classical reactionary and authoritarian movements.

734 "Cos'e la reazione?", *Avanti*, 20 November 1920 in *Ordine Nuovo*, pp. 365-7.
735 "La forza dello Stato", *Avanti* (Piedmont), 11 December 1920 in Caprioglio, pp. 150-2.
736 "Cos'e la reazione?", in *ON*, p. 366.
737 *Livorno*, pp. 91-2.
738 "Popolo delle scimmie", *Ordine Nuovo*, 2 January 1921 in *SF*, pp. 9-12.
739 L. Salvatorelli, *Nazional fascismo* (Gobetti, Turin, 1923), *Introduction*. See the debate on this issue between him and the reformist Ansaldo in *Il Lavoro*, IV, 3, 1923 and *Rivoluzione liberale*, XI, No. 13, 1923 in Valeri, pp. 575-520.
740 This party document was republished by R. de Felice as "La Guerra civile 1919-1922", *Rivista storica del socialismo*, IX, No. 27 January-April 1966 and the excerpts are from Spriano, *Storia*, I, pp. 124-5.
741 *Ibid.*
742 "La guerra e le guerra", *Ordine Nuovo*, 31 January 1921, in *SF* pp. 57-9. this became the PCI policy after its leader Lavagnini was killed. See the appeal of the PCI: "The slogan of the Communist Party is thus to accept battle on the ground of the bourgeoisie; to reply to preparation with preparation; to organisation with organisation; to grouping with grouping, to discipline with discipline, to force with force, to arms with arms."
743 "Italia e Spagna", *Ordine Nuovo*, 11 March 1921 in *SF*, pp. 101-3.
744 "Il fascismo italiano", *Ordine Nuovo*, 24 March 1921 in *SF*, p. 117, "Il manifesto dei socialisti", *Ordine Nuovo*, 13 August 1921 in *SF*, p. 137.
745 "Forze elementari", *Ordine Nuovo*, 26 April 1921, in *SF*, p. 150-1.
746 See the work of Reich, Neumann, and later Kohn, Mosse, and Weber.
747 "Fiume", *Ordine Nuovo*, 11 January 1921 in *SF*, pp. 35-6.
748 S. F. Romano, pp. 457-8.
749 *Ibid.*, pp. 457.
750 "Marinetti rivoluzionario?" *Ordine Nuovo*, 5 January 1921, in *SF*, pp. 20-22. See also the postscript to Trotsky's *Literature and Revolution*.
751 S. Caprioglio, "Un mancato incontro a Gardone etc.," All the account of this abortive meeting with d'Annunzio is taken from this source.
752 Articles like "Fascisti e legionari", *Ordine Nuovo*, 19 February 1921 in *SF*, pp. 76-9 support this judgement.
753 Togliatti and Danieli disagree over whether the mission was known at headquarters. See "Un mancato incontro etc ..."
754 See Spriano, *Storia*, I, pp. 143-5.
755 The article "Gli arditi del popolo" *Ordine Nuovo*, 15 July 1921 is republished in Spriano ed., *Gramsci, Scritti Politici*, pp. 450-2.
756 "Reazione?" *Ordine Nuovo*, 23 April 1921 in *SF*, pp. 144-7.
757 "Socialisti e fascisti", *Ordine Nuovo*, 11 June 1921 in *SF*, pp. 186-8; "I capi e le masse", *Ordine Nuovo*, 3 July 1921 in *SF*, pp. 224-6.
758 "Socialisti e fascisti" *Ordine Nuovo*, 11 June 1921, in *SF*, pp. 257-9.
759 "La crisi del fascismo", *Ordine Nuovo*, 9 August 1921 cited by Leonetti, "L'Analisi del fascismo".
760 "Il sasso nello stagno", *Ordine Nuovo*, 12 March 1922, in *SF*, p. 469. See *La formazione*, p. 192.
761 "Les Origines du cabinet Mussolini", *passim*.
762 "Le Parlementarisme et le fascisme en Italie", *op. cit., passim*.
763 "L'echec du syndicalisme fasciste", *La Correspondance internationale*, 3 January 1924.
764 *La formazione*, pp. 152-3.

765 "Les elections italiennes", *La Correspondance internationale,* 17 April 1924.
766 "Le Vatican", in *ibid.,* 12 March 1924.
767 See Spriano, *Storia,* I, p. 238.
768 This view was advanced by Togliatti who wished to emphasise the differences between both men and hence Gramsci's "bolshevik discipline", See *La formazione,* p. 22; see *contra* Humbert Droz, *Archives,* I, p. 157; Spriano, *Storia,* I. p. 190.
769 From a letter in the PCI archives cited by *ibid.,* p. 218.
770 Gramsci to Togliatti and Scoccimarro, 1 March 1924, in *La Formazione,* pp. 228-9.
771 From an interview in the Leonetti Archives cited by Spriano, *Storia,* I, p. 249, fn. 1.
772 *La Formazione,* p. 229.
773 *Stato operaio,* II, 7, 13 March 1924; *Materialismo storico,* pp. 278-9.
774 *Ibid.*
775 *Ibid.*
776 Droz, *Il Contrasto,* pp. 35, 39.
777 *Ibid.*
778 Droz, *Il Contrasto,* p. 40; *Mémoires,* p. 124.
779 *Report of the Moscow Conference 1922* (Great Britain, 1922), pp. 278-9.
780 Degras, I, pp. 434-5.
781 Droz, *Il Contrasto,* p. 35.
782 *Sul movimento operaio,* p. 191.
783 Droz, *Mémoires,* p. 161.
784 Humbert Droz to Zinoviev and Trotsky, 21 April 1923, in *Archives,* I, pp. 466-473.
785 Cited by Spriano, *Storia,* I, p. 257.
786 Droz to Zinoviev and Trotsky, 21 april 1923, *Archives,* I, p. 471.
787 *Stato operaio,* II, 13 24 April 1924.
788 Letter republished in *Alba nuova,* III, 10, 17 March 1923, cited by Spriano, *Storia,* I, p. 260.
789 See Ferrata and Galli, II, p. 25; Togliatti to Gramsci, 1 May 1923, *La Formazione,* p. 59.
790 *Ibid,* p. 58.
791 Gramsci to Togliatti, 18 May 1923 in *La Formazione,* pp. 67-9.
792 Spriano, *Storia,* I, pp. 294-5.
793 *La Formazione,* p. 102.
794 The letter is republished by S. Merli in *Rivista storica del socialismo,* VI, 18, January-April 1965, pp. 115-6.
795 *Stato operaio,* I, 8, 18 October 1923, reprinted in Spriano, *Scritti politici,* pp. 532-6.
796 Spriano, *Storia,* I, p. 300.
797 *Verbale della riunione del Comitato centrale* in *La Formazione,* pp. 104-122. See also *Ibid.,* pp. 122-5.
798 Spriano, *Storia,* I, p. 300.
799 Droz, *Mémoires,* p. 166-8.
800 I. Silone, *Uscita di sicurezza* (Florence, 1965), pp. 81-2.
801 Gramsci to Giulia, 18 January 1924, in Ferrata and Gallo, II, p. 30.
802 G. Zamis, "Gramsci a Vienna nel 1924", *Rinascita,* 28 November 1964, passim.
803 Gramsci to Giulia, 18 January 1924 in Ferrata and Gallo, II, p. 30.
804 Victor Serge, *Memoirs of a Revolutionary* (OUP, London, 1963), p. 186; Gramsci to Giulia, 6 March 1924, in Ferrata and Gallo, II, pp. 32-5.

301

804 Victor Serge, *Memoirs of a Revolutionary* (OUP, London, 1963), p. 186; Gramsci to Giulia, 6 March 1924, in Ferrata and Gallo, II, pp. 32-5.
805 Scoccimarro to Gramsci, 23 December 1923 and Togliatti to Gramsci, 29 December 1923 in *La Formazione,* pp. 137-143.
806 Gramsci to Scoccimarro, 5 January 1924 in *ibid.,* p. 150.
807 Gramsci to Togliatti et al, 9 February 1924 in *La Formazione,* p. 195 See also *Passato e presente,* pp. 58-9.
808 Terracini to Gramsci, 21 January 1924; Gramsci to Terracini, 13 January 1924 in *La Formazione,* pp. 145-7, 155.
809 *Il Prometeo,* 7 February 1924; see also Gramsci's comments in *La formazione,* p. 254.
810 Leonetti, "La terza seria del *Ordine Nuovo*" in *Note su Gramsci,* pp. 84-104.
811 *Ibid.,* p. 93; See article in Spriano, *Scritti politici,* pp. 553-557.
812 "Contro il pessimismo", *Ordine Nuovo,* 15 March 1924 in Spriano *Scritti politici,* pp. 544-8.
813 Gramsci to Togliatti, Terracini et al., 9 February 1924, in *La Formazione,* pp. 196-7.
814 "Il programma dell 'Ordine Nuovo'", in *Ordine Nuovo,* 1-15 April 1924 in Spriano, *Scritti politici,* pp. 552-7.
815 Togliatti in Gramsci, 20 March 1924, in *La Formazione,* p. 236; See by comparison the *Rapport de la minorité ... à l'Executif elargi* in *La Formazione,* pp. 73-87.
816 Scoccimarro to Gramsci, 30 March 1924 in *La Formazione,* p. 267.
817 Droz, *Mémoires,* p. 201; Droz to Zinoviev, 1 February 1924 in *Il Contrasto* pp. 71-2.
818 Droz to Kolarov, 15 February 1924 in *Il Contrasto,* pp. 80-81; *Mémoires,* p. 204.
819 *Ibid.*
820 Droz to Zinoviev, 15 February 1924 in *Il Contrasto,* p. 86.
821 *Ibid.*
822 Droz, *Mémoires,* p. 214; Togliatti to Terracini 15 March 1924 in *La Formazione* pp. 231-2.
823 Togliatti to Gramsci, 20 March 1924 in *La Formazione,* pp. 236-7.
824 Gramsci to Togliatti, 27 March 1924 in *Ibid.,* pp. 254-5.
825 Gramsci to Giulia, 22 June 1924 in Ferrata and Gallo, II, p. 45.
826 Verbale della riunione del Comitato centrale del 19 aprile 1924 in *La Formazione,* pp. 299-300.
827 *Ibid.,* pp. 297-326.
828 Spriano, *Storia,* I, pp. 352-3; Gramsci to Giulia, 21 July 1924 in Ferrata and Gallo, II, p. 50.
829 35 of the 45 secretaries voted for Bordiga's position and 5 for that of the "right". The "centre" could muster only 4 votes. Spriano, *Storia,* I, p. 358-9.
830 Montagnana, *Ricordi,* p. 258; the report of the *Convegno* is in *Annali Feltrinelli,* 1966 where Gramsci's comments are much shorter.
831 Droz, *Il Contrasto,* p. 156; Spriano, I, p. 358.
832 *Ordine Nuovo,* 1-15 April 1924, in Spriano, *Scritti politici,* pp. 558-560.
833 *Ibid.,* p. 564.
834 Tasca to Rakosi (n.d) in *La Formazione,* p. 329.
835 See Ferrata and Gallo, II, pp. 49-72 passim; Montagnana, *Ricordi,* p. 266.
836 Franco Restaino, "Con Gramsci a Is Arenas", *Rinascita Sarda* I, 7,

25 April 1963, pp.8-9; a rather less reliable (police) report is included in D. Zucàro, "Antonio Gramsci e la Sardegna. Carteggio inedito Gramsci Lussu", *Mondo operaio*, V, I, 6 June 1952, pp. 18-20.

837 See Spano, "Gramsci sardo", pp. 106-8; Negarville, "Gramsci, Maestro e Capo", pp. 125-6; for Gramsci's account see Gramsci to Giulia, 10 November 1924 in Ferrata and Gallo, II, pp. 62-3.

838 "Una lezione di Gramsci sul movimento socialista italiano", *Movimento operaio e contadino in Liguria*, III, 2-3 May-June 1957, pp. 35-7.

839 Cammett, pp. 167-70; "introduction" to *Selections from the Prison Notebooks* (Lawrence and Wishart, London, 1971), lxxi.

840 See *La Formazione*, p. 186.

841 Droz, *Il Contrasto*, p. 176.

842 For the V Congress and the PCI see Spriano, *Storia*, I, pp. 362-380. It is worth noting that Tasca supported Zinoviev apparently for personal reasons, but perhaps because he saw through the "leftism".

843 Droz to Presidium, 6 October 1924 in *Il Contrasto*, pp. 185-8.

844 Silverio Corvisieri, *Trotskij e il comunismo italiano* (Samona and Savelli, Rome, 1969), p. 200.

845 *l'Unita*, 18 February 1925 republished in Corvisieri, pp. 185-191.

846 The distinctions between the practical implications of the two views can be seen from a near-contemporary report by Droz to the Presidium in *Il Contrasto*, p. 227; "Soccimarro still supports Bordiga's view, according to which the party should establish its own long-term tactics down to the smallest particulars and not change them at all, no matter what happens ... Gramsci in particular defended the view that in so changing and complex a situation as that in Italy, the party should lay down broadly defined tactics, leaving itself free to manoeuvre in particular application of those tactics.

847 Gramsci to Giulia, 22 June 1924, in Ferrata and Gallo, II, p. 45; see also "La caduta del fascismo", *Ordine Nuovo*, 15 November 1924 in Spriano, *Scritti politici*, p. 590.

848 Gramsci to Giulia, 4 August 1924 in *ibid.*, p. 52.

849 Spriano, *Storia*, I, p. 397; Report to CC (July 1924) in *Rinascita*, 16 25 August 17, 1 September 1962.

850 Spriano, *Scritti politici*, pp. 677-685; *Il Contrasto*, pp. 192-197.

851 *Il Contrasto*, pp. 195-8, 209, 226.

852 *l'Unita*, 4 July 1925, reprinted in Corvisieri, pp. 205-214; compare Gamsci's "Contro il pessimismo", *op. cit.* and his letter to Togliatti and others of 9 February 1925 in *La Formazione*, pp. 196-7.

853 He did not believe that the "left" or its leader would force the issue to this point: Bodiga was "... a practical man, not a don Quixote ..." Gramsci to P. Tresso, April 1924 in *La Formazione*, pp. 335-6.

854 See Berti, p. 213.

855 "La scuola del partito", *Ordine Nuovo*, 1 April 1925; "La volonta delle masse", *l'Unita*, 24 June 1925 in Spriano, *Scritti politici*, pp. 595-7, 620-4.

856 "La situazione interna del nostro partito ed i compiti del prossimo congresso", *l'Unita* 3 July 1925 in *Critica marxista*, 5-6 September-December 1963, pp. 289ff; "L'organizzazione per cellule e il II congresso mondiale", l'Unita, 29 July, 1925, in Spriano, *Scritti politici*, pp. 638-641; "L'organizzazione base del Partico", *l'Unita*, 15 August 1925.

857 See *Lo Stato operaio*, March-April 1931.

858 *La Formazione*, p. 375-80.

859 *Lo\Stato operaio*, II, 3, March 1928, pp. 82-88. To our knowledge, this was the last of his writings before he was jailed.

860 "Operai e contadini" (Three articles with the same title) in *Ordine Nuovo*, 2 August 1919, 3 January 1920 and *Avanti*, 20 February 1920; "Mezzogiorno e fascismo" in *ON*, 15 March 1924 in Spriano, *Scritti politici*, pp. 549-552; A. Gramsci, *La Questione meridionale* (Riuniti, Rome, 1969), p. 137-140 and ff.

861 See Trent'anni di vita e lotta etc., II, pp. 93-103; *l'Unita*, 24 February 1929.

862 *Lettere*, p. 58.

863 "Alcuni temi della questione meridionale" in Gramsci, *La Questione meridionale*, pp. 131-160.

864 "Il significato e i risultati del III congresso del Partito Comunista d'Italia", l'Unita, 24 February 1926; G. Galli, *Storia del Partito Comunista italiano* (Schwarz, Milan, 1958), p. 152.

865 *Ibid.*, Spriano *Storia*, I, pp. 482, 507; Droz, *Mémoires*, p. 263; V. Spano, "Il Congresso di Lione", *Rinascita*, April 1956, pp. 235-240.

866 Spriano, *Storia*, I, pp. 494-5, 504-5, 508; Droz, *Il Contrasto*, p. 217.

867 Gramsci to Giulia, 25 May 1925 in Ferrata and Gallo, II, pp. 72-3; *l'Unita*, 27 May 1925 in Spriano, *Scritti politici*, pp. 605-615; there is an interesting but unverified story that Mussolini tried to congratulate Gramsci after his maiden speech, but that Gramsci ignored his outstretched hand.

868 D. Zucàro, "Antonio Gramsci e la Sardegna, Carteggio inedito Gramsci-Lussu", *Mondo operaio*, V, 2, 6 June 1952.

869 See Camilla Ravera to Togliatti 16(?) November 1926 in *Rinascita*, 5 December 1964; for speculation why Gramsci did not leave see Fiori, *Vita*, ch. 22.

870 Zucàro, "Antonio Gramsci e la Sardegna", *passim*.

871 Droz to Comintern, 6 October 1924, in *Il Contrasto*, pp. 191-2.

872 The account of his trial is based mainly on D. Zucàro ed., *Il processone: Gramsci e i dirigenti comunisti dinanzi al tribunale speciale* (Riuniti, Rome, 1961) and Spriano, *Storia*, II, ch. 4. For Gramsci's own assessment of his lawyer see Casucci, p. 421.

CHAPTER V

873 According to Dr Irina Grigoreva, the leading Soviet specialist on Gramsci, there is only one record of a proposed meeting with Lenin and none that it actually took place. Personal interview 27 March 1974.

874 Ferrata and Gallo, II, pp. 27-8; The Italian edition appeared in 1931-7.

875 "Capo" in Antonio Gramsci, *La Costruzione del partito comunista 1923-1926* (Einaudi, Turin, 1972), pp. 13-15.

876 "Il Programma del Ordine Nuovo" in *La Costruzione*, p. 21.

877 "La situazione interna del nostro partito ed i compiti del prossimo congresso", (11-12 May 1925) in *La Costruzione*, pp. 62-73.

878 See *La Costruzione*, pp. 69, 90, 187.

879 "Liquidatori di sinistra", *La Costruzione*, pp. 220-3.

880 Citing G. Zinoviev, *Against the Current*.

881 *La Costruzione*, p. 246.

882 *La Costruzione*, pp. 62-73, 270-1.

883 *Ibid.*, p. 270; for Bordiga's position see A. de Clementi, *Amadeo Bordiga*

(Einaudi, Turin, 1971), Chs. 6 and 7, esp. pp. 216-7.

884 "L'Organizzazione Base del Partito", *La Costruzione,* pp. 272-6.

885 "Critica sterile e negativa", *La Costruzione,* p. 293.

886 "Vecchiume imbellettato", (22 September, 1926) *La Costruzione,* pp. 331-3.

887 See *Clarté,* 29 November 1919.

888 Alfred Rosmer, *Moscou sous Lenine* (Maspéro, Paris, 1970).

889 "Come non si deve scrivere la storia della rivoluzione bolshevica; A proposito del *1917* di Leo Trotsky", (19 November 1924), *La Costruzione,* pp. 211-2.

890 Victor Serge, *op. cit.,* p. 186; See also the letter to Gramsci's wife of 13 January 1924 in Ferrata and Gallo, II, p. 29.

891 *Rinascita,* 30 May 1964.

892 Ferrata and Gallo, II, p. 29.

893 *Rinascita,* 30 May 1964.

894 *La Costruzione,* pp. 133-137.

895 See *Rinascita,* 30 May 1964 for Togliatti's lame explanation and denial that a copy of the last letter existed.

896 See Ferrata and Gallo, II, pp. 27-8, 35, 51; *La Costruzione,* p. 25.

897 D. Ryazanoff, *The Communist Manifesto* (Martin Lawrence, London, 1930), pp. 105, 132, 173, 179.

898 Ryazanoff, p. 132.

899 *Lettere dal Carcere,* pp. 1-9.

900 *Ibid.,* p. 76.

901 Casucci, p. 443 contains a very interesting report by Professor Filippo Saporito to the Director General of Prisons, which supports his assertion.

902 *Ibid.*

903 *Lettere,* pp. 52, 88.

904 *Ibid.,* p. 268-270.

905 *Ibid.,* pp. 58-9.

906 We recall to readers that the essay on the Southern Question was linked directly to the practical issue of how to free the southern peasant through organising in the villages, and thus referred back to the central theme in Gramsci's activity: workers' councils.

907 *Lettere,* p. 157.

908 See the letter from Gramsci to the judge in Carbone, "I libri del carcere di Antonio Gramsci", p. 641.

909 *Lettere,* p. 235.

910 *Lettere,* pp. 92-5; Valentino Gerratana, "Sulla preparazione di un edizione critica dei 'Quaderni del carcere'" in *Gramsci e la cultura contemporanea,* II, p. 465.

911 These are listed in the Preface of *Materialismo storico e la filosofia di Benedetto Croce* (Einaudi, Turin, 1966), p. XIV.

912 *Lettere,* pp. 263-64.

913 *Lettere,* p. 309.

914 *Lettere,* p. 313.

915 Louis Althusser, *Lire le Capital* (Maspéro, Paris, 1967), II, Ch. 5.

916 *Lettere,* p. 363.

917 *Ibid.,* p. 344.

918 See Gerratana, "Sulla preparazione ...", pp. 466-7.

919 G. Ceresa, "In carcere con Gramsci, in *Gramsci,* p. 76. This disintegration could be dated back to Christmas 1928. See *Lettere,* p. 502.

920 See D. Zucàro, *Vita di Carcere di Antonio Gramsci* (Avanti, Milan/Rome 1954), p. 61.
921 As M.A. Macciocchi's recent interview with Professor P. Sraffa reveals. See Macciocchi, *Pour Gramsci* (Seuil, Paris, 1974), p. 289.
922 A. Leonetti, *Note su Gramsci,* pp. 191-209; Fiori, *Vita,* pp. 291-3.
923 Fiori, *Vita,* p. 292.
924 Athos Lisa, "Discussione politica con Gramsci in Carcere", *Rinascita* 12 December 1964: The substantial correctness of Lisa's report is confirmed by Giovanni Lay, "Colloqui con Gramsci nel carcere di Turin in *ibid.,* 22 February 1965.
925 Ceresa, *op. cit.,* who was one of his closest friends in prison recalls his position thus. So do Lisa and Lay.
926 *Ibid.*
927 Lay; see *Lettere,* p. 422 and Carbone, pp. 544-6 as well. Some prisoners had even resented that he has served first at mealtimes although this was owed only to the location of his cell. See Tatiana Schucht, "Colloqui con Gramsci ... in Carcere", *Rinascita,* 23 January 1970, p. 18.
928 Garuglieri, p. 696.
929 *Ibid.*
930 Leonetti, "Guerra di posizione" e 'guerra di movimento'", in *Note,* pp.181-190; and "Il cazzotto nell'occhio o della costituente" in *ibid,* pp. 191-208.
931 *Ibid.,* p. 197.
932 L. Trotsky, "Et Maintenant" in *Ecrits,* 1928-40, (Quatrière Internationale, Paris), p. 160.
933 *R,* pp. 89-90; pp. 71.
934 *Mach,* pp. 114-5.
935 *Mach,* pp. 114-5.
936 *R,* pp. 89-90, n.
937 *Lettere,* p. 422 (28 March 1931).
938 *PP,* pp. 136-7.
939 *Mach,* p. 18.
940 *Lettere,* pp. 464-5.
941 This feeling had been compounded by his last experiences with his family, who came to Rome in 1926, where his wife was employed at the Soviet Embassy. Gramsci had, of course, enjoyed having them near him, and had tried to teach his son Delio to play the piano. His wife was again pregnant. But there had been fundamental disagreements about how to bring up the children and he was made to feel an outsider on occasion, for example when his son called him "uncle". Moreover, he disapproved of the excessively close relationship between the child and Eugenia Schucht. The dispute about the rearing of children continued in his prison letters.
942 Guaruglieri, pp. 694-5; *Lettere,* p. 597.
943 *Ibid.*
944 *Lettere,* p. 431.
945 See Gerratana, "Sulla preparazione ...", pp. 467-8.
946 This means inferentially that Gramsci's notes begin with *MS* and then proceed to *Mach* and the *Intellectuali* in the Einaudi edition. It also means that the Nowell-Smith and Hoare edition of the *Notebooks* should start with the excerpts where it ends.
947 See *MS,* pp. 198-200, which were written in 1932.

Notes

948 See this manuscript at pp. 247-8.
949 *Lettere,* pp. 378-380.
950 *Lettere,* pp. 459-460.
951 *Lettere,* p. 466.
952 For the grouping see *Lettere,* p. 576. For the only example of this development at present available see V. Gerratana, "Inediti dei Quaderni del Carcere", *Rinascita,* 14 April 1967, pp. 16-19. As Gerratana says in "Sulla preparazione ...", p. 456: "It can be said that a critical edition fulfills its purpose if it offers not so much an interpretation as the necessary philological support which is essential to a correct and reliable interpretation." Gerratana's critical edition appeared too late to be used for this book.
953 *Lettere,* pp. 607-9.
954 *Ibid.,* p. 612-13.
955 *Ibid.,* p. 616.
956 *Ibid.,* p. 619.
957 *Ibid.,* p. 620.
958 *Ibid.,* p. 632-3.
959 *Ibid.,* p. 665.
960 Piero Sraffa was introduced to Gramsci in 1919 by Umberto Cosmo, joined the student socialist group in 1920, and was in the *Ordine Nuovo* circle in 1919-20. In 1921 he wrote a couple of articles for the second series of *Ordine Nuovo.* In 1924, he wrote letters to Gramsci which provoked a statement of Gramsci's political position. In 1927, through the good graces of Gaetano Salvemini, he was appointed to a lectureship at Cambridge. After 1928 he started to arrange for books to be sent to the imprisoned Gramsci.
961 See *Rinascita,* 23 June 1970, p. 19.
962 See *Manchester Guardian,* 29 October 1929.
963 See Spriano, "Gli ultimi anni di Gramsci in un colloquia con Piero Sraffa", *Rinascita,* 4 April 1967, p. 14.
964 *Lettere,* p. 627.
965 Spriano, "Gli ultimi anni di Gramsci ..."; "Relazioni di Tatiana: Antonio Gramsci nel Carcere di Turi", p. 17; Fiori, *Vita,* pp. 312-3.
966 Fiori, *Vita,* p. 313.
967 *Lettere,* pp. 676-8.
968 *Ibid.,* pp. 762-3.
969 Guaruglieri, p. 701.
970 "Relazioni di Tatiana, ...", p. 19.
971 "Inediti di Gramsci. Nota autobiografica (1933)", *Europa Letteraria* 13-14, February-April 1962, pp. 8-9; see also *Lettere,* p. 757.
972 The report is reproduced in *Lettere,* p. 763.
973 *Ibid.,* p. 785.
974 Fiori, *Vita,* p. 324.
975 Lombardo Radice and Carbone, *Vita,* pp. 95-232. See also Cusumano's report in Casucci, p. 444.
976 The twenty-one exercise books are listed by Gerratana, "Sulla preparazione ...", pp. 475-6.
977 Casucci, pp. 426-7; "Gli ultimi anni di Gramsci", *passim;* Fiori, *Vita,* p. 330; *Lettere,* p. 841.
978 Casucci, p. 443.
979 *Ibid.,* p. 444.

980 "Gli ultimi anni ..." p. 15; "Relazione di Tatiana ..." See Spriano, *Storia*, III, p. 150.

981 See the list of publications for 1934 in comparison with those of 1933 in Fubini, *Gramsci e la cultura contemporanea*, II, p. 485.

982 There is dispute about this, but I follow Gerratana, *opera citata*.

983 See the recollection of his sister Edmea in *Rinascita sarda*, 15 January-15 February 1965, p. 13.

984 *Lettere*, pp. 915-9.

985 See "Gli ultimi anni ..."

986 *Ibid.*, p. 15.

987 *Passato e presente*, p. 3.

988 Compare the positions of Tamburrano and Agazzi with Togliatti and with Leonetti and Corvisieri (see bibliography) and how they arrived at these positions.

989 *Passato presente*, p. 70.

990 *Passato e presente*, p. 5.

991 "La sovranita della legge" (1 June 1919); "La conquista dello Stato" (12 July 1919) in *Ordine Nuovo*, pp. 3-5, 13-19.

Except for the writings of Gramsci himself, only books, articles, manuscripts and interviews cited in footnotes in this book are listed in this bibliography. There is an almost complete list of all titles on Gramsci to 1967 in Fubini, *op.cit.* in *Gramsci e la Cultura contemporanea*, II and a full list of titles in English to 1968 in Davidson, *Antonio Gramsci The Man His Ideas*. Readers who are able to read French should consult the bibliographies in Macciocchi, *Pour Gramsci* or H. Portelli, *Gramsci et la Question Réligieuse* (Anthropos, Paris, 1974).

Bibliography

GRAMSCI'S WRITINGS

COLLECTIONS & ANTHOLOGIES

Ferrata, G. & Gallo, N., eds., *2000 Pagine di Gramsci* (Il Saggiatore, Milan, 1964) 2 vols. Vol. 1, *Nel Tempo della lotta* (1914-1926). Vol. 2, *Lettere edite e inedite* (1912-1937)

Salinari, C. & Spinelli M., eds., *Antonio Gramsci, antologia degli scritti* (Editori Riuniti, Rome, 1963), 2 vols

L'Albero del Riccio (Milano Sera, Milan, 1949)

Americanismo e fordismo. Edited by F. Platone (Universale economica, Milan, 1950)

Elementi di politica. Edited and presented by M. Spinelli (Editori Riuniti, Rome, 1964)

The Modern Price and Other Writings. Translated with an Introduction by L. Marks (International publishers, New York, 1959)

The Open Marxism of Antonio Gramsci. Translated and annotated by C. Marzani (Cameron Associates, New York, 1957)

La Questione meridionale. Third Edition (Editori Riuniti, Rome, 1957)

Sul Risorgimento. Edited by E. Fubini with preface by G. Candeloro (Editori Riuniti, Rome, 1959)

Il Vaticano e l'Italia. Edited by E. Fubini with preface by A. Cecchi (Editori Riuniti, Rome, 1961)

COLLECTED WORKS

Opere di Antonio Gramsci (Einaudi, Turin, 1947-1972) Vol.1 *Lettere dal Carcere* 1947. Rev. edit. 1965, edited by S. Caprioglio & E. Fubini

Vol. 2. *Il Materialismo Storico e la filosofia di Benedetto Croce,* 1949

Vol. 3 *Gli Intellettuali e l'organizzione della cultura,* 1949

Vol. 4. *Il Risorgimento,* 1949

Vol. 5 *Note sul Machiavelli, sulla politica, e sullo stato moderno,* 1949

Vol. 6. *Letteratura e vita nazionale,* 1950

Vol. 7. *Passato e presente,* 1951

Vol. 8. *Scritti giovanili, 1914-18,* 1958

Vol. 9. *L'Ordine Nuovo, 1919-1920,* 1954

Vol. 10. *Sotto la Mole,* 1916-1920, 1960

Vol. 11. *Socialismo e Fascismo, L'Ordine Nuovo, 1921-22,* 1967

Vol. 12. *La Construzione del Partito Comunista 1923-26,* 1972

Bibliography

OTHER WRITINGS IN CHRONOLOGICAL ORDER OF COMPOSITION

La Città futura ("Numero Unico Pubblicato dalla Federazione Giovanile Socialista Piemontese") Turin, 11 February 1917

Letter to Giusseppe Lombaro Radice, March (?) 1918, in *Rinascita*, 7 March 1964

"Nuovi Contributi agli scritti giovanili di Gramsci", *Rivista Storica del socialismo*, Vol. 3, No. 10, May-August 1960. Edited by Luigi Ambrosoli

"Gli Editoriali di Gramsci nei tre Giorni che Precedettero il Congresso di Livorno," *Rinascita*, Vol. 21, No. 3, 18 January 1964

"Note Sulla Situazione Italiana 1922-1924 (A cura di Aldo Romano)", *Rivista Storica del Socialismo*, Vol. 4, Nos. 13-14, May-December 1961

"Les Origines du Cabinet Mussolini", *La Correspondence internationale*, 20 November 1922

"Le parlementarisme et le fascisme en Italie", in *La Correspondence internationale*, 28 December 1923

"Lettera inedita per la fondazione de L'Unità", 12 September, 1923, *Rivista Storica del Socialismo*, Vol. 6, No. 18, January-April 1963

Letter of 1923 in S. Merli, *Rivista Storica del Socialismo*, Vol. 6, No. 18, January-April 1965 contains Gramsci's view of the role of the Press

"L'echec du syndicalisme fasciste", *La Correspondance internationale*, 3 January 1924

"Le Vatican", *La Correspondance internationale*, 12 March 1924

"Les elections italiennes", *La Correspondance internationale*, 17 April 1924

"1924 Al professore Zino Zini, collaboratore dell'Ordine Nuovo: Due lettere inedite di Gramsci," *Rinascita*, Vol. 21, No. 18, 25 April 1964

Report to the C.C. (July 1924), in *Rinascita*, Vol. 16, No. 17, 25 August-1 September 1962

"Il Discorso al parlamento italiano nel maggio, 1925", *Rinascita*, Vol. 6, 9 June 1962

"1925: In una lettera all Esecutivo dell'Internazionale comunista Gramsci respinge le critiche del compagno Manuilski: "Legalismo" e "Carbonarismo" nel Partito comunista d'Italia," *Rinascita*, Vol. 20, No. 34, 31 August 1963

"La Relazione di Antonio Gramsci sul III Congresso (Lione) del PCI", *Rinascita*, Vol. 12, No. 10, October 1956. First published in *L'Unita*, 24 February 1926

"Come si determinano le nostre prospettive e i nostri compiti," in *Lo Stato operaio* (Rome, Editori Riuniti, 1964) Vol. 1. Gramsci's Report to the central committee of the PCI in August 1926

"Gramsci al CC del PC(b); (1926) Togliatti a Gramsci", *Rinascita*, Vol. 21, No. 22, 30 May 1964

"Alcuni Temi della quistione meridionale", *Stato operaio*, Vol. 4, No. 1, January 1930

"Tesi sulla situazione italiana e sui compiti del PCI, approvate dal III Congresso nazionale nel gennaio 1926", *Stato operaio*, Vol. 2, Nos. 6-7, June-July 1928

"Notes on anti-semitism", *The Promethean Review*, Vol. 1, No. 4, October-November 1959 Transl. Hamish Henderson. From letters to his sister-in-law, 1931

"Benedetto Croce and his Concept of Liberty", *Science & Society*, Vol. 10, Summer 1946. Transl. by Samuel Putnam. From letters to his sister-in-law, 1932

311

Antonio Gramsci

"Inediti di Gramsci. Nota autobiografica 1933", *Europa Letteraria*, Nos. 13-14, February-April 1962

"In Search of the Educational Principle", *New Left Review*, No. 32, July-August 1965 Translation with an Introduction by Quintin Hoare. A Translation of "per la ricerca del principio educativo", in *Gli Intellettuali e l'organizzazione della cultura*

OTHER SOURCES

Alghero, M.L.S. di *Mémoire pour Napoleon* (Giuffré, Milan, 1967)

Althusser, L., *Lire le Capital* (Maspéro, Paris, 1967)

Alziator, Francisco, *Il folklore sardo* (La Zattera, Bologna, 1957)

Amoretti, G., "Con Gramsci sotto la Mole", in *Gramsci Scritti di P. Togliatti ed altri* (Unita, Rome, 1945)

Anfossi, A., *Socialità e Organizzazioni in Sardegna* (Franco Angeli, Milan, 1968)

Angioy, Giovanni Maria, "Mémoire sur la Sardaigne (1799)" in C. Sole ed., *La Sardegna di Carlo Felice e il Problema Della Terra* (Fossataro, Cagliari, 1968)

Archives de Jules Humbert-Droz, 1, Origines et Débuts des Partis Comunistes Des Pays Latins 1919-31 (Reidel, 1970)

Arfé Gaetano, *il movimento giovanile socialista* (Avanti, Milan, 1966)

———, *Storia dell'Avanti* (Avanti, Milan, 1956)

———, (ed.) *Gaetano Salvemini. Movimento socialista e questione meridionale. Opere, IV,* Vol. 2 (Feltrinelli, Milan, 1968)

———, *Storia del Socialismo italiano (1892-1926)* (Einaudi, Turin, 1965)

Avigdor, E., "Il movimento operaio torinese durante la prima guerra mondiale", in A. Caracciolo & G. Scalià eds., *La Citta Futura* (Feltrinelli, Milan, 1959)

Azuni, Domenico Alberto, "Projet des reformes à faire en Sardaigne" (1802), in C. Sole, *La Sardegna di Carlo Felice e il Problema della Terra* (Fossataro, Cagliari, 1968)

Balabanoff, A., *Impressions of Lenin* (Ann Arbor, Michigan, 1968)

Banfield, E., *The Moral Basis of a Backward Society* (Free Press, New York, 1958)

Bergson, H., *L'évolution créatrice* (Alcan, Paris, 1911)

Berti, G., "Il gruppo del *Soviet* nella formazione del PCI," *Stato operaio*, Vol. 9, No. 1, January 1935

———, *I Primi dieci anni di vita del P.C.I. Documenti inediti dell archivio Angelo Tasca* (Feltrinelli, Milan, 1967)

Bezveselny S.F., & Grunberg, D.Y., *They Knew Lenin* (Foreign languages publishing House, Moscow, 1968)

Bobbio, Norberto, Introduction to R. Mondolfo, *Umanismo di Marx: Studii filosofici, 1908-1966* (Einaudi, Turin, 1968)

———, "Profilo ideologico del Novecento" in *Storia della Letteratura italiana* (Garzanti, 1969)

———, "Tre Maestri", in *Italia Civile* (Lacaita, Manduria, Bari, Perugia, 1964)

Boscolo, A., ed., *Feudalismo in Sardegna* (Fossataro, Cagliari, 1967)

Bottiglioni, G., *Vita Sarda, Note di Folklore, Cante e Legende* (Luigi Trevisini, Milan, 1925)

Bresciani, Padre Antonio, *Dei Costumi dell' isola di Sardegna comparati con gli antichissimi popoli orientali*

Bibliography

Brett, V., *Henri Barbusse, Sa Marche vers la clarté, Son mouvement Clarté* (Editions de l'Academie Tshecoslovaque des Sciences, Prague, 1963)

Cabitza, C., *La Sardegna davanti ad una svolta decisiva* (Feltrinelli, Milan, 1968)

———, *Sardegna, Rivolta contro la colonizzazione* (Feltrinelli, Milan, 1968)

Cajati, A., "Gli Anni liceali di Gramsci e gli strafalcioni di alcuni suoi biografi", *Annali del Liceo Classico G.M. Dettori di Cagliari, 1,* 1962-3 (Bari, 1963)

Cammett, John M., *Antonio Gramsci and the Origins of Italian Communism* (Stanford University Press, Stanford, 1967)

Caprioglio, Sergio, Letter to *Rinascita,* Vol. 22, No. 11, 13 March 1965

———, "Un Articolo di Gramsci alla vigilia dell 'Ottobre'", *Rinascita,* 13 October 1967

———, "Il Movimento Torinese dei consigli di fabbrica", *Mondo operaio,* 2 February 1958

Caracciolo, A. & Scalià, Gianni, eds., *La Citta Futura* (Feltrinelli, Milan, 1959)

———, "Serrati, Bordiga, e la polemica gramsciana contro il 'blanquismo' e il Settarismo di partito", in A. Caracciolo & G. Scalià eds., *La Citta Futura* (Feltrinelli, Milan, 1959)

Carbone, G., "I Libri del carcere di Antonio Gramsci", *Movimento operaio,* Vol. 4, July-August 1952

Carbone, G. & L. Lombardo-Radice, *Vita di Antonio Gramsci* (Critica Sociale, Rome, 1957)

Carena, Pia, interviewed by Giovanni Bosca in A. Leonetti, *Note Sur Gramsci* (Argalià, Urbino, 1971)

Casucci, C., "Il Carteggio di Antonio Gramsci conservato nel Casellario politico centrale", *Rassegna degli archivi di Stato,* Vol. 25, No. 3, September-December 1965

Caute, D., *Communism and the French Intellectuals* (Deutsch, London, 1964)

———, *Fanon* (Fontana, London, 1970)

Clementi A, de., *Amadeo Bordiga* (Einaudi, Turin, 1971)

———, "La politica del Partito comunista d'Italia nel 1921-22 e il rapporto Bordiga-Gramsci", *Rivista storica del socialismo,* No. 28, 1966

Coffin, J.F., "Mémoire sur la situation politique de la Sardaigne" (1798-9), in C. Sole ed., *La Sardegna di Carlo Felice e il Problema della terra* (Fossataro, Cagliari, 1968)

Communist International, Vol. 1, No. 1, May 1919 & No. 5, 1919

Communist International Vol. 2, No. 13, August 1920

Contini, G., *L'influenza culturale di Benedetto Croce* (Riccardo Ricciardi, Naples, 1957)

Cortesi, Luigi, ed. *Il socialismo italiano tra riforme e rivoluzione 1892-1921 Atti congressuali del PSI* (Laterza, Bari, 1969)

Corvisieri, S., *Trotskij e il Comunismo italiano* (Samona and Savelli, Rome, 1969)

Cosmo, U., *Con madonna poverta* (Laterza, Bari, 1940)

Croce, Benedetto, "Come Nacque e come Morì il marxismo teorico in Italia", in Antonio Labriola, *La Concezione materialistica della storia* (Laterza, Bari, 1953)

———, "Intorno all'idealismo attuale", *La Voce,* Vol. 5, No. 46, 1913

———, *Filosofia della practica* (Laterza, Bari, 1st published 1913)

———, *Saggio sullo Hegel* (Laterza, Bari, 1948)

———, *Storia d'Italia 1870-1915* (Laterza, Bari, 1943)

———, *Storia del Regno di Napoli* (Laterza, Bari, 1925)

_____, *Teoria della storia della storiografia* (Laterza, Bari, 1954)

Cutri, M., 'Nella Casa di Ghilarza'', *L'Unita*, 27 April 1947, Interview with Teresina and Grazietta Gramsci

Daniels, R.V., *A Documentary History of Communism* (Vintage Books, New York, 1960)

Davidson, Alastair, "Banditi nel vecchio Mezzogiorno", *Lingua Bella* (Brisbane, March 1970)

_____, "Benedetto Croce, Philosopher and Historian", *Quaderni dell 'Instituto italiano de cultura*, No. 3 (Melbourne, 1968)

_____, 'Marxism & Anarchism,'' *Australian Left Review*, No. 33, November 1971

_____, "The Russian Revolution and the Formation of the Italian Communist Party", *The Australian Journal of Politics and History*, Vol. 10, No. 3, December 1964

_____, "The Varying Seasons of Gramscian Studies", *Political Studies*, Vol. 20, No. 4, December 1972

_____, in *Lot's Wife* (Melbourne), 14 September 1970

Dawson, R.E. & Prewitt, K., *Political Socialisation; An Analytical Study,* (Little Brown, Boston, 1969)

Deledda, Grazia, *Canne al Vento* (Mondadori, Milan, 1941)

_____, *Cosima* (Mondadori, Milan, 1941)

_____, *Elias Portolu* in *Romanzi e Novelle* (Mondadori, Milan, 1957)

Delogu, Ignazio, "Casa Gramsci", *Rinascita Sarda*, Vol. 5, No. 7, 20 April-5 May 1967

Dizionario enciclopedico della Letteratura italiana

Dollard, J., *Criteria for the Life History,* (Peter Smith, New York, 1949)

Dolléans, E., *Histoire du mouvement ouvrier 1871-1920* (Colin, Paris, 1957), Vol. 2

Douglas, Norman, *Old Calabria,* (Penguin, London, 1962)

Erikson, E. H., *Childhood and Soceity,* (Norton, New York, 1950)

Felice, R de., "Un corso di glottologia di Matteo Bartoli negli appunti di Antonio Gramsci", *Rivista storica del socialismo,* Vol. 2, No. 2, January-April 1964

_____, "La Guerra civile 1919-1922,'' *Rivista Storica del socialismo,* Vol. 9, No. 27, January-April 1966

Felice, R. de & Parlato, V. eds., *La Questione Meridionale: Gramsci* (Editori Riuniti, Rome, 1969

Ferrara, M & M., *Conversando con Togliatti, Note biografiche* (Edizioni di Cultura sociale, Rome, 1953)

Ferrata, Giansiro, ed., *La Voce 1908-1916* (Landi, Rome, 1961)

Ferri, F., "La situazione interna della sezione socialista torinese nell' estate del 1920'', *Rinascita,* April 1958

Finnochiaro, B. ed., *L'Unita di Gaetano Salvemini* (Neri Pozza, Venice, 1958)

Fiori, Giuseppe, *Antonio Gramsci Life of a Revolutionary* (NLB, 1970)

_____, "La giovinezza di Gramsci", *Rinascita sarda,* Vol. 5, No. 7, 20 April-5 May 1967

_____, *Vita di Gramsci* (Laterza, Bari, 1966)

Freud, Sigmund, *Introductory Lectures on Psychoanalysis* (George, Allen & Unwin, London, 1961)

Fromm, Erich, *The Fear of Freedom* (Routledge & Kegan Paul, London, 1966)

Galli, G., *Storia del Partito comunista italiano* (Schwarz, Milan, 1958)

Bibliography

Garin, Eugenio, *Cronache di filosofia italiana 1900-1943* (Laterza, Bari, 1959)
_____, "La Formazione di Gramsci e Croce", in *Prassi rivolutionaria e storicismo in Gramsci, Quaderni di Critica marxista* No. 3
Garosci, A., "Palmiro Togliatti", *Survey,* No. 53, 1964
_____, "Totalitarismo e storicismo nel pensiero di Antonio Gramsci", in *Pensiero politico e storiografia moderna* (Nistri-Lischi, Pisa, 1954)
Genovesi, A., Essay on Campania in R. Villari ed., *Il Sud nella Storia d'Italia* (Laterza, Bari, 1966) Vol. 1
Gentile, P., Translation of K. Marx *Theses on Feuerbach,* in P. Gentile (Trans.) *La Filosofia di Marx* (Spoerri, Pisa, 1899)
Germanetto, Giovanni, *Memoirs of a Barber* (Co-Operative Publishing Society of Foreign Workers in the USSR, Moscow/Leningrad, 1934)
Gerratana, V., "Inediti dei Quaderni di Carcere", *Rinascita,* 14 April 1967
Ghisalberti, I., "La questione demaniale del Mezzogiorno", in B. Finnochiaro ed. *L'Unita di Gaetano Salvemini* (Neri Pozza, Venice, 1958)
Giolitti, G., "Discorso per le elezioni della XXV Legislatura" (12 October 1919), in *Discorsi etraparlamentari* (Einaudi, Turin, 1952)
Gobetti, Piero, "Le Commissione interne", *La Rivoluzione liberale,* Vol. 4, No. 22, 20 September 1925
_____, *Opere complete di Piero Gobetti,* edited by P. Spriano (Einaudi, Turin, 1960)
_____, "Il problema Sardo", in P. Spriano ed., *Opere complete di Piero Gobetti, I, Scitti politici* (Einaudi, Turin, 1969)
_____, "La Russia dei Soviet" *Rivista di Milano,* 20 February 1921
_____, "Storia dei communisti torinesi scritto da un liberale", *Rivoluzione Liberale,* Vol. 4, No. 2, 1922
_____, "L'Universita e la cultura: Torino", in P. Spriano (1960), *op. cit.sopra*
Grieco, R., Article critical of Gramsci in *Il Prometeo,* 7 February 1924
Guarnieri, Mario, *I consigli di Fabbrica* (Il Solco, Citta di Castello, 1921)
Guerin, D., *Anarchism* (Monthly Review, London, 1970)
Hall, C.S. & Lindzey, G., "Freud's Psychoanalytic theory of Personality", in R. Hunt ed. *Personalities and Cultures* (Natural History Press, New York, 1967)
Hertz, F.O., *Nationality in History and Politics: A Study of the Psychology and Sociology of National Sentiment and Character* (London, 1944)
Hess, R. D. & Torney, J. V., *The Development of Political Attitudes in Children* (Aldone, Chicago, 1967)
Hulse, J., *The Forming of the Communist International* (Stanford, California, 1964)
Humbert-Droz, J., *Il Contrasto tra l 'Internazionale e il P.C.I. 1922-28. Documenti inediti dall' archivio di Jules Humbert-Droz, Segretario dell' Inter nazionale Comunista* (Feltrinelli, Milan, 1965)
_____, *Mémoires: De Lenine a Staline. Dix ans au Service de L'Internationale Communiste 1921-1931* (Baconnière, Neuchatel, 1971)
Hunt, R. ed., *Personalities and Cultures* (Natural History Press, New York, 1967)
Jaco, Aldo de ed., *Il Brigantaggio Meridionale* (Editori Riuniti, Rome, 1969)
_____, "Visita a Ghilarza. Lettere di A. Gramsci studente alla famiglia," *L'Unita,* Vol. 43, No. 22, 23 January 1966
Kardiner, A. et alia, *The Psychological Frontiers of Society* (Columbia University Press, New York, 1963)
Kriegel, A., *Aux origines du communisme francais* (Flammarion, Paris, 1969)

Labriola, Antonio, *La Concezione materialistica della storia* (Laterza, Bari, 1953)
———, *Discorrendo di socialismo e filosofia* (Laterza, Bari, 1947)
——— Arturo, Lecture, Rome, 28 March 1910 at Collègio dei Parrucchieri, in Nino Valeri, *La Lotta politica in Italia dall' Unita al 1925* (Le Monnier, Florence, 1962)
———, *Storia di dieci anni 1899-1909* (Milan, 1910)
Langevin L. & Cogniot, G., "Les Premiers intellectuals communistes francais", *La Pensée*, No. 136, December 1967
Lawrence, D. H., *Sea and Sardinia* (Martin Secker, London, 1923)
Lay, G., "Colloqui con Gramsci nel carcere di Turin", *Rinascita,* 22 February 1965
Lenin, V.I., *Sul movimento operaio italiano* (Rinascita, Rome, 1952)
———, *The State and the Revolution* (F.L.P.H., Moscow, 1949)
Leonetti, A., "L'analisi del fascismo", *Paese Sera,* 8 November 1963
———, "Coerenza di Gramsci", *Paese sera,* 6 March 1964, now in A. Leonetti, *Note su Gramsci* (Argalia, Urbino, 1971)
———, "Guerra di posizione e 'guerra di movimento'", in A. Leonetti, *ibid*
———, "Romain Rolland e Gramsci", *Rinascita,* 20 June 1969
———, "La terza seria del *Ordine Nuovo*", in *Note su Gramsci,* op. cit.
Lepre, A., "Bordiga e Gramsci di fronte alla guerra e alla Rivoluzione d' Ottobre", *Critica marxista,* Vol. 5, Nos. 4-5, July-October 1967
Levi, P., *Unser Weg wider den Putschismus* (Berlin, 1921)
"Una Lezione di Gramsci sul movimento socialista italiano", *Movimento operaio e contadino in Liguria,* Vol. 3, Nos. 2-3, May-June 1957
Lisa, A., "Discussione politica con Gramsci in Carcere", *Rinascita,* 12 December 1964
Livorno 1921, Resoconto stenografico del XVII Congresso Nazionale del Partito socialista italiano (Leghorn 15-20 January 1921) (Avanti, Milan, 1962)
Lukacs, George, *Political Writings 1919-1929* (New Left Books, London, 1972)
Macciocchi, M.A., *Pour Gramsci* (Seuil, Paris, 1974)
Mack Smith, D., *Italy* (University of Michigan, Ann Arbor, 1959)
———, *The Latifundia in Modern Sicilian History* (Proceedings of British Academy, 51, O.U.P. Oxford 1965)
"Un mancato incontro Gramsci D'Annunzio a Gardone nell' Aprile 1920", *Rivista Storica del socialismo,* Vol. 5, Nos. 15-16, January-August 1962
Manchester Guardian, 29 October 1929
Manno, G., *Storia di Sardegna* (3rd ed) (Placido Maria Visaj, Milan, 1835), Vol. 1
Mautino, A., *La Formazione delle filosofia politica di Benedetto Croce* (Laterza, Bari, 1953)
Mondolfo, Rodolfo, *Umanismo di Marx: Studi filosofici 1908-1966* (Einaudi, Turin, 1968
Mondolfo, Ugo, "Terre e classi sociali in Sardegna nel periodo feudale," in A. Boscolo ed., *Feudalesimo in Sardegna* (Fossataro, Cagliari, 1967)
Montagnana, Rita, "La Sua grandezza e la sua semplicita", in *Gramsci Scritti di Togliatti ed altri* (Unita, Rome, 1945)
Montagnana, M., *Ricordi di un operaio torinese* (Rinascita, Rome, 1949)
Müller, Richard, "Comment nacquirent les conseils revolutionnaires d'Unsine", *Spartacus,* 1 July 1921
Mussolini, B., in *Popolo d'Italia,* 15 November 1914

Bibliography

Negarville, Cesar, "Gramsci, Maestro e Capo", in *Gramsci, Scritti di Togliatti ed altri* (L'Unita, Rome, 1945)

Nenni, Pietro, *Storia di Quattro anni [1919-1922]* (Einaudi, Rome, 1946)

Niceforo, A., *La delinquenza in Sardegna* (Remo Sandron, Palermo, 1897)

Nitti, F.S., "Agricultural contracts in Southern Italy", *Economic Review*, Vol. 3, July 1893

―――, *Nord e Sud Prime linee di un Inchiesta sulla ripartizione territoriale della entrate e delle spese* (Roux and Viarengo, Turin, 1900), *Introduction*

―――, "Poor Relief in Italy", in *Scritti sulla questione meridionale* (Laterza, Bari, 1958)

Nolte, E., *Three Faces of Fascism* (Holt, Chicago, 1967)

Olla, D., *Il Vecchio e il Nuovo dell'economia agropastorale in Sardegna* (Feltrinelli, Milan, 1969)

Paggi, Leonardo, *Gramsci e il moderno principe* (Riuniti, Rome, 1971) Vol.1

―――, "La Redazione Culturale del Grido del Popolo", in *Prassi revoluzionaria e storicismo in Gramsci Quaderni di Critica marxista No. 3*

Parodi, G., "La Fiat Centro in mano agli operai", *Stato operaio*, No. 10, 1930

―――, "Gramsci con gli operai", in *Gramsci Scritti di P. Togliatti ed altri* (L'Unita, Rome, 1945)

Parsons, A., "Is the Oedipus Complex Universal? A Southern Italian 'Nuclear Complex'", in R. Hunt ed. *Personalities and Cultures* (Natural History Press, New York, 1967)

Pastore, O., "Il problema delle commissioni interne", *Ordine Nuovo*, Vol. 1, No. 14, 15 August 1919

Péguy, Charles, *Oeuvres en prose, 1909-14* (Pléiade, Paris, 1957)

Piaget, J., & Weil, A.M., "The development in Children of the idea of the homeland and relations with other countries", *International Social Science Bulletin*, Vol. 3, No. 3, 1951

Pigliarù, A., *La vendetta barbaricina come ordinamento giuridico* (Giuffré, Milan, 1959)

Pirastu, I., "Che fare contro il banditismo in Sardegna," *Problemi di Ulisse*, Vol. 22, No. 10, April 1969

Pinna, Gonario, *Il Pastore Sardo e la giustizia* (Fossataro, Cagliari, 1967)

Prezzolini, G., "Alle sorgenti dello spirito", in *Leonardo*, No. 3, 1903 in G. Frigessi, *Introduction to La cultura italiana del' 900 attraverso le riviste, I, Leonardo Hermes, Il Regno* (Einaudi, Turin, 1960)

Procacci, G., "La classe operaia italiana agli inizi del secolo XX", *Studi storici*, Vol. 3, No. 1, January-March 1962

Protokoll des Dritten Kongressen der Kommunistischen Internazionale, Moskau 21 Juin 1921, Hamburg, 1921

Ravera, C., Letter to Togliatti 16(?) November 1926, in *Rinascita*, 5 December 1964

Reich, W., *The Mass Psychology of Fascism* (New York, 1946)

Report to the *Convegno 1924*, in *Annali Feltrinelli*, 1966

Report of the Moscow Conference 1922 (Great Britain, 1922)

Restaino, F., "Con Gramsci a Is Arenas", *Rinascita Sarda*, Vol. 1, No. 7, 25 April 1963

Robinson, P.A., *The Freudian Left: Wilhelm Reich, Geza Roheim, Herbert Marcuse* (Colophon, New York, 1969)

Rolland, Romain, "Au-dessus de la mélée" in R. Rolland, *l'Esprit libre*

(Michel, Paris, 1953)

_____, *Jean-Christophe* (Michel, Paris, 1956)

Romano, Aldo, "Antonio Gramsci, Note Sulla Situazione italiana 1922-24", *Rivista storica del socialismo,* Vol. 4, Nos. 13-14, May-December 1961

_____, "Antonio Gramsci tra guerra revoluzione", *Rivista storica del Socialismo,* Vol. 1, No. 1, 1958

Romano S.F., *Antonio Gramsci* (UTET, Turin, 1965)

Romeo, R., *Breve storia della grande industria in Italia* (Capelli, Bologna, 1961)

Russo, L., "Antonio Gramsci e l'educazione democratica", in *De vera religione* (Einaudi, Turin, 1949) originally in *Belfagor,* Vol. 2, No. 4, 15 July 1947

Ryazanoff, D., *The Communist Manifesto* (Martin Lawrence, London, 1930)

Salvadori, M., "L'attuale storiografia sul Partito Communista (1921-1926)", in *Gramsci e il problema storica della democrazia* (Einaudi, 1970)

_____, *Gramsci e il problema storio della democrazia* (Einaudi, 1970)

Salvatorelli, L., *Nazionalfascismo* (Gobetti, Turin, 1923), *Introduction*

Salvemini, Gaetano, *The French Revolution* (Cape, London, 1954)

_____, *Problemi educativi e sociali d'oggi* (Batiato, Catania, 1914)

_____, in *l'Unita,* 28 November 1913

_____, in *Critica Sociale,* Vol. 12, 1902, in M. Spinella, A. Caracciolo, R. Amaduzzi, G. Petronio eds., *Critica Sociale* (Feltrinelli, Milan, 1959), Vol. 1

_____, in *La Voce* Vol. 44, No. 11, 1910 in *La Cultura italiana del 1900 attraverso le riviste,* Vol. 3, La Voce (Einaudi, Turin, 1960)

Santhià, Battista, *Con Gramsci all 'Ordine Nuovo* (Riuniti, Rome, 1956)

_____, Letter to A. Leonetti 18 June 1964, in A. Leonetti *Note su Gramsci* (Argalià, Urbino, 1971)

Schucht, T., "Colloqui con Gramsci in Carcere", *Rinascita,* 23 January 1970

Serge, Victor, *Memoirs of a Revolutionary* (OUP, London, 1963)

Schichilone, G., *Documenti sulle condizioni della Sicilia dal 1860* al 1870 (Ateneo, Rome, 1952)

Silone, I., *Uscita di sicurezza* (Florence, 1965)

Soave, E., "Appunti sulle origini teoriche e practiche dei consigli di fabbrica a Torino", *Rivista storica del socialismo,* Vol. 2, No. 21, January-April 1964

Solari, Gioele, Introduction to Aldo Mautino, *La formazione delle filosofia politica di Benedetto Croce* (Laterza, Bari, 1953)

Sole, C. ed., *La Sardegna di Carlo Felice e il problema della terra* (Fossataro, Cagliari, 1968)

Sonnino, S., "I contadini in Sicilia" (Florence, 1877), in R. Villari ed. *Il Sud nella storia d'Italia* (Laterza, Bari, 1966) Vol. 1

Spano, G., *Proverbi Sardi* (Cagliari, 1871), cited in G. Pinna, *Il pastore sardo e la giustizia* (Fossataro, Caliari, 1967)

Spano, Velio, "Il congresso di Lione", *Rinascita,* April 1956

_____, "Gramsci sardo", in *Gramsci Scritti di P. Togliatti ed altri* (L'Unita, Rome, 1945)

Spinella, M., Caracciolo, A., Amaduzzi, R., Petroni, G., (eds.), *Critica Sociale* (Feltrinelli, Milan, 1959)

Spriano, P., "Gli ultimi anni di Gramsci in un colloquio con Piero Sraffa", *Rinascita,* 4 April 1967

_____, *Gramsci e l'Ordine Nuovo* (Riuniti, Rome, 1965)

_____, *Opere complete di Piero Gobetti* (Einaudi, Turin, 1960)

_____, *L'Ordine Nuovo* (Einaudi, Turin, 1963)

_____. "La Scelta di Gramsci", in *Rinascita,* 27 July 1967

_____ *Socialismo e classe operaia a Torino dal 1892 al 1913* (Einaudi, Turin, 1958)

Bibliography

————, *Storia del Partito Comunista italiano, I, Da Bordiga a Gramsci* (Einaudi, 1967)

————, *Torino operaia nella grande guerra 1914-1918* (Einaudi, Turin, 1960)

S.V.I.M.E.Z. *Statistiche sul Mezzogiorno d'Italia 1861-1953* (Rome, 1954)

Tasca, A., 'I prima dieci anni del partito comunista italiano'', *Il Mondo* Vol. 5, Nos. 33-38, 18 August-22September 1953

————, in *Energie Nove,* 12 March 1919 cited in P. Spriano, *Gramsci e l'Ordine Nuovo* (Riuniti, Rome, 1965)

Tarozzi, L., "Ricordo di Gramsci", *Vie Nuove,* 4 May 1947

Terracini, U., "I Consigli di fabbrica: vicende e problemi dall'Inghilterra alla Russia, dalla Germania a Torino", *L'Almanacco socialista,* 1920

————, "Three Meetings with Lenin" in S.F. Bezveselny & D.Y. Grunberg, *They Knew Lenin* (Foreign languages publishing House, Moscow, 1968)

Togliatti, P., ed., *La formazione del gruppo dirigente del Partito Comunista italiano* (Riuniti, Rome, 1962)

————, "Il leninismo nel pensiero e nell'azione di A. Gramsci", in *Studi gramsciani atti del convegno tenuto a Roma nel giorni,* 11-13 gennaio 1958 (Riuniti, Rome, 1969)

"Trent 'anni di vita e lotte del PCI", *Quaderni di Rinascita,* 2

Trombetti, G., "In cellula con la matricola 7047", *Rinascita,* September 1946

Trotsky, L., *Literature and Revolution* (University of Michigan Press, Ann Arbor, 1960) *Postscript*

————, *The New Course* (1922)

Turati, A., *Agli elettori di Milano* (Critica sociale, Milan, 1919)

————, reply to article by A. Labriola in support of Leninism, in M. Spinella et alia, *Critica Sociale* (Feltrinelli, Milan, 1959)

————, "Trent 'anni di Critica Sociale" in N. Valeri, *La Lotta politica in Italia dall 'Unita al 1925* (Le Monnier, Florence, 1962)

Tyndale, J.W., *Island of Sardinia* (Richard Bentley, London, 1849), III vols

Valeri, N., *La Lotta politica in Italia dall 'Unita al 1925* (Le Monnier, Florence, 1962)

Valiani, L., "Il Problema delle 'grandi reforme' fra i socialisti italiani dal 1900 al 1914", in *Questioni di storia del socialismo* (Einaudi, Turin, 1958)

Villari R. ed., *Il Sud nella Storia d'Italia* (Laterza, Bari, 1966)

Editorial, *La Voce* 2, 1909 in *La cultura italiana del '900 attraverso le riviste,* 3, La Voce 1908-14 (Einaudi, Turin 1960)

La Voce, Vol. 5, No. 6, 1913, expresses opposition to anti-clericalism.

Vochting, F., *La questione meridionale* (Instituto Editoriale del Mezzogiorno, Naples, n.d.)

Wagner, M.L., *La lingua sarda, Storia, spirito, forma* (Francke, Bern, n.d.)

White, S., "Gramsci and the Italian Communist Party", *Government and Opposition,* Vol. 7, No. 2, 1972

Zamis, G., "Gramsci a Vienna nel 1924", *Rinascita,* 28 November 1964

Zucàro, D., "Antonio Gramsci all'universita di Torino", *Società,* December 1957

————, "Antonio Gramsci e la Sardegna. Carteggio inedito Gramsci — Lussu", *Mondo operaio,* Vol. 5, No. 1, 6 June 1952

————, *Il Processone Gramsci e i dirigenti comunisti dinanzi al tribunale speciale* (Riuniti, Rome, 1961)

————, *Vita di Carcere di Antonio Gramsci* (Avanti, Milan/Rome, 1954)

Index

Index